Also by George Packer

Interesting Times

Interesting Times

Writings from a Turbulent Decade

GEORGE PACKER

Farrar, Straus and Giroux

New York

Farrar, Straus and Giroux
18 West 18th Street, New York 10011

Distributed in Canada by D&M Publishers, Inc.
Printed in the United States of America
First edition, 2009

Grateful acknowledgment is made to the following publications, in which these essays originally appeared, in slightly different form: *The Boston Globe, Dissent, The Fight Is for Democracy* (Harper Perennial, 2003), *Mother Jones, The New Yorker, The New York Times Magazine,* and *World Affairs.*

Library of Congress Cataloging-in-Publication Data
Packer, George, 1960–
    Interesting times : writings from a turbulent decade / George Packer.
        p.   cm.
    ISBN: 978-0-374-17572-6 (hardcover : alk. paper)
    1. Packer, George, 1960–   2. Authors—Political and social views.   I. Title.

PS3566.A317I58 2009
814'.54—dc22

                                                                2009010186

Designed by Jonathan D. Lippincott

www.fsgbooks.com

1   3   5   7   9   10   8   6   4   2

For Bill Finnegan

Contents

Introduction

The decade covered by this collection of essays is actually seven years, from the morning of September 11, 2001, to the night of November 4, 2008. The margins of a historical period don't conform to the turning of a new zero; eras are defined less precisely but more truly by events, a prevailing moral atmosphere, what it felt like to live during a certain time. With just a little simplification, it's possible to see from a distance that the thirties began on October 24, 1929, and ended on December 7, 1941; that the sixties began on November 22, 1963, and ended on—well, maybe on December 6, 1969 (the Altamont Speedway concert), or January 27, 1973 (the signing of the Paris Peace Accords), or August 9, 1974 (Nixon's resignation). ("It is easy to see the beginnings of things," Joan Didion wrote, "and harder to see the ends.") Only a year on, is it too soon to define the period between the attacks on American soil and the election of Barack Obama as a distinct era? I'm going to anyway. It was the era of terror and of waste, when America, at the dizzying height of its powers, was given a chance to change the world in a new direction, failed miserably, and responded to the failure by changing itself. The era began with an unprecedented American tragedy; it ended, and a new era began, with one of those occasional moments of national renewal that have been among our saving graces.

These seven years, following an earlier time of domestic tranquillity and triviality, were crowded with drama: wars, suicide bombings, secret prisons, partisan combat, wild gyrations in the stock market, economic collapse, the disappearance of entire industries, political transformation. In retrospect, all this agitation had the quality of the various stages of some prolonged illness, during which the patient sweated, tossed, became

delirious with visions incubated by a strange logic, spoke incomprehensi-
bly, suffered delusions of possessing enormous strength, inflicted inadvertent pain on himself and others, collapsed and lay prostrate, and slowly
began to recover. When I was in Baghdad in 2007, I had lunch in the
Green Zone with an American official who said to me, "Do you think this
is all going to seem like a dream? Is it just going to be a fever dream that
we'll wake up from and say, 'We got into this crazy war, but now it's over'?"
It isn't over, but now that the country has begun to emerge, we can look
back and ask: What was it all about? Perhaps those seven years were the
last spasm of the world's greatest power at its apogee, the beginning of its
slow decline. Perhaps they were a painful working out of certain malignancies that had been dormant within the country for years, while other
malignancies erupted around the world. History confers on events the ex
post facto aura of narrative coherence and inexorability—perhaps it was
all accident and needless folly.

For most Americans, September 11 and all that it unleashed dominated the decade. This revealed, among other things, our besetting narcissism, the vice that leads us to imagine ourselves the best or the worst
but at any rate the center of everything. The shock of that morning can
still be felt years later, but for an Iraqi or a Congolese the human loss on
September 11 would have been, proportionate to population, an average
day. It's just that we hadn't seen it coming and never felt so helpless before. I had erroneously and perhaps inappropriately hoped that the force
of the blows would jolt America out of the long daydream of the Reagan
and Clinton years, into a consciousness of responsibility at home and
abroad. Things didn't quite work out that way—America's reputation sank
to a fathomless global low. And yet, partly for this reason, the years right
after the attacks saw a period of unusual openness to the world on the
part of this most insular nation. Until we grew weary of the bad news and
set up real and mental barriers to the world, Americans expressed a willingness to learn about other countries and to understand why so many
people regarded us with ambivalence, if not outright fury. Oprah devoted
a show to Islam, and the front page of *The New York Times* ran story after
story, year after year, under unpronounceable headlines.

But because Americans do nothing in restrained measures, the news
of the world was swallowed in great gulps, large quantities of it on the
Web and cable networks as well as more established outlets, often with-

out the help of background or context. The torrents of images from alien places pouring into the minds of Americans and everyone else, pictures of air strikes, beheadings, charred corpses, terrified children, elicited anguish and outrage but above all the consciousness of being unable to do anything about it. Too much information and not enough understanding or power: globalization and violence merged to create a particular kind of psychosis, with well-founded fears and judgments warped into paranoia and hallucination by nonstop media saturation. The world beyond your street was never closer, and never more out of reach.

The years after September 11 saw, strangely enough, a golden age of American journalism, a late-life flowering even as the traditional news business was dying thanks to the Internet. Not in Washington—where the press covered the Bush presidency the way it's covered politics for the past several decades, as entertainment and sports, even when the story was as serious as war and a corps of insiders with high-level access failed to see what was under their noses—but in Jalalabad and Jeddah and Falluja. During these years, the curiosity of readers and generosity of editors allowed me to travel to foreign places that ordinarily didn't show up on the map of the American media, and to devote considerable time, resources, and words to conveying the stories of their obscure inhabitants as something more than exotica or horror show. Long-form narrative journalism, that luxury of an earlier, slower time, like the three-volume novel or the three-martini lunch, turned out to be the means by which much of the reading public at the start of the twenty-first century started to understand what had been done to America and what America was doing in return. On the surface, all was chaos and violence—if causes and truths lay anywhere, they were down below. And now that the country is pulling inward again, to its habitual focus on its own concerns, we may soon look back at the period after September 11 as a rare moment when Americans became interested in people other than themselves.

The center of my journalistic world during these years was Iraq. I began writing about the coming war in the months before it began, made six trips to Iraq after the invasion, and only stopped thinking obsessively about it after most of my Iraqi friends had left the country in 2007 and 2008. But there's a gap in this collection between the start of the war and its later years, a period covered by reporting that is not included here because it became the basis for *The Assassins' Gate*, my book about Iraq. The reader expecting a continuous, if fragmentary, chronicle will find instead a sudden jump from nail-biting pre-war forecasts to grim late-war reporting. The discontinuity highlights certain changes in my thinking and writing that came with the war.

The past decade was as intensely ideological as the 1930s. After September 11, it seemed to me necessary not just to understand the worldview that had turned passenger planes into missiles, but to answer its mental force with a counterforce. The conservative administration in Washington mustered its own very quickly and assertively: it was nationalistic, militaristic, and almost religiously certain. My political inclinations pointed in a different, though not an opposite, direction. The interventions and failures to intervene of the 1990s had shown that, in certain circumstances, America could be an instrument—often of last resort—for good in the world, and that liberalism's problem was too much hesitation in the face of this possibility, not too little. I wrote several essays after September 11 in the belief that more was required in the wake of the Islamist assault and the conservative reaction than just liberal criticism.

Today, the ambition of these essays makes me a little uneasy—something in the tone and language no longer sits well. There's a tendency toward overreach, driven by uncertainty more than overconfidence, and by an unreliable excitement in the thick of world-historical events. After a few trips to Iraq, words like "democracy" and "totalitarianism," appeals to grand ideological struggles, and comparisons with the Cold War began to sound a little too glib. The analysis was still relevant and, in a sense, intellectually justified, but it did not tell you what to do or how to do it, and in the case of Iraq—a war I supported, for reasons that had more to do with strong emotions than global strategy—it gave the wrong answer. Abstractions and sweeping statements suddenly seemed dangerous. "Ideas scare me. They get people killed," Dexter Filkins of the *Times*, who has seen as much of the latter as any journalist, said when we met in Baghdad.

One alternative to intellectual journalism is reportage that approaches pointillism: the patient accretion of local knowledge, building story upon story one fact at a time, while restraining the impulse to generalize, with the awareness that the subject is too complex, maybe even unknowable, for any kind of summary judgment. For a while my pieces from Iraq, under the chastening influence of experience, moved in this direction. But answering bad or misleading ideas with no ideas at all is hardly satisfying. The war in Iraq introduced me to new ideas about war, developed by dissidents inside the government and military; but the theories they propose are closer to the ground than philosophy or ideology, less intellectually stimulating but better informed and more strategically useful.

My ambition as a journalist is always to combine narrative writing with political thought. Finding the balance is a continuous struggle, but each needs the other and is poorer without it.

The ideological battles of the past decade left out large swaths of the globe. The poor countries of the Southern Hemisphere, where religion is a way of life and not a political weapon, had begun to push their way into the consciousness of enlightened people in wealthy countries during the 1990s, when the end of the Cold War lifted the ideological shadow of the two superpowers. Without the American-Soviet rivalry to consume the world's attention and resources, these trouble spots, plagued by poverty, mass killing, disease, and tyranny, became the object of a kind of consensus on the part of humanitarians: outsiders had a moral interest in what went on inside distant borders and an obligation to ameliorate it. In certain circumstances, this obligation even came at the expense of national sovereignty, for in the post–Cold War world, as an awareness of the contagious effects of local problems grew, borders became less sacrosanct and sometimes disappeared right off the map. Like any new idea, this humanitarian consensus was extremely controversial in practice and the source of a great deal of hypocrisy and evasion. But double standards and violated standards are better than no standards at all; desperate people don't care very much about the moral consistency of people who are not desperate. At the very least, worldwide media made it harder to ignore what was happening to small boys in Sierra Leone and teenage girls in Cambodia.

But after September 11, American foreign policy once again divided the world into ideological camps, and neither Ivory Coast nor Burma fit into one. Traveling through Africa and Southeast Asia during these years, I heard a number of people crack the same bleak joke: that their country's obvious problem was a lack of terrorists. If a suicide bomber blew himself up next to an appropriate target, media attention and development money and other lifelines would flow their way. For even when the outside world wasn't thinking about them, people in these forgotten places were acutely aware of the outside world. In a town near Ivory Coast's border with Liberia, I saw a drunken young rebel fighter in a T-shirt showing the faces of George W. Bush and Osama bin Laden, like the stars of an action film, side by side, as if to say: Don't make me choose—I'm with the guy who wins. In Rangoon, a dissident artist earnestly explained to me that a single well-placed American bomb dropped on Burma's remote new capital could make up for all the harm done by all the bombs in Iraq.

The inhabitants of countries like these find themselves in a situation of existential absurdity. From the global media we know something about their plight—occasionally enough to want to act and alleviate it. And from the same global media they know something about us, too, enough to borrow freely—the fighters on both sides of the civil war in Ivory Coast styled themselves after American gangsta rappers, while people all over Africa dress themselves in our castoff clothing. But the information never leads to meaningful action. From across this great gulf we look at them, and they look at us, and nothing happens. A French scholar in Abidjan had a phrase for the condition of young people there: *lèche-vitrines*. The closest they can come to matching their aspirations with possibility is window-shopping. In this context, the Internet and satellite television become torments.

When the Iraq War began, Ivorians demonstrated in their capital for America to invade their country, too, and end French interference in their civil war (that week I happened to be in the only country on earth where the invasion of Iraq was wildly popular). The coincidence of these events contained an irony that became clear only later: the idea of outside rescue perished in Iraq. The humanitarian consensus of the 1990s collapsed after it was invoked to justify the most controversial war in recent history—to the great benefit of Robert Mugabe, Omar al-Bashir, and Than Shwe. After Iraq, the burden of working out their own destiny falls more and more on young people living under tyranny in Burma, on self-employed Nigerians scavenging a living in the thronged streets of Lagos. The West, with its staggering abundance, its music and images, and its freedoms, remains a model and a temptation. But the sense that a quick and simple answer to human misery lies somewhere *out there* no longer holds many people on either side of the gulf under its spell. If this is a case of wising up, it's also a sign of atrophied imaginations.

To some degree, almost every essay in this collection deals with the problem of idealism. Why is it a problem? Because, whether on the scale of individuals or nations, good intentions prompt actions that always lead to unintended consequences. Because, for all our saturation in media, we never really know enough until, one way or another, it's too late. Because, as Lionel Trilling wrote in *The Liberal Imagination*, "Some paradox of our natures leads us, when once we have made our fellow men the objects of our enlightened interest, to go on to make them the objects of our pity, then of our wisdom, ultimately of our coercion. It is to prevent this corruption, the most ironic and tragic that man knows, that we stand in need of the moral realism which is the product of the free play of the moral imagination." The corruption that begins in enlightenment and ends in force is a particularly American one, and the era of terror was rotten with it, producing along the way innumerable critics, internal and external, of American self-righteousness. They are all in one way or another descendants of Graham Greene, who identified the original sin of innocence at the start of the American war in Vietnam. When a new movie version of *The Quiet American* was released just before the Iraq War, Greene's ghost stirred and spoke as a new generation of Americans apparently headed down another road to hell.

But idealism would hardly be a problem at all if it were as easily disposed of as it is in Greene's theology of anti-Americanism. When the perils of interfering stop human beings from making one another the object of enlightened interest, that won't be the exercise of moral realism, but its death. The antidote to the dangerous innocence of Greene's Alden Pyle, and of the scheming visionaries who gathered in London just before the invasion of Iraq, is not an ennui that shrugs in the presence of hubris and folly, as if to say, "What did you expect?" This is more often than not the pose of observers who are comfortable and secure enough that they can afford to be unimpressed when evil enters the room. It's a more callous form of "innocence." For the writers who mean the most to me, experience in the world makes the moral imagination *more* capable of registering and resisting the injustice of things, not less. V. S. Naipaul, the soul of skepticism, devoted his novels and essays to stripping away with supreme precision the illusions of and about people in the former colonial world. But in spite of his famous cruelty, at the heart of his work is an abiding belief in individual striving, the pursuit of happiness, man's perfectibility. George Orwell saw firsthand the betrayal of the Spanish revolution by the Stalinist left, but unlike Hemingway, he didn't adopt a false cynicism toward it, nor did he allow it to unhinge him, as it did John Dos Passos. In Spain, Orwell witnessed the worst of his own side and the other side, and "the effect," he wrote in *Homage to Catalonia*, "was to make my desire to see Socialism established much more actual than it had been before."

During the Spanish Civil War, writers very publicly took sides. A few ran risks; more adopted stances. And many of them, including some great ones, ended up violating their calling—looked the other way, took refuge from the messiness of facts in ideology, used pretty words for ugly things, settled scores or satisfied vanities in the name of high principles, wrote out of sheer ignorance, told outright lies. The analogies to our own time don't need to be spelled out. Whenever writers wade into the mucky shoals of ideology and war, they do so at their peril. One understandable reaction is to insist on a kind of purity of craft that restricts the writer's role to that of scrupulous witness, distrusting all claims not founded in particulars. But the moral, for me, is not that writers shouldn't take sides. In a tumultuous time like the one we've been living through, only those who draw entirely on inwardness or imagination for their subjects could avoid having and, in some way, expressing a view about the world-shaking events happening every week. Partisanship is inevitable, and it's better not to pretend that it doesn't exist or try to cut it out like a cancer. One can only be honest about having a point of view while remaining open to aspects of reality—the human faces and voices—that might demolish it. The best means I know for doing this is journalism.

"What I truly detested was American liberalism," Graham Greene once said. He meant our materialism, our shallowness, our lack of a tragic sense. But it turns out that even after the era of terror, with all its waste, the world still expects something from America. When a new face of idealism, tempered and restrained by self-knowledge, appeared in the shape of a new political figure, the country revealed that criticism and change are as integral to American democracy as innocence and arrogance. The election of Barack Obama was made possible during the course of an extraordinary year by a series of tectonic shifts: the collapse of the conservative ideology that dominated American politics since Reagan, the implosion of the country's financial system after years of erosion in its political economy, a new mass politics of youth in a new technological era, and the tremors of a resurgent liberalism.

It was clear from the beginning that Obama, in his personal story and his political style, represented something novel, but its shape took time to materialize. The year 2008 saw one of those rare convergences between individual character and public events that can produce a decisive turn in national history. Obama's signature word was "hope," but by election night what he offered was something closer to a sense of limits, an acceptance of responsibility in the conduct of individuals and of the country, at home and abroad. His victory did not close the book on the era that began on September 11, 2001—the wars continue, the threat of terrorism still hangs over us, the failure of markets will haunt us for years, the times will remain interesting. But it did mark—and so decisively that you could hear the click of change on the night of November 4—a shift in moral consciousness. The country gave itself a second chance to fulfill the promise lost seven years before.

The pieces from the 2008 campaign come with certain birthmarks that already date them. The same is true of almost everything in this collection, because the nature of journalism is to be topical and transient. This is its well-known weakness, but it is also the surprising source of whatever lasts. The best way to tell the future what it was like to live in a previous era is to be engaged in its passions and concerns.

—March 2009

PART ONE

After September 11

Living Up to It

Adapted from the introduction to *The Fight Is for Democracy*, ed. George Packer (New York: Harper Perennial, 2003).

I

In the minutes after the South Tower fell on September 11, 2001, an investment banker had an epiphany. Having escaped with his life just ahead of the collapse, he wandered through the smoke and confusion of lower Manhattan until he found himself in a church in Greenwich Village. Alone at the altar, covered in ash and dust, he began to shake and sob. Feeling a hand on his shoulder, he looked up. It was a policeman.

"Don't worry," the cop said, "you're in shock."

"I'm *not* in shock," the investment banker answered. "I like this state. I've never been more cognizant in my life."

Around the same time that the banker noticed his changed consciousness and a hundred blocks north, I thought, or felt, because there were really no words yet: Maybe this will make us better. That was all; I didn't know what it meant. The feeling made me ashamed because it seemed insufficiently horror-stricken. But like any repressed feeling, it continued to lurk. And in the hours and days that followed, it seemed to be borne out on the streets of New York.

I spent most of two days sitting on a sidewalk in downtown Brooklyn, waiting to give blood with hundreds of other people. I had long conversations with those near me, in the temporary intimacy between strangers that kept breaking out all over the city. There was Matthew Timms, a twenty-eight-year-old unemployed video producer who had tried to film the attacks from across the East River in Williamsburg, only to find his camera battery had gone dead. His own detachment, he said—which extended to his whole life—so disturbed him that he wanted his blood drawn in order to overcome it. "I volunteered so I could be a part of something," he said. "All over the world people do something for an ideal. I've been at no point in my life when I could say something I've done has affected mankind. Like when the news was on, I was thinking, What if there was a draft? Would I go? I think I would." Lauren Moynihan, a lawyer in her thirties, had traveled all over the city pleading with hospitals and emergency centers to take her blood and been turned away by all of them. As a "civilian," without skills, she felt useless. "This is like a little bit short of volunteering to go for the French Foreign Legion," said Dave Lampe, a computer technician from Jersey City who was wearing suspenders decorated with brightly colored workman's tools. A sixteen-year-old girl named Amalia della Paolera, passing out juice and cookies along the line, said, "This is the time when we need to be, like, pulling together and doing as much as we can for each other and not, like, sitting at home watching it on TV and saying, like, 'Oh, there's another bomb.'"

Everyone wanted to be of use and no one knew how, as if citizenship were a skilled position for which none of us had the right experience and qualifications. People seemed to be feeling the same thing: they had not been living as they would have liked; the horrors of the day before had woken them up; they wanted to change. So they had come to stand in line, and they continued to wait long after it became clear that no blood was going to be needed.

The mood that came over New York after September 11—for me it will always be tied to the "Missing" picture posted at my subway stop of a young woman named Gennie Gambale, and then all the other pictures that appeared overnight around the city; the flags sprouting in shop windows; the clots of melted candle wax on sidewalks; the bitter smell of smoke from lower Manhattan; the clusters of people gathering in the Brooklyn Heights Promenade or Union Square to sing or write messages or read them; the kindness on the subway; the constant wail of sirens for no obvious purpose; the firemen outside a station house in midtown accepting flowers at midnight; the rescue workers at the end of their shift trudging up West Street with gray dust coating their faces and clothes; the people waiting at barricades on Canal Street with pots of foil-covered food; the garrulousness of strangers; the sleeplessness, the sense of being on alert all the time and yet useless—this mood broke over the city like a storm at the end of a season of languid days stretching back longer than anyone could remember. People became aware, as if for the first time, that they were not merely individuals with private ends. Whitman's spirit walked down every street: "What is more subtle than this which ties me to the woman or man that looks in my face?" The embarrassment of strong emotions felt by sophisticated people in peaceful times dropped away, and strangers looked at one another differently. We became citizens.

This mood lasted around two weeks, then it began to fade. The cleanup was taken out of the hands of volunteers and entrusted to experts with heavy machinery. Elected officials told the public to resume normal life as quickly as possible. Average people could show they cared by going out to dinner and holding on to stocks. Then came the anthrax scare, which created more panic than the air attacks had, replacing solidarity with hysteria; and then the Afghanistan war, which signaled the return of the familiar, since the public in whose name it was fought had no more to do with it than with other recent wars. By now, it's hard to believe that anything as profound as the banker's epiphany really happened at all.

I thought that the attacks and the response would puncture a bloated era in American history and mark the start of a different, more attractive era. I thought that without some such change we would not be able to win this new war—that the crisis that mattered most was internal. One undercurrent of the mood of those days was a sense of shame: we had had it too good, had gotten away with it for too long. In the weeks afterward, W. H. Auden's poem "September 1, 1939" kept appearing in e-mails and on websites and on subway walls, with its suddenly apt first stanza:

> I sit in one of the dives
> On Fifty-second Street
> Uncertain and afraid
> As the clever hopes expire
> Of a low dishonest decade:
> Waves of anger and fear
> Circulate over the bright
> And darkened lands of the earth,
> Obsessing our private lives;
> The unmentionable odour of death
> Offends the September night.

For at least a low dishonest decade, large numbers of Americans had been living in an untenable state, a kind of complacent fantasy in which the dollar is always strong; the stock market keeps going up; investments always provide a handsome return; wars are fought by other people, end quickly, and can be won with no tax increases, no civilian sacrifices, and few if any American casualties; global dominance is maintained on the strength of technological and economic success without the taint or burden of an occupying empire; power and wealth demand no responsibility; and history leaves Americans alone. It didn't matter whether a Democrat or a Republican was in the White House, or whether we were bombing some foreign country or not. Public concerns had nothing to do with politics or citizenship, those relics of the eighteenth century, and everything to do with the market—"Where," Auden wrote, "blind skyscrapers use / Their full height to proclaim / The strength of Collective Man."

This fantasy took on its most lavish and triumphant expression in New York, and it was frozen in place there when the towers fell. Several weeks later, a journalist wandered into the ghostly executive dining room of Deutsche Bank, across Liberty Street from where the South Tower had stood, and noted the breakfast menu for September 11: smoked-salmon omelettes and chocolate-filled pancakes. The remains of a meal for two— half-drunk juice turning dark, a mostly eaten omelette, withering fruit— sat abandoned on a table. The whole scene was finely coated in the ubiquitous gray dust and ash, like the tableaux of Romans caught eating and sleeping by the lava of Vesuvius; except that Pompeii was entirely destroyed, whereas the American civilization at which the nineteen radical Islamist hijackers aimed passenger planes still persists in roughly its old shape, though ragged at the edges and shaky in the nerves.

Political predictions usually come true when reality and wish coincide, and as it turned out, I was wrong. September 11 has not ushered in an era of reform. It has not made America or Americans very much better, more civic-minded. It has not replaced market values with democratic values. It has not transformed America from the world's overwhelming economic and military power into what it has often been in the past—a light of freedom and equality unto the nations. None of this has happened, because America is currently governed by bad leaders, because the opposition is weak, because our wealth and power remain so enormous that even an event as dramatic as the terrorist attacks can't fully penetrate them, because a crisis doesn't automatically bring down the curtain on an era, because change usually comes in the manner of a cork-screw rather than a hammer.

Yet my first response on the morning of September 11 still seems the one worth holding on to. The investment banker jerked awake, the aspira-tions up and down the line of those wanting to give blood, revealed some-thing about the moral condition of Americans at this moment in our history. Like any crisis, the attacks brought buried feelings to the surface and showed our society in a collective mirror. That day changed America less than most people anticipated, but it made Americans think about change—not just as individuals, but as a country.

2

The hijackers believed they were striking a blow at a decadent civiliza-tion, and they were partly right. Islamic terrorists had been trying for years to make Americans aware of their implacable hostility. In 1996 Osama bin Laden declared war on American interests in the Arab world, and in 1998 he extended it to American and Jewish civilians everywhere, telling a reporter that he had learned from Somalia that Americans were too soft and cowardly to fight back. No one here noticed. Only a deeply insular, perpetually distracted people with a short memory, a vague notion of the rest of the world, and no firsthand experience of tyranny could have absorbed all the blows of the past decade without understanding that a serious movement wanted to destroy us. Imagine what the hijackers saw in their last days on earth—a society so capacious and free that it opened itself wide to the agents of its own destruction and gave them the tools to do it. The soulless motels and parking lots of small towns from Florida to Maine, the promiscuous street mix of colors and sexes and faiths, the lack of prayer, the half-dressed women, the fat people in tight clothes, the world empty of Allah, the supreme thrill of knowing in advance what every ignorant idiot around them did not, the endless stock market news on airport lounge televisions, the drowsy security guards, and finally the towers coming into view, thrusting up out of the clear blue sky in their dazzling white arrogance. The hijackers would have seen, and hated, both

America's best and its worst—the rowdy polychrome energy, the moral emptiness of wealth and power.

To imagine a new, and a better, American response, it's necessary to look hard at where we are now and how we got here. One of the features of American life that had fallen into decay by September 11, 2001, was our democracy. The reasons are numerous and have a complex history, but I want to discuss three. The first has to do with government, and with ancient (and more recent) American attitudes toward it. The second has to do with money, and how it's distributed in American society. The third has to do with an idea, which I will call liberalism, and the people whose business is ideas, who are called intellectuals.

Suspicion of government was seared into Americans' minds before there was a United States. But the Enlightenment pamphleteers and politicians—Thomas Paine, Thomas Jefferson, and others—distrusted government in a way almost opposite that of modern people. The eighteenth-century mind that gave birth to the new republic believed human beings to be rational creatures with a nearly limitless capacity for finding happiness if only they are free. "Government in a well-constituted republic," Paine wrote in *The Rights of Man*, his scathing response to Edmund Burke's *Reflections on the Revolution in France*, the founding document of conservatism, "requires no belief in man beyond what his reason can give." In this sense all men are indeed created equal—endowed not just with rights but with reason. Liberal government, of which America gave the world the first example, was government based on reason rather than tradition (or ignorance, as Paine would have it; or faith, in the Islamists' terms). This confidence in the human mind to work out its own destiny meant that government, set up by consent to limit freedom only enough to ensure the public good, should remain small. If it got too big, it would concentrate too much power in privileged hands and turn back toward favoritism and distinctions, and against freedom and its rational use. Limited government, then, was a means, not an end; the end was human happiness, best achieved when men are free.

Individualism is part of our national character—the most famous part. But so is moralism, and this, too, goes back several centuries. The utopian fantasies of the pilgrims were submerged under the commercial practices of republican society, but they were never completely buried. The main theme of American history since independence has been the cheerful, vulgar, brutal, wantonly innocent pursuit of happiness, from the frontiersman to the venture capitalist. But a minor theme keeps recurring, a moralism so rigid that it baffles Europeans—from John Brown to Kenneth Starr. Just as American individualism can appear either healthy and dynamic or blindly selfish, American moralism swings wildly between high-minded idealism and hysterical intolerance. At certain moments—our entry into World War I was one—the transformation happens almost overnight: the muckraker gave way to the night rider, the Progressive city commission to the Red Scare, without any letup in the sense of a national crusade.

The most potent political idea of my lifetime has been hostility to government—from Goldwater's crankish "extremism in the defense of liberty," to Reagan's triumphant "government isn't the solution to the problem; government is the problem," to Clinton's final tactical surrender: "The era of big government is over." In this thinking, the government doesn't embody the will of the people—in fact, it's something alien, and a threat to their well-being. The creed reached a reductio ad absurdum in the last days of the 2000 campaign, when George W. Bush proclaimed that the Democrats "want the federal government controlling the Social Security like it's some kind of federal program. We understand differently, though. You see, it's your money, not the government's money." The superficial similarity of modern conservatism to the language of the founders is misleading. Jefferson and his generation saw *democratic* government—a new beginning of human history—as the collective embodiment of rational man. It served the public good. Conservatives today have no concept of the public good. They see Americans as investors and consumers, not citizens.

Like most victorious ideologies, antigovernment conservatism grew as complacent as the welfare-state liberalism it replaced—and far more extreme. The thinking of Timothy McVeigh wasn't far from the core of the "respectable" American right in the 1990s. The doctrinal rigidity hardened to the point where, in the absence of government interventions, untreated problems, from the health care system to the electoral system, continued to fester, and still do. Among other things, September 11 reminded Americans that they need a government: inside the towers, public employees were going up while private ones went down.

One of the strangest things about the antigovernment era is that it coincided with the first prolonged drop in wages in American history. While free-market thinking was reigning triumphant, the middle class was contracting; even the brief pause during Clinton's second term turned out to be riding on a mountain of personal debt and a stock market bubble that had to burst. So why was there no protest movement, not even a moderate legislative program, against the concentration of 50 percent of the nation's wealth among 1 percent of its people, the lopsided effects of tax cuts, the massive economic dislocations caused by deindustrialization and globalization? When you come to think of it, less calamitous forces sparked the American Revolution.

But the change from an industrial to a high-tech economy, along with the movement of jobs and investment around the world, has been too incremental and various and complex to arouse any focused resistance. Most of the influential voices in society—the politicians, scholars, and journalists who, along with other professional classes, seemed to do better and better—said that the change was inevitable and ultimately beneficial, and the public believed them. Meanwhile, the money kept adding up in the winners' column, staggering amounts that no longer meant anything—hundred-and-fifty-million-dollar compensation packages for a CEO having a subpar year. This money bought unprecedented political power. Some businessmen spent their fortunes running for office; others paid for their influence indirectly.

The relationship between democracy and economic inequality creates a kind of self-perpetuating cycle: the people hold government in low esteem; public power shrinks against the awesome might of corporations and rich individuals; money and its influence claim a greater and greater share of political power; and the public, priced out of the democratic game, grows ever more cynical about politics and puts more of its energy into private ends. Far from creating a surge of reform, the erosion of the middle class has only deepened the disenchantment. For thirty years or more the musculature of democracy has atrophied, culminating in 2000 with a stolen presidential election.

For the past century, the political philosophy of collective action on behalf of freedom and justice has been liberalism. For most of that time, it was an expansive, self-confident philosophy, and history was on its side. Since around 1968, liberalism has been an active participant in its own decline. A creed that once spoke on behalf of the desire of millions of Americans for a decent life and a place in the sun shrank to a set of rigid pieties preached on college campuses and in eccentric big-city enclaves.

It turned insular, defensive, fragmented, and pessimistic. The phenomenon of political correctness, which for a period during the 1980s and early '90s became the most visible expression of liberalism, amounted to a desire to control reality by purifying language and thought, to make the world better by changing a syllabus, or a name, or a word. It was a kind of cargo cult. At bottom, it represented a retreat from politics.

During these years, the energy that had once gone into struggles for justice under the heading of labor or civil rights balkanized and propelled narrower causes, defined not by any universal principles but along the lines of identity. This turned liberalism's original project on its head: Two centuries ago, and up until the late 1960s, it was conservatives who argued for the importance of tradition, tribe, culture, for all the things given, while liberals put their faith in the free individual, who transcended any specificities of time and place, and whose rights were universal, by virtue of being human. Rhetorically, at least, all of that changed in the past few decades. The right took up the universalist language of reason, freedom, and truth, while multiculturalism spoke for group grievances based on the accident of birth. Many of them were real and redress was long overdue, but the idea of social justice ended up being someone else's business.

While liberalism slept, the country became more corporate, less democratic, less equal, more complacent. Liberalism has been a kind of enzyme in America's democratic system, periodically catalyzing reactions, speeding up change, making the organism more vital. Without it, our democracy tends to get fat and sluggish, as the pursuit of happiness guaranteed in the Declaration of Independence becomes a wholly private matter. In the tension between individual and community that every democracy has to negotiate, what we saw in America in the years leading up to September 11 was the triumph of market individualism, without commitments. The polis was routed and the sense of civic responsibility died on both the left and the right. Instead, they offered a choice of hedonisms.

Dissatisfaction with the condition of democracy isn't new. It recurs among writers and intellectuals throughout American history, almost always couched in images of rot or decay or slackness, as periods of intense civic activism give way to ages of business dominance. The republicans of the Revolutionary era saw their new country release the massive energy of a free people into the getting of wealth, and it was not the republic for which men had pledged their lives, their fortunes, and their sacred honor.

By 1809 Philip Freneau, a Jeffersonian poet and journalist, beheld his countrymen "besotted by prosperity, corrupted by avarice, abject from luxury," and in 1812 he proposed another war against the British as a dubious restoration of the spirit of '76. After the supreme sacrifices of the Civil War, Walt Whitman began to wonder what the fighting had all been for—whether making America safe for Jay Gould and John D. Rockefeller and a victorious people "with hearts of rags and souls of chalk" had merited Gettysburg's last full measure of devotion. "Is not Democracy of human rights humbug after all?" Whitman asked. In his 1949 book *The Vital Center*, Arthur Schlesinger, Jr., tried to suck new life into the lungs of the New Deal and antitotalitarianism as the stagnant waters of the television era started to rise around him: "Why does not democracy believe in itself with passion? Why is freedom not a fighting faith?" Democracy, it turns out, is a muscle that needs more frequent exercise than Americans have generally been interested in mustering.

In our own gilded age—whose obituary some commentators wrote after September 11—intellectuals played a curiously muted role. Who will be regarded as the Freneau, the Whitman, or the Schlesinger of the Nasdaq era? There was no convincing critique, no passionate dissent, no partisan literature that moved significant numbers of people and stands a chance of being read in ten years. The reasons for this intellectual vacuum are many. Academic thinking, infatuated with postmodernist theory, has satisfied itself with a fake-specialist jargon and a coy relativism that prefers dancing circles around important questions to the risk of trying to answer them. Political dissidence suffers, as it has in this country at least since Thoreau, from a sneering contempt for average American life and a sentimental insistence that reality simply fall in line behind enlightened feelings. The best imaginative writers withdrew into the inner life and its discontents, or else wrote about American society with such compulsive irony that nothing could be affirmed beyond a style of narrative brilliance. There is also the possibility that most intellectuals, in universities and think tanks and journals, have no authentic quarrel with American life. Seduction by iced latte, mutual fund, and *The Sopranos* is a slow, nearly invisible disease; it can happen without leaving a trace in print, yet at some point the organism has lost the impulse to object. An opposition that is financially secure, mentally insincere, and generally ignored isn't likely to produce *Common Sense* or *Democratic Vistas*. Very few intellectuals today—and this goes for conservatives as well, including those who have made careers out of loudly claiming otherwise—feel a strong enough attachment to their country to want to change it. The idea that anything of great consequence depends on the condition of America's democracy sounds quaint.

This is the landscape on which the sun rose that late-summer Tuesday morning, as the polls opened in New York for a primary election that bored everyone, and the bankers rode the escalator toward their smoked-salmon omelettes. Then out of the blue sky came what Hannah Arendt called a new thing in the world. It was the worst thing most Americans alive today have ever known. And the task was now ours to understand how the world was, and was not, new.

3

We are engaged in a war for world opinion, a war of ideas. No one should doubt that we are losing it—and that this has something to do with the condition of American democracy. Our leaders have failed to articulate what we are fighting for beyond our own security and the assertion of our power around the world; and the failure is no accident or "missed opportunity." It comes from the fact that they themselves have no ardor for democracy. The ideals of freedom and equality, secularism, tolerance, and critical inquiry that have lain at the heart of the American experiment from the beginning get lip service from those in power; much of the world, with some reason, sees America's commitment to them as shallow and hypocritical.

The fight against political Islam isn't a clash of civilizations, and it isn't an imperialist campaign. As Paul Berman has written, it is a conflict of ideologies, and they come down to the century-old struggle between totalitarianism and liberal democracy. There is no possibility of a negotiated peace, because the ideologies are incompatible—they can't coexist. "Between democracy and totalitarianism there can be no compromise," said an authority on the subject, Benito Mussolini. Leaving aside the implacable foes who want us dead, America has to persuade people around the world that this is their fight, too; that the side of liberal democracy is where their hope lies.

In the war on terror, the ultimate enemy isn't a method, even one as apocalyptically menacing as Al Qaeda–style terrorism. It's the outlook that produced Al Qaeda—in this case, political Islam, but at bottom the view of all people who fear and hate the modern democratic world, with its fluidity, its openness, its assertion of the individual's freedom and of human equality. America is the most vibrant example. America is also the world's leading power, constantly racking up resentments. It's this combination of facts that makes our situation as complex and delicate as it is.

America is seen by much of the world as an empire without actual colonies, perhaps the most dominant since Rome. To Americans this view is bewildering. Unlike the British or the French, Americans have never had an interest in empire building. They elect presidents who have barely traveled abroad, eliminate the U.S. Information Service and shut down cultural centers in foreign capitals, resent being "the world's policeman," and pride themselves on their ignorance of other countries. Throughout the decade after the Cold War ended, American military action and inaction, corporate dominance, and cultural influence were making us the object of hope and confusion and anger among hundreds of millions of people, from Kigali to Jakarta. Meanwhile, it's difficult to think of a period when Americans showed less interest in the rest of the world. Genocide, famine, plague, economic upheaval, filthy wars on every continent, and, of course, international terrorism—an incredibly tumultuous period (at what was supposed to be the end of history), but citizens of the world's superpower largely succeeded in not paying attention. While we were absorbed with Internet chat rooms and a blue Gap dress, power and resentment accumulated in front of our noses or behind our backs. Even the battle over multiculturalism turned out to have nothing to teach us about anyone else—it was an internal fight and a ritualized one, the narcissism of small differences. September 11 came as an immense slap to this immense complacency.

The real question is not whether America is an empire, but what to do with the power we have. It's a question with which Americans are instinctively uncomfortable, none more than those who think of themselves as liberals. Much of what made up liberal thinking in the past few decades will be of no help from now on. The reluctance to make judgments, the finely ironic habits of thought, the reflexive contempt for patriotism, the suspicion of uniforms and military qualities, the sentimentality about oppressed peoples, the irresponsibility about hard choices, the embarrassment with phrases like "democratic values" and "Western civilization"—the softheadedness into which liberalism sank after the 1960s seems as useless today as isolationism in 1941 or compromise in 1861. If there is any guide to this strange new era in our recent past, it could be the liberal anticommunism of the postwar period, which confidently defended democracy in the face of totalitarianism but also took economic justice and nation building seriously. It was both tough and wise; it had a decent respect for the opinion of mankind; it understood the struggle against Communism to be a struggle for hearts and minds.

Breaking the seal of tyranny in the Arab world and letting in fresh liberal air is a matter of our security as much as their freedom. But the ultimate audience for this fight is neither in the West nor in the Arab countries, but among the vast majority of the world's poor. Beyond the struggle to survive—to avoid disease, find enough to eat, educate their children, stay out of the way of men with guns—people in Asia and Africa and Latin America increasingly wonder whether the modern world holds a place for them, whether dignity and a decent life and a sense of identity are possible. This is an economic problem, but not only that—it's also cultural and, in a way, existential. Globalization didn't lose its importance on September 11. Just the opposite: it underlies everything else, and the shape it takes in the new century will determine whether the world's poor see America as a beacon or a blackmailer.

Without a vibrant, hardheaded liberalism in America, the era that began on September 11, 2001, will continue in the direction that we now see: narrow, defensive, chauvinistic, an American war for American security that leaves the rest of the world feeling ignored or threatened. The title of a conservative manifesto proclaimed *Why We Fight: Moral Clarity and the War on Terrorism*. Moral clarity is not why we should fight; it is why the other side fights. Our idea of the good society is secular and democratic—an idea of human possibility, not fixed and eternal truth. Beyond sheer physical survival, a liberal civilization like ours should fight for the ability to remain open to what's foreign or unknown, tell leaders what they don't want to hear, tolerate moral uncertainty, act in spite of self-criticism, and ask questions like: Can a civilization remain liberal when it's as heavily armed as ours? Can a fight for democracy be led by the world's greatest power?

Liberals have an uneasy relationship with force. Force has no sense of complexity. It reduces everything to the elemental level where thinking is trampled underfoot. When America entered World War I, an argument broke out among the first generation of Americans to call themselves liberals. On one side, people like the editors of *The New Republic* saw the war as an international extension of Progressive reform. In language as exalted as their hero Woodrow Wilson's, they proclaimed the world's first humanitarian war. On the other side stood skeptics like *The New Republic*'s own young contributor Randolph Bourne. To him, liberal intellectuals urging war were like children who imagined they could control a wild elephant by riding on its back. "Willing war means willing all the evils that are organically bound up with it," he wrote (but not in *The New Republic*, which banned his criticism). "A good many people still seem to believe in a peculiar kind of democratic and antiseptic war. The pacifists opposed the war because they knew this was an illusion, and because of the myriad hurts they knew war would do the promise of democracy at home. For once the babes and sucklings seem to have been wiser than the children of light." Intellectuals like John Dewey, Bourne said, were too rational to understand war. On airships of idealism, they unleashed a barrage of violence that fell on American towns as well as the trenches in France. The war whipped up a frenzy of intolerance all over the country that destroyed what was left of the Progressive era, mocked Wilson's vision of a just new world order, and produced a backlash against reform lasting for the next decade.

Liberalism has a tendency to respond to its doubts by overreaching. There are good reasons in history and principle—Vietnam is one—to keep Randolph Bourne's warning in mind. But there are equally good reasons—the war against fascism—to imagine exceptions. We have to answer the demands of our own age. And what we need today is more, not less, confidence in liberal democracy. America has always swung feverishly between its individualism and its moralism—between periods of business dominance, when the rest of the world can go to hell, and bursts of reformist zeal, when America shines a light unto the nations. September 11 was a hinge between two such eras—and our current conservative leadership wants to take the country into one without leaving the other. It wants to wage war on terrorism and still preserve all the privileges and injustices of a low dishonest age. It wants lockstep unity and unequal sacrifice.

Citizens of a democracy need to know what they're fighting for, and to believe in it. We are fighting the wrong fight if corporations can move offshore to avoid taxes while the working poor get audited; if the vice president's former company profiteers off the war while Americans taking care of old people make six dollars an hour; if millionaires buy elections here while generals win them by fraud and force overseas; if security becomes an excuse for taking away some liberties while self-censorship removes others; if Saudi oil princes are coddled while Muslim students can't get U.S. visas; if Afghan warlords are left in power while returning refugees are allowed to starve. In the long run we will lose if this fight isn't for something. It ought to be for democracy.

Stop Making Sense

Mother Jones, May/June 2003

On the table by my bed sits a stack of half-read books—a volume of poetry, a couple of novels, a history of the Middle East, Camus's *The Rebel*, a new book about the lure of war. I have no hope of finishing any of them. I can't spare the time from the all-consuming task of keeping up with the news.

These days I buy my daily paper, *The New York Times*, with dread and resentment—not just for the content, but for the weight. Since September 12, 2001, it seems to have ballooned to double its old size. The ink of international disaster rubs off on my fingers from no fewer than six full theme pages in the A section. So intense is the competition for space that a massive car bombing in Colombia is relegated deep into the inside pages. While reading the paper, I also scan www.nytimes.com for breaking news, as well as the wire services and the BBC. By midmorning, after swallowing the great lump of the *Times* and digesting it along with a dose of radio news and half a dozen articles e-mailed by various friends and Listservs, I'm jittery with crises. And there's still the rest of the day to get through.

"May you live in interesting times" is not, in fact, an ancient Chinese curse. According to the experts, the only Chinese proverb that comes close says, "It's better to be a dog in a peaceful time than a man in a chaotic time." The "curse" is Western, probably American, in origin. We've lived under its spell for going on two years now. Lately I've been thinking about the effect this is having on our minds.

It's the nature of the age to expose us to an endless amount of information about wars, planned wars, threats, atrocities, grievances, hatreds—

and, simultaneously, to our own inability to do much about any of it. These days everyone's brain is a situation room, but the activity flows only one way—inward. The response team inside is flooded with updates, warning lights, alarms, but the crisis atmosphere never resolves itself in constructive action. It's the mental equivalent of a permanent orange alert, with words in place of duct tape. Add to this the persistent sense of unreality that infects the consciousness: while relatively few Americans have been directly affected by anything that's happened on the terror front since September 11, every day's news involves us in the most personal way, because we're responsible or outraged or threatened. On my block of Brooklyn, not two miles from Ground Zero, it's hard to believe that there's a war on anywhere. Every morning the elderly Arab who sells me my paper and I smile and say "How are you?" while the headlines on the counter between us tell of Arabs and Americans inflicting terrible deaths on one another, or promising to.

This mental state of emergency—high readiness alert, nonstop intelligence chatter, response dysfunction—is a recipe for a severe kind of civic neurosis. It's an anxiety all its own—not the classic trauma of actual events, but the disturbance of excessive awareness. There's nothing new about information overload; the twenty-four-hour news cycle arose in the nineties with cable and the Internet, and it was considered at the time to be a technological breakthrough, part of the general speeding up of life that came with the boom. What's peculiar to this moment is round-the-clock saturation with bulletins from an unfamiliar, complex, and frightening world. The ticker at the bottom of the screen is no longer tracking the fluctuation of stocks; it's announcing the latest mass threat. What we don't know could kill us, yet the more information we absorb, the less we truly understand and the more helpless we feel (and the more we lose trust in the policymakers and experts who are supposed to help us sort it all out).

In these circumstances, the besieged mind inevitably develops strategies to continue functioning. But they tend to be insufficient, if not misleading and even dangerous. They distort reality more than they clarify it. Lately I've tried to perform a diagnosis, taking myself as a starting point, to analyze our mental response to the inner disturbances of the times. What I've found are a variety of coping strategies that seem to allow us to handle the flow of information, but at the same time keep us from thinking clearly about it.

Nerve-Agent Words

These are the kinds of words that give us the illusion of having said something definite, scored a point, solved a problem, disabled an opponent. They include "imperial," "anti-American," "security," "preemptive," "blowback," "good," "evil," "democracy." Given definition and context, many of them could be the basis for an argument, but most of the time they are deliberately converted to an anesthetizing gas.

Defining abstract concepts is notoriously difficult. But these words are particularly dangerous at a time when everyone wants to achieve moral clarity, yet all the options are bad. (Which is the right course—supporting an increasingly autocratic Pervez Musharraf, or abandoning him to the radical forces in his own military?) In my own case, the word I've found myself resorting to again and again is democracy. It stands for whatever I think is good. Recently I offered it as the solution to the problems of the Muslim world without offering any detailed guide to what that meant or how it could be achieved. Depending on your viewpoint, you can pull out a term like "anti-American" or "imperialist" to dismiss your opponent's entire worldview—without any of the work of trying to understand what that worldview actually is.

One striking thing about the new political vocabulary is that it obfuscates with what sounds like clarity. A few decades ago, the characteristic examples of propaganda were Latinate, quasi-technical terms like "pacification" or "counterrevolutionary." Now an apparently simple, tough-minded word like "blowback" or "evildoer" releases just as much theatrical smoke as the jargon of the Pentagon or the Soviet Central Committee once did. The new style of deception reflects the pervasiveness of ad lingo, just as older political language accompanied the rise of twentieth-century bureaucracies; in the mouths of public figures after September 11, "Let's roll" was a variation on Nike's "Just do it."

Liquid Facts

Living in a state of permanent confusion—in some ways the only appropriate response to the current crisis—is more than most of us are capable of. We badly want the world to make sense; we want a unified field theory that explains everything and justifies all our views. But unified field theories require you to pour large batches of facts into small, oddly shaped containers, and to throw out whatever won't fit. If, for example, you oppose Saudi Arabia's ruling family for its corruption, repressiveness, and hypocrisy, and you advocate liberal reform for the sake of people there as well as our own security, then it's easy to overlook the fact that the main engine of reform in that country is the ruling family, and that "the people" tend to be more conservative, more anti-Western, and more open to Islamist extremism than their leaders. The more confusing and contradictory reality becomes, the more we cling to our fantasies of how things should be; facts, it turns out, can be far less stubborn things than opinions.

Vanishing Positions

If, on the other hand, it becomes too hard (or inconvenient or unpopular) to maintain a particular belief, you can always pretend you never held it. Once you've concealed the change from others, it's only a matter of time before you've hidden it from yourself. The same person who once wanted to shut down the CIA can still score points by jeering at the agency's failure to head off the terror attacks. The president himself campaigned not long ago for a more "humble" foreign policy. These days, each of us has an inner press secretary who delivers "clarifications" with a straight face, a psychological mechanism by which yesterday's statement automatically becomes inoperative.

A shifting position is much easier to notice in someone other than yourself, especially if he happens to be a columnist whose views are regularly published. Thomas Friedman of *The New York Times* made his reputation as a pundit by writing about the inevitability of globalization—the idea that trade, technology, and information flow are making the world more integrated and ultimately more peaceful. This is an idea that the events since September 11 have at the very least complicated; yet now Friedman writes twice a week about a world in perpetual conflict with every bit as much assurance as he used to write about a world becoming one. Former *Nation* columnist Christopher Hitchens has dumped many of the positions of an entire career (two years ago he chastised the Clinton and Bush administrations for refusing to cooperate with international institutions;

today he endorses unilateral war), with no suggestion that any reconsideration took place. Hitchens's willingness to change after September 11 shows an intellectual courage that many of his detractors lack (it's also more interesting), but a public accounting would have shown more.

The Told-You-So Principle

Perhaps the easiest way to win an argument—including one with yourself—is simply to declare that the other side is wrong. You might not know what to do about a nuclear North Korea, but you can be certain that the Bush administration is making the situation worse. You might not know the rights and wrongs of the Pakistan-India standoff, but you're against nuclear weapons and you're convinced that the United States should have done much more to prevent their proliferation—so you throw up your hands and say, essentially, "I told you so."

All these strategies are a natural and often unconscious response to unimaginably complex times. They are not unique to this country or this moment, but crisis requires their overuse—and eventually they make all of us coconspirators in the demise of honest public debate. What Hannah Arendt called a new thing in the world—a response to crisis that goes beyond simply repeating history—requires an openness to uncertainty and confusion that few of us can now tolerate, especially in public.

Clarity and conviction are wonderful things; I wouldn't want to be told that I can never have them again. But a better test of mental health and civic responsibility just now may be whether you can endure inconsistency, hold a fact without manipulating its shape, use words that will expose the falseness of your own thoughts, and accept that you will be embarrassed tomorrow by much of what you think and say today.

On the Morning After Saddam

The New York Times Magazine, March 2, 2003 (under the title "Dreaming of Democracy")

Last summer, the State Department convened a number of Iraqi exiles to advise the United States government on the problems that Iraq would face after the fall of Saddam Hussein. It was called, rather grandly, the Future of Iraq Project. Among the topics was democracy, and among the Iraqis invited to join was a dissident named Kanan Makiya. He seemed a natural choice. In 1989, under the pseudonym Samir al-Khalil, Makiya published a book called *Republic of Fear*, which relentlessly dissected the totalitarian nature of Saddam's regime. The pseudonym wasn't a whim; in those years Iraq's overseas dissidents were frequently bumped off. Ignored upon publication, the book became a bestseller the next year with the outbreak of the Persian Gulf War, and Makiya, the son of Iraq's most distinguished architect and a trained architect himself, was thrust into the turbulence of Middle Eastern politics. At the end of the war, during a forum at Harvard, the author revealed his identity for the first time and urged President George H. W. Bush to finish the job the war had left undone by getting rid of Saddam Hussein. Makiya's ideas cut deeply against the grain of Arab intellectual life and won him both powerful admirers and powerful enemies.

But when the State Department's invitation came last year, Makiya balked. He assumed that the Future of Iraq Project wasn't serious. "Some people in the government are talking democratic change," he told me recently, referring to the civilian hawks in the Pentagon, "and there are other people who think that's all a pile of garbage. These others are in the State Department and the CIA today. They are very powerful players."

The history of the Iraqi opposition's relationship with the United States government is a tangled and unhappy one, leaving deep suspicions between and within them. Iraq is one of the most diverse countries in the Arab world, with a majority population of Shiite Arabs, who predominate in the south, as well as large minorities of Sunni Arabs in the center, Kurds in the north, and smaller groups of Assyrians, Turkomans, Armenians, and a surviving handful of Jews. This ethnic makeup explains some of the Iraqi opposition's notorious divisions, but the political differences are even more rancorous. And nothing Iraqis say about one another quite equals the vitriol of the feuding over Iraq within the American government.

The Iraq question seems to exist on the far side of a looking glass where everyone turns into his opposite. The State Department and the CIA, considered the moderate wing of the Bush foreign policy apparatus, favor working through Iraq's traditional politics, which would mean removing Saddam but letting power stay with his ruling Baath Party, mainly minority Sunni Arabs. The State Department wants stability above all. Meanwhile, the hard-line hawks at the Pentagon and in the vice president's office, with their professed devotion to sweeping transformation in Iraq, want the transition to democracy to be led by the Western-oriented exiles grouped since 1992 under the loose umbrella of the Iraqi National Congress, whose chairman, Ahmad Chalabi, is close to Makiya.

The battle is less between left and right than between realists and revolutionaries. It has simmered throughout the buildup to war, and it could haunt and possibly sabotage the postwar reconstruction. It makes an odd kind of sense that Makiya, fifty-three, who was once a Trotskyist and supporter of radical Palestinian politics, has ended up as a liberal in the camp of neoconservative zealots, who see a democratic Iraq as a lever for moving the entire Arab world toward the West.

In the end, Makiya decided to call the State Department's bluff—to "hoist them on their own petard." He joined the Future of Iraq Project's Democratic Principles Working Group, and along with a few allies from the exile community in Washington and London, he took over the writing of a detailed report on democracy after Saddam. There's something in it to offend everyone. The report proposes, among other radical ideas, a representative "transitional authority" chosen by Iraq's opposition exiles and ready to operate inside the country as the regime crumbles; the postwar demilitarization of Iraq; the dismantling of the Baath Party along the lines of German denazification; war crimes trials and a truth commission; thoroughgoing secularism; a constitution in which individual and minority group rights would be guaranteed in advance of local and then national elections, so that democracy does not lead to tyranny of the majority; a decentralized federal government in which the regions would be drawn along geographic rather than ethnic lines; and an end to ethnic identity as a basis for the state. As long as Iraq is defined as an Arab state, other ethnic groups, such as Kurds and Assyrians, will continue to be second-class citizens. In Kanan Makiya's blueprint, Iraq would officially cease to be an Arab country.

"It's the architect in me," he says, nursing a cold over Japanese tea in Cambridge, Massachusetts, where he lives. Makiya is a balding and somewhat disheveled Brandeis University professor of Middle East studies with a soft, intense manner. His office in a Cambridge apartment is lined with leatherbound books on Islamic history and literature. When his cell phone rings, he apologizes for having temporarily acquired one—"a disaster for a writer." The immediate world of waitresses and crosswalks constantly surprises Makiya out of his thoughts, which these days are elsewhere. This unlikely revolutionary is taking the huge gamble that by riding on the back of an American war, he can hold the Americans to their own talk and help direct the outcome.

"We've played a kind of game," he says. "It's not a game, it's serious—we've emerged with something very hard to disown even though it comes up with conclusions opposite to what the State Department wanted. They never wanted that kind of document in the first place."

In December, Makiya went to London to present the report at a meeting of the hundreds of mullahs, monarchists, ex-officers, party bosses, businessmen, intellectuals, and schemers who make up Iraq's fractious exiled opposition. In London I saw that the qualities that make Makiya a powerful thinker also make him a bad politician—the most eloquent spokesman for Iraqi democracy and at times his own worst advocate. In the weeks since London, the pressure on him has only grown, along with the difficulty of the task. The closer we get to war, the harder it is to believe that the liberal democracy Makiya envisions will be the outcome. The problem isn't just the Iraqis. It's also the Americans.

• • •

No one knows what will happen when Saddam Hussein's death grip on his country is finally broken. Prediction is a dangerous business in politics generally, but in the case of Iraq, where since 1968 the only political activity that won't get you killed is unambiguous loyalty to the Baath Party, the future is especially opaque. For the past several months the country has been crawling with foreign journalists, yet the security apparatus is so extensive and terror so deeply internalized that most of what we know about Iraqis' unofficial thoughts is confined to facial expressions and buried meanings. When Makiya and two other Iraqis were invited to the Oval Office in January, he told President Bush that invading American troops would be greeted with "sweets and flowers." More fancifully, Professor Fouad Ajami, a Middle East scholar at the Johns Hopkins School of Advanced International Studies, predicts "kites and boom boxes."

A recent report compiled by the International Crisis Group, a policy organization based in Brussels, from secret interviews held in three Iraqi cities last fall gives perhaps the most thorough account of political thought in Iraq today, and it lends some support to the optimists. With unexpected homogeneity, Iraqis voiced an acceptance of the inevitability of war and a change of government. "We have nothing to lose," one Iraqi said. According to the report, "A significant number of those Iraqis interviewed, with surprising candor, expressed their view that if such a change required an American-led attack, they would support it." Though fear of a destructive war and anarchy afterward runs deep, "the overwhelming sentiment among those interviewed was one of frustration and impatience with the status quo."

But when it comes to the Iraqi landscape after the dictator's fall, the International Crisis Group report has more sobering news for those who imagine a swift transition to democracy. "Thoughts about a post-Saddam Iraq remain extremely vague and inarticulate," it found. In the words of one Iraqi, "We have become political dwarfs." Questions about successor regimes and federal democracy met with indifference. On the other hand, according to the report, the opposition in exile "is viewed with considerable suspicion"—far more than a foreign occupier would be—"and the desire for a long-term U.S. involvement is higher than anticipated."

When Saddam suddenly ordered the release of tens of thousands of prisoners from the notorious Abu Ghraib prison last fall, the surge of inmates from within the walls and family members from without overwhelmed

prison guards and crushed a number of people to death at the very moment of freedom. Reporters who ventured into the bowels of the prison
were struck by the appalling odors of long human confinement. When
the seal on Iraq is broken, the surge will be just as intense, and the smell
of decades of repression just as rank. "With the removal of the dictator,"
says Thomas Carothers, a democracy expert at the Carnegie Endowment
for International Peace, "political life will begin immediately," and unless
American troops are able to provide civil order while they hunt down
weapons depots and resisting units of the Special Republican Guard, it
will initially look more like vigilantism than party building. Peter Galbraith, a professor at the National Defense University in Washington,
says: "As the American troops sweep north, they'll pass Basra in the early
days. Presumably they won't go into the city. Then who's going to govern
the city? Will there be another uprising? I think there's a good chance."

In 1991, when Kurds in the north and Shiites in the south rose up
against Saddam after his defeat in Kuwait, the score settling and looting
were so extreme that Makiya later wrote of a "basic nihilistic impulse."
Today, Iraqi Kurdistan, under the protection of an allied no-fly zone, has a
flourishing civil society and the beginnings of democratic self-government.
Peter Galbraith, who as a Senate aide in the late 1980s saw the effects of
genocide in Kurdish villages and unsuccessfully tried to turn Reagan administration policy against Saddam, says: "A unified and democratic Iraq
is an oxymoron. The important point about the north is that the Iraqi
identity is disappearing there."

A breakaway Kurdistan is a long-term possibility; civil violence in the
south is the more immediate threat. The Shiites there have been especially persecuted by Saddam since their 1991 uprising was put down with
tens of thousands of deaths. Joseph Braude, a young Iraqi American
whose book *The New Iraq* will be published this month, says that the
impoverished Shiite south is "not an existential threat to the map of Iraq.
It's more of a terrible social challenge of Iraqi society." The distribution of
wealth, more than the ethnic division of power, he says, will determine
whether there will ever be social peace in Iraq. Iraq's Shiites—the most
disenfranchised group, with the freshest grievances and the strongest
claim on a share of power—will challenge the policing and diplomatic
skills of an army of occupation after the flowers, sweets, kites, and boom
boxes disappear. Patrick Clawson, deputy director of the Washington In-

stitute for Near East Policy and editor of the book *How to Build a New Iraq After Saddam*, thinks that Iraq's disintegration into ethnic pieces is less of a threat than a series of "revolving-door coups," and for that reason the United States military should keep intact elements of Iraq's army to maintain order and even join a new government.

To the crucial questions of who will take power after Saddam and for how long, the administration has been loath to give a public answer. For months, a surprisingly public argument has raged between the State Department and the Pentagon over the shape of Iraq after a war. People close to the administration's decision making about the postwar period describe a confused, largely day-to-day process, in contrast with the disciplined long-term planning for the war itself. In the Pentagon version, Iraqi exiles would form a provisional government prepared to take power under American protection. The State Department, which intensely dislikes the Iraqi National Congress and its chairman, Ahmad Chalabi, has done everything possible to block this possibility and either encourage a coup or plan for the American military to run Iraq for months or years until it would gradually hand over power to Iraqis.

Chalabi is a banker with an aristocratic manner and a controversial reputation who has devoted a considerable part of his fortune and the past decade of his life to building up the Iraqi National Congress, which is based in London. He elicits strong reactions of admiration or contempt in Washington. David L. Phillips, a senior fellow at the Council on Foreign Relations who worked closely with the State Department on its Future of Iraq Project, says, "If Ahmad Chalabi walked down a street in Baghdad today, nobody would recognize him." In the view of the State Department's Middle East hands, there's something inauthentic about Iraqi exiles, soaked for years in nostalgia, grand ideas, and impotence. Some of them haven't set foot in Baghdad for more than three decades; Makiya left to attend MIT in 1968, the year the Baath Party seized total power, and has lived in Cambridge or London ever since. Condoleezza Rice, to whom both American factions have appealed as an arbiter, told one Iraqi, referring to Poland's World War II–era, self-proclaimed government in exile, "The trouble with the Iraqi opposition is they're like the London Poles." But the Pentagon hawks and their neoconservative allies argue just as passionately that the exiles are the only Iraqis capable of forming a government, all political life inside Iraq having long since been extinguished. In this view, the State Department's scorn for the Iraqi National Congress amounts to a disbelief in Arab democracy.

It now seems that the State Department has won this fight. As Peter Galbraith suggested, half in jest, the Pentagon will get its war and State will get its postwar. In mid-February, administration officials finally announced plans for an American military government to run the country for at least two years, guaranteeing security and overseeing the reconstruction of Iraq and the election of an Iraqi government. Baath Party officials would be removed from the top levels of the bureaucracy, but those a notch down would be kept on to work with their American superiors. Gen. Tommy Franks of the United States Central Command would take a job that the Pentagon never wanted to exist, acting as a sort of discreet and colorless MacArthur. Iraq's exiles would be the losers, relegated to seats on an advisory council to be shared with American-picked Iraqis from inside the country. This proposed course of action, played down for months by the administration, suggests that in the absence of a strong coalition of countries, a largely American war will be followed by a largely American peace.

There are other projections for what might take place—ones that follow the law of unintended consequences. The Turkish army occupies northern Iraq to prevent an independent Kurdistan on its border, prompting Turkish and Iraqi Kurds to join forces against the Turks and Iraqi Turkomans. The Kurds refuse to rejoin the country that once tried to exterminate them unless federalism gives them control over the oil reserves of Kirkuk. The two Kurdish parties resume the fighting that broke out between them in 1996. The Iranian hard-liners, realizing that Iraq's territorial integrity has become a theoretical matter, take the opportunity to finish off the opposition mujahideen across the border. Shiite mullahs, finding themselves locked out of power again, resist American authority and form antioccupation militias. A Sunni officer in the Iraqi army pulls off an eleventh-hour coup, declares himself friendly to the United States, and stops the process cold. Makiya calls this last "my greatest fear."

In Arabic, "Iraq" means "well-rooted country," which suggests the kind of promotional thinking that makes urban planners christen a concrete housing project "Metropolitan Gardens." The country was assembled at Versailles after World War I out of three former Ottoman provinces and handed over by the League of Nations in 1920 to be a British mandate, breaking the promise of postwar independence that T. E. Lawrence, better known as Lawrence of Arabia, had made to Britain's Arab allies. But the British found this unruly concoction of peoples more trouble to govern than it was worth, even with Lawrence's friend King Faisal I on the throne, and in 1932 Iraq became an independent constitutional monarchy, though the imperial power didn't leave without securing favorable oil concessions. Within four years Iraq gave the Arab world its first modern coup. After that, the violence never really stopped, with coups, ethnic pogroms, and massacres among political parties. (The Arab Baath movement emerged in World War II as a pro-Nazi group.) But the most turbulent decade followed the overthrow of the constitutional monarchy in 1958. One military regime was toppled by the next. In 1968 the Arab Baath Socialist Party finally consolidated power, destroying its opponents among the Communists and the other Arab nationalists. Saddam, the head of internal security, quickly acquired de facto power but assumed the presidency only in 1979 amid a bloody purge. Chaos gave way to dictatorship, two ruinous foreign wars, and the Kurdish genocide.

Iraqis today, depending on their age, express deep nostalgia either for the cosmopolitan Baghdad of the years before the Jews were made to flee upon the creation of Israel; or for the constitutional monarchy before the 1958 coup; or for the oil-rich years of the 1970s. But while Iraq might once have been stable or wealthy or tolerant, it was never really democratic. Makiya first got to know Ahmad Chalabi when they sat together on an airplane and Makiya was impressed to find the chairman of the Iraqi National Congress reading a thick tome on the reconstruction of postwar Germany. But anyone seeking historical lessons for a democratic Iraq has to face the fact that Germany before Hitler was liberal compared with Iraq before Saddam.

This bloody history has produced a hopeful new idea. Call it Iraqi exceptionalism. It's the idea that Iraqis have suffered so intensely under a radical nationalist regime that they are by now immune to the anti-Western rhetoric that remains potent in the rest of the Arab world. Iraqis crushed by Saddam's brand of Arab nationalism do not see America and Israel as their eternal enemies. The real enemy is the one within.

This thinking took hold of Makiya during the Iran-Iraq War. He left his father's London architectural practice when Mohamed Makiya began to receive commissions from Saddam to rebuild Baghdad in monumental fashion; he threw himself into the research for *Republic of Fear*. It changed him from a revolutionary Marxist to a liberal democrat. He began to think outside the dominant lines of Middle Eastern ideologies: rather than an anti-imperialist resistance leader, he became a dissident in the Eastern European way, diagnosing the pathology of homegrown tyranny. "It wasn't the United States, it was Iraqis and Iranians who were bleeding themselves to death," he told me. "This sense that the malaise was principally in my world, and not principally in the United States, was the seismic shift in my politics."

The implications of the shift are far-reaching, for the lens through which most of the Arab world views Israel and America might no longer fit Iraq. Without denying the justice of the Palestinian cause, Makiya says, Arabs shouldn't regard it as the key to solving regional problems. The crucial issue is no longer national liberation, but democracy based on human rights. These ideas came to a head during the Gulf War, when most of the Arab world supported Saddam. *Republic of Fear*, copies of which had been smuggled into Iraq, made Makiya famous among his countrymen, and after the war, when he traveled through the Kurdish region to film a BBC documentary, *Saddam's Killing Fields*, Iraqis sought him out to tell their stories of the genocide and the bloody repression of the 1991 uprisings. If Makiya had simply collected them in his next book and called it *Cruelty*, he wouldn't have become a lightning rod in the Arab world. But his anger at the Arab intelligentsia's complacency before Saddam's crimes was burning too high, and *Cruelty and Silence*, which came out in 1993, was not a cool meditation but a cri de coeur that named names. "There can be no more romance and no more false heroics in the Arab world," Makiya wrote. "There is only the legacy of pain which must be grappled with by a new language and in a new style."

Not surprisingly, the idea of Iraqi exceptionalism has brought denunciation from many Arab quarters, including the leading Arab intellectual in the West, the literary critic Edward Said. Writing in an Arabic newspaper in December, Said, who teaches at Columbia University, accused Makiya of being an inauthentic Arab and of selling himself to American imperialism and Zionism out of sheer vanity. For Said, a Palestinian who sees the Israeli occupation as the primary problem of the Middle East, Makiya has made himself the tool of Israel's right wing and of America's interest in Arab oil. This fight is far more than personal: it suggests an intellectual turning point in the history of Arab politics.

One striking feature of Iraqi exceptionalism is the attitude toward Jews. Before their exodus in the early 1950s, Jews made up an estimated one-third of Baghdad's highly diverse population. Among certain exiles, Jewish music and culture have become part of the lore of pre-Baathist Iraq. The Iraqi National Congress newspaper *Al Mutamar* recently published an article by an Israeli writer and articles about Iraqi Jewish poetry. A London coffee shop owner named Dia Kashi went so far as to travel to Israel, meet with Iraqi Jews, and help found the Iraqi-Israeli Friendship Committee. Several Jews were invited as delegates to the London opposition conference.

The champions of Iraqi exceptionalism include the neoconservatives in the administration—Donald Rumsfeld, Paul Wolfowitz, and Douglas Feith at the Pentagon; John Bolton at the State Department; Lewis Libby in the vice president's office; Richard Perle, who is chairman of the Defense Policy Board, a panel that advises the Pentagon—and numerous scholars, columnists, and activists, most of them identified with the pro-Israel American right. In recent weeks, President Bush himself has appeared to embrace the idea as a geopolitical rationale for war. The story being told goes like this:

The Arab world is hopelessly sunk in corruption and popular discontent. Misrule and a culture of victimhood have left Arabs economically stagnant and prone to seeing their problems in delusional terms. The United States has contributed to the pathology by cynically shoring up dictatorships; September 11 was one result. Both the Arab world and official American attitudes toward it need to be jolted out of their rut. An invasion of Iraq would provide the necessary shock, and a democratic Iraq would become an example of change for the rest of the region. Political Islam would lose its hold on the imagination of young Arabs as they watched a more successful model rise up in their midst. The Middle East's center of political, economic, and cultural gravity would shift from the region's theocracies and autocracies to its new, oil-rich democracy. And finally, the deadlock in which Israel and Palestine are trapped would end as Palestinians, realizing that their Arab backers were now tending their own democratic gardens, would accept compromise. By this way of thinking, the road to Damascus, Tehran, Riyadh, and Jerusalem goes through Baghdad.

The idea is sometimes referred to as a new domino theory, with tyrannies collapsing on top of one another. Among the harder heads at the State Department, I was told, it is also mocked as the Everybody Move Over One theory: Israel will take the West Bank, the Palestinians will get Jordan, and the members of Jordan's Hashemite ruling family will regain the Iraqi throne once held by their relative King Faisal I.

At times this story is told in the lofty moral language of Woodrow Wilson, the language that President Bush used religiously in his State of the Union address. Others—both advocates and detractors—tell the story in more naked terms of power and resources. David Frum, the former Bush speechwriter who wrote the first two words in the phrase "axis of evil," argues in his new book, *The Right Man*, "An American-led overthrow of Saddam Hussein—and a replacement of the radical Baathist dictatorship with a new government more closely aligned with the United States—would put America more wholly in charge of the region than any power since the Ottomans, or maybe the Romans."

It's an audacious idea, and part of its appeal lies in the audacity. It shoves history out of a deep hole. To the idea's strongest backers, status quo caution toward the sick, dangerous Middle East is contemptible, almost unbearable. "You have to start somewhere," says Danielle Pletka, a vice president of the American Enterprise Institute, a conservative research group. "There are always a million excuses not to do something like this." Who wouldn't choose amputation over gangrene? If we have the will and imagination, the thinking goes, we can strike one great blow at terrorism, tyranny, underdevelopment, and the region's hardest, saddest problem.

"It's called magical realism, Middle East style," says Thomas Carothers of the Carnegie Endowment for International Peace. Exactly how, he wonders, would this chain reaction occur? Arab countries are stuck between autocratic governments and Islamist opposition, he says, and "our invasion of Iraq isn't going to remove those political forces. They're going to be sitting there the next day." The war, which is vastly unpopular in the Arab world, is far more likely to improve the fortunes of the Islamists, he says, and provoke governments to tighten their grip, than to ventilate the region with an Arab spring.

The chances of democracy's succeeding even in Iraq under American occupation are highly questionable, Carothers argues. War seldom creates democracy; according to a recent article in *The Christian Science*

Monitor, of the eighteen regime changes forced by the United States in the twentieth century, only five resulted in democracy, and in the case of wars fought unilaterally, the number goes down to one—Panama. Democracy takes root from within, over a long period of time, in conditions that have never prevailed in Iraq. For democracy to have a chance would require a lengthy and careful American commitment to nation building— which could easily look to Iraqis and other Arabs like colonialism. Nor can we be sure that democracy, in Iraq or elsewhere, will lead to pro-American regimes; it might lead to the opposite. "The idea that there's a small democracy inside every society waiting to be released just isn't true," Carothers says. "If we're pinning our hopes on the idea that this will lead to a democratic change throughout the region, then we're invading for the wrong reason." Jessica T. Mathews, president of the Carnegie Endowment, adds, "'We've suffered so much that the only alternative is democracy'—as soon as you say it, you realize there's a mile between the beginning and end of that sentence."

One premise of the strategic rationale for war is that Arab public opinion—the resentment turning to fury that will probably greet an American invasion—doesn't matter, because it is wrong, even delusional. "America," Fouad Ajami writes, "ought to be able to live with this distrust and discount a good deal of this anti-Americanism as the 'road rage' of a thwarted Arab world—the congenital condition of a culture yet to take full responsibility for its self-inflicted wounds."

I ran these notions by Hussein Ibish, the Lebanese-born communications director of the American-Arab Anti-Discrimination Committee. He pointed out that some Arab views, especially about the Palestinians, are based on reality, not manipulated paranoia, and that anyone genuinely interested in Arab democracy had better take the popular will into account, delusional or not. If, on the other hand, Iraq is to be turned back into a colonial mandate as it was eighty years ago, inching toward *Heart of Darkness*, as Ibish said, we should openly admit that the anticolonial values of the intervening decade are being cast aside. "How do you think this discussion will sound translated into Arabic and broadcast on Al Jazeera?" he asked. "This war will only reinforce the Arab feeling of humiliation and impotence. It could be a giant television commercial for Al Qaeda."

As Arab regimes try to weather popular discontent, they will be far happier with the State Department's postwar scheme for regional stability than with the Pentagon hawks' notions about regional transformation— especially if Iraq's oil is used by the Americans to rebuild Iraq and not to undermine OPEC. Iran, which has taken a surprisingly benign view of the war gathering on its horizon, might change its mind once American troops settle into Iraq for the long haul and events across the border make themselves felt among Iranian reformers. France and Russia, with their extensive interests in Iraqi oil and other contracts, might sit out the war but cut to the front of the line during the reconstruction to claim their share of the spoils. America's closest ally in the neighborhood, Turkey, with its troops in Iraq's north possibly provoking a Kurdish revolt, could turn out to be the most problematic player of all. Except, of course, for the Iraqis and the Americans themselves.

The London Hilton Metropole is a garish hotel near Paddington Station, and over a December weekend it seemed that most of Iraq's three million to four million exiles were there, in turbans and robes, in kaffiyehs, in English-cut business suits, huddled in conspiratorial-looking groups, clutching cell phones to ears. Among them Makiya was an anomalous sight, looking rumpled in shirtsleeves, baggy corduroys, and all-weather shoes, his face clean-shaven. (One Iraqi told me that the country's next president must either be a woman or a man without a mustache.) The politicos from the Kurdish, Shiite, and ex-military parties complained that Makiya's casual appearance lacked respect. The rumored contents of his report, copies of which most of them hadn't yet received, troubled them, too. Worst of all was the bluntness with which Makiya and some of his young, Western-educated allies in the Iraqi National Congress were talking about the need to move beyond the "old politics" of the ethnic parties, which had all been born in the image of the Baath.

Before the conference, American officials made it clear that they were opposed to any votes being taken in London; no transitional government would be elected, no report on democracy approved. The State Department had won out. Just before the conference began, Makiya sat down in a café across from the British Museum to survey the damage with Salim Chalabi, a London lawyer and nephew of Ahmad Chalabi, who had helped draft the document.

"They want to come out of this as one big happy family," Makiya said of the traditional parties. "They want to show unity and support for the Americans. I want to win something concrete." He wanted the Iraqi opposition to commit itself to a proposal and make itself relevant before the shooting started and the logic of war took its course. "But I'm afraid we're fighting a losing battle."

Chalabi told Makiya that his outspokenness was hurting his own cause. Makiya is an old friend of the Kurds; in addition to having made the documentary *Saddam's Killing Fields*, he directs Harvard's Iraq Documentation Project, which is organizing and translating millions of documents left behind by the Baath Party as records of the genocide. But the Kurdish parties at the conference were vehemently opposed to the proposal for a nonethnic federation in Iraq. They had fought hard to gain recognition and equal status with the Arabs, and they were not going to relinquish it easily. The views of the Shiites on the section dealing with secularism had not been solicited. The Sunnis were less represented than anyone. There had been a lack of inclusiveness. Makiya agreed—but he couldn't help adding: "I've begun to hate the word 'inclusive' here. I know it's going to mean the lowest common denominator. Nothing will be said that means anything."

Makiya was sweating, the lines deepening in his high forehead. The conference, the months of work, the political storm that always swirled around him, seemed to be placing him under an intolerable strain. Finally he relented.

"Okay, what should we do?" he asked.

"You have to play it more like a game," Chalabi said. He suggested emphasizing the points on which there was agreement, like human rights, and muting the controversial ones. He urged Makiya to lower his profile.

On the first day of the conference, at a press briefing, Makiya sat alongside Ahmad Chalabi and a few others, content to listen. But when a reporter asked him a question, he leaned forward and said: "The report carries forward a completely new idea that doesn't exist in the Arab-Muslim world. This is something tremendous, something unbelievable. We're talking above all of an idea of democracy that isn't only majority rule—an idea of democracy that is about minority rights and above all individual rights." He added: "This is a fighting document, by the way. We intend to fight for it on the floor of the conference."

I had seen it before: when Makiya spoke, the energy in the room became focused. Afterward a swarm of reporters gathered around him. Into the room walked a furious Hoshyar Zebari, a leading official of the Kurdistan Democratic Party, whose own press conference had been sparsely attended. Later, I asked Zebari about the document and about Makiya. Zebari smiled through his answer, but he kept thumping me in the chest as he spoke. "We are rooted in the country, we are the ones who have suffered," he said. "What Kanan Makiya has done, I appreciate his intellectual work, but it's just an intellectual exercise."

Makiya, I suggested, was trying to give it teeth.

"He's the only one," said an American who was hovering around the conversation. It was David L. Phillips, who had worked with the State Department on the Future of Iraq Project. "The report is not a political document—it's not a blueprint. If it becomes one it will be divisive." Phillips later expressed sharp anger at Makiya for hijacking the writing of the report and then lobbying so hard for its provisions.

Back in Washington, officials thanked the Democratic Principles Working Group for its advice and shelved the report that the State Department had solicited. Makiya had called their bluff, and now they were calling his. The London conference ended with expressions of unity and vague support for that thing called democracy in Iraq; Makiya was named to a sixty-five-member transitional coordinating committee. But the report of the Democratic Principles Working Group, printed and bound with hundreds of pages of appendices and dissents, was never officially discussed. It struck me as inauspicious that of all the committees in the Future of Iraq Project—on water, electricity, agriculture, and a host of other topics—only the committee on democracy was deemed a failure.

The longer you try to look at Iraq on the morning after Saddam, the more you see the truth of what many people told me: getting rid of him will be the easy part. After that, the United States will find itself caught in a series of conundrums that will require supreme finesse: to liberate without appearing to dominate, to ensure order without overstaying, to secure its interests without trampling on Iraq's, to oversee democratization without picking winners, to push for reforms in the neighborhood without unleashing demons. It's hard to know whether to be more worried by the State Department's complacency or by the Pentagon civilians' zealotry.

On the day that Saigon fell in 1975, the British writer James Fenton found a framed quotation on a wall of the looted American embassy: "Better to let them do it imperfectly than to do it perfectly yourself, for it is their country, their way, and your time is short." The words are from T. E. Lawrence. Vietnam remains the shadow over every American war, but never more than the one we're poised to fight, for no war since Vietnam has professed greater ambitions: to change the political culture of a country, maybe a whole region. Ever since Woodrow Wilson worked to put democracy and self-determination on the agenda at Versailles, this strain of high-mindedness in the American character has drawn the world's admiration and its scorn. In Graham Greene's novel *The Quiet American*, which was recently released as a film, the title character is a young idealist sent to Vietnam in the early 1950s to find a democratic "Third Force" between the French and the Communists. The book's narrator, a jaded British journalist, remarks, "I never knew a man who had better motives for all the trouble he caused." Americans have never been very good at imperialism, or much interested in it; we're too innocent, too impatient, too intoxicated with our own sense of selfless purpose. Several Iraqis expressed the wish that their occupiers could be the British again, who took the trouble to know them so much better, who wrote whole books on the Marsh Arabs and the flora and fauna of Kuwait. Afghanistan lost America's attention as soon as Kandahar fell, and it remains unfinished business. As for Iraq, Jessica Mathews of the Carnegie Endowment says, "Our country is not remotely prepared for what this is going to take."

If so, the fault mainly lies with President Bush. His articulation of political aims and postwar plans has been sketchy to the point of empty cliché. He has never discussed the human costs of war, nor its price. The Yale economist William D. Nordhaus estimates the military expenditure between $50 billion and $140 billion; far more daunting, his study finds, the postwar costs to the United States of occupying and rebuilding Iraq, along with the impact on oil markets and the economy, could run as high as $2 trillion. This is a calculation that no one in the administration has dared to make, at least publicly. Privately, some officials suggest that Iraqi oil will pay for it.

More than anything, the president hasn't readied Americans psychologically to commit themselves to a project of such magnitude, nor has he made them understand why they should. He has maintained his spirit of hostility to nation building while reversing his policy against it. Bush is a man who has never shown much curiosity about the world. When he met with Makiya and two other Iraqis in January, I was told by someone not present, the exiles spent a good portion of the time explaining to the president that there are two kinds of Arabs in Iraq, Sunnis and Shiites. The very notion of an Iraqi opposition appeared to be new to him. War has turned Bush into a foreign policy president, but democratizing an Arab country will require a subtlety and sophistication that have been less in evidence than the resolve to fight.

I asked John W. Dower, a history professor at MIT and author of a Pulitzer Prize–winning book about the American occupation of Japan, to compare that project with the democratization of Iraq. The difference between Japan and Iraq is great enough, he answered; the difference between America in 1945 and 2003 is even greater. "We do not have the moral legitimacy we had then, nor do we have the other thing that was present when we occupied Japan—the vision of the American public that we would engage in serious and genuinely democratic nation building and that we would do this in the context of an international order." Even Fouad Ajami, a strong believer in the war's potential for regional reform, told me: "The country is depressed, psychologically and economically. There is no great calling toward planting our truth in Mesopotamia. The war will have an ideological claim, but tempered by the difficulty of Iraq, by the fact that we don't know this land."

The unease among Americans, even those who support the president, about the war and its aftermath is certainly due to fear of unknown consequences. It might also come from the sense that we're trying to have it both ways—guns and butter, war without sacrifice, intervention without commitment. If Iraq succeeds in becoming a democracy under American protection, it will represent the triumph of hope over experience for both countries. It's a notion that I always found easier to imagine when I was within earshot of Kanan Makiya.

In mid-January, Makiya emerged from his meeting at the Oval Office to declare himself "deeply reassured" by the president's dedication to Iraqi democracy. Within a few days Makiya had flown to Tehran with Ahmad Chalabi and a few other Iraqi National Congress members to hold talks with Iraqi Shiite leaders. At the end of January, under the protection of Iranian security, they crossed the snow-covered mountains into northern Iraq. One recent morning, Makiya called me from Sulaimaniya, in Iraqi Kurdistan. He and the Kurds had patched up their differences, and one of the two Kurdish parties—the Patriotic Union of Kurdistan— had embraced the principle of nonethnic federalism. "The opposition is trying to get its act together, basically," he said.

When the United States revealed a few weeks ago its intent to impose a military government after the war, Makiya took the news as a betrayal. "It is Baathism with an American face," he declared. In his view, the odds for democracy have never looked longer, and he now wonders aloud if his harshest critics, who accused him of naïveté and worse, will be proved right after all. The exiles who gathered in late February to hold a second confer- ence in northern Iraq won't declare a provisional government against Amer- ican wishes, Makiya told me, but they are trying to forge an Iraqi leadership that will be capable of forming one after the war sweeps through.

What Makiya is trying to do is think his way out of Iraq's bloodstained history. After the Gulf War, when he and other dissidents drafted what they called Charter 91, outlining principles of tolerance for a new Iraq, Makiya received a severe letter from an old friend that he was willing to reprint in *Cruelty and Silence*: "I think—and please allow me to tell you this—that the ideas of the Charter issue from an ivory tower which has elevated itself so high up into the sky that we who are standing down below can hardly see or hear where they are coming from. You see, our society today has become like *1984*. There is no one who remembers or who even dares to remember the meaning of words like 'freedom,' 'democ- racy,' 'brotherhood,' or 'humanity.' They no longer know what 'human rights' are. I mean, what does this have to do with them! . . . Their only preoccupation is to survive and to live, like sheep."

It's possible that Makiya's ideas are too lofty to stand a chance of be- ing realized soon. David L. Phillips may be right to say that "Iraqis aren't quite ready for the new politics. The tribal structures, the ethnic group- ings—they matter to Iraqis. They're important. This isn't a university laboratory." It's also possible that Makiya was foolish ever to imagine American cooperation with his exile dreams, and that he is out of his ele- ment in the dangerous labyrinth of Iraqi power politics. Meanwhile, ahead of the war, an Arabic translation of the report is being smuggled from Iraqi Kurdistan into Baghdad in miniature editions disguised as cig- arette cartons.

"The document is just paper at the end of the day," Makiya told me one snowy evening at his Cambridge apartment. "One of the less grandiose impulses behind it was this: there's a world of people out there deeply, deeply skeptical about whether or not this country can make it to democracy. And I know deep down that they have good reason to be skeptical. I'm not really as rosy, I'm not as naïve as sometimes I appear on this question. But it seems to me, for history's sake, important to have a group of Iraqis turn out a decent document that can be taken seriously, that will be picked up and remembered and churned over and used as some kind of a test, some kind of a yardstick against which to measure the progress of things afterward. And it was, after all, produced by Iraqis—so that Iraqis can lift their heads up a bit and go out there in the world and say: 'We meant it. It wasn't all a word game. Some of us tried to give it a shot.'"

A Democratic World

The New Yorker, February 16, 2004

In December 2001, after the fall of the Taliban, President Bush asked Senator Joseph Biden, a Delaware Democrat who was then the chairman of the Foreign Relations Committee, to draft a legislative proposal for winning the minds of young people around the Muslim world. The following month, Biden went to Kabul, where he toured a new school—one that was bitterly cold, with plastic sheeting over the windows and a naked bulb hanging from the ceiling. When the visit was over and Biden started to leave, a young girl stood ramrod straight at her desk and said, "You cannot leave. You cannot leave."

"I promise I'll come back," Biden told her.

"You cannot leave," the girl insisted. "They will not deny me learning to read. I will read, and I will be a doctor like my mother. I will. America must stay."

As Biden put it in a recent interview, the Afghan girl was telling him, "Don't fuck with me, Jack. You got me in here. You said you were going to help me. You better not leave me now."

Biden described the encounter as "a catalytic event for me." Its lesson was one that he had already begun to absorb in the Balkans, where he had traveled extensively during the 1990s. There is a worldwide struggle, he explained, between the values of liberal democracy and the destructive ideologies that fester with dictatorship, misery, and humiliation; in this struggle, America needs to expand the conditions for democracy in the most concrete ways, with serious commitments of energy and resources, or risk greater instability. After September 11, this insight became a matter of urgent national security. When Biden returned from Kabul, he followed up on the president's request and wrote a proposal to build, staff, and supply a thousand schools in Afghanistan, at a cost of twenty thousand dollars each. By thinking small, Biden believed, he had a better chance of success: "You could shove twenty million dollars anywhere in a two-trillion budget, and this was something specific." The schools would employ teachers, many of them women, who had been jobless and desperate under the Taliban, and they would teach a modern curriculum to children who, if they had any schooling at all, knew only the Islamist education of the madrassa. "It was something concrete we could show the Afghanis we're doing," Biden said. "It was something other than the butt of a gun."

The idea went nowhere. Biden's Democratic colleagues didn't get behind it, and very soon the administration moved on. The most important front in the worldwide struggle largely dropped from Washington's view, and the senator stopped receiving invitations to the White House.

By the fall of 2002, the Bush administration had begun mobilizing for the invasion of Iraq. Biden's view was that Saddam Hussein, who had violated every international agreement he had signed but was not an immediate threat, would have to be confronted sooner or later. But he also worried that a unilateral war with Iraq would distract America from the tasks it had only just begun—stabilizing Afghanistan and defeating Al Qaeda—and seriously damage the alliances necessary to eliminate terrorism and other problems that freely cross borders: weapons proliferation, disease, environmental damage, ethnic conflict, impoverishment. "The burden was on Saddam," Biden said. "But I would not have prematurely forced the world's hand on whether or not to go to war, because I'd get the wrong answer."

Instead, he tried to slow the administration's momentum without shifting the burden from Saddam. It was in his party's power to do so—Democrats still held the majority in the Senate (though they were about to lose it, in part because the public didn't trust them on the issue of national security). Together with Senator Richard Lugar of Indiana, the committee's ranking Republican, Biden drafted an alternative to the administration's Iraq resolution that would have placed various restraints on the president, making it harder for him to wage war unilaterally and forcing him to bolster his case that Saddam possessed weapons of mass destruction. Lugar had assembled a surprisingly large number of Republicans—twenty-five or so out of the forty-nine—who were uneasy with the administration's bellicose stance. In order to deliver their votes, Lugar needed Biden to line up at least forty Democrats; and Biden was sure of only thirty-eight.

As Biden recalled, on September 30, Lugar, who was in touch with the White House, called him. "Joe, I fear in the next twenty-four, forty-eight hours, the president's going to cut a deal with Gephardt," he said.

Biden was stunned. "Gephardt? Gephardt's not going to do this."

"Joe, I'm telling you. They're working two sides here. They're working us, keeping us occupied, but they're working just as hard meeting with him. Whoever they reach an agreement with first, they're going to go with."

If Richard Gephardt, the House Democratic minority leader, came out for the administration's resolution, it would be politically almost impossible for any Republican to support the Biden-Lugar alternative. Biden had to gather the Democratic holdouts immediately and persuade them to stand behind his resolution so that he and Lugar could move it onto the Senate floor the next day.

That evening, Biden met with half a dozen leading Democrats who were opposed to any war resolution at all. "They said, 'It's not right, you're not principled, asking us to do this,'" Biden recalled. "I said, 'Wait, wait, wait. Please spare me the lecture. I thought our job was to do as much as we could to prevent this president from going off to war half-cocked. Does anybody in here believe that we're going to get any resolution remotely approaching the constraints this resolution has?'" Biden warned his colleagues, "Guess what? Your principle is going to kill a lot of Americans." But the antiwar Democrats were intractable. At the end of the meeting, Senator Paul Wellstone of Minnesota and Senator Barbara Boxer of California left the room arm in arm, chuckling.

Two days later, with no alternative making its way through the Senate, Gephardt appeared at Bush's side in the Rose Garden and announced his support for the administration's war resolution. Nine days later, both houses of Congress approved it, and the president had all the authority he needed to invade Iraq.

Biden told me these stories in answer to a simple question: Why hasn't the Democratic Party played a serious role in shaping the national debate about foreign policy since September 11? Biden has been one of the few Democrats to try. His views defy party orthodoxy. He has criticized the administration relentlessly, not for doing too much in the war on terrorism but for doing too little, and in the wrong way—for failing to understand that this war has to be waged on many fronts, the most important of which is ideological. The fate of the schoolgirl in Kabul is as critical to ultimate victory as the next generation of unmanned aircraft.

Biden's own party has all but forfeited the chance to make this case. The two complementary tendencies that doomed his effort on Iraq have characterized Democrats since the war on terrorism began: on one side, the urge to take cover under Republican policies in order not to be labeled weak; on the other, a rigid opposition that invokes moral principle but often leads to the very results it seeks to prevent. Neither posture shows a willingness to grapple with the world as it is, to do the hard work of imagining a foreign policy for the post–September 11 era.

The Democratic Party hasn't always been stymied by foreign policy. A half century ago, the party's ideas were ascendant, transforming America's international role in the postwar years as dramatically as President Bush has since September 11. In 1945, the United States had more relative power and prestige than it has today. Instead of seizing the occasion to strip the country of constraints and dominate the world, the ruling Democrats, most of whom were New Dealers, realized that the global fight against Communism required partners. The postwar Democratic leadership under President Truman helped bring into being institutions and alliances—the United Nations, NATO, the World Bank—through which the country's goals could be met. These goals were as much economic and political as military. The thinking behind Truman's speech in March 1947, asking Congress for economic as well as military aid to Greece and Turkey against Communist insurgents, and the speech by his secretary of state, George C. Marshall, a few months later, calling for a massive reconstruction package for a devastated Europe, was the same: containing and ultimately defeating totalitarianism required an investment in countries where conditions made Communism a threat. It also required the participation of Americans at every level of society. Anticommunist liberals in the labor movement and the Democratic Party funded social-democratic parties in Western Europe as alternatives to Communism; politicians and intellectuals organized themselves in associations like Americans for

Democratic Action and around magazines like *Encounter* to fight the war of ideas. These liberals understood that the new war could not afford to be rigidly doctrinaire; it required a practical effort to understand realities in Europe and elsewhere, in order to know what would be necessary to prevent Communism from winning over individuals and countries. It had to be wise as well as tough. Above all, it needed the help of other democracies—there had to be alliances, reciprocity. This is what was meant by liberal internationalism.

Vietnam, of course, badly divided Democrats, turning some into Republicans and others into pacifists. And here is a remarkable fact: since the 1960s, the Democratic Party has had no foreign policy. Its leaders have continued to speak the language of liberal internationalism, but after Vietnam most Democrats haven't wanted to back up the talk with power. They continued to put their faith in institutions like the United Nations (where Saddam's Iraq was a member in good standing and Libya chaired the human rights commission) long after it was apparent that these institutions needed repair. By the 1990s, liberal internationalism had become an atrophied muscle, with little fiber or sinew left. The Clinton administration allowed a genocidal war to bleed away in the Balkans for two and a half years before acting to end it. In the dot-com decade, a lot of Democrats simply lost interest in the rest of the world. Clinton's foreign policy was globalization: encouraging the economic interconnectedness of the world, without developing a mechanism to prevent threats and conflicts from becoming catastrophes without borders.

The exception was Kosovo. NATO's intervention in the Balkans, in the spring of 1999, was one of the successes of the Clinton years, stopping the ethnic cleansing of hundreds of thousands of Kosovar Albanians, preventing the Balkan wars from spreading into Macedonia and Albania, and ultimately making possible Slobodan Milošević's removal from power and his current trial at The Hague. However flawed aspects of the military strategy were—three months of aerial bombing with no contingency for ground troops—the Kosovo war was a singular example of American power creating international cooperation on behalf of stability and human rights.

But Kosovo never became the Clinton Doctrine. Clinton himself seemed ambivalent about the war, and obstacles thrown up by a Republican Congress kept NATO's first war from becoming the foundation of post–Cold War American foreign policy.

The humanitarian interventions of the nineties—Haiti, Bosnia, Kosovo—and the glaring failure in Rwanda made a minority of Democrats willing, sometimes even eager, advocates of the use of American power for liberal ends abroad. But the party's base remains instinctively uncomfortable with activism and armed force. In Biden's words, most Democrats still "worship at the shrine of multilateral institutions, and without absolute consensus there's no action."

While the Democrats held the White House, the ideological children of Ronald Reagan were thinking hard about America's place in the world after the Cold War. At conferences and in journal articles, the singular idea of these conservatives was that with no Soviet threat, the United States was uniquely positioned to exert power all over the world—to discourage rivals, to pursue interests, to spread values, with or without partners. Coalitions might be temporary; force might be used unilaterally and preventively, not just as a matter of convenience but as a point of doctrine. Their view admitted no daylight between American interests and democratic ideals: our motives are good, therefore our unleashed power will have good effects. These thinkers were also skilled publicists, and they defined the difference between the two parties as the difference between strength and weakness.

Within hours of the September 11 attacks, Defense Secretary Donald Rumsfeld and his deputy, Paul Wolfowitz, were suggesting that Iraq—the unflagging obsession of the conservatives throughout the nineties—should receive the brunt of American wrath. Whether or not this was a sound analysis of the threat, the conservatives were organized; they had ideas, and they were poised to put them into action. The Iraq War was nothing if not a war of ideas—an elective war that came of arguments and theories about America and the world. It was exactly on this level that Democrats were ill prepared to join the contest.

But from the start, and at its core, the administration's idea of the war on terrorism has been flawed. This flaw, which is often discussed as a matter of tone, is so substantive that the administration constantly undermines even its own best efforts.

President Bush has given a number of speeches in support of global democracy, and they have been some of his finest. Nine days after the attacks in New York and Washington, he went before Congress and described the war on terrorism as a continuation of the twentieth-century conflict between freedom and totalitarianism. More recently, in the wake of the Iraq War, he has championed the spread of democracy through the world's meanest precincts. "Iraqi democracy will succeed," the president said in November, "and that success will send forth the news from Damascus to Tehran that freedom can be the future of every nation."

The soaring language recalls that of Bush's hero Ronald Reagan. It gives the new conservative foreign policy its poetry. The first President Bush never made such proclamations about Iraq, or about any other benighted country, for he belonged to the Nixon-Kissinger wing of the Republican Party—"realists" who believe in a balance of power and distrust idealistic talk of "global democratic revolution." But there is a problem with the language of Bush the son: his actions rarely measure up to his rhetoric. A case in point was the president's November speech at the National Endowment for Democracy's twentieth anniversary celebrations. After the fall of Baghdad, an institute funded by the endowment sent a team to Iraq to organize a series of focus groups so that Iraqis could talk about their collective future. The institute wanted to follow up with workshops that would train Iraqis in forming moderate civic groups and political parties, but its money soon ran out. Despite repeated requests, the funding wasn't replenished until last month.

It happens often enough to form a pattern: the president talks of a Marshall Plan for Afghanistan at the Virginia Military Institute in April 2002, and then he fails to include any dollars for Afghanistan in his 2004 budget proposal; the president gives a landmark speech at the American Enterprise Institute in February 2003, proposing a democratic Iraq as a model for the transformation of the entire Middle East, and within two months the Pentagon's minimalist planning for postwar Iraq has that country in chaos, its state institutions gutted, its people demoralized; the State Department sets out to improve public diplomacy in the Islamic world, then puts the campaign in the hands of Charlotte Beers, a Madison Avenue executive, who produces a slick video about Muslims in the United States that is widely ridiculed; the administration vows to get tough on Saudi sources that finance terrorism and the spread of extremist ideology, then suppresses the section of a congressional report on September 11 having to do with Saudi Arabia; after the Iraq War the president vows to resolve the Israeli-Palestinian conflict, only to stand aside a few months later.

In Iraq, at least, the administration, having accepted that its initial democracy efforts were wholly inadequate, has begun to make serious commitments. In a frantic rush to educate voters and strengthen institutions before its June 30 deadline for the transfer of sovereignty, it is about to flood the country's civic desert with almost half a billion dollars, including twelve and a half million for building political parties.

Elsewhere, the administration remains averse to such commitments. The president and his chief advisers have long expressed disdain for the "soft" uses of American power. In the 2000 campaign, Bush ran against the nation-building efforts of the Clinton administration. In an article in *Foreign Affairs* in 2000, Condoleezza Rice called for an end to such missions, asserting that the United States Army "is not a civilian police force." "Peacekeeping" is a dirty word at the Rumsfeld Pentagon: its peacekeeping division was renamed the Office of Stability Operations, and its importance was downgraded, even after war created the need for such an operation in Afghanistan and then again, on an even larger scale, in Iraq. In Afghanistan, the peacekeepers never ventured beyond Kabul and Kunduz, and the country's admirable new constitution is jeopardized by warlords and the resurgent Taliban.

The Bush administration has always been more interested in military power than in any of the other tools that are available to advance its goals. The hostility to nation building, the attitude that treaties and international institutions are disposable nuisances, the treatment of alliances as matters of convenience—all these reflect a belief that the country will be safer, and the world ultimately better off, if America is free to use its awesome strength.

The president speaks idealistically of spreading democracy around the world. "The advance of freedom is the calling of our time," he said in November. "It is the calling of our country." Since Bush took office, favorable views of America have plunged globally—especially in the Muslim world. The Pew Research Center found that in Turkey, our secular Muslim NATO ally, favorable opinion of the United States fell from 52 percent three years ago to 15 percent last spring. For an administration rhetorically devoted to the calling of freedom, this trend ought to cause great concern. But Bush expresses only bewilderment, and his hard-line advisers scoff that we can't make decisions about American security based on opinion polls in foreign countries. Since September 11, the president and his spokesmen have regarded the crisis as a test of personal will. Do you pass or not? So they've waged the war by self-assertion, guided by the assumption that American might always equates with freedom. But when promoting democracy seems in practice to mean bullying other people into doing what you want, the poetry is lost on the world, and not even the overthrow of tyrants is taken as proof of America's sincerity.

In treating the war on terrorism as a mere military struggle, the administration's mistake begins with the name itself. "Terrorism" is a method; the terror used by the Tamil Tigers in Sri Lanka is not the enemy in this war. The enemy is an ideology—in the German foreign minister Joschka Fischer's phrase, "Islamist totalitarianism"—that reaches from Karachi to London, from Riyadh to Brooklyn, and that uses terror to advance its ends. The administration's failure to grasp the political nature of the war has led to many crucial mistakes, most notably the Pentagon's attitude that postwar problems in Afghanistan and Iraq would essentially take care of themselves, that we could have democracy on the cheap: once the dictators and terrorists were rooted out, the logic went, freedom would spontaneously grow in their place. As Lakhdar Brahimi, the former United Nations envoy to Afghanistan, recently told the *Times*, "There is now a very well-meaning and welcome Western interest in supporting democracy everywhere, but they want to do it like instant coffee." Instead, in both countries the real struggle has just begun, and it will last a generation or more, with little international help in sight and victory not at all assured.

"They don't get it, because they don't believe this is an ideology," Ivo H. Daalder, a political scientist at the Brookings Institution, said of the administration. "They believe that this is a state-based threat—that if you get rid of evil people, who are in finite supply, you will have resolved the problem. And the proof of the pudding is a very simple statement that the president keeps repeating: 'It's better to kill them there than to have them kill us here.' Which assumes there are a finite number."

Remarkably, this narrow approach has met with no systematic criticism from the Democratic Party. Democratic leaders attack the administration for its unilateralism, but, with a few exceptions, they have been unprepared to reckon with the nature and scale of the conflict; and this has to do with the party's own intellectual shortcomings. Certain mental traits that have spread among Democrats since the Vietnam War get in the way—not just the tendency toward isolationism and pacifism but a cultural relativism (going by the name of "multiculturalism") that makes it difficult for them to mount a wholehearted defense of one political system against another, especially when the other has taken root among poorer and darker-skinned peoples. Like the Bush administration, the Democrats have failed to grasp the political dimensions of the struggle. They, too, have cast it narrowly, as a matter of security (preferring the notion of police action to that of war). They've pushed the administration only for greater effort on the margins, such as upgrading communications equipment for firemen and federalizing airport security. And the Iraq War let Democrats off the hook, allowing them to say what they wouldn't do rather than what they would do.

Another approach remains available to the Democrats—one that draws on the party's own not so distant history. The parallels between the early years of the Cold War and our situation are inexact. The Islamist movement doesn't have the same hold on Westerners that Communism had. It draws on cultures that remain alien to us; the history of colonialism and the fact of religious difference make it all the harder for the liberal democracies of the West to effect change in the Muslim world. Waving the banner of freedom and mustering the will to act aren't enough. Anyone who believes that September 11 thrust us into a Manichaean conflict between good and evil should visit Iraq, where the simplicity of that formula lies half buried under all the crosscurrents of foreign occupation and social chaos and ethnic strife. Simply negotiating the transfer of sovereignty back to Iraqis has proved so vexing that an administration that jealously guarded the occupation against any international control has turned to the battered and despised United Nations for help in dealing with Iraq's unleashed political forces. Iraq and other battlegrounds require patience, self-criticism, and local knowledge, not just an apocalyptic moral summons.

Nonetheless, for Democrats and for Americans, the first step is to realize that the war on terrorism is actually a war for liberalism—a struggle to bring populations now living under tyrannies and failed states into the orbit of liberal democracy. In this light, it makes sense to think about the strategy and mind-set that the postwar generation brought to their task: the marriage of power and cooperation. Daalder said, "The fundamental challenge—just as the fundamental challenge in '46 and '47 and '48 in France and Italy was to provide Italians and Frenchmen with a real constructive alternative to Communism, to defeat it politically—is to provide people in the Islamic world with an alternative that gives them hope in a period where they have only despair." He pointed out that America now spends forty times more on defense than it does on foreign aid, and that half of this aid goes to Israel and Egypt. "This is like the new Cold War, and we've got to fight it as a generational fight in which we need to invest," he said.

As it happens, an increasing number of Democrats are pursuing this theme. Wesley Clark talks about a "new Atlantic Charter" that would make NATO the first resort of American military power, starting in Iraq. "Uncertainties, nations looking for leadership, a multidimensional challenge on a global scale—all of that is similar" to the early Cold War, he told me. "As is the indefinite duration of the challenge." Clark argued that NATO's war in Kosovo, which he conducted as supreme allied commander, could become the basis for a new foreign policy. "You could call it efficient multilateralism—the recognition that if you link diplomacy, law, and force, you can achieve decisive results without using decisive force."

Senator John Kerry of Massachusetts has for some time advocated the extension of NATO forces in Kabul to the whole of Afghanistan, and he recently called for expanding public diplomacy in the Muslim world and imposing international sanctions against countries and institutions that fund terrorism, a money flow that the Bush administration has had little success in shutting off. In a recent debate, Kerry said, "Most importantly, the war on terror is also an engagement in the Middle East economically, socially, culturally, in a way that we haven't embraced, because otherwise we're inviting a clash of civilizations." Senator John Edwards of North Carolina proposes publishing an annual list of dissidents imprisoned around the world, and forming an organization of Western democracies and Arab countries moving toward liberalization which would be modeled on efforts to reform the former Eastern Bloc. Invoking Truman and Marshall, Senator Biden talks about a Prevention Doctrine: long-term engagement in troubled regions to head off threats before they lead to war—for example, by funding programs to destroy nuclear weapons in the former Soviet Union. (The Bush administration's remarkably sluggish approach to securing "loose nukes" is one consequence of a policy aimed narrowly at terrorists and their state sponsors, like cards in a deck.) All these Democrats advocate a domestic policy that would acknowledge the reality of wartime, including alternative energy, tax fairness, and greater spending on security. But Biden reminded me, "It took the Democratic Party after World War II six years to get that figured out."

If you're paying attention, you can hear the sound of Democratic leaders straining to pry the party away from its long aversion to America's world leadership. The ghosts of Wilson, Roosevelt, Truman, and Kennedy are frequently summoned. These leaders have a thankless job, and, politically, a difficult one. Whatever they thought of the Iraq War, the struggle there is now the epicenter of the war of ideas, and leading Democrats have to show more commitment to the new Iraq's success than they did in opposing the administration's reconstruction package. A broader approach to the war includes a willingness to fight—and for Democrats out of power, it's all the harder to persuade a skeptical public that they will fight. But this approach also demands an ability to make judgments about when and where and how to fight—or not. Compared with "axis of evil," "efficient multilateralism" is a pallid phrase. Millions won't rally behind the banner of the Prevention Doctrine. Spending twenty million dollars on schools in Afghanistan is a harder sell than spending four hundred billion on defense; fear is more compelling than foresight. Biden admitted, "This is a place where the president's bragging to me, 'Mr. Chairman, I don't do nuance'—where he has an advantage."

I asked Thomas Carothers, an expert on democracy at the Carnegie Endowment for International Peace, to name one project that might help change the political culture of the Arab world. He mentioned a nonprofit group, the Center for International Private Enterprise, that is working to spread the idea among Arab business associations that transparency and the rule of law will attract foreign investment. Carothers has studied democracy-building programs for two decades, and he compared them to painting the Golden Gate Bridge. His experience has left him wary of the rhetoric coming out of Washington these days. Compared with the revolutions of 1989 in Central Europe, he said, "this is a made-in-Washington

democratic transformation. It's very hard to do it when there are no democratic trends in the area." Success can come only over a period of years,
mainly by finding local groups and helping them do what they already
want to do. The United States achieved this in Serbia during the late
nineties—funding pro-democracy student groups that helped in the overthrow of the Milošević dictatorship. It's possible for something of the
kind to occur in Muslim countries. Government agencies and nonprofit
groups could fund new organizations like the Iranian dissident Ladan
Boroumand's democracy foundation, whose website will post a library of
liberal ideas for young people in Iran to read behind the privacy of their
computer screens. But all this will take more time and commitment than
American administrations, including the present one, have been interested in showing.

"It's long-term, it's not flashy, it's not expensive," Carothers said. "All
of our programs now are showy, expensive, big-impact. And maybe we
need to do that, but we also need to do things for fifteen to twenty years
down the line." When we spoke, he had just returned from the former
Soviet republics, which he described as "a democratic wasteland." A decade ago, reform in those countries seemed as urgent as it now seems in
the Middle East; but America's attention moved on, and the administration has made its peace with the region's post-Soviet strongmen. The
president, Carothers said, has failed to make the struggle to liberalize the
Muslim world the concern of ordinary Americans—to take one small example, by creating high school exchange programs. "He's unable to connect it to us in any way other than fear," Carothers said. "And I don't think
that's going to do it."

A political struggle on the part of a democracy requires the involvement of the public, not as frightened spectators but as active participants.
In recent decades, our leaders—both Democrats and Republicans—have
asked very little of us as citizens, to the point where the word itself
sounds quaint. The dominant theme of American politics since the 1960s
has been freedom: cultural freedoms under Democrats, economic freedoms under Republicans. The pursuit of happiness became a private
affair, and the sense of civic responsibility withered among liberals and
conservatives alike. The political choice was between two versions of
hedonism.

In the days that followed the September 11 attacks, we saw the early stages of something like a national self-mobilization. The long lines of would-be blood donors, the volunteers converging on lower Manhattan from around the country, the fumbling public efforts at understanding Islam: the response took on very personal tones. People spoke as if they wanted to change their lives. A generation legendary for its self-centeredness seemed to grasp that here was a historic chance to aim for something greater.

It has been much remarked that President Bush did nothing to tap this palpable desire among ordinary people to join a larger effort. Americans were told to go shopping and watch out for suspicious activity. Nothing would ever be the same, and everything was just the same. "How urgent can this be if I tell you this is a great crisis and, at the time we're marching to war, I give the single largest tax cut in the history of the United States of America?" Biden said. The tax cuts haven't just left the country fiscally unsound during wartime; their inequity has been terrible for morale. But the president's failure to call for shared, equal sacrifice followed directly on the governing spirit of the modern Republican Party. After years of a sustained assault on the idea of collective action, there was no ideological foundation left on which Bush could stand up and ask what Americans can do for their country. We haven't been asked to study Arabic, to join the foreign service or international aid groups, to form a national civil reserve for emergencies—or even to pay off the cost of the war in our own time. The war's burdens are borne solely by a few hundred thousand volunteer soldiers.

Perhaps this was a shrewd political intuition on Bush's part—a recognition that Americans, for all their passion after September 11, would inevitably slouch back to their sofas. It's fair to ask, though, how a body politic as out of shape as ours is likely to make it over the long, hard slog of wartime; how convincingly we can export liberal democratic values when our own version shows so many signs of atrophy; how much solidarity we can expect to muster for Afghanis and Iraqis when we're asked to feel so little for one another.

"Why does not democracy believe in itself with passion?" Arthur Schlesinger, Jr., asked in *The Vital Center*, his 1949 book about totalitarianism and America's anxious postwar mood. "Why is freedom not a fighting faith?" The only hope (Schlesinger turned to Walt Whitman for the words—who else?) lay in "the exercise of Democracy." The process of struggling for freedom, accepting conflict, tolerating uncertainty, joining community—this would allow democracy to survive and not die. What if we now find ourselves, at this stage of thickening maturity, in the middle of a new crisis that requires us to act like citizens of a democracy? It's impossible to know how the public would respond to a political party that spoke about these things—because, so far, no party has.

The Lesson of Tal Afar

The New Yorker, April 10, 2006

Tal Afar is an ancient city of a quarter million inhabitants, situated on a smuggling route in the northwestern desert of Iraq, near the Syrian border. In January, when I visited, the streets had been muddied by cold winter rains and gouged by the tracks of armored vehicles. Tal Afar's stone fortifications and narrow alleys had the haggard look of a French town in the First World War that had changed hands several times. In some neighborhoods, markets were open and children played in the streets; elsewhere, in areas cordoned off by Iraqi checkpoints, shops remained shuttered, and townspeople peered warily from front doors and gates.

Since the Iraq War began, American forces had repeatedly driven insurgents out of Tal Afar, but the Army did not have enough troops to maintain a sufficient military presence there, and insurgents kept returning to terrorize the city. In early 2004, the division that had occupied northwestern Iraq was replaced by a brigade, with one-third the strength. A single company—about a hundred and fifty soldiers—became responsible for protecting Tal Afar. Insurgents soon seized the city and turned it into a strategic stronghold.

Last fall, thousands of American and Iraqi soldiers moved in to restore government control. This time, a thousand Americans stayed, and they slowly established trust among community leaders and local residents; by January, a tenuous peace had taken hold. The operation was a notable success in the administration's newly proclaimed strategy of counterinsurgency, which has been described by Secretary of State Condoleezza Rice as "clear, hold, and build." Last month, in a speech in

Cleveland, President Bush hailed the achievement in Tal Afar as evidence that Iraq is progressing toward a stable future. "Tal Afar shows that when Iraqis can count on a basic level of safety and security, they can live together peacefully," he said. "The people of Tal Afar have shown why spreading liberty and democracy is at the heart of our strategy to defeat the terrorists."

But the story of Tal Afar is not so simple. The effort came after numerous failures, and very late in the war—perhaps too late. And the operation succeeded despite an absence of guidance from senior civilian and military leaders in Washington. The soldiers who worked to secure Tal Afar were, in a sense, rebels against an incoherent strategy that has brought the American project in Iraq to the brink of defeat.

The "I" Word

Colonel H. R. McMaster, the commander of the 3rd Armored Cavalry Regiment, is forty-three years old, a small man, thick in the middle, with black eyebrows that are the only signs of hair on a pale, shaved head. His features are deeply furrowed across the brow and along the nose, as if his head had been shaped from modeling clay; but when he grins, mischief creases his face, and it's easy to imagine him as an undaunted ten-year-old, marching around and giving orders in his own private war. The first time I saw him, he had a football in his hands and was throwing hard spirals to a few other soldiers next to his plywood headquarters on a muddy airfield a few miles south of Tal Afar.

McMaster and the 3rd ACR had been stationed in Tal Afar for nine months. When they arrived, in the spring of 2005, the city was largely in the hands of hard-core Iraqi and foreign jihadis, who, together with members of the local Sunni population, had destabilized the city with a campaign of intimidation, including beheadings aimed largely at Tal Afar's Shiite minority. By October, after months of often fierce fighting and painstaking negotiations with local leaders, McMaster's regiment, working alongside Iraqi army battalions, had established bases around the city and greatly reduced the violence. When I met McMaster, his unit was about to return home; the men were to be replaced by a brigade of the 1st Armored Division that had no experience in Tal Afar, and no one knew if the city would remain secure. (Within weeks, there were reports that sectarian killings were on the rise.)

The lessons that McMaster and his soldiers applied in Tal Afar were learned during the first two years of an increasingly unpopular war. "When we came to Iraq, we didn't understand the complexity—what it meant for a society to live under a brutal dictatorship, with ethnic and sectarian divisions," he said, in his hoarse, energetic voice. "When we first got here, we made a lot of mistakes. We were like a blind man, trying to do the right thing but breaking a lot of things." Later, he said, "You gotta come in with your ears open. You can't come in and start talking. You have to really listen to people."

McMaster is a West Point graduate who earned a Silver Star for battlefield prowess during the 1991 Gulf War: his armored cavalry troop stumbled across an Iraqi mechanized brigade in the middle of a sandstorm and destroyed it. That war was a textbook case of what the military calls "kinetic operations," or major combat in relatively uncomplicated circumstances; the field of battle was almost easier, some Gulf War veterans say, than the live fire exercises at the National Training Center in Fort Irwin, California. After the war, McMaster earned a doctorate in history from the University of North Carolina. His dissertation, based on research in newly declassified archives, was published in 1997, with the title *Dereliction of Duty: Lyndon Johnson, Robert McNamara, the Joint Chiefs of Staff, and the Lies That Led to Vietnam.* The book assembled a damning case against senior military leaders for failing to speak their minds when, in the early years of the war, they disagreed with Pentagon policies. The Joint Chiefs of Staff, knowing that Johnson and McNamara wanted uncritical support rather than honest advice, and eager to protect their careers, went along with official lies and a split-the-difference strategy of gradual escalation that none of them thought could work. *Dereliction of Duty* won McMaster wide praise, and its candor inspired an ardent following among post-Vietnam officers.

In April 2003, at the moment when General Tommy Franks's "shock and awe" campaign against the regime of Saddam Hussein appeared to be a clean victory, the Army War College's Center for Strategic Leadership approved the release of a monograph by McMaster entitled "Crack in the Foundation: Defense Transformation and the Underlying Assumption of Dominant Knowledge in Future War." McMaster, who describes himself as "a bit of a Luddite," argued against the notion that new weapons technology offered the promise of certainty and precision in warfare. The success of the Gulf War, he wrote, had led military thinkers to forget that war is, above all, a human endeavor. He examined the messier operations of the 1990s, beginning with the debacle in Somalia, and concluded, "What is certain about the future is that even the best efforts to predict the conditions of future war will prove erroneous. What is important, however, is to not be so far off the mark that visions of the future run counter to the very nature of war and render American forces unable to adapt to unforeseen challenges."

In the spring of 2003, McMaster joined the staff of General John Abizaid at Central Command. Abizaid soon took over from Franks, who got out of Iraq and the military just as his three-week triumph over the Baathist regime showed signs of turning into a long ordeal. Although the violence in Iraq was rapidly intensifying, no one at the top levels of the government or the military would admit that an insurgency was forming.

"They didn't even want to say the 'i' word," one officer in Iraq told me. "It was the specter of Vietnam. They did not want to say the 'insurgency' word, because the next word you say is 'quagmire.' The next thing you say is 'the only war America has lost.' And the next thing you conclude is that certain people's vision of war is wrong."

The most stubborn resistance to the idea of an insurgency came from Donald Rumsfeld, the defense secretary, who was determined to bring about a "revolution in military affairs" at the Pentagon—the transformation of war fighting into a combination of information technology and precision firepower that would eliminate the need for large numbers of ground troops and prolonged involvement in distant countries. "It's a vision of war that totally neglects the psychological and cultural dimensions of war," the officer said. Rumsfeld's denial of the existence of the insurgency turned on technicalities: insurgencies were fought against sovereign governments, he argued, and in 2003 Iraq did not yet have one.

In October of that year, a classified National Intelligence Estimate warned that the insurgency was becoming broad-based among Sunni Arabs who were unhappy with the American presence in Iraq, and that it would expand and intensify, with a serious risk of civil war. But Rumsfeld, President Bush, and other administration officials continued to call the escalating violence in Iraq the work of a small number of Baathist "dead-enders" and foreign jihadis. For Rumsfeld, this aversion became a permanent condition. Over Thanksgiving weekend last year, he had a self-described "epiphany" in which he realized that the fighters in Iraq didn't deserve the word "insurgents." The following week, at a Pentagon press conference, when the new chairman of the Joint Chiefs of Staff, Marine Corps general Peter Pace, said, rather sheepishly, "I have to use the word 'insurgent,' because I can't think of a better word right now," Rumsfeld cut in, " 'Enemies of the legitimate Iraqi government'—how's that?"

The refusal of Washington's leaders to acknowledge the true character of the war in Iraq had serious consequences on the battlefield: in the first eighteen months, the United States government failed to organize a strategic response to the insurgency. Capt. Jesse Sellars, a troop commander in the 3rd ACR, who fought in some of the most violent parts of western Iraq in 2003 and 2004, told me about a general who visited his unit and announced, "This is not an insurgency." Sellars recalled thinking, "Well, if you could tell us what it is, that'd be awesome." In the absence of guidance, the 3rd ACR adopted a heavy-handed approach, conducting frequent raids that were often based on bad information. The regiment was constantly moved around, so that officers were never able to form relationships with local people or learn from mistakes. Eventually, the regiment became responsible for vast tracts of Anbar province, with hundreds of miles bordering Saudi Arabia, Jordan, and Syria; it had far too few men to secure any area.

A proper strategy would have demanded the coordinated use of all the tools of American power in Iraq: political, economic, and military. "Militarily, you've got to call it an insurgency," McMaster said, "because we have a counterinsurgency doctrine and theory that you want to access." The classic doctrine, which was developed by the British in Malaya in the 1940s and '50s, says that counterinsurgency warfare is 20 percent military and 80 percent political. The focus of operations is on the civilian population: isolating residents from insurgents, providing security, building a police force, and allowing political and economic development to take place so that the government commands the allegiance of its citizens. A counterinsurgency strategy involves both offensive and defensive operations, but there is an emphasis on using the minimum amount of force necessary. For all these reasons, such a strategy is extremely hard to carry out, especially for the American military, which focuses on combat

operations. Counterinsurgency cuts deeply against the Army's institutional instincts. The doctrine fell out of use after Vietnam, and the Army's
most recent field manual on the subject is two decades old.

The Pentagon's strategy in 2003 and 2004 was to combat the insurgency simply by eliminating insurgents—an approach called "kill-capture."
Kalev Sepp, a retired Special Forces officer who now teaches at the Naval
Postgraduate School in Monterey, California, said of the method, "It's all
about hunting people. I think it comes directly from the Secretary of
Defense—'I want heads on a plate.' You'll get some people that way, but
the failure of that approach is evident: they get Hussein, they get his sons,
they continue every week to kill more, capture more, they've got facilities
full of thousands of detainees, yet there's more insurgents than there were
when they started." In *Dereliction of Duty*, McMaster wrote that a strategy of attrition "was, in essence, the absence of a strategy."

During the first year of the war, Lt. Gen. Ricardo Sanchez was the
commander of military operations in Iraq. He never executed a campaign
plan—as if, like Rumsfeld, he assumed that America was about to leave.
As a result, there was no governing logic to the Army's myriad operations.
T. X. Hammes, a retired Marine colonel who served in Baghdad in early
2004, said, "Each division was operating so differently, right next to the
other—absolutely hard-ass here, and hearts-and-minds here." In the first
year of the war, in Falluja and Ramadi, Maj. Gen. Charles Swannack, of the
82nd Airborne Division, emphasized killing and capturing the enemy, and
the war grew worse in those places; in northern Iraq, Maj. Gen. David
Petraeus, of the 101st Airborne Division, focused on winning over the
civilian population by encouraging economic reconstruction and local government, and had considerable success. "Why is the 82nd hard-ass and
the 101st so different?" Hammes asked. "Because Swannack sees it differently than Petraeus. But that's Sanchez's job. That's why you have a corps
commander." Lieutenant General Sanchez, who never received his fourth
star, remains the only senior military official to have suffered professionally for the failures of the Iraq War. (He is now stationed in Germany.)

From his post in Central Command, McMaster pushed for a more
imaginative and coherent response to an insurgency that he believed was
made up of highly decentralized groups with different agendas making
short-term alliances of convenience. By August 2004, Falluja had fallen
under insurgent control, Mosul had begun to collapse, and Najaf had

become the scene of a ferocious battle. On August 5, General George Casey, Sanchez's successor, signed the Operation Iraqi Freedom campaign plan. The document, which was largely written on Sanchez's watch, remains classified, but Kalev Sepp described it to me in general terms. (In early 2004, McMaster had recruited him to be an adviser on Iraq.) Sepp said, "It was a product that seemed to be toning itself down. It was written as if there were knowledge of this bad thing, an insurgency, that was coming up underfoot, and you had to deal with it, but you had to be careful about being too direct in calling it an insurgency and dealing with it that way, because then you would be admitting that it had always been there but you had ignored it up to that point. It did not talk about what you had to do to defeat an insurgency. It was not a counterinsurgency plan."

In the fall of 2004, Sepp went to work under Casey in the strategy division of Multi-National Force Iraq, MNF-I. In Baghdad, a small group of officers, led by an Army colonel named Bill Hix, worked with Sepp and two analysts from the RAND Corporation to turn the campaign plan into a classic counterinsurgency strategy that focused, above all, on the training of Iraqi security forces, with American advisers embedded in Iraqi units and partnerships between the two armies.

By November 2004, MNF-I had outlined a strategy, and the military command in Baghdad finally had a plan for fighting the insurgency. Much time had been lost, and putting the plan into effect in numerous units was a formidable task. Counterinsurgency, by its nature, is highly dependent on local knowledge and conditions. Changes had to be made at the level of the platoon, the company, and the battalion; the campaign plan helped officers catch up with what some local commanders had already learned to do.

By then, Colonel McMaster had arrived in Fort Carson, Colorado, and he had assumed command of the 3rd ACR. He had just a few months to get the regiment ready for its second deployment to Iraq. The unit ended up in Tal Afar—a place that was being called the next Falluja.

A War for People

In Colorado, McMaster and his officers, most of them veterans of the war's first year, improvised a new way to train for Iraq. Instead of preparing for tank battles, the regiment bought dozens of Arab dishdashas, which the Americans call "man dresses," and acted out a variety of realistic scenarios, with soldiers and Arab Americans playing the role of Iraqis. "We need training that puts soldiers in situations where they need to make extremely tough choices," Captain Sellars, the troop commander, said. "What are they going to see at the traffic control point? They're possibly going to have a walk-up suicide bomber—okay, let's train that. They're going to have an irate drunk guy that is of no real threat—let's train that. They're going to have a pregnant lady that needs to get through the checkpoint faster—okay, let's train that." Pictures of Shiite saints and politicians were hung on the walls of a house, and soldiers were asked to draw conclusions about the occupants. Soldiers searching the house were given the information they wanted only after they had sat down with the occupants three or four times, accepted tea, and asked the right questions. Soldiers filmed the scenarios and afterward analyzed body language and conversational tone. McMaster ordered his soldiers never to swear in front of Iraqis or call them "hajjis" in a derogatory way (this war's version of "gook"). Some were selected to take three-week courses in Arabic language and culture; hundreds of copies of *The Modern History of Iraq*, by Phebe Marr were shipped to Fort Carson; and McMaster drew up a counterinsurgency reading list that included classic works such as T. E. Lawrence's *Seven Pillars of Wisdom*, together with *Learning to Eat Soup with a Knife*, a recent study by Lt. Col. John Nagl, a veteran of the Iraq War.

Sellars told me, "I don't know how many times I've thought, and then heard others say, 'Wish I'd known that the first time.'" The rehearsals in Colorado, he said, amounted to a recognition that "this war is for the people of Iraq." Sellars, who grew up in a family of lumber millers in rural Arkansas, described it as a kind of training in empathy. "Given these circumstances, what would be my reaction?" he asked. "If I was in a situation where my neighbor had gotten his head cut off, how would I react? If it was my kid that had gotten killed by mortars, how would I react?"

By the time two squadrons of the 3rd ACR reached the outskirts of Tal Afar, in the spring of 2005, the city was being terrorized by *takfirin*—Sunni extremists who believe that Muslims who don't subscribe to their brand of Islam, especially Shiites, are infidels and should be killed. The city was central to the strategy of the Jordanian terrorist Abu Musab al-Zarqawi;

Tal Afar had become a transit point for foreign fighters arriving from Syria, and a base of operations in northern Iraq. Zarqawi exploited tribal and sectarian divisions among the city's poor and semiliterate population, which consists mostly of Turkomans, rather than Arabs, three-quarters of them Sunni and one-quarter Shiite. The mayor was a pro-insurgent Sunni. The police chief, appointed by the government of Prime Minister Ibra-him al-Jaafari, was a Shiite. His all-Shiite force was holed up in an area of high ground in the middle of the city known as the Castle, which is sur-rounded by sixteenth-century Ottoman ramparts. Unable to control the city, the Shiite police sent out commandos (McMaster described them as a "death squad") to kidnap and kill Sunnis. Outside the Castle, radical young Sunnis left headless corpses of Shiites in the streets as a warning to anyone who contemplated cooperating with the Americans or the Iraqi government. Shiites living in mixed neighborhoods fled. "The Shia and Sunni communities fell in on themselves," McMaster said. "They be-came armed camps in direct military competition with one another."

McMaster's point man in the effort to stabilize the city was Lt. Col. Chris Hickey, a squadron commander. Hickey, a good-looking man who has soft brown eyes and an aquiline nose, almost never raises his voice and seems as ordinary and steady as McMaster is intellectually restless and gregarious. He's the father of two girls, and it's easy to picture him at a parent-teacher conference. His soldiers spoke of him with reverence; a major in the squadron described Hickey as "the sort of quiet man who feels things very deeply," and Jesse Sellars spoke of his "tactical patience." Last summer, while American and Iraqi soldiers moved block by block into the city, encountering heavy resistance that often took the form of three-hour firefights, Hickey began to study the local power structure. For several months, he spent forty or fifty hours a week with sheikhs from Tal Afar's dozens of tribes: first the Shiite sheikhs, to convince them that the Americans could be counted on to secure their neighborhoods; and then the Sunni sheikhs, many of whom were passive or active supporters of the insurgency.

"The Shia freaked out," Hickey told me inside his cramped head-quarters, in a derelict cluster of cement buildings behind the crenellated ramparts of the Castle. "'Don't we give you information? So why are you meeting with the Sunnis?' 'Because I'm trying to be balanced. I'm try-ing to stabilize your city. If I just talk to you, I'm not going to stabilize your city.' We tried to switch the argument from Sunni versus Shia, which was what the terrorists were trying to make the argument, to Iraqi versus *takfirin*."

Hickey's first attempts to persuade Sunnis to join the Tal Afar police force yielded only three recruits, but he did not give up. In painstakingly slow and inconclusive encounters, each one centering on the same sectarian grievances and fears, Hickey tried to establish common interests between the Sunnis and the Shiites. He also attempted to drive a wedge between nationalist-minded Sunnis and extremists, a distinction that, in the war's first year or two, American soldiers were rarely able to make; they were simply fighting "bad guys." At the highest levels of the administration, the notion of acknowledging the enemy's grievances was dismissed as defeatist. But in Tal Afar I heard expressions of soldierly respect for what some Americans called the Iraqi resistance. "In a city that's seventy-five percent Sunni, if you approach it from a point of view of bringing in or killing everyone who's had anything to do with the insurgency you're bound to fail," Maj. Michael Simmering said. "Imagine how many people in this town have picked up a rifle and taken a shot at coalition forces. Do we really want to try to arrest them all?" Lt. Brian Tinklepaugh explained, "You can't sever your ties with anyone—even your enemy. People with ties to the insurgents have us over for tea."

Hickey, during his conversations with sheikhs, was educating himself in the social intricacies of Tal Afar's neighborhoods, so that his men would know how a raid on a particular house would be perceived by the rest of the street. ("Effects-based operations," a term of art in counterinsurgency, rolled off the tongue of every young officer I met in Tal Afar.) He was also showing his soldiers what kind of war he wanted them to fight. It required unlearning Army precepts, under fire. "The tedium of counterinsurgency ops, the small, very incremental gains—our military culture doesn't lend itself to that kind of war," Jack McLaughlin, a major on Hickey's staff, told me. "There are no glorious maneuvers like at the National Training Center, where you destroy the Krasnovian hordes. It's just a slow grind, and you have to have patience."

At the same time, the 3rd ACR engaged in frequent combat; ultimately, the regiment lost twenty-one soldiers in northwestern Iraq, and one platoon suffered a casualty rate of 40 percent. Last September, Colonel McMaster staged a push into Surai, the oldest, densest part of the city, which had become the base of insurgent operations; there were days of heavy fighting, with support from Apache helicopters shooting Hellfire missiles. Most of the civilians in the area, who had been warned of the coming attack, fled ahead of the action (unknown numbers of insurgents escaped with them), and though many buildings were demolished, the damage to the city wasn't close to the destruction of Falluja in November 2004. "There are two ways to do counterinsurgency," Major McLaughlin said. "You can come in, cordon off a city, and level it, à la Falluja. Or you can come in, get to know the city, the culture, establish relationships with the people, and then you can go in and eliminate individuals instead of whole city blocks."

After McMaster's offensive, Hickey and a squadron of a thousand men set up living quarters next to Iraqi army soldiers, in primitive patrol bases without hot water, reliable heat, or regular cooked meals. One afternoon, I walked with Hickey a hundred yards from his headquarters—past soldiers on guard duty warming themselves over a barrel fire—to the mayor's office, in the Castle. The new mayor, Najim Abdullah al-Jabouri, is a secular Sunni Arab and a former brigadier general from Baghdad who speaks no Turkmen, Tal Afar's main language. The city was so polarized that the provincial authorities had turned to an outsider to replace the corrupt former mayor and win a measure of confidence from all sides. Najim, a chain-smoker, wore a dark suit and a purple shirt without a tie; his face was drawn and he had dark pouches under his eyes. On his wall hung a photograph of him with McMaster. The mayor had written a letter to Bush, Rumsfeld, and Congress asking them to extend the 3rd ACR's deployment in Tal Afar for another year.

"If a doctor makes an operation and the operation succeeds, it's not a good thing to put the patient under the care of another doctor," the mayor told me. "This doctor knows the wound, he knows the patient." He added, "Hickey knows my children by name."

I asked what would happen if, as before, the Americans withdrew from Tal Afar.

"What? No American forces?" The mayor could hardly comprehend my question. "It will take only one month and the terrorists will take over. At a minimum, we need three years for the Iraqi army to be strong enough to take control of the country—at least three years. You can't measure the army only by weapons. It's building people, too."

The mayor had once been tempted to join the insurgency. He lost his military career in 2003, when L. Paul Bremer III, the administrator of the Coalition Provisional Authority—the American occupation government—dissolved the old Iraqi army. "Bremer gave the order that whole families die," he said. "I decided that if my children died I would pick up my gun in revenge." But the dynamic in Tal Afar, where the U.S. Army seemed to be cleaning up after its own mistakes, had improved his opinion of the Americans. "I began to work with the Americans here and saw a new picture. I thought before that all Americans, like Bremer and the people we saw on TV, were killers and turned guns on Iraqis. But when I worked with them and saw them more, I realized they were different. Before, we were just sitting and watching Al Jazeera and believing it. Now I see it's a lying network."

The intensity of the mayor's attachment to the Americans was understandable. They were in the same position, outsiders trying to hold the city together and persuade its tribes and sects to find a common national identity. I once saw Hickey ask a group of police trainees at a new station whether they were Sunni or Shiite, and when they started to answer he said, "No—Iraqi!" Hickey had seen the mayor demonstrate the lesson to an elementary school classroom.

Down the hall from the mayor's office was a small conference room dominated by a thirty-foot table. Along each side, behind clouds of cigarette smoke, Tal Afar's notables sat grimly in tribal dress and business clothes: Sunnis on one side, Shiites on the other. It was only the second time the two groups had met in the Castle. The mayor had told me that cold drinks were among his main negotiation tools, and everyone was sipping a Pepsi or a Sprite. The mayor took his place at the head of the table. On the wall behind him hung a giant Iraqi flag.

The meeting soon deteriorated. There were complaints about the slow pace of rebuilding, the uneven distribution of contracts, the lack of government funds, and the inability of Shiite families who had fled Tal Afar to return to the mixed neighborhoods. "The rebuilding is something horrible," the mayor said, in agreement. "But it contains a wonderful thing: it's not accepted by both sectors. So that's proof they can be united."

Shiite sheikhs accused the Sunnis of tolerating the presence of terrorists, and Sunni sheikhs accused the Shia of making unwarranted generalizations about them. "This is our second meeting, and we're saying the same things," a Shiite sheikh complained. "What is the point?"

"Sitting here is the point," the mayor, relentlessly cheerful, said; I was beginning to understand his look of exhaustion. "It's wonderful that you are at least sitting together. We're supposed to have a meeting of the reconstruction committee, but the important thing is we should reconstruct ourselves—then everything will be easier."

A Sunni sheikh demanded, "If you want to make things better, why do you ask people applying to be police whether they are Sunni or Shiite? Asking will only consolidate the problems."

"We want to create a balance between Shiite and Sunni," the mayor answered. "If the Sunnis come, believe me, after a while we won't ask this question."

After listening to the complaints of the Sunnis, a Shiite sheikh lost his temper and stood up to face the other side of the table: "The people who are fighting—where do they come from? They don't pop up from the ground. Some of you know who they are." The sheikh's father had been ambushed and killed on the way to a reconciliation meeting with a Sunni tribe. "Only Shia have these problems," he said.

That night, I visited the jail at a police station between Hickey's headquarters and the mayor's office. Forty-seven prisoners were squeezed into a cell so tight that they had to take turns sleeping; four or five others were crammed into the latrine. When a guard slid aside a plywood sheet covering the cell's barred door, the prisoners, dazed and wide-eyed, protested their innocence and asked for blankets. One boy said that he was twelve years old. A fat, middle-aged man who claimed to be a teacher from Mosul told me in fluent English that he'd been arrested because a roadside bomb had happened to go off near a taxi in which he was riding. He hadn't seen a judge in a month, and hadn't seen a lawyer at all.

Next door to the cell, in an unlit room whose roof had partially caved in, offering a view of the starry desert sky, several policemen were trying to stay warm around a gasoline burner. With one exception, they were Shiites. Police work was the only job they could find, they said; Sunnis had taken their old jobs. The chief, whose name was Ibrahim Hussein, said, "My wife and children can't leave the house." A slight young cop named Hassan said that seventy members of his tribe had been killed by terrorists, including a cousin whose corpse turned up one day with the head severed.

The policemen offered me the only chair in their squalid little room. One of their colleagues was sleeping under a blanket on the cement floor. It was bitterly cold. They said that they wanted the Americans to leave Tal Afar and create a perimeter around the city to keep terrorists out; inside the city, they said, the Americans were preventing the police from eliminating the terrorists, releasing most prisoners after just a few days. The men had been trained for two months in Jordan, and I asked whether they had been instructed in human rights. They said that they had studied the subject for a week.

"What about the rights of the guy who gets kidnapped and beheaded?" Hussein said. Hassan added, "If the Americans weren't here, we could get more out of our interrogations."

"You mean torture?"

"Only the terrorists."

"How do you know that they're terrorists?"

"Someone identifies them to me. We have evidence. The innocent ones, we let go."

"How many terrorists and sympathizers are there in Tal Afar?"

Hassan considered it for a moment. "A hundred and fifty thousand." This was approximately the number of Sunnis in the city.

When I got up to leave, the policemen begged me to ask Colonel Hickey for blankets and heaters.

The Tal Afar police were better informed about local realities than either the Americans or the Iraqi army, but they were ill-trained, quick to shoot, likelier to represent parochial interests, and reluctant to take risks. "There are some police that would go after the Sunnis," Chris Hickey said. "So, yes, we are a constraint on them. Their head's not there yet." A soldier in the squadron, who was departing on a mission with Iraqi policemen to distribute food packages in a mixed area, went further: "These guys are worthless."

The American patrol bases around the city stand next to Iraqi army battalion headquarters; this allows for daily conversations among counterparts in the two armies and frequent sharing of information. The Americans are not just training an Iraqi army; they are trying to build an institution of national unity before there is a nation.

Hickey and other Americans spoke highly of Lt. Col. Majid Abdul-Latif Hatem, an Iraqi battalion deputy commander. One evening, Colonel Majid invited me into his spartan quarters on the grounds of Tal Afar's granary, across a marshy field from the American patrol base. A Shiite from Nasiriya, in the south, he had a comically large handlebar mustache and mirthless eyes under droopy eyelids. In the corner of the room was a cot with a military blanket; on the wall was a map of his battalion's area of operations. As he began to talk, an orderly prepared tea in a blackened brass pot.

Colonel Majid, who had been in Tal Afar for a month, had an unsentimental view of the city's problems. "If we evacuated Tal Afar of Shiites or of Sunnis, it would be a calm, lovely city. The main issue in Iraq now is the sectarian one: one group wants to destroy the other group. The people need a long, long time, so that they can learn democracy, because they were raised on a sectarian basis. Second, to get rid of the problems we should divide Iraq into three parts: Sunni, Shiite, and Kurd. If there is one Iraq on the map, but inside the people are divided, what's the point of being one? The people are tired of war and instability—they just want to live in peace, even by dividing. The time of Jesus and the Prophet Muhammad is past. There are no more miracles."

Colonel Majid took out a piece of white paper and carefully drew the outline of Iraq, then carved it into sectors. "This area is Shiite," he said. "This area is Sunni: Mosul, Tikrit, Samarra, Anbar. Take oil from here"— he pointed to Basra and Kirkuk—"and give some of it to here. The Sunnis will have to accept. If the oil was in their area, they would ask for division."

I asked if the American and Iraqi armies could prevent a civil war.

"At any moment, there will be war between the two sects," he said. "I want to tell you the truth." He repeated the word in English. "Right now, you are observing the men of the Iraqi army, and seeing what's on the outside. But I know the interior of them. My men are not coming here for nationalist beliefs, for one Iraq. They are here because they need work. So don't be surprised if they stand and watch killing between the people here."

We drank tea and talked, and as the night wore on, Colonel Majid disappeared into the darkness; I could see only his mustache, his eyes, and the orange glow of the gasoline burner. I asked if Iraq could be divided without huge population transfers and terrible bloodshed.

"How much do the Americans spend on their army every month here? Six billion dollars. One billion of this can build houses or apartment complexes in the south, for the Shia here up north. You have to offer many things if you're going to move people: transportation, houses, jobs. It's a very complicated situation, and I'm not George Washington to arrange everything for you. God says: no one can change the people if they don't change themselves. America is the biggest power in the world, but it cannot get control over the explosions here and the insurgency. It cannot change the way people think." He added, "Saddam Hussein brought all of us to the point where we all hate Iraq."

I asked if Iraqi minds could change over time.

"Maybe," Colonel Majid said. "But it will take years."

In Tal Afar, I began to imagine the Americans as sutures closing a deep wound. If they were removed too quickly, the wound would open again, and there would be heavy bleeding; at the same time, their presence was causing an infection in the surrounding flesh. This was a dilemma that required careful timing. It was also possible that the wound was too deep to ever be repaired. This would be less a dilemma than a defeat.

The Americans' achievement in Tal Afar showed that, in the war's third year, individuals and units within the Army could learn and adapt on their own. On my last night in the city, Colonel McMaster sat in his makeshift office and said, "It is so damn complex. If you ever think you have the solution to this, you're wrong, and you're dangerous. You have to keep listening and thinking and being critical and self-critical. Remember General Nivelle, in the First World War, at Verdun? He said he had the solution, and then destroyed the French army until it mutinied."

During the 3rd Armored Cavalry Regiment's final weeks in Iraq, morale was remarkably high. Some soldiers expressed, almost under their breath, a reluctance to leave. Many of them had established strong bonds with Iraqis and didn't want to abandon the work they had done together. They brought gifts for the Iraqis' children when they returned from leave. The Iraqi army units in Tal Afar had been watching McMaster's men carefully and were showing signs of competence, taking the lead in small operations, learning to win the trust of local civilians, and often proving more adept than the Americans at securing good intelligence. They still faced enormous logistical problems—they lacked armored vehicles and a reliable system of paying salaries, and their Ministry of Defense was so weak and corrupt that Iraqi soldiers still depended on the American military's supply system to eat and to stay warm. As for the Iraqi police, they resembled less a neutral security force than a faction in the city's conflicts. Nonetheless, the American soldiers in Tal Afar felt that they had achieved something. At the headquarters of Hickey's squadron, in the Castle, young officers who, in the war's second year, had concluded that the cause was lost now talked about a fragile success.

"If we're not stupid, and we don't quit, we can win this thing," Major McLaughlin said. "History teaches you that war, at its heart, is a human endeavor. And if you ignore the human side—yours, the enemy's, and the civilians'—you set yourself up for failure. It's not about weapons. It's about people."

"If we are smart enough to see this through, we can win it," Major Simmering said. "If we're not careful, we could destroy everything we've done in the last six months in a matter of minutes by doing something stupid—taking an action that could alienate the Sunni population. It takes months to make somebody like you; it can take just a minute to make them hate you." All the soldiers worried about what one general in Iraq called a "rush to failure." As Simmering put it, "There's a lot of political pressure back home to turn this over to the Iraqis."

"A Good-Enough Solution"

From Tal Afar, I flew by helicopter to an airfield a few miles north of Tikrit, called Forward Operating Base Speicher. The headquarters of the 101st Airborne Division, Speicher is an "enduring FOB"—one of a handful of gigantic bases around Iraq to which American forces are being pulled back, as smaller bases are handed over to the Iraqi army. Speicher has an area of twenty-four square miles and the appearance of a small, flat, modular Midwestern city; there is a bus system, a cavernous dining hall that serves four flavors of Baskin-Robbins ice cream, a couple of gyms, and several movie theaters. At least nine thousand soldiers live there, and many of them seemed to leave the base rarely or not at all: they talked about "going out," as if the psychological barrier between them and Iraq had become daunting. After three months on the base, an Army lawyer working on the Iraqi justice system still hadn't visited the Tikrit courts. A civil affairs major who had been in Iraq since May needed to consult a handbook when I asked him the names of the local tribes. A reporter for the military newspaper *Stars & Stripes* had heard a bewildered sergeant near Tikrit ask his captain, "What's our mission here?" The captain replied sardonically, "We're here to guard the ice cream trucks going north so that someone else can guard them there."

Much of the activity at an enduring FOB simply involves self-supply. These vast military oases raise the specter of American permanence in Iraq, but to me they more acutely suggested American irrelevance. Soldiers have even coined a derogatory term for those who never get off the base: "fobbits." I spent two days at Speicher without seeing an Iraqi.

After Tal Afar, it was dismaying how little soldiers at Speicher knew about the lives of Iraqis. When I drove with the civil affairs major into Tikrit, we stopped along the way at an elementary school just outside the base. The major wanted to see if the teachers had pursued his request to have the children become pen pals with kids at an elementary school in his hometown in California. It sounded like a fine idea, but two nervous female teachers who received us in their office gave a number of reasons that the children hadn't yet written letters. The major pressed them for a few minutes, and then he was ready to let the project go. As soon as he left the room, the women showed me a thick stack of pictures that their students had drawn for the children in California, along with a letter from the teachers asking for school supplies and "lotion for dry skin." The letter concluded, "Good luck U.S.A. Army." But the women were too frightened to give the bundle to the major; a relationship with an elementary school in America could make them targets of local insurgents. All this was lost on the major. The teachers said that they rarely saw American soldiers anymore.

Speicher provides a more representative picture of the American military's future in Iraq than Tal Afar. The trend is away from counterinsurgency and toward what, in Washington, is known as an "exit strategy." Commanders are under tremendous pressure to keep casualties low, and combat deaths have been declining for several months as patrols are reduced and the Americans rely more and more on air power. (During the past five months, the number of air strikes increased 50 percent over the same period a year ago.) More than half the country is scheduled to be turned over to Iraqi army control this year. This is the crux of the military strategy for withdrawal, and it is happening at a surprisingly fast pace. President Bush has always insisted that the turnover and "drawdown" will be "conditions-based"—governed by the situation in Iraq and by the advice of commanders, not by a timetable set in Washington. But everywhere I went in Iraq, officers and soldiers spoke as if they were already preparing to leave. A sergeant in Baquba, northeast of Baghdad, said, "We'll be here for ten years in some form, but boots-on-the-ground-wise? We're really almost done." He said that the U.S. Army doesn't allow itself to fail, and when I suggested that Iraq hardly looked like a victory the sergeant replied, "So you adjust the standard of success. For me, it's getting all the Joes home. It's not that I don't give a damn about what's going on here. But that's how it is."

A field-grade officer in the 101st Airborne said, "The algorithm of success is to get a good-enough solution." There were, he said, three categories of assessment for every aspect of the mission: optimal, acceptable, and unacceptable. He made it clear that optimal wasn't in the running. "We're handing a shit sandwich over to someone else," the officer said. "We have to turn this over, let them do it their way. We're like a frigging organ transplant that's rejected. We have to get the Iraqi army to where they can hold their own in a frigging firefight with insurgents, and get the hell out." The Iraqi national security adviser, Mowaffak al-Rubaie, who chairs a high-level committee in Baghdad on American withdrawal, gave the same forecast that was mentioned by a planner on General Abizaid's staff at Central Command: fewer than a hundred thousand foreign troops in Iraq by the end of this year, and half that number by the middle of 2007.

In other words, "conditions-based" withdrawal is a flexible term. The conditions will be evaluated by commanders who know what results are expected back in Washington. I suggested to Senator Chuck Hagel, the Nebraska Republican, who has been a critic of the administration's war policy, that this sounded like a variation on the famous advice that Senator George Aiken of Vermont gave President Johnson about Vietnam in 1966: declare victory and go home. "In a twenty-first-century version, yes, probably," Hagel said. "It won't be quite that stark." The administration, he said, is "finding ways in its own mind for back-door exits out of Iraq." He added, "We have an election coming up in November. The fact is, we're going to be pulling troops out, and I suspect it'll be kind of quiet. We're going to wake up some morning, probably in the summer, and all of a sudden we'll be forty thousand troops down, and people will say, 'Gee, I didn't know.'"

A senior military officer defended Generals Abizaid and Casey, and said that they would not simply bow to pressure from Washington. "I don't think commanders are so ambitious that they're willing to sell their men and their endeavor up the river so they can tell their bosses what they want to hear." But he admitted that there was considerable pressure for withdrawal, saying, "A blind man on a dark night can see people want the recommendation to be drawdown." The pressure is partly driven by the strain on the military and partly by the fear that thousands of junior officers and senior sergeants, who face future deployments, may quit if the war extends many more years. Divorce rates among Army officers have doubled since the war began. The Army is so short-staffed that it has promoted 97 percent of its captains. "If you're not a convicted felon, you're being promoted to major," a Pentagon official said.

As Americans pull back to the isolated megabases, further reducing the daily death toll, Iraq will likely become a lighter burden for Republicans in Congress and for the administration. A number of American officials, both civilian and military, along with Sunni politicians in Tal Afar and Tikrit, told me that this scenario was not only inevitable but healthy. Contact between Americans and Iraqis had led to mistakes, deaths, and mutual exhaustion.

But a good-enough counterinsurgency is really none at all. There is no substitute for the investment of time, effort, and risk that was so evident in Tal Afar. The retreat to the enduring FOBs seems like an acknowledgment that counterinsurgency is just too hard. "If you really want to reduce your casualties, go back to Fort Riley," Kalev Sepp, the Naval Postgraduate School professor, said. "It's absurd to think that you can protect the population from armed insurgents without putting your men's lives at risk." The policy of gathering troops at enormous bases, he added, "is old Army thinking—centralization of resources, of people, of control. Counterinsurgency requires decentralization."

Some military leaders are feverishly trying to institutionalize the hard-won knowledge from cities like Tal Afar in time to make a difference in this war. At the training base in Taji, just north of Baghdad, there is now a counterinsurgency academy where incoming officers attend classes taught by those they've come to relieve. (Jesse Sellars told me that his main lesson to his successors was to educate themselves and their soldiers about the Iraqis.) Sepp sat in on a class led by General Casey, after which a newly arrived brigade commander said, "This is the first time I've been told my primary mission is to train Iraqi forces." Until then, he had thought that his mission was to kick down doors and haul people in. Many commanders in Iraq still think so.

In the first year of the war, Maj. Gen. David Petraeus achieved a temporary success when, as a divisional commander in northern Iraq, he applied the basic ideas of counterinsurgency. He is now a lieutenant general and commander of the Combined Arms Center at Fort Leavenworth in Kansas. Petraeus is overseeing a group of active duty and former officers in the writing of a new joint Army/Marine Corps counterinsurgency field manual. "It is, as with many things in life, much easier to explain than to do," he told me. "But it is very important to get that basic understanding right again, and the power of a field manual is its ability to communicate relatively straightforward concepts. The basic concepts and principles are not rocket science or brain surgery, but they can be very hard to apply." Counterinsurgency begins, he said, when military leaders "set the right tone."

In February, I attended a two-day workshop at Fort Leavenworth, where the authors of the draft heard suggestions from an assembly of critics. Petraeus had invited not just military and civilian officials but academics, journalists, and human rights activists, and the workshop was cosponsored by the Carr Center for Human Rights Policy, at Harvard's Kennedy School—in keeping with the draft manual's claim that counterinsurgency is 20 percent military and 80 percent political. Also in attendance was Brigadier Nigel Aylwin-Foster, a British general who had just published an article in *Military Review*, out of Fort Leavenworth, which delivered an attack on the American military's cultural ineptitude in fighting the Iraqi insurgency. Aylwin-Foster, who had served under Petraeus in 2004, when Petraeus led the training mission in Baghdad, told me, "It seemed to be an enigma, the U.S. military as an entity. They're polite, courteous, generous, humble, in a sense. But you see some of the things going on—if I could sum it up, I never saw such a good bunch of people inadvertently piss off so many people." When Aylwin-Foster's article appeared, in December, General Peter Schoomaker, the Army chief of staff, ordered it to be sent to every general in the Army; I saw it on a number of desks in Iraq.

The question hanging unasked over the workshop at Fort Leavenworth was whether it was already too late to change the military's approach in Iraq. When Kalev Sepp discussed the field manual with students in his class on insurgency at the Naval Postgraduate School, a Special Forces captain said, "If this manual isn't written soon, you'll have it ready just in time to give one to each soldier leaving Iraq."

Civil War?

Just as the Americans have begun to learn how to fight a counterinsurgency war, they find themselves in the middle of a growing civil conflict, and what succeeds in the former may backfire in the latter. Training Iraqi security forces and turning responsibility over to them makes sense if the Americans are trying to buttress an embattled government against insurgents; but as sectarian violence rises, with the police and the Army dominated by one group, the Americans could also be arming one side of an approaching civil war.

On February 22, the Shiite shrine in Samarra was bombed, almost certainly by elements of Al Qaeda; its golden dome was destroyed. The sectarian violence that followed was widely interpreted as the first definitive sign that Iraq was coming apart, but Baghdad and the mixed towns around it had already shown clear symptoms of civil war. In the capital, Shiite families were being driven out of Sunni neighborhoods by a campaign of threats and assassinations. Young Sunni men were being rounded up by Shiite militiamen, some of whom wore police uniforms; they disappeared into secret prisons or turned up on the street, bound and shot to death.

Dora, a middle-class neighborhood of Sunnis, Shiites, and Christians in southern Baghdad, has become the epicenter of the low-grade civil war. A businessman from Dora told me that it began with the killing of barbers: Sunni extremists believed that shaving a man's beard was against

Islam, and they extended the ban to Western-style haircuts. "After the barbers, they went on to the real estate agents," the businessman said. A fatwa was issued, declaring that in the time of the Prophet there was no buying or selling of property. Then an ice vendor was shot dead on the street because ice wasn't sold in the seventh century.

The next targets were grocery shop owners, exchange shop owners, clothing shop owners. "At first, they were giving reasons, but then things developed, and they started killing for no reason," the businessman said. Every day in the heart of Dora, around the Assyrian Market, a list of intended victims—mostly merchants, and always Shiites—circulates by word of mouth. Within a few days, people on the list who don't take precautions are shot to death in broad daylight. Police at the local stations don't get involved, and American soldiers rarely enter the district, though the businessman said that he goes to sleep at night to the sound of gunfire, helicopters overhead, and bombs dropping, as if he were on the front line of a battle. "Dora is out of the government's control," the businessman said, and Shiites who can afford to escape are leaving.

A senior Iraqi official who has access to classified intelligence said that the campaign of violence is part of a strategic effort by Sunni insurgents to "shape the battlefield": to clear the district of potential enemies and use it as a staging area for attacks in Baghdad. Dora has an oil refinery and a power plant, and it lies along the route from the Sunni-dominated tribal areas south of Baghdad to the heart of the city. The killings in Dora, the official said, are part of a trend away from attacks on American and Iraqi military units, which expose insurgents to great risk, toward killings of local officials and ordinary citizens, intended to undermine the public's confidence that the government can protect it. In January, he said, there were seven hundred of these murders, the highest number of the war up until that month. "So 2006, maybe, will be the year of assassinations and infrastructure attacks," the official said.

The killings have created an atmosphere of sectarian hysteria that residents of Baghdad have never known before. Fear and hatred of one's neighbor are expressed in extreme language. I met a Shiite butcher, Muhammad Kareem Jassim, who owns a small shop on a busy thoroughfare, the doorway obstructed by the hanging carcasses of skinned lambs. His brother was also a butcher, with a shop in Dora. One morning in January, the brother was cutting meat for two women customers when a man walked into the shop, asked the women to excuse him, came up to the counter, and said "Good morning." The brother looked up, said "Good morning," and was shot in the face and killed. His grown son rushed into the room shouting "Daddy, Daddy!" and he, too, was shot dead. A second brother, also a butcher, came running from an adjacent shop with a carving knife in his hand; he was also killed.

When I sat down, ten days later, to talk with Jassim, a stout, bearded man in his fifties, he was hyperventilating with rage. "Dirty fuckers, sons of bitches—they have no faith, no religious leaders, since the time of Omar and Abu Bakr until now," he said of Sunnis, going straight back to the seventh century. "The only reason for this is that we are Shia." He expressed great bitterness that Sunni religious and political leaders rarely condemn the killings of Shiites, and he despaired of being protected by American or Iraqi security forces. The butcher's shoulders heaved, and he said, "If our religious leaders gave a fatwa, there would be no more Sunnis in Iraq anymore! Because everybody now has a broken heart. I wish I could catch them with my hands and slaughter them. I could do it—I'm a butcher."

In the past year, Shiites have begun to engage in deadly retaliatory strikes against Sunnis. Many ordinary Shiites have lost patience with the calls for restraint from religious leaders like Grand Ayatollah Ali al-Sistani. And Shiite party militias have taken up kidnapping and assassination, creating widespread fear among Sunnis for the first time.

The Iraqi Islamic Party is the country's largest Sunni party. Its headquarters, in western Baghdad, has a human rights office with pictures on the walls of Sunni corpses bearing marks of torture allegedly inflicted by Shiites. While I was in the office, an elderly couple arrived in a state of panic. A week before, at six in the morning, fifteen commandos had broken into their house and taken their grown son from his bed. Since then, the parents had been unable to get any information about him. The woman described the commandos as members of the Badr Corps, the largest Shiite militia in Iraq, which was formed during the Iran-Iraq War by the Iranian Revolutionary Guards. One of its leaders, Bayan Jabr, is now the Minister of the Interior; Sunnis accuse him of allowing Shiite militiamen to infiltrate Iraqi police forces. Sunnis routinely call Shiite politicians like Jabr "Iranians." The mother cried, "In all my life, I never saw something like this. They are coming from Iran, the Persian people—Iran, which is trying to get the nuclear bomb to destroy the world."

A party official, Omar Hechel al-Jabouri, told the old couple that he would contact the Interior Ministry about the case, in order to prevent their son from being tortured or killed. Every day, he said, a hundred people come to his office with complaints, so many that he has taken to sleeping on a cot in a corner of the room. "Our brothers, the Shia, are very smart in crying about their suffering," he said. "We others are not as smart." (An American Embassy official told me that in Iraq each side has perfected its own "victimology.")

American troops have been struggling to purge Shiite militiamen from the Iraqi police and recruit Sunnis, with the goal of making it a nonsectarian force. Maj. Gen. Joe Peterson, who is leading the police training effort, said that the goal was to have two hundred thousand police trained and equipped by the end of the year. (As of mid-March, a hundred and thirty thousand had been trained.) "We captured a Shiite death squad last week," he said. "There are guys going out in the middle of the night." The squad, which was out to avenge the death of a member's relative, included twenty-two employees of the Interior Ministry. "We have some very bad groups out there who are bent on ensuring that the government fails," he said.

An American intelligence official said that he considers the increasingly aggressive Shiite militias a bigger long-term threat to Iraq than the Sunni insurgency. These groups raise the prospect not just of a Sunni-Shiite civil war but also of an intra-Shiite fight, between the Badr Corps—widely perceived as a front for Iran—and the Mahdi Army of Moqtada al-Sadr, the radical Iraqi populist. When I asked Colonel McMaster what Americans could do if a full-scale Iraqi civil war breaks out, he said, "Not a whole hell of a lot."

Plan B

Fort Leavenworth has a Center for Army Lessons Learned. There is no equivalent at the White House or the Office of the Secretary of Defense. Last November, the Pentagon issued DOD Directive 3000.05, which declared that "stability operations," or peacekeeping and security maintenance—which Rumsfeld had denigrated in the run-up to the invasion of Iraq, questioning why the Pentagon had such a division—were now "a core U.S. military mission that the Department of Defense shall be prepared to conduct and support." The directive went on, "They shall be given priority comparable to combat operations." In the obscure world of "stability ops," DOD 3000.05 was a historic, if belated, document. Careful readers noticed that it was signed not by Rumsfeld but by his deputy Gordon England. In February, Rumsfeld released his Quadrennial Defense Review, a congressionally mandated report setting out long-term military policy. Its language seemed unassailable, focusing on the need for greater capability in civil affairs, military policing, cultural and language expertise, and counterinsurgency, all as part of what the document called "the long war" against global terrorism. But in its budget choices, which reveal the real priorities of the defense secretary, the Iraq War had hardly registered. Instead of cutting back on hugely expensive weapons programs in order to build more troop divisions—Iraq has made it painfully obvious that a larger army is necessary for fighting counterinsurgency wars—the review favored the fighter jets and carriers that are the lifeblood of military contractors and members of Congress.

It's an open secret in Washington that Rumsfeld wants to extricate himself from Iraq. But President Bush's rhetoric—most recently, in a series of speeches given to shore up faltering public support—remains resolute. For three years, the administration has split the difference between these two poles, committing itself halfheartedly to Iraq. (Through every turn in the war, the number of troops in Iraq has remained remarkably stable—between a hundred and fifteen thousand and a hundred and sixty thousand.) In 2006, maintaining the status quo no longer seems viable. The midterm elections and the president's flagging popularity will force Bush to make a choice: either he will devote the rest of his presidency to staying in Iraq or he will begin a withdrawal.

In *Dereliction of Duty*, McMaster's book on Vietnam, he described how Lyndon Johnson's top generals allowed the president to mire American troops in Vietnam with no possible strategy and no public candor. He wrote, "As American involvement in Vietnam deepened, the gap between the true nature of that commitment and the President's depiction of it to the American people, the Congress, and members of his own Administration widened. Lyndon Johnson, with the assistance of Robert S. McNamara and the Joint Chiefs of Staff, had set the stage for America's disaster in Vietnam." In Tal Afar, I told McMaster that there were more than a few echoes of the Iraq War in his book. He laughed and said, "I can't even touch that."

A president who projects a consistently unrealistic message of success to the public; a defense secretary who consolidates power in his office and intimidates or ignores the uniformed military; senior generals—Tommy Franks, John Abizaid, Ricardo Sanchez, Richard Myers, and now Peter Pace, Myers's successor as chairman of the Joint Chiefs—who appear before congressional committees and at news conferences and solemnly confirm that they have enough troops to win: the parallels between Vietnam and Iraq, in terms of the moral abdication of leaders, are not hard to see. In one sense, though, the two wars are inversely analogous: in Vietnam, Johnson claimed to be staying out while he was getting in; in Iraq, something like the opposite is happening.

It isn't easy to know how much unwelcome information reaches the president. On December 16, the day after elections for a constitutional government in Iraq, a group of senators and representatives met with the president and his top national security advisers in the Roosevelt Room at the White House, while General Casey and Zalmay Khalilzad, the U.S. ambassador to Iraq, joined in from Baghdad on a large video screen. According to Senator Joseph Biden, the Delaware Democrat, who had flown back from Iraq that morning, Vice President Cheney was characteristically sanguine about the war, saying, "It's been a great election, Mr. President—we're well on our way." The president talked at length about the need to continue fighting terrorism. When it was Biden's turn to speak, he said, "With all due respect, Mr. President, if every single Al Qaeda–related terrorist were killed tomorrow, done, gone, you'd still have a war on your hands in Iraq." On the video screen, Khalilzad and Casey nodded. When the discussion turned to the need for a political solution, with nonsectarian heads of the Defense and Interior Ministries, Rumsfeld began nodding vigorously—as if to say, Biden thought, "Hey, this is Condi's problem. This ain't my problem."

Condoleezza Rice now finds herself trying to win the kinds of fights with Rumsfeld that Colin Powell lost long ago. As secretary of state, she has begun to repair alliances that Powell was helpless to keep the administration from shredding. By most accounts, Stephen Hadley, her replacement as national security adviser, is a weak figure in the White House, and Cheney's influence has waned in the second term, allowing Rice to consolidate foreign policy decision making in her department, as Powell never could. But Rumsfeld remains a formidable bureaucratic force. Recently,

Rice and Rumsfeld have battled over the question of how to protect Iraq's infrastructure. Insurgents have become so adept at hitting pipelines, power stations, and refineries that fuel and electricity shortages have become nationwide crises; meanwhile, some Iraqi army units and tribes that are being paid to guard these facilities are collaborating in the destruction. At the State Department, these attacks have become a full-time preoccupation. One official there described the strategy of Sunni insurgents this way: "The one thing we can do is strangle Baghdad, the crown jewel of Iraq. You don't have a country without dealing with us. You may have the oil in the north, Kurds—but how are you going to get it out?" For several months, Rice has tried to force a decision on whether to commit American troops to protecting key sites. Rumsfeld has resisted, and—as with so many issues in Iraq—the White House has made no decision.

The defense secretary has even objected to soldiers providing security for the small reconstruction teams that Khalilzad wants to establish in provincial capitals. (Rumsfeld insists that private contractors be used instead.) Final word on the mission has been held up at the White House for months. An administration official said that the delay showed how badly reality can be "disconnected from the president's rhetoric of Iraq as the most important thing on the planet." The official went on, "Certain people at the Pentagon want to get out of Iraq at all costs." He added, "These provincial reconstruction teams should be resolved in an afternoon. But Rumsfeld doesn't want to do it, and nobody wants to confront him."

As a State Department official was preparing to leave for Baghdad recently, a colleague told him, "When you get there, the big sucking sound you'll hear is DOD moonwalking out of Iraq as fast as it can go. Your job is to figure out how we can fill the gap." But the State Department has nothing like the resources—money, equipment, personnel—of Defense. It is having trouble persuading enough foreign service officers to risk their lives by filling the vacant slots at the embassy in Baghdad or on ministerial assistance teams, even though raises are being offered; for a brief period, the State Department considered reactivating, for the first time since Vietnam, a policy of forced assignments. In 1970, at the height of the pacification program in Vietnam, the U.S. reconstruction teams included seventy-six hundred civilians and military officials; in a country the size of Iraq, that would mean eleven thousand people, but barely a thousand positions are planned for the provincial teams in Iraq. The administration asked an increasingly skeptical Congress for just $1.6 billion in reconstruction funds for the coming year, which means that, though the output of electricity, water, oil, and other utilities still falls well short of prewar levels, the major reconstruction effort in Iraq is now over.

In February, I met Secretary Rice in her office at the State Department. On one wall was an old recruiting poster, in which the pointing figure of Uncle Sam is saying, "We're at War. Are You Doing All You Can?" I asked Rice whether she would alert the president if she saw a rush to disengage from Iraq. "If I thought there was a drawdown that was going to endanger our ability to deliver a foundation for stability that outlasts whatever presence we had—absolutely, I would," she said. She quickly added that this isn't happening, and that the president won't allow it to happen: "Even though there is violence, there is a process that is moving, I think rather inexorably, actually, toward an outcome that will one day bring a stable Iraq."

Rice admitted that the American public is "uneasy" about Iraq. Speaking in her precise, academic manner, she analyzed one or two of the administration's mistakes. But she kept falling back on the strategy of hope. I asked in several ways about the danger of civil war; her answer was that Iraq won't have one, because Iraqis don't want one. And when she turned to the larger questions about the president's legacy in the Middle East, Rice sounded almost mystically optimistic: "I think all the trends are in the right direction. I can see a path where this turns out as we would want to see it turn out." She narrowed her eyes. "I can see that path clearly."

At the embassy in Baghdad, Khalilzad gave me the impression that he worries about the focus and staying power of the administration, as if his own sense of urgency had to be constantly signaled to Washington. As the military draws down, he said, he isn't certain that the American effort will be redoubled in other crucial areas, such as education, or on the provincial teams. He was blunt about his fears for 2006. The United States will stay engaged in Iraq on one condition, he said. "The condition is whether we, the people who have responsibility here and in Washington, project to the American people that we know what we're doing: that we have reasonable goals, that we have good means to achieve those goals, and that we're making progress. I think the American people lose confidence when they think either the war is not important or we don't know what the hell we're doing. So it behooves us, those of us who believe that we know what we're doing, to communicate to the American people that there is a strategy that can produce results, and to communicate it effectively, without hyping." He added, "Happy talk is not the way to gain the confidence of the people."

The American strategy is for Khalilzad to push the Iraqi factions toward a government of national unity, so that political compromise will drain away support for the violence, while the Iraqi security forces become capable national institutions. Considering that just a year ago Sunni Arabs stood completely outside the political game, and the Iraqi army was only a few months into a serious training program, the strategy has been at least partly successful; the high Sunni turnout in the December elections was a tribute to Iraqis' political maturity and Khalilzad's skills as a broker. But if a government forms and the violence—whether sectarian, insurgent, criminal, or some indistinguishable mixture of them all—continues at this extraordinary level, or even intensifies, the United States will have played its last card. Then there will be no more milestones to celebrate, only the incremental effort of fighting an insurgency and rebuilding a failed state, without the prospect of a dramatic turn that could restore the support of the American public. People with experience in insurgencies talk about five, eight, ten years.

Recently, Senator Biden noticed a change in the tone of administration officials. After the Samarra mosque bombing, Stephen Hadley, the national security adviser, called him to say that perhaps Iraqi leaders had "looked over the precipice" of civil war and would now pull back. What Biden heard in Hadley's voice was not the unshakable conviction normally expressed by White House officials. It was something closer to "wistfulness," he said—a prayer more than a belief.

In recent remarks, the president and administration officials, such as Cheney and Rumsfeld, have made it clear that in the case of an American defeat, they will have a Plan B ready: they will blame the press for reporting bad news. They will blame the opposition for losing the war. In mid-March, on *Face the Nation*, Cheney, who has offered consistently rosy forecasts on Iraq, was asked whether his statements had deepened public skepticism about the war. "I think it has less to do with the statements we've made, which I think were basically accurate and reflect reality, than it does with the fact that there's a constant sort of perception, if you will, that's created because what's newsworthy is the car bomb in Baghdad."

In Congress, there has been remarkably little public pressure on the administration from Republicans or Democrats to take drastic action, at least until the formation of the Iraqi government is complete. Among Republicans, though, the anxiety over Iraq is barely concealed—midterm elections are now seven months away—and has been expressed partly through criticism of the administration on other national security issues, such as wiretapping and the Dubai port controversy.

"Most Republicans know that they're connected to Bush and his fortunes and his poll numbers," Chuck Hagel said. "Iraq has been consistently the number one issue in the polls." Since the call for withdrawal, several months ago, by Representative John Murtha, the Pennsylvania Democrat, members of his party seem to be content to watch in silence as the administration destroys its domestic standing over Iraq. Three years into the war, there is still no coherent political opposition.

"There's an old saying in politics: when your opponent's in trouble, just get out of the way," Senator Barack Obama, the Illinois Democrat, told me. "In political terms, I don't think that Democrats are obligated to solve Iraq for the administration." He added, "I think that, for the good of the country, we've got to be constructive in figuring out what's going to be best. I've taken political hits from certain quarters in the Democratic Party for even trying to figure this out. I feel that obligation. I'll confess to you, though, I haven't come up with any novel, unique answer so far."

After the Samarra bombing, when the prospect of civil war was added to an intractable insurgency, many Democrats and Republicans concluded that Iraq was lost. Conservatives like George F. Will and William F. Buckley, Jr., who, for philosophical reasons, never held out much hope for Iraq, have given up on the reconstruction. But most politicians remain paralyzed between staying and leaving, unable to decide which is the lesser evil. The deaths of more Americans and the spending of billions more dollars offer no promise of success beyond the prevention of wider chaos and, perhaps, a slow consolidation of the Iraqi state. Yet an American withdrawal would leave behind killings on a larger scale than anything yet seen; Iraqis from every background expressed this fear. Baghdad and other mixed cities would be divided up into barricaded sectors, and a civil war in the center of the country might spread into a regional war. The

Shiite south would fall deeper under Iranian control, Kurdistan would try to break away, and the Sunni areas would go the way of Tal Afar at its worst. This is where comparisons to Vietnam do not apply: in Southeast Asia, the domino theory turned out to be false, but Iraq in the hands of militias and terrorists, manipulated by neighboring states, would threaten the Middle East and the United States for many years. The truth is that no one in Washington knows what to do.

A former administration official said, "All of us—not just the administration but Congress and the American people—own the problem of Iraq. But I'm afraid we're going to cut. We're unwilling to make the sacrifice and spend the political capital." He summed up the three years of the Iraq War as three successive kinds of failure: "There was an intellectual failure at the start. There was an implementation failure after that. And now there's a failure of political will."

Beyond the White House, various analysts have offered alternative strategies, all of them based on the notion that 2006 is the year in which Iraq's long-term future, for better or worse, will be decided. Barry Posen, a political scientist at the Massachusetts Institute of Technology, has offered a more radical proposal than any officials have dared to entertain. In a recent article in *Boston Review*, Posen concluded that a unified, democratic Iraq is highly unlikely and that American interests require a strategic withdrawal over the next eighteen months. Posen is known as a foreign policy realist; when I met him at his office at MIT, he said, "I've been depicted as a villain. I just want the American polity to consider all sides of the equation before undertaking armed philanthropy." Posen has decided that America can afford to leave behind a civil war in Iraq—one that we will "manage" on our way out, so that its result will be, in his words, "a hurting stalemate." If one side seems about to win, the United States can tip the board in the other direction. "We managed a civil war in Bosnia from the outside," Posen said. "Whether we knew it or not, we were generating a hurting stalemate." In the end, after much violence, Iraq's factions will conclude that no one can win, and then they will come to their own arrangement.

Posen's version of withdrawal is realpolitik with a vengeance, offering the cold comfort of hardheaded calculations rather than grand illusions; but it's difficult to imagine how America, without troops in Iraq, could control events on the ground any better than it can now. When I asked

Posen about the moral obligation to Iraqis, who will surely be massacred in large numbers without American forces around, he replied, "No one talks about the terrible things that can happen if we stay the course. The insurgents are trying for a Beirut Marine barracks bombing." He added that he doesn't imagine his ideas will be heard in Washington. "These people are stubborn. A rational person would think that they've learned something about the limits of American power. They've learned nothing."

Kenneth Pollack, who served on the National Security Council under President Clinton—and whose book *The Threatening Storm* made an influential case for the war in 2002—recently led a small group at the Brookings Institution in writing a detailed report on a new strategy for Iraq. It calls for the administration to shift the focus from the pursuit of insurgents in the Sunni heartland and, instead, to concentrate overstretched American and Iraqi forces in cities where the reconstruction effort is still somewhat popular—providing security while allowing economic development to flourish. This strategy, known in counterinsurgency doctrine as the "ink spot" approach (because zones of security gradually spread out from population centers), has also been proposed by the military expert Andrew Krepinevich. It was put into practice in Tal Afar. Pollack's proposal demands that, in spite of intense political pressures at home, there be no troop withdrawals anytime soon, since the total number of American and Iraqi forces is now only half of what experts say is required to secure the country. It also counts on a level of international help that the Bush administration has never shown the ability, or the desire, to muster. In a sense, the report asks the country to offer the same commitment and imagination, to take the same risks and make the same sacrifices, as the soldiers in Tal Afar.

"Paradise"

On a quiet street in eastern Baghdad, behind a garden with lawn chairs arranged in rows, there is a small, unremarkable two-story building. A sign in front, which says AL JANNA CENTER, is barely visible from the street, for reasons of safety. "Al Janna" means "Paradise," and Dr. Baher Butti, who directs Al Janna, had been warned by anonymous fundamentalists that paradise cannot be found on earth.

Dr. Butti is a psychiatrist and a secular Christian in his mid-forties, a small, stoop-shouldered man with thinning hair and an air of stoical gloom. I first met him in the summer of 2003, and on each subsequent visit to Iraq I looked him up. Over the past three years, he has grown increasingly skeptical about the motives of the Americans, Iraqi politicians, religious leaders, and the country's neighbors. Yet he pursued with great persistence an idea that had first come to him after the fall of Saddam: he wanted to open a "psychosocial rehabilitation clinic" that would rebuild the humanity of his countrymen. Dr. Butti believed that after decades of dictatorship, wars, sanctions, and occupation, Iraqis need to learn to talk, to think, to tolerate. He had registered his proposal for the clinic with the occupation authority and successive Iraqi ministries, but none of them had given him support. Last year, a Baghdad newspaper owner donated funds, and in January the Al Janna Center finally opened.

In the waiting room, brightly colored abstract paintings by patients hung on the walls. Up a narrow flight of stairs, there were several small meeting rooms where Dr. Butti planned to hold lectures, poetry readings, computer training courses, and women's mental health group meetings. The center was humble and barely furnished, but amid the grinding ugliness and violence of Baghdad, it felt like an oasis of calm. "If we gain humanitarian care for our patients, then the rebound will be a humanitarian movement in all the society," Dr. Butti said. "This place is not just a scientific institute. It's also a place for literature and arts. We are trying to educate people about communication."

Dr. Butti lives in Dora, the mixed neighborhood in south Baghdad that has been particularly violent. "There are no direct clashes in the streets, but when every day you have one or two of your acquaintances killed, this is civil war," he said. Most of his friends and colleagues are leaving Iraq, along with much of the country's professional class.

When we sat down in his office, with cups of tea, he said, "Let me tell you about my own conflict." His conflict was simple: to stay or to leave. Last May, his young daughter was badly injured when her school bus was hit by a suicide car bomb. After that, his wife, who is also a doctor, insisted that the family move to Abu Dhabi. Yet Dr. Butti has finally achieved something tangible in Iraq, and to leave now would be like abandoning a child. "I feel like someone who's been cut from the roots," he said.

Dr. Butti's decision depends on what happens in the next few months, and on the formation of a new government. He doesn't have much hope for improvement anytime soon, but he is looking for some sign of stability. "Or it will go into a civil war, and all will be lost, and there will be nothing to be done here anymore. It's either this year or none." He added, "Not one of the Iraqis believes that you Americans should leave tomorrow. Even the Sunni leaders—they announce it in the media, but that's for, let's say, public use. They know that we can't have the American Army leaving the country right now, because, excuse me to say, George Bush did a mess, he must clean it." He shrugged and smiled, in his pained way. "We are attached in a Catholic marriage with our occupiers. It's not possible to have a divorce."

He walked me outside into the sunlit garden. On the street, a car passed by slowly. For an hour, I had forgotten to be afraid, and now that we were saying goodbye I was reluctant to go. In the past we had always shaken hands, but on this occasion Dr. Butti kissed my cheeks, in the Iraqi way. Perhaps he felt, as I did, that we might not meet again for a long time.

Knowing the Enemy

The New Yorker, December 18, 2006

In 1993, a young captain in the Australian army named David Kilcullen was living among villagers in West Java, as part of an immersion program in the Indonesian language. One day, he visited a local military museum that contained a display about Indonesia's war, during the 1950s and '60s, against a separatist Muslim insurgency movement called Darul Islam. "I had never heard of this conflict," Kilcullen told me recently. "It's hardly known in the West. The Indonesian government won, hands down. And I was fascinated by how it managed to pull off such a successful counterinsurgency campaign."

Kilcullen, the son of two left-leaning academics, had studied counterinsurgency as a cadet at Duntroon, the Australian West Point, and he decided to pursue a doctorate in political anthropology at the University of New South Wales. He chose as his dissertation subject the Darul Islam conflict, conducting research over tea with former guerrillas while continuing to serve in the Australian army. The rebel movement, he said, was bigger than the Malayan Emergency—the twelve-year Communist revolt against British rule, which was finally put down in 1960, and which has become a major point of reference in the military doctrine of counterinsurgency. During the years that Kilcullen worked on his dissertation, two events in Indonesia deeply affected his thinking. The first was the rise—in the same region that had given birth to Darul Islam, and among some of the same families—of a more extreme Islamist movement called Jemaah Islamiya, which became a Southeast Asian affiliate of Al Qaeda. The second was East Timor's successful struggle for independence from Indonesia. Kilcullen witnessed the former as he was carrying out his field work; he participated in the latter as an infantry company commander in a United Nations intervention force. The experiences shaped the conclusions about counterinsurgency in his dissertation, which he finished in 2001, just as a new war was about to begin.

"I saw extremely similar behavior and extremely similar problems in an Islamic insurgency in West Java and a Christian separatist insurgency in East Timor," he said. "After 9/11, when a lot of people were saying, 'The problem is Islam,' I was thinking, It's something deeper than that. It's about human social networks and the way that they operate." In West Java, elements of the failed Darul Islam insurgency—a local separatist movement with mystical leanings—had resumed fighting as Jemaah Islamiya, whose outlook was Salafist and global. Kilcullen said, "What that told me about Jemaah Islamiya is that it's not about theology." He went on, "There are elements in human psychological and social makeup that drive what's happening. The Islamic bit is secondary. This is human behavior in an Islamic setting. This is not 'Islamic behavior.'" Paraphrasing the American political scientist Roger D. Petersen, he said, "People don't get pushed into rebellion by their ideology. They get pulled in by their social networks." He noted that all fifteen Saudi hijackers in the September 11 plot had trouble with their fathers. Although radical ideas prepare the way for disaffected young men to become violent jihadists, the reasons they convert, Kilcullen said, are more mundane and familiar: family, friends, associates.

Indonesia's failure to replicate in East Timor its victory in West Java later influenced Kilcullen's views about what the Bush administration calls the "global war on terror." In both instances, the Indonesian military used the same harsh techniques, including forced population movements, coercion of locals into security forces, stringent curfews, and even lethal pressure on civilians to take the government side. The reason that the effort in East Timor failed, Kilcullen concluded, was globalization. In the late nineties, a Timorese international propaganda campaign and ubiquitous media coverage prompted international intervention, thus ending the use of tactics that, in the obscure jungles of West Java in the fifties, outsiders had known nothing about. "The globalized information environment makes counterinsurgency even more difficult now," Kilcullen said.

Just before the 2004 American elections, Kilcullen was doing intelligence work for the Australian government, sifting through Osama bin Laden's public statements, including transcripts of a video that offered a list of grievances against America: Palestine, Saudi Arabia, Afghanistan, global warming. The last item brought Kilcullen up short. "I thought, Hang on! What kind of jihadist are you?" he recalled. The odd inclusion of environmentalist rhetoric, he said, made clear that "this wasn't a list of genuine grievances. This was an Al Qaeda information strategy." Ron Suskind, in his book *The One Percent Doctrine*, claims that analysts at the Central Intelligence Agency watched a similar video, released in 2004, and concluded that "bin Laden's message was clearly designed to assist the president's reelection." Bin Laden shrewdly created an implicit association between Al Qaeda and the Democratic Party, for he had come to feel that Bush's strategy in the war on terror was sustaining his own global importance. Indeed, in the years after September 11, Al Qaeda's core leadership had become a propaganda hub. "If bin Laden didn't have access to global media, satellite communications, and the Internet, he'd just be a cranky guy in a cave," Kilcullen said.

In 2004, Kilcullen's writings and lectures brought him to the attention of an official working for Paul Wolfowitz, then the deputy secretary of defense. Wolfowitz asked him to help write the section on "irregular warfare" in the Pentagon's *Quadrennial Defense Review*, a statement of department policy and priorities, which was published earlier this year. Under the leadership of Donald Rumsfeld, who resigned in November, the Pentagon had embraced a narrow "shock-and-awe" approach to war fighting, emphasizing technology, long-range firepower, and spectacular displays of force. The new document declared that activities such as "long-duration unconventional warfare, counterterrorism, counterinsurgency, and military support for stabilization and reconstruction efforts" needed to become a more important component of the war on terror. Kilcullen was partly responsible for the inclusion of the phrase "the long war," which has become the preferred term among many military officers to describe the current conflict. In the end, the Rumsfeld Pentagon was unwilling to make the cuts in expensive weapons systems that would have allowed it to create new combat units and other resources necessary for a proper counterinsurgency strategy.

In July 2005, Kilcullen, as a result of his work on the Pentagon document, received an invitation to attend a conference on defense policy, in Vermont. There he met Henry Crumpton, a highly regarded official who had supervised the CIA's covert activities in Afghanistan during the 2001 military campaign that overthrew the Taliban. The two men spent much of the conference talking privately, and learned, among other things, that they saw the war on terror in the same way. Soon afterward, Condoleezza Rice, the secretary of state, hired Crumpton as the department's coordinator for counterterrorism, and Crumpton, in turn, offered Kilcullen a job. For the past year, Kilcullen has occupied an office on the State Department's second floor, as Crumpton's chief strategist. In some senses, Kilcullen has arrived too late: this year, the insurgency in Iraq has been transformed into a calamitous civil war between Sunnis and Shiites, and his ideas about counterinsurgency are unlikely to reverse the country's disintegration. Yet radical Islamist movements now extend across the globe, from Somalia to Afghanistan and Indonesia, and Kilcullen—an Australian anthropologist and lieutenant colonel, who is "on loan" to the U.S. government—offers a new way to understand and fight a war that seems to grow less intelligible the longer it goes on.

Kilcullen is thirty-nine years old and has a wide pink face, a fondness for desert boots, and an Australian's good-natured bluntness. He has a talent for making everything sound like common sense by turning disturbing explanations into brisk, cheerful questions: "America is very, very good at big, short conventional wars? It's not very good at small, long wars? But it's even worse at big, long wars? And that's what we've got." Kilcullen's heroes are soldier-intellectuals, both real (T. E. Lawrence) and fictional (Robert Jordan, the flinty, self-reliant schoolteacher turned guerrilla who is the protagonist of Hemingway's *For Whom the Bell Tolls*). On his bookshelves, alongside monographs by social scientists such as Max Gluckman and E. E. Evans-Pritchard, is a knife that he took from a militiaman he had just ambushed in East Timor. "If I were a Muslim, I'd probably be a jihadist," Kilcullen said as we sat in his office. "The thing that drives these guys—a sense of adventure, wanting to be part of the moment, wanting to be in the big movement of history that's happening now—that's the same thing that drives me, you know?"

More than three years into the Iraq War and five into the conflict in Afghanistan, many members of the American military—especially those with combat experience—have begun to accept the need to learn the kind of counterinsurgency tactics that it tried to leave behind in Vietnam.

On December 15, the Army and the Marine Corps will release an ambitious new counterinsurgency field manual—the first in more than two decades—that will shape military doctrine for many years. The introduction to the field manual says, "Effective insurgents rapidly adapt to changing circumstances. They cleverly use the tools of the global information revolution to magnify the effects of their actions . . . However, by focusing on efforts to secure the safety and support of the local populace, and through a concerted effort to truly function as learning organizations, the Army and Marine Corps can defeat their insurgent enemies."

One night earlier this year, Kilcullen sat down with a bottle of single-malt Scotch and wrote out a series of tips for company commanders about to be deployed to Iraq and Afghanistan. He is an energetic writer who avoids military and social science jargon, and he addressed himself intimately to young captains who have had to become familiar with exotica such as *The Battle of Algiers*, the 1966 film documenting the insurgency against French colonists. "What does all the theory mean, at the company level?" he asked. "How do the principles translate into action—at night, with the GPS down, the media criticizing you, the locals complaining in a language you don't understand, and an unseen enemy killing your people by ones and twos? How does counterinsurgency actually happen? There are no universal answers, and insurgents are among the most adaptive opponents you will ever face. Countering them will demand every ounce of your intellect." The first tip is "Know Your Turf": "Know the people, the topography, economy, history, religion and culture. Know every village, road, field, population group, tribal leader, and ancient grievance. Your task is to become the world expert on your district." "Twenty-eight Articles: Fundamentals of Company-Level Counterinsurgency"—the title riffs on a T. E. Lawrence insurgency manual from the First World War—was disseminated via e-mail to junior officers in the field, and was avidly read.

Last year, in an influential article in the *Journal of Strategic Studies*, Kilcullen redefined the war on terror as a "global counterinsurgency." The change in terminology has large implications. A terrorist is "a kook in a room," Kilcullen told me, and beyond persuasion; an insurgent has a mass base whose support can be won or lost through politics. The notion of a "war on terror" has led the U.S. government to focus overwhelmingly on military responses. In a counterinsurgency, according to the classical doctrine, which was first laid out by the British general Sir Gerald Templar during the Malayan Emergency, armed force is only a quarter of the effort; political, economic, and informational operations are also required. A "war on terror" suggests an undifferentiated enemy. Kilcullen speaks of the need to "disaggregate" insurgencies: finding ways to address local grievances in Pakistan's tribal areas or along the Thai-Malay border so that they aren't mapped onto the ambitions of the global jihad. Kilcullen writes, "Just as the Containment strategy was central to the Cold War, likewise a Disaggregation strategy would provide a unifying strategic conception for the war—something that has been lacking to date." As an example of disaggregation, Kilcullen cited the Indonesian province of Aceh, where, after the 2004 tsunami, a radical Islamist organization tried to set up an office and convert a local separatist movement to its ideological agenda. Resentment toward the outsiders, combined with the swift humanitarian action of American and Australian warships, helped to prevent the Acehnese rebellion from becoming part of the global jihad. As for America, this success had more to do with luck than with strategy. Crumpton, Kilcullen's boss, told me that American foreign policy traditionally operates on two levels, the global and the national; today, however, the battlefields are also regional and local, where the U.S. government has less knowledge and where it is not institutionally organized to act. In half a dozen critical regions, Crumpton has organized meetings among American diplomats, intelligence officials, and combat commanders, so that information about cross-border terrorist threats is shared. "It's really important that we define the enemy in narrow terms," Crumpton said. "The thing we should not do is let our fears grow and then inflate the threat. The threat is big enough without us having to exaggerate it."

By speaking of Saddam Hussein, the Sunni insurgency in Iraq, the Taliban, the Iranian government, Hezbollah, and Al Qaeda in terms of one big war, administration officials and ideologues have made Osama bin Laden's job much easier. "You don't play to the enemy's global information strategy of making it all one fight," Kilcullen said. He pointedly avoided describing this as the administration's approach. "You say, 'Actually, there are sixty different groups in sixty different countries who all have different objectives. Let's not talk about bin Laden's objectives— let's talk about your objectives. How do we solve that problem?'" In other words, the global ambitions of the enemy don't automatically demand a monolithic response.

• • •

The more Kilcullen travels to the various theaters of war, the less he
thinks that the lessons of Malaya and Vietnam are useful guides in the
current conflict. "Classical counterinsurgency is designed to defeat insurgency in one country," he writes in his *Strategic Studies* article. "We need
a new paradigm, capable of addressing globalised insurgency." After a recent trip to Afghanistan, where Taliban forces have begun to mount large
operations in the Pashto-speaking south of the country, he told me, "This
ain't your granddaddy's counterinsurgency." Many American units there,
he said, are executing the new field manual's tactics brilliantly. For example, before conducting operations in a given area, soldiers sit down
over bread and tea with tribal leaders and find out what they need—Korans,
cold weather gear, a hydroelectric dynamo. In exchange for promises of
local support, the Americans gather the supplies and then, within hours
of the end of fighting, produce them, to show what can be gained from
cooperating.

But the Taliban seem to be waging a different war, driven entirely by
information operations. "They're essentially armed propaganda organizations," Kilcullen said. "They switch between guerrilla activity and terrorist
activity as they need to, in order to maintain the political momentum, and
it's all about an information operation that generates the perception of an
unstoppable, growing insurgency." After traveling through southern Afghanistan, Kilcullen e-mailed me:

> One good example of Taliban information strategy is their use of
> "night letters." They have been pushing local farmers in several
> provinces (Helmand, Uruzgan, Kandahar) to grow poppy instead
> of regular crops, and using night-time threats and intimidation to
> punish those who don't and convince others to convert to poppy.
> This is not because they need more opium—God knows they
> already have enough—but because they're trying to detach the
> local people from the legal economy and the legally approved
> governance system of the provinces and districts, to weaken the
> hold of central and provincial government. Get the people doing
> something illegal, and they're less likely to feel able to support the
> government, and more willing to do other illegal things (e.g. join

the insurgency)—this is a classic old Bolshevik tactic from the early cold war, by the way. They are specifically trying to send the message: "The government can neither help you nor hurt us. We can hurt you, or protect you—the choice is yours." They also use object lessons, making an example of people who don't cooperate—for example, dozens of provincial-level officials have been assassinated this year, again as an "armed propaganda" tool—not because they want one official less but because they want to send the message "We can reach out and touch you if you cross us." Classic armed information operation.

Kilcullen doesn't believe that an entirely "soft" counterinsurgency approach can work against such tactics. In his view, winning hearts and minds is not a matter of making local people like you—as some American initiates to counterinsurgency whom I met in Iraq seemed to believe—but of getting them to accept that supporting your side is in their interest, which requires an element of coercion. Kilcullen met senior European officers with the NATO force in Afghanistan who seemed to be applying "a development model to counterinsurgency," hoping that gratitude for good work would bring the Afghans over to their side. He told me, "In a counterinsurgency, the gratitude effect will last until the sun goes down and the insurgents show up and say, 'You're on our side, aren't you? Otherwise, we're going to kill you.' If one side is willing to apply lethal force to bring the population to its side and the other side isn't, ultimately you're going to find yourself losing." Kilcullen was describing a willingness to show local people that supporting the enemy risks harm and hardship, not a campaign like the Phoenix program in Vietnam, in which noncombatants were assassinated; besides being unethical, such a tactic would inevitably backfire in the age of globalized information. Nevertheless, because he talks about war with an analyst's rationalism and a practitioner's matter-of-factness, Kilcullen can appear deceptively detached from its consequences.

An information strategy seems to be driving the agenda of every radical Islamist movement. Kilcullen noted that when insurgents ambush an American convoy in Iraq, "they're not doing that because they want to reduce the number of Humvees we have in Iraq by one. They're doing it because they want spectacular media footage of a burning Humvee." Last year, a letter surfaced that is believed to have been sent from Ayman al-Zawahiri, bin Laden's deputy, to the leader of Al Qaeda in Iraq, Abu Musab al-Zarqawi, nine months before Zarqawi's death; the letter urged Zarqawi to make his videotaped beheadings and mass slaughter of Shiite civilians less gruesome. Kilcullen interpreted the letter as "basically saying to Zarqawi, 'Justify your attacks on the basis of how they support our information strategy.'" As soon as the recent fighting in Lebanon between Hezbollah and Israeli troops ended, Hezbollah marked, with its party flags, houses that had been damaged. Kilcullen said, "That's not a reconstruction operation—it's an information operation. It's influence. They're going out there to send a couple of messages. To the Lebanese people they're saying, 'We're going to take care of you.' To all the aid agencies it's like a dog pissing on trees: they're saying, 'We own this house—don't you touch it.'" He went on, "When the aid agencies arrive a few days later, they have to negotiate with Hezbollah because there's a Hezbollah flag on the house. Hezbollah says, 'Yeah, you can sell a contract to us to fix up that house.' It's an information operation. They're trying to generate influence."

The result is an intimidated or motivated population, and a spike in fund-raising and recruiting. "When you go on YouTube and look at one of these attacks in Iraq, all you see is the video," Kilcullen said. "If you go to some jihadist websites, you see the same video and then a button next to it that says, 'Click here and donate.'" The Afghan or Iraqi or Lebanese insurgent, unlike his Vietnamese or Salvadoran predecessor, can plug in to a global media network that will instantly amplify his message. After Kilcullen returned from Afghanistan last month, he stayed up late one Saturday night ("because I have no social life") and calculated how many sources of information existed for a Vietnamese villager in 1966 and for an Afghan villager in 2006. He concluded that the former had ten, almost half under government control, such as Saigon radio and local officials; the latter has twenty-five (counting the Internet as only one), of which just five are controlled by the government. Most of the rest—including e-mail, satellite phone, and text messaging—are independent but more easily exploited by insurgents than by the Afghan government. And it is on the level of influencing perceptions that these wars will be won or lost. "The international information environment is critical to the success of America's mission," Kilcullen said.

In the information war, America and its allies are barely competing. America's information operations, far from being the primary strategy, simply support military actions, and often badly: a Pentagon spokesman announces a battle victory, but no one in the area of the battlefield hears him (or would believe him anyway). Just as the Indonesians failed in East Timor, in spite of using locally successful tactics, Kilcullen said, "We've done a similar thing in Iraq—we've arguably done okay on the ground in some places, but we're totally losing the domestic information battle. In Afghanistan, it still could go either way."

However careful Kilcullen is not to criticize administration policy, his argument amounts to a thoroughgoing critique. As a foreigner who is not a career official in the U.S. government, he has more distance and freedom to discuss the war on jihadism frankly, and in ways that his American counterparts rarely can. "It's now fundamentally an information fight," he said. "The enemy gets that, and we don't yet get that, and I think that's why we're losing."

In late September, Kilcullen was one of the featured speakers at a conference in Washington, organized by the State and Defense Departments, on bringing the civilian branches of the government into the global counterinsurgency effort. In the hallway outside the meeting room, he made a point of introducing me to another speaker, an anthropologist and Pentagon consultant named Montgomery McFate. For five years, McFate later told me, she has been making it her "evangelical mission" to get the Department of Defense to understand the importance of "cultural knowledge." McFate is forty years old, with hair cut stylishly short and an air of humorous cool. When I asked why a social scientist would want to help the war effort, she replied, only half joking, "Because I'm engaged in a massive act of rebellion against my hippie parents."

McFate grew up in the sixties on a communal houseboat in Marin County, California. Her parents were friends with Jack Kerouac and Lawrence Ferlinghetti, and one of her schoolmates was the daughter of Jefferson Airplane's Grace Slick and Paul Kantner. Like Kilcullen, she was drawn to the study of human conflict and also its reality: at Yale, where she received a doctorate, her dissertation was based on several years she spent living among supporters of the Irish Republican Army and then among British counterinsurgents. In Northern Ireland, McFate discovered something very like what Kilcullen found in West Java: insurgency runs in families and social networks, held together by persistent cultural narratives—in this case, the eight-hundred-year-old saga of "perfidious Albion." She went on to marry a U.S. Army officer. "When I was little in California, we never believed there was such a thing as the Cold War," McFate said. "That was a bunch of lies that the government fed us to keep us paranoid. Of course, there was a thing called the Cold War, and we nearly lost. And there was no guarantee that we were going to win. And this thing that's happening now is, without taking that too far, similar." After September 11, McFate said, she became "passionate about one issue: the government's need to actually understand its adversaries," in the same way that the United States came to understand—and thereby undermine—the Soviet Union. If, as Kilcullen and Crumpton maintain, the battlefield in the global counterinsurgency is intimately local, then the American government needs what McFate calls a "granular" knowledge of the social terrains on which it is competing.

In 2004, when McFate had a fellowship at the Office of Naval Research, she got a call from a science adviser to the Joint Chiefs of Staff. He had been contacted by battalion commanders with the 4th Infantry Division in a violent sector of the Sunni Triangle, in Iraq. "We're having a really hard time out here—we have no idea how this society works," the commanders said. "Could you help us?" The science adviser replied that he was a mathematical physicist, and turned for help to one of the few anthropologists he could find in the Defense Department.

For decades, the Pentagon and the humanistic social sciences have had little to do with each other. In 1964, the Pentagon set up a program called, with the self-conscious idealism of the period, Project Camelot. Anthropologists were hired and sent abroad to conduct a multiyear study of the factors that promote stability or war in certain societies, beginning with Chile. When news of the program leaked, the uproar in Chile and America forced Defense Secretary Robert McNamara to cancel it. "The Department of Defense has invested hardly any money in conducting ethnographic research in areas where conflict was occurring since 1965," McFate told me. After Project Camelot and Vietnam, where social scientists often did contract work for the U.S. military, professional associations discouraged such involvement. ("Academic anthropologists hate me for working with DOD," McFate said.) Kilcullen, who calls counterinsurgency "armed social science," told me, "This is fundamentally about the broken relationship between the government and the discipline of anthropology. What broke that relationship is Vietnam. And people still haven't recovered from that." As a result, a complex human understanding of societies at war has been lost. "But it didn't have to be lost," McFate said. During the Second World War, anthropologists such as Margaret Mead, Gregory Bateson, Geoffrey Gorer, and Ruth Benedict provided the Allied war effort with essential insights into Asian societies. Gorer and Benedict suggested, for example, that the terms of Japan's surrender be separated from the question of the emperor's abdication, because the emperor was thought to embody the country's soul; doing so allowed the Japanese to accept unconditional surrender. McFate sees herself as reaching back to this tradition of military-academic cooperation.

By 2004, the military desperately needed cooperation. McFate saw Americans in Iraq make one strategic mistake after another because they didn't understand the nature of Iraqi society. In an article in *Joint Force Quarterly*, she wrote, "Once the Sunni Ba'thists [*sic*] lost their prestigious jobs, were humiliated in the conflict, and got frozen out through de-Ba'thification [*sic*], the tribal network became the backbone of the insurgency. The tribal insurgency is a direct result of our misunderstanding the Iraqi culture." In the course of eighteen months of interviews with returning soldiers, she was told by one Marine Corps officer, "My marines were almost wholly uninterested in interacting with the local population. Our primary mission was the security of Camp Falluja. We relieved soldiers from the 82nd Airborne Division, and their assessment was that every local was participating or complicit with the enemy. This view was quickly adopted by my unit and framed all of our actions (and reactions)." Another marine told McFate that his unit had lost the battle to influence public opinion because it used the wrong approach to communication: "We were focused on broadcast media and metrics. But this had no impact because Iraqis spread information through rumor. We should have been visiting their coffee shops."

The result of efforts like McFate's is a new project with the quintessential Pentagon name Cultural Operations Research Human Terrain. It began in the form of a "ruggedized" laptop computer, loaded with data from social science research conducted in Iraq—such as, McFate said,

"an analysis of the eighty-eight tribes and subtribes in a particular province." Now the project is recruiting social scientists around the country to
join five-person "human terrain" teams that would go to Iraq and Afghanistan with combat brigades and serve as cultural advisers on six- to nine-
month tours. Pilot teams are planning to leave next spring.

Steve Fondacaro, a retired Army colonel who for a year commanded
the Joint Improvised Explosive Device Defeat Task Force in Iraq, is in
charge of the Human Terrain project. Fondacaro sees the war in the same
terms as Kilcullen. "The new element of power that has emerged in the
last thirty to forty years and has subsumed the rest is information," he
said. "A revolution happened without us knowing or paying attention.
Perception truly now is reality, and our enemies know it. We have to fight
on the information battlefield." I asked him what the government should
have done, say, in the case of revelations of abuse at the Abu Ghraib
prison. "You're talking to a radical here," Fondacaro said. "Immediately be
the first one to tell the story. Don't let anyone else do it. That carries so
much strategic weight." He added, "Iraqis are not shocked by torture. It
would have impressed them if we had exposed it, punished it, rectified
it." But senior military leadership, he said, remains closed to this kind of
thinking. He is turning for help to academics—to "social scientists who
want to educate me," he said. So far, though, Fondacaro has hired just
one anthropologist. When I spoke to her by telephone, she admitted that
the assignment comes with huge ethical risks. "I do not want to get anybody killed," she said. Some of her colleagues are curious, she said; others
are critical. "I end up getting shunned at cocktail parties," she said. "I see
there could be misuse. But I just can't stand to sit back and watch these
mistakes happen over and over as people get killed, and do nothing."

At the counterinsurgency conference in Washington, the tone among the
uniformed officers, civilian officials, and various experts was urgent, almost desperate. James Kunder, a former marine and the acting deputy of
the U.S. Agency for International Development, pointed out that in Iraq and
Afghanistan "the civilian agencies have received 1.4 percent of the total
money," whereas classical counterinsurgency doctrine says that 80 percent of the effort should be nonmilitary. During Vietnam, his agency had
fifteen thousand employees; it now has two thousand. After the end of

the Cold War, foreign service and aid budgets were sharply cut. "Size matters," Kunder said, noting that throughout the civilian agencies there are shortages of money and personnel. To staff the embassy in Baghdad, the State Department has had to steal officers from other embassies, and the government can't even fill the provincial reconstruction teams it has tried to set up in Iraq and Afghanistan. While correcting these shortages could not have prevented the deepening disaster in Iraq, they betray the government's priorities.

In early 2004, as Iraq was beginning to unravel, Senator Richard Lugar, the Indiana Republican who chairs the Senate Foreign Relations Committee, and Senator Joseph Biden, the Delaware Democrat, introduced legislation for a nation-building office, under the aegis of the State Department. The office would be able to tap into contingency funds and would allow cabinet department officials, along with congressional staff people and civilian experts, to carry out overseas operations to help stabilize and rebuild failed states and societies shattered by war—to do it deliberately and well rather than in the ad hoc fashion that has characterized interventions from Somalia and Kosovo to Iraq. Lugar envisioned both an active duty contingent and a reserve corps.

The bill's biggest supporter was the military, which frequently finds itself forced to do tasks overseas for which civilians are better prepared, such as training police or rebuilding sewers. But Colin Powell, then the secretary of state, and other administration officials refused to give it strong backing. Then, in the summer of 2004, the administration reversed course by announcing the creation, in the State Department, of the Office of the Coordinator for Reconstruction and Stabilization; the office was given the imprimatur of National Security Presidential Directive 44. At the September conference in Washington, Kilcullen held up the office as a model for how to bring civilians into counterinsurgency: "True enough, the words 'insurgency,' 'insurgent,' and 'counterinsurgency' do not appear in NSPD 44, but it clearly envisages the need to deploy integrated whole-of-government capabilities in hostile environments."

But the new office was virtually orphaned at birth. Congress provided only seven million of the hundred million dollars requested by the administration, which never made the office a top presidential priority. The State Department has contributed fifteen officials who can manage overseas operations, but other agencies have offered nothing. The office thus has no ability to coordinate operations, such as mobilizing police trainers, even as Iraq and Afghanistan deteriorate and new emergencies loom in places like Darfur and Pakistan. It has become insiders' favorite example of bureaucratic inertia in the face of glaring need.

Frederick Barton, an expert at the Center for Strategic and International Studies, a Washington think tank, considers failures like these to be a prime cause of American setbacks in fighting global jihadism. "Hard power is not the way we're going to make an impression," he told me, and he cited Pakistan, where a huge population, rising militancy, nuclear weapons, and the remnants of Al Qaeda's leadership create a combustible mix. According to Barton's figures, since 2002 America has spent more than six billion dollars on buttressing the Pakistani military, and probably a similar amount on intelligence (the number is kept secret). Yet it has spent less than a billion dollars on aid for education and economic development, in a country where Islamist madrassas and joblessness contribute to the radicalization of young people. On a recent visit to Nigeria, Barton heard that American propaganda efforts are being outclassed by those of the Iranians and the Saudis. "What would Pepsi-Cola or Disney do?" he asked. "We're not thinking creatively, expansively. We are sclerotic, bureaucratic, lumbering—you can see the U.S. coming from miles away."

If, as Kilcullen says, the global counterinsurgency is primarily an information war, one place where American strategy should be executed is the State Department office of Karen Hughes, the under secretary for public diplomacy and public affairs. Hughes is a longtime Bush adviser from Texas. One of her first missions, in September 2005, took her to the Middle East, where her efforts to speak with Muslim women as fellow "moms" and religious believers received poor reviews. Last year, she sent out a memo to American embassies urging diplomats to make themselves widely available to the local press, but she also warned them against saying anything that might seem to deviate from administration policy. The choice of a high-level political operative to run the government's global outreach effort suggests that the Bush administration sees public diplomacy the way it sees campaigning, with the same emphasis on top-down message discipline. "It has this fixation with strategic communications— whatever that is," an expert in public diplomacy with close ties to the State Department told me. "It's just hokum. When you do strategic communications, it fails, because nothing gets out." She cited a news report that the Voice of America wanted to produce on American-funded AIDS programs in Africa. The VOA was told by a government official that the Office of the U.S. Global AIDS Coordinator would have to give its approval before anything could be broadcast. (The decision was later overruled.) "We're spending billions of dollars on AIDS," the expert said—an effort that could generate considerable gratitude in African countries with substantial Muslim populations, such as Somalia and Nigeria. "But no one in Africa has a clue."

After the Cold War, the government closed down the United States Information Service, and with it a number of libraries and cultural centers around the world. Since September 11, there has been an attempt to revive such public diplomacy, but with American embassies now barricaded or built far from city centers, only the most dedicated local people will use their resources. To circumvent this problem, the State Department has established what it calls American Corners—rooms or shelves in foreign libraries dedicated to American books and culture. "It's a good idea, but they're small and marginal," the expert said. She recently visited the American Corner in the main library in Kano, Nigeria, a center of Islamic learning. "I had to laugh," she said. "A few Africans asleep at the switch, a couple of computers that weren't working, a video series on George Washington that no one was using." She mentioned one encouraging new example of public diplomacy, funded partly by Henry Crumpton's office: Voice of America news broadcasts will begin airing next February in the language of Somalia, a country of increasing worry to counterterrorism officials. In general, though, there is little organized American effort to rebut the jihadist conspiracy theories that circulate daily among the Muslims living in populous countries such as Indonesia, Pakistan, and Nigeria.

According to the expert, an American diplomat with years of experience identified another obstacle to American outreach. "Let's face it," he told her. "All public diplomacy is on hold till George Bush is out of office."

I once asked David Kilcullen if he thought that America was fundamentally able to deal with the global jihad. Is a society in which few people spend much time overseas or learn a second language, which is impatient

with chronic problems, whose vision of war is of huge air and armor battles ended by the signing of articles of surrender, and which tends to assume that everyone is basically alike cut out for this new "long war"?

Kilcullen reminded me that there was a precedent for American success in a sustained struggle with a formidable enemy. "If this is the Cold
War—if that analogy holds—then right now we're in, like, 1953. This is a
long way to go here. It didn't all happen overnight—but it happened." The
Cold War, he emphasized, was many wars, constructed on many different
models, fought in many different ways: a nuclear standoff between the
superpowers, insurgencies in developing countries, a struggle of ideas in
Europe. "Our current battle is a new Cold War," Kilcullen said, "but it's
not monolithic. You've got to define the enemy as narrowly as you can get
away with."

President Bush has used the Cold War as an inspirational analogy
almost from the beginning of the war on terror. Last month, in Riga, Lat-
via, he reminded an audience of the early years of the Cold War, "when
freedom's victory was not so obvious or assured." Six decades later, he
went on, "freedom in Europe has brought peace to Europe, and freedom
has brought the power to bring peace to the broader Middle East." Bush's
die-hard supporters compare him to Harry S. Truman, who was reviled in
his last years in office but has been vindicated by history as a plainspoken
visionary.

An administration official pointed out that the president's speeches
on the war are like the last paragraph of every Churchill speech from the
Second World War: a soaring peroration about freedom, civilization, and
darkness. But in Churchill's case, the official went on, nineteen pages of
analysis, contextualization, and persuasion preceded that final paragraph.
A Bush speech gives only the uplift—which suggests that there is no
strategy beyond it. Bush's notion of a titanic struggle between good and
evil, between freedom and those who hate freedom, recalls the rigid anti-
communism of Whittaker Chambers, William F. Buckley, Jr., and Barry
Goldwater. Montgomery McFate noted that the current avatars of right-
wing cold warriors, the neoconservatives, have dismissed all Iraqi insurgents as "dead-enders" and "bad people." Terms like "totalitarianism" and
"Islamofascism," she said, which stir the American historical memory,
mislead policymakers into greatly increasing the number of our enemies
and coming up with wrongheaded strategies against them. "That's not

what the insurgents call themselves," she said. "If you can't call some-thing by its name—if you can't say, 'This is what this phenomenon is, it has structure, meaning, agency'—how can you ever fight it?" In other words, even if we think that a jihadi in Yemen has ideas similar to those of an Islamist in Java, we have to approach them in discrete ways, both to prevent them from becoming a unified movement and because their par-ticular political yearnings are different.

Kilcullen is attempting to revive a strain of Cold War thought that saw the confrontation with Communism not primarily as a blunt military struggle but as a subtle propaganda war that required deep knowledge of diverse enemies and civilian populations. By this standard, America's per-formance against radical Islamists thus far is dismal. Bruce Hoffman of Georgetown University, a former RAND Corporation analyst who began to use the term "global counterinsurgency" around the same time as Kil-cullen, pointed to two Cold War projects: RAND's study of the motiva-tion and morale of the Vietcong in the mid-sixties, based on extensive interviews with prisoners and former insurgents, which led some analysts to conclude that the war was unwinnable; and a survey by Radio Free Europe of two hundred thousand émigrés from the Eastern Bloc in the eighties, which used the findings to shape broadcasts. "We haven't done anything like that in this struggle," Hoffman said, and he cited the thou-sands of detainees in Iraq. "Instead of turning the prisons into insurgent universities, you could have a systematic process that would be based on scientific surveys designed to elicit certain information on how people joined, who their leaders were, how leadership was exercised, how group cohesion was maintained." In other words, America would get to know its enemy. Hoffman added, "Even though we say it's going to be the long war, we still have this enormous sense of impatience. Are we committed to doing the fundamental spadework that's necessary?"

Kilcullen's thinking is informed by some of the key texts of Cold War social science, such as Eric Hoffer's *The True Believer*, which analyzed the conversion of frustrated individuals into members of fanatical mass movements, and Philip Selznick's *The Organizational Weapon: A Study of Bolshevik Strategy and Tactics*, which described how Communists sub-verted existing social groups and institutions like trade unions. To these older theoretical guides he adds two recent studies of radical Islam: *Glo-balized Islam*, by the French scholar Olivier Roy, and *Understanding Terror*

Networks, by Marc Sageman, an American forensic psychiatrist and former covert operator with the mujahideen in Afghanistan. After September 11, Sageman traced the paths of 172 alienated young Muslims who joined the jihad, and found that the common ground lay not in personal pathology, poverty, or religious belief but in social bonds. Roy sees the rise of "neo-fundamentalism" among Western Muslims as a new identity movement shaped by its response to globalization. In the margin of a section of Roy's book called "Is *jihad* closer to Marx than to the Koran?" Kilcullen noted, "If Islamism is the new leftism, then the strategies and techniques used to counter Marxist subversion during the Cold War may have direct or indirect relevance to combating Al Qaeda–sponsored subversion."

Drawing on these studies, Kilcullen has plotted out a "ladder of extremism" that shows the progress of a jihadist. At the bottom is the vast population of mainstream Muslims, who are potential allies against radical Islamism as well as potential targets of subversion, and whose grievances can be addressed by political reform. The next tier up is a smaller number of "alienated Muslims," who have given up on reform. Some of these join radical groups, like the young Muslims in North London who spend afternoons at the local community center watching jihadist videos. They require "ideological conversion"—that is, countersubversion, which Kilcullen compares to helping young men leave gangs. (In a lecture that Kilcullen teaches on counterterrorism at Johns Hopkins, his students watch *Fight Club*, the 1999 satire about anticapitalist terrorists, to see a radical ideology without an Islamic face.) A smaller number of these individuals, already steeped in the atmosphere of radical mosques and extremist discussions, end up joining local and regional insurgent cells, usually as the result of a "biographical trigger—they will lose a friend in Iraq, or see something that shocks them on television." With these insurgents, the full range of counterinsurgency tools has to be used, including violence and persuasion. The very small number of fighters who are recruited to the top tier of Al Qaeda and its affiliated terrorist groups are beyond persuasion or conversion. "They're so committed you've got to destroy them," Kilcullen said. "But you've got to do it in such a way that you don't create new terrorists."

When I asked him to outline a counterpropaganda strategy, he described three basic methods. "We've got to create resistance to their message," he said. "We've got to co-opt or assist people who have a countermessage. And we might need to consider creating or supporting the creation of rival organizations." Bruce Hoffman told me that jihadists have posted five thousand websites that react quickly and imaginatively to events. In 2004, he said, a jihadist rap video called "Dirty Kuffar" became widely popular with young Muslims in Britain: "It's like Ali G wearing a balaclava and having a pistol in one hand and a Koran in the other." Hoffman believes that America must help foreign governments and civil society groups flood the Internet with persuasively youthful websites presenting anti-jihadist messages—but not necessarily pro-American ones, and without leaving American fingerprints.

Kilcullen argues that Western governments should establish competing "trusted networks" in Muslim countries: friendly mosques, professional associations, and labor unions. (A favorite Kilcullen example from the Cold War is left-wing anticommunist trade unions, which gave the working class in Western Europe an outlet for its grievances without driving it into the arms of the Soviet Union.) The United States should also support traditional authority figures—community leaders, father figures, moderate imams—in countries where the destabilizing transition to modernity has inspired Islamist violence. "You've got to be quiet about it," he cautioned. "You don't go in there like a missionary." The key is providing a social context for individuals to choose ways other than jihad.

Kilcullen's proposals will not be easy to implement at a moment when the government's resources and attention are being severely drained by the chaos in Iraq. And if some of his ideas seem sketchy, it's because he and his colleagues have only just begun to think along these lines. The U.S. government, encumbered by habit and inertia, has not adapted as quickly to the changing terrain as the light-footed, mercurial jihadists. America's many failures in the war on terror have led a number of thinkers to conclude that the problem is institutional. Thomas Barnett, a military analyst, proposes dividing the Department of Defense into two sections: one to fight big wars and one for insurgencies and nation building. Lawrence Wilkerson, a retired Army colonel and Colin Powell's former chief of staff, goes even further. He thinks that the entire national security bureaucracy, which was essentially set in place at the start of the Cold War, is incapable of dealing with the new threats and should be overhauled, so that the government can work faster to prevent conflicts or to intervene early. "Especially in light of this administration, but also other recent ones, do we really want to concentrate power so incredibly in the White House?" he asked. "And, if we do, why do we still have the departments, except as an appendage of bureaucracy that becomes an impediment?" In Wilkerson's vision, new legislation would create a "unified command," with leadership drawn from across the civilian agencies, which "could supplant the existing bureaucracy."

Since September 11, the government's traditional approach to national security has proved inadequate in one area after another. The intelligence agencies habitually rely on satellites and spies, when most of the information that matters now, as Kilcullen pointed out, is "open source"—available to anyone with an Internet connection. Traditional diplomacy, with its emphasis on treaties and geopolitical debates, is less relevant than the ability to understand and influence foreign populations—not in their councils of state but in their villages and slums. And future enemies are unlikely to confront the world's overwhelming military power with conventional warfare; technology-assisted insurgency is proving far more effective. At the highest levels of Western governments, the failure of traditional approaches to counter the jihadist threat has had a paralyzing effect. "I sense we've lost the ability to think strategically," Field Marshal Sir Peter Inge, the former chief of the British armed forces, has said of his government. He could have been describing the White House and the Pentagon.

Kilcullen's strategic mind, by contrast, seems remarkably febrile. I could call him at the office or at home at any hour of the night and he'd be jotting down ideas in one of his little black notebooks, ready to think out loud. Kilcullen, Crumpton, and their colleagues are desperately trying to develop a lasting new strategy that, in Kilcullen's words, would be neither Republican nor Democratic. Bruce Hoffman said, "We're talking about a profound shift in mind-set and attitude"—not to mention a drastic change in budgetary and bureaucratic priorities." And that may not be achievable until there's a change in administration." Kilcullen is now in charge of writing a new counterinsurgency manual for the civilian government, and early this month he briefed Condoleezza Rice on his findings in Afghanistan. But his ideas have yet to penetrate the fortress that is the Bush White House. Hoffman said, "Isn't it ironic that an Australian is spearheading this shift, together with a former covert operator? It shows that it's almost too revolutionary for the places where it should be discussed—the Pentagon, the National Security Council." At a moment when the Bush administration has run out of ideas and lost control, it could turn away from its "war on terror" and follow a different path—one that is right under its nose.

Betrayed

The New Yorker, March 26, 2007

On a cold, wet night in January, I met two young Iraqi men in the lobby of the Palestine Hotel in central Baghdad. A few Arabic television studios had rooms on the upper floors of the building, but the hotel was otherwise vacant. In the lobby, a bucket collected drips of rainwater; at the gift shop, which was closed, a shelf displayed film, batteries, and sheathed daggers covered in dust. A sign from another era read, WE HAVE GREAT PLEASURE IN ANNOUNCING THE OPENING OF THE INTERNET CAFÉ 24 HOUR A DAY. AT THE BUSINESS CENTER ON THE FIRST FLOOR. THE MANAGEMENT. The management consisted of a desk clerk and a few men in black leather jackets slouched in armchairs and holding two-way radios.

The two Iraqis, Othman and Laith, had asked to meet me at the Palestine because it was the only place left in Baghdad where they were willing to be seen with an American. They lived in violent neighborhoods that were surrounded by militia checkpoints. Entering and leaving the Green Zone, the fortified heart of the American presence, had become too risky. But even the Palestine made them nervous. In October 2005, a suicide bomber driving a cement mixer had triggered an explosion that nearly brought down the hotel's eighteen-story tower. An American tank unit that was guarding the hotel eventually pulled out, leaving security in the hands of Iraqi civilians. It would now be relatively easy for insurgents to get inside. The one comforting thought for Othman and Laith was that, four years into the war, the Palestine was no longer worth attacking.

The Iraqis and I went up to a room on the eighth floor. Othman smoked by the window while Laith sat on one of the twin beds. (The names of most of the Iraqis in this story have been changed for their protection.) Othman was a heavyset doctor, twenty-nine years old, with a gentle voice and an unflappable ironic manner. Laith, an engineer with rimless eyeglasses, was younger and taller, and given to bursts of enthusiasm and displeasure. Othman was Sunni, Laith was Shiite.

It had taken Othman three days to get to the hotel from his house, in western Baghdad. On the way, he was trapped for two nights at his sister's house, which was in an ethnically mixed neighborhood: gun battles had broken out between Sunni and Shiite militiamen. Othman watched the home of his sister's neighbor, a Sunni, burn to the ground. Shiite militiamen scrawled the words "Leave or else" on the doors of Sunni houses. Othman was able to leave the house only because his sister's husband—a Shiite, who was known to the local Shia militias—escorted him out. Othman took a taxi to the house of Laith's grandfather; from there, he and Laith went to the Palestine, where they enjoyed their first hot water in several weeks.

They had a strong friendship, based on a shared desire. Before the war, they had both longed for the arrival of the Americans, expecting them to change their lives. They had told each other that they would try to work with the foreigners. Othman and Laith were both secular, and despised the extremist militias on each side of Iraq's civil war, but the ethnic conflict had led them increasingly to quarrel, to the point that one of them—usually Laith—would refuse to speak to the other.

Laith began to describe these strains. "It started when the Americans came with Shia leaders and wanted to give the Shia leadership—"

"And kick out the Sunnis," Othman interrupted. "You admit this? You were not admitting it before."

"The Americans don't want to kick out the Sunnis," Laith said. "They want to give Shia the power because most Iraqis are Shia."

"And you believe the Sunnis did not want to participate, right?" Othman said. "The Americans didn't give them the chance to participate." He turned to me: "You know I'm not just saying this because I'm a Sunni—"

Laith rolled his eyes. "Whatever."

"But I think the Shia made the Sunnis feel that they're against them."

"This is not the point, who started it," Laith said heatedly. "Everybody is getting killed, the Shia and the Sunnis." He paused. "But if we think who started it, I think the Sunnis started it!"

"I think the Shia," Othman repeated, with calm knowingness. He said to me, "When I feel that I'm pushing too much and he starts to become so angry, I pull the brake."

Laith had a job with an American organization, affiliated with the National Endowment for Democracy, that encouraged private enterprise in developing countries. Othman had worked with a German group called Architects for People in Need, and then as a translator for foreign journalists. These were coveted jobs, but over time they had become so dangerous that Othman and Laith could talk candidly about their lives with no one except each other.

"I trust him," Othman said of his friend. "We've shared our experiences with foreigners—the good and the bad. We don't have a secret life when we are together. But when we go out we have to lie."

Othman's cell phone rang: a friend was calling from Jordan. "I had a vision that you'll be killed by the end of the month," he told Othman. "Get out now, please. You can stay here with me. We'll live on pasta." Othman said something reassuring and hung up, but his phone kept ringing, the friend calling back; his vision had made him hysterical.

A string of bad events had given Othman the sense that time was running out for him in Iraq. In November, members of the Mahdi Army—the Shia militia commanded by the radical cleric Moqtada al-Sadr—rounded up Othman's older brother and several other Sunnis who worked in a shop in a mixed neighborhood. The Sunnis were taken to a local Shia mosque and shot. Othman's brother was only grazed in the head, but a Shiite soldier noticed that he was still alive and shot him in the eye. Somehow he survived this, too. Othman found his brother and took him to a hospital for surgery. The hospital—like the entire Iraqi health system—was under the Mahdi Army's control, and Othman decided that his brother would be safer at their parents' house. The brother was now blind, deranged, and vengeful, making life unbearable for Othman's family. A few days later, Othman's elderly maternal aunts, who were Shia and lived in a majority Sunni area, were told by Sunni insurgents that they had three days to leave. Othman's father, a retired Sunni officer, went to their neighborhood and convinced the insurgents that his wife's sisters were, in fact, Sunnis. And then, one day in January, Othman's two teenage brothers, Muhammad and Salim, on whom he doted, failed to come home from school. Othman called the cell phone of Muhammad, who was fifteen. "Is this Muhammad?" he said.

A stranger's voice answered: "No, I'm not Muhammad."

"Where is Muhammad?"

"Muhammad is right here," the stranger said. "I'm looking at him now. We have both of them."

"Are you joking?"

"No, I'm not. Are you Sunni or Shia?"

Thinking of what had happened to his older brother, Othman lied: "We're Shia." The stranger told him to prove it. The boys had left their identity cards at home, for their own safety.

Othman's mother took the phone, sobbing and begging the kidnapper not to hurt her boys. "We're going to behead them," the kidnapper told her. "Choose where you want us to throw the bodies. Or do you prefer us to cut them to pieces for you? We enjoy cutting young boys to pieces." The man hung up.

After several more phone conversations, Othman realized his mistake: the kidnappers were Sunnis, with Al Qaeda. Shiites are not Muslims, the kidnappers told him—they deserve to be killed. Then they stopped answering the phone. Othman called a friend who belonged to a Sunni political party with ties to insurgents; over the course of the afternoon, the friend got the kidnappers back on the phone and convinced them that the boys were Sunnis. They were released with apologies, along with their money and their phones.

It was the worst day of Othman's life. He said he would never forget the sound of the stranger's voice.

Othman began a campaign of burning. He went into the yard or up on the roof of his parents' house with a jerrican of kerosene and set fire to papers, identity badges, books in English, photographs—anything that might incriminate him as an Iraqi who worked with foreigners. If Othman had to flee Iraq, he wanted to leave nothing behind that might harm him or his family. He couldn't bring himself to destroy a few items, though: his diaries, his weekly notes from the hospital where he had once worked. "I have this bad habit of keeping everything like memories," he said.

Most of the people Othman and Laith knew had left Iraq. House by house, Baghdad was being abandoned. Othman was considering his options: move his parents from their house (in an insurgent stronghold) to his sister's house (in the midst of civil war); move his parents and brothers to Syria (where there was no work) and live with his friend in Jordan (going crazy with boredom while watching his savings dwindle); go to

London and ask for asylum (and probably be sent back); stay in Baghdad for six more months until he could begin a scholarship that he'd won, to study journalism in America (or get killed waiting). Beneath his calm good humor, Othman was paralyzed—he didn't want to leave Baghdad and his family, but staying had become impossible. Every day, he changed his mind.

From the hotel window, Othman could see the palace domes of the Green Zone directly across the Tigris River. "It's sad," he told me. "With all the hopes that we had, and all the dreams, I was totally against the word 'invasion.' Wherever I go, I was defending the Americans and strongly saying, 'America was here to make a change.' Now I have my doubts."

Laith was more blunt: "Sometimes, I feel like we're standing in line for a ticket, waiting to die."

By the time Othman and Laith finished talking, it was almost ten o'clock. We went downstairs and found the hotel restaurant empty, with no light or heat. A waiter in a white shirt and black vest emerged out of the darkness to take our orders. We shivered for an hour until the food came.

There was an old woman at the cash register, with long, dyed-blond hair, a shapeless gown, and a macramé beret that kept falling off her head. I recognized her: she had been the cashier in 2003, when I first came to the Palestine. Her name was Taja, and she had worked at the hotel for twenty-five years. She had the smile of a mad hag.

I asked if there had been any other customers tonight. "My dear, no one," Taja said, in English. The sight of me seemed to jar loose a bundle of memories. Her brother had gone to New Orleans in 1948 and forgotten all about her. There was music here in the old days, she said, and she sang a few lines from the Spaniels'"Goodnight, Sweetheart, Goodnight":

> Goodnight, sweetheart, well, it's time to go,
> I hate to leave you, but I really must say,
> Goodnight, sweetheart, goodnight.

When the Americans first came, Taja said, the hotel was full of customers, including marines. She took the exam to work as a translator three times, but kept failing, because the questions were so hard: "The spider is an insect or an animal?" "Water is a beverage or a food?" Who could answer such questions?

Taja smiled at us. "Now all finished," she said.

My Time Will Come

Millions of Iraqis, spanning the country's religious and ethnic spectrum, welcomed the overthrow of Saddam Hussein. But the mostly young men and women who embraced America's project so enthusiastically that they were prepared to risk their lives for it may constitute Iraq's smallest minority. I came across them in every city: the young man in Mosul who loved Metallica and signed up to be a translator at a U.S. Army base; the DVD salesman in Najaf whose plans to study medicine were crushed by Baath Party favoritism, and who offered his services to the first American Humvee that entered his city. They had learned English from American movies and music, and from listening secretly to the BBC. Before the war, their only chance at a normal life was to flee the country—a nearly impossible feat. Their future in Saddam's Iraq was, as the Metallica fan in Mosul put it, "a one-way road leading to nothing." I thought of them as oddballs, like misunderstood high school students whose isolation ends when they go off to college. In a similar way, the four years of the war created intense friendships, but they were forged through collective disappointment. The arc from hope to betrayal that traverses the Iraq War is nowhere more vivid than in the lives of these Iraqis. America's failure to understand, trust, and protect its closest friends in Iraq is a small drama that contains the larger history of defeat.

An interpreter named Firas—he insisted on using his real name—grew up in a middle-class Shia family in a prosperous Baghdad neighborhood. He is a big man in his mid-thirties with a shaved head, and his fierce, heavily ringed eyes provide a glimpse into the reserves of energy that lie beneath his phlegmatic surface. As a young man, Firas was shut out of a government job by his family's religious affiliation and by his lack of connections. He wasted his twenties in a series of petty occupations: selling cigarettes wholesale; dealing in spare parts; peddling books on Mutanabi Street in old Baghdad. Books, more than anything, shaped

Firas's passionately melancholy character. As a young man, he kept a credo on his wall in English and Arabic: "Be honest without the thought of Heaven or Hell." He was particularly impressed by *The Outsider*, a 1956 philosophical work by the British existentialist Colin Wilson. "He wrote about the 'nonbelonger,'" Firas explained. Firas felt like an exile in his own land, but, he recalled, "There was always this sound in the back of my head: the time will come, the change will come, my time will come. And when 2003 came, I couldn't believe how right I was."

Overnight, everything was new. Americans, whom he had seen only in movies, rolled through the streets. Men who had been silent all their lives cursed Saddam in front of their neighbors. The fall of the regime revealed traits that Iraqis had kept hidden: the greed that drove some to loot, the courage that made others stay on the job. Firas felt a lifelong depression lift. "The first thing I learned about myself was that I can make things happen," he said. "When you feel that you are an outcast, you don't really put an effort in anything. But after the war I would run here and there, I would kill myself, I would focus on one thing and not stop until I do it."

Thousands of Iraqis converged on the Palestine Hotel and, later, the Green Zone, in search of work with the Americans. In the chaos of the early days, a demonstrable ability to speak English—sometimes in a chance encounter with a street patrol—was enough to get you hired by an enterprising Marine captain. Firas began working in military intelligence. Almost all the Iraqis who were hired became interpreters, and American soldiers called them "terps," often giving them nicknames for convenience and, later, security (Firas became Phil). But what the Iraqis had to offer went well beyond linguistic ability: each of them was, potentially, a cultural adviser, an intelligence officer, a policy analyst. Firas told the soldiers not to point with their feet, not to ask to be introduced to someone's sister. Interpreters assumed that their perspective would be valuable to foreigners who knew little or nothing of Iraq.

Whenever I asked Iraqis what kind of government they had wanted to replace Saddam's regime, I got the same answer: they had never given it any thought. They just assumed that the Americans would bring the right people, and the country would blossom with freedom, prosperity, consumer goods, travel opportunities. In this, they mirrored the wishful thinking of American officials and neoconservative intellectuals who failed to plan for trouble. Almost no Iraqi claimed to have anticipated videos of beheadings, or Moqtada al-Sadr, or the terrifying question "Are you Sunni or Shia?" Least of all did they imagine that America would make so many mistakes, and persist in those mistakes to the point that even fair-minded Iraqis wondered about ulterior motives. In retrospect, the blind faith that many Iraqis displayed in themselves and in America seems naïve. But now that Iraq's demise is increasingly regarded as foreordained, it's worth recalling the optimism among Iraqis four years ago.

Ali, an interpreter in Baghdad, spent his childhood in Pennsylvania and Oklahoma, where his father was completing his graduate studies. In 1987, when Ali was eleven and his father was shortly to get his green card, the family returned to Baghdad for a brief visit. But it was during the war with Iran, and the authorities refused to let them leave again. Ali had to learn Arabic from scratch. He grew up in Ghazaliya, a Baathist stronghold in western Baghdad where Shia families like his were rare. Iraq felt like a prison, and Ali considered his American childhood a paradise lost.

In 2003, soon after the arrival of the Americans, soldiers in his neighborhood persuaded him to work as an interpreter with the 82nd Airborne Division. He wore a U.S. Army uniform and a bandanna, and during interrogations he used broken Arabic in order to make prisoners think he was American. Although the work was not yet dangerous, an instinct led him to mask his identity and keep his job to himself around the neighborhood. Ali found that although many soldiers were friendly, they often ignored information and advice from their Iraqi employees. Interpreters would give them names of insurgents, and nothing would happen. When Ali suggested that soldiers buy up locals' rocket-propelled grenade launchers so that they would not fall into the hands of insurgents, he was disregarded. When interpreters drove onto the base, their cars were searched, and at the end of their shift they would sometimes find their car doors unlocked or a mirror broken—the cars had been searched again. "People came with true faces to the Americans, with complete loyalty," Ali said. "But from the beginning, they didn't trust us."

Ali initially worked the night shift at a base in his neighborhood and walked home by himself after midnight. In June 2003, the Americans mounted a huge floodlight at the front gate of the base, and when Ali left for home the light projected his shadow hundreds of feet down the street. "It's dangerous," he told the soldiers at the gate. "Can't you turn it off when we go out?"

"Don't be scared," the soldiers told him. "There's a sniper protecting you all the way."

A couple of weeks later, one of Ali's Iraqi friends was hanging out with the snipers in the tower, and he thanked them. "For what?" the snipers asked. For looking out for us, Ali's friend said. The snipers didn't know what he was talking about, and when he told them they started laughing.

"We got freaked out," Ali said. The message was clear: You Iraqis are on your own.

A Person In Between

The Arabic for "collaborator" is *aameel*—literally, "agent." Early in the occupation, the Baathists in Ali's neighborhood, who at first had been cowed by the Americans' arrival, began a shrewd whispering campaign. They told their neighbors that the Iraqi interpreters who went along on raids were feeding the Americans false information, urging the abuse of Iraqis, stealing houses, and raping women. In the market, a Baathist would point at an Iraqi riding in the back of a Humvee and say, "He's a traitor, a thug." Such rumors were repeated often enough that people began to believe them, especially as the promised benefits of the American occupation failed to materialize. Before long, Ali told me, the Baathists "made the reputation of the interpreter very, very low—worse than the Americans'."

There was no American campaign to counter the word on the street; there wasn't even a sense that these subversive rumors posed a serious threat. "Americans are living in another world," Ali said. "There's an Iraqi saying: 'He's sleeping and his feet are baking in the sun.'" The United States typically provided interpreters with inferior or no body armor, allowing the Baathists to make a persuasive case that Americans treated all Iraqis badly, even those who worked for them.

"The Iraqis aren't trusting you, and the Americans don't trust you from the beginning," Ali said. "You became a person in between."

• • •

Firas met the personal interpreter of L. Paul Bremer III, the head of the Coalition Provisional Authority—which governed Iraq for fourteen months after the invasion—in the fall of 2003. Soon, Firas had secured a privileged view of official America, translating documents at the Republican Palace, in the Green Zone.

He liked most of the American officials who came and went at the palace. Even when he saw colossal mistakes at high levels—for example, Bremer's decision to abolish the Iraqi army—Firas admired his new colleagues, and believed that they were helping to create institutions that would lead to a better future. And yet Firas kept being confronted by fresh ironies: he had less authority than any of the Americans, although he knew more about Iraq; and the less that Americans knew about Iraq the less they wanted to hear from him, especially if they occupied high positions.

One day, Firas accompanied one of Bremer's top political advisers to a meeting with an important Shiite cleric. The cleric's mosque, the Baratha, is an ancient Shiite bastion, and Firas, whose family came from the holy city of Najaf, knew a great deal about the mosque and the cleric. On the way, the adviser asked, "Is this a mosque or a shrine or what?" Firas said, "It's the Baratha mosque," and he started to explain its significance, but the adviser cut him short: "Okay, got it." They went into the meeting with the cleric, who was from a hard-line party backed by Tehran but who spoke as if he represented the views of all Iraqis. He didn't represent the views of many people Firas knew, and, given the chance, Firas could have told the adviser that the mosque and its imam had a history of promoting Shia nationalism. "There were a million comments in my head," Firas recalled. "Why the hell was he paying so much attention to this imam?"

Bremer and his advisers—Scott Carpenter, Meghan O'Sullivan, and Roman Martinez—were creating an interim constitution and negotiating the transfer of power to Iraqis, but they did not speak Arabic and had no background in the Middle East. The Iraqis they spent time with were, for the most part, returned exiles with sectarian agendas. The Americans had little sense of what ordinary Iraqis were experiencing, and they seemed oblivious of a readily available source of knowledge: the Iraqi employees who had lived in Baghdad for years and who went home to its neighborhoods every night. "These people would consider themselves too high to listen to a translator," Firas said. "Maybe they were interested more in telling D.C. what they want to hear instead of telling them what the Iraqis are saying."

Later, when the Coalition Provisional Authority was replaced by the U.S. embassy and political appointees gave way to career diplomats, Firas found himself working for a different kind of American. The embassy's political counselor, Robert Ford, his deputy, Henry Ensher, and a younger official in the political section, Jeffrey Beals, spoke Arabic, had worked extensively in the region, and spent most of their time in Baghdad talking to a range of Iraqis, including extremists. They gave Firas and other "foreign-service nationals" more authority, encouraging them to help write reports on Iraqi politics that were sometimes forwarded to Washington. Beals would be interviewed in Arabic on Al Jazeera and then endure a thorough critique by an Iraqi colleague—Ahmed, a tall, handsome Kurdish Shiite who lived just outside Sadr City and who was obsessed with Iraqi politics. When Firas, Ali, and Ahmed visited New York during a training trip, Beals's brother was their escort.

Beals quit the foreign service after almost two years in Iraq and is now studying history at Columbia University. He said that, with Americans in Baghdad coming and going every six or twelve months, "the lowest rung on your ladder ends up being the real institutional memory and repository of expertise—which is always a tension, because it's totally at odds with their status." The inversion of the power relationship between American officials and Iraqi employees became more dramatic as the dangers increased and American civilians lost almost all mobility around Baghdad. Beals said, "There aren't many people with pro-American eyes and the means to get their message across who can go into Sadr City and tell you what's happening day to day."

Badges

On the morning of January 18, 2004, a suicide truck bomber detonated a massive payload amid a line of vehicles waiting to enter the Green Zone by the entry point known as the Assassins' Gate. Most Iraqis working in the Green Zone knew someone who died in the explosion, which incinerated twenty-five people. Ali was hit by the blowback but was otherwise uninjured; two months later, he narrowly escaped an assassination attempt while driving to work. Throughout 2004, the murder of interpreters and other Iraqi employees became increasingly commonplace. Seven of Ali's friends who worked with the U.S. military were killed, which prompted him to leave the Army and take a job at the embassy.

In Mosul, insurgents circulated a DVD showing the decapitations of two military interpreters. American soldiers stationed there expressed sympathy to their Iraqi employees, but, one interpreter told me, there was "no real reaction": no offer of protection, in the form of a weapons permit or a place to live on base. He said, "The soldiers I worked with were friends and they felt sorry for us—they were good people—but they couldn't help. The people above them didn't care. Or maybe the people above *them* didn't care." This story repeated itself across the country: Iraqi employees of the U.S. military began to be kidnapped and killed in large numbers, and there was essentially no American response. Titan Corporation of Chantilly, Virginia, which until December held the Pentagon contract for employing interpreters in Iraq, was notorious among Iraqis for mistreating its foreign staff. I spoke with an interpreter who was injured in a roadside explosion; Titan refused to compensate him for the time he spent recovering from second-degree burns on his hands and feet. An Iraqi woman working at an American base was recognized by someone she had known in college, who began calling her with death threats. She told me that when she went to the Titan representative for help he responded, "You have two choices: move or quit." She told him that if she quit and stayed home, her life would be in danger. "That's not my business," the representative said. (A Titan spokesperson said, "The safety and welfare of all employees, including, of course, contract workers, is the highest priority.")

A State Department official in Iraq sent a cable to Washington criticizing the Americans' "lackadaisical" attitude about helping Iraqi employees relocate. In an e-mail to me, he said, "Most of them have lived secret lives for so long that they are truly a unique 'homeless' population in Iraq's war zone—dependent on us for security and not convinced we will take care of them when we leave." It's as if the Americans never imagined that the intimidation and murder of interpreters by other Iraqis would undermine the larger American effort, by destroying the confidence of Iraqis who wanted to give it support. The problem was treated as managerial, not moral or political.

• • •

One day in January 2005, Riyadh Hamid, a Sunni father of six from the embassy's political section, was shot to death as he left his house for work. When Firas heard the news at the embassy, he was deeply shaken: he, Ali, or Ahmed could be next. But he never thought of quitting. "At that time, I believed more in my cause, so if I die for it, let it be," he said.

Americans and Iraqis at the embassy collected twenty thousand dollars in private donations for Hamid's widow. At first, the U.S. government refused to pay workmen's compensation, because Hamid had been traveling between home and work and was not technically on the job when he was killed. (Eventually, compensation was approved.) A few days after the murder, Robert Ford, the political counselor, arranged a conversation between Ambassador John Negroponte and the Iraqis from the political section, whom the ambassador had never met. The Iraqis were escorted into a room in a secure wing of the embassy's second floor.

Negroponte had barely expressed his condolences when Firas, Ahmed, and their colleagues pressed him with a single request. They wanted identification that would allow them to enter the Green Zone through the priority lane that Americans with government clearance used, instead of having to wait every morning for an hour or two in a very long line with every other Iraqi who had business in the Green Zone. This line was an easy target for suicide bombers and insurgent lookouts (known in Iraq as *alaasa*—"chewers"). Iraqis at the embassy had been making this request for some time, without success. "Our problem is badges," the Iraqis told the ambassador.

Negroponte sent for the embassy's regional security officer, John Frese. "Here's the man who is responsible for badges," Negroponte said, and left.

According to the Iraqis, they asked Frese for green badges, which were a notch below the official blue American badges. These allowed the holder to enter through the priority lane and then be searched inside the gate.

"I can't give you that," Frese said.

"Why?"

"Because it says 'Weapon permit: yes.'"

"Change the 'yes' to 'no' for us."

Frese's tone was peremptory: "I can't do that."

Ahmed made another suggestion: allow the Iraqis to use their embassy passes to get into the priority lane. Frese again refused. Ahmed turned to one of his colleagues and said, in Arabic, "We're blowing into a punctured bag."

"My top priority is embassy security, and I won't jeopardize it, no matter what," Frese told them, and the Iraqis understood that this security did not extend to them—if anything, they were part of the threat.

After the meeting, a junior American diplomat who had sat through it was on the verge of tears. "This is what always calmed me down," Firas said. "I saw Americans who understand me, trust me, believe me, love me. This is what always kept my rage under control and kept my hope alive."

When I recently asked a senior government official in Washington about the badges, he insisted, "They are concerns that have been raised, addressed, and satisfactorily resolved. We acted extremely expeditiously." In fact, the matter was left unresolved for almost two years, until late 2006, when verbal instructions were given to soldiers at the gates of the Green Zone to let Iraqis with embassy passes into the priority lane—and even then individual soldiers, among whom there was rapid turnover, often refused to do so.

Americans and Iraqis recalled the meeting as the moment when the embassy's local employees began to be disenchanted. If Negroponte had taken an interest, he could have pushed Frese to change the badges. But a diplomat doesn't rise to Negroponte's stature by busying himself with small-bore details, and without his directive the rest of the bureaucracy wouldn't budge.

In Baghdad, the regional security officer had unusual power: to investigate staff members, to revoke clearances, to block diplomats' trips outside the Green Zone. The word "security" was ubiquitous—a "magical word," one Iraqi said, that could justify anything. "Saying no to the regional security officer is a dangerous thing," according to a second former embassy official, who occasionally did say no in order to be able to carry out his job. "You're taking a lot of responsibility on yourself." Although Iraqi employees had been vetted with background checks and took regular lie detector tests, a permanent shadow of suspicion lay over them because they lived outside the Green Zone. Firas once attended a briefing at which the regional security officer told newly arrived Americans that no Iraqi could be trusted.

The reminders were constant. Iraqi staff members were not allowed into the gym or the food court near the embassy. Banned from the military PX, they had to ask an American supervisor to buy them a pair of sunglasses or underwear. These petty humiliations were compounded by security officers who easily crossed the line between vigilance and bullying.

One day in late 2004, Laith, who had never given up hope of working for the American embassy, did well on an interview in the Green Zone and was called to undergo a polygraph. After he was hooked up to the machine, the questions began: Have you ever lied to your family? Do you know any insurgents? At some point, he thought too hard about his answer; when the test was over, the technician called in a security officer and shouted at Laith: "Do you think you can fuck with the United States? Who sent you here?" Laith was hustled out to the gate, where the technician promised to tell his employers at the National Endowment for Democracy to fire him.

"That was the first time I hated the Americans," Laith said.

Corridors of Power

In January 2005, Kirk Johnson, a twenty-four-year-old from Illinois, arrived in Baghdad as an information officer with the United States Agency for International Development. He came from a patriotic family that believed in public service; his father was a lawyer whose chance at an open seat in Congress, in 1986, was blocked when the state Republican Party chose a former wrestling coach named Dennis Hastert to run instead. Johnson, an Arabic speaker, was studying Islamist thought as a Fulbright scholar in Cairo when the war began; when he arrived in Baghdad, he became one of USAID's few Arabic-speaking Americans in Iraq.

Johnson, who is rangy, earnest, and baby-faced, thought that he was going to help America rebuild Iraq, in a mission that was his generation's calling. Instead, he found a "narcotic" atmosphere in the Green Zone. Surprisingly few Americans ever ventured outside its gates. A short drive from the embassy, at the Blue Star Café—famous for its chicken fillet and fries—contractors could be seen, in golf shirts, khakis, and baseball caps, enjoying a leisurely lunch, their Department of Defense badges draped around their necks. At such moments, it was hard not to have uncharitable thoughts about the war—that Americans today aren't equipped for something of this magnitude. Iraq is that rare war in which people put on weight. An Iraqi woman at the embassy who had seen many Americans come and go—and revered a few of them—declared that 70 percent of them were "useless, crippled," avoiding debt back home or escaping a bad marriage. I met an American official who, during one year, left the Green Zone less than half a dozen times; unlike many of his colleagues, he understood this to be a problem.

The deeper the Americans dug themselves into the bunker, the harder they tried to create a sense of normalcy, resulting in what Johnson called "a bizarre arena of paperwork and booze." There were karaoke nights and volleyball leagues, the Baghdad Regatta, and "Country Night—One Howdy-Doody Good Time." Halliburton, the defense contractor, hosted a Middle Eastern night. The cubicles in USAID's new Baghdad office building, Johnson discovered, were exactly the same as the cubicles at its headquarters in Washington. The more chaotic Iraq became, the more the Americans resorted to bureaucratic gestures of control. The fact that it took five signatures to get Adobe Acrobat installed on a computer was strangely comforting.

Johnson learned that Iraqis were third-class citizens in the Green Zone, after Americans and other foreigners. For a time, Americans were ordered to wear body armor while outdoors; when Johnson found out that Iraqi staff members hadn't been provided with any, he couldn't bear to wear his own around them. Superiors eventually ordered him to do so. "If you're still properly calibrated, it can be a shameful sort of existence there," Johnson said. "It takes a certain amount of self-delusion not to be brought down by it."

In October 2004, two bombs killed four Americans and two Iraqis at a café and a shopping center inside the Green Zone, fueling the suspicion that there were enemies within. The Iraqi employees became perceived as part of an undifferentiated menace. They also induced a deeper, more elusive form of paranoia. As Johnson put it, "Not that we thought they'd do us bodily harm, but they represented the reality beyond those blast walls. You keep your distance from these Iraqis, because if you get close you start to discover it's absolute bullshit—the lives of people in Baghdad aren't safer, in spite of our trend lines or ginned-up reports by contractors that tell you everything is going great."

After eight months in the Green Zone, Johnson felt that the impulse that had originally made him volunteer to work in Iraq was dying. He got a transfer to Falluja, to work on the front lines of the insurgency.

The Iraqis who saw both sides of the Green Zone gates had to be as alert as prey in a jungle of predators. Ahmed, the Kurdish Shiite, had the job of reporting on Shia issues, and his feel for the mood in Sadr City was crucial to the political section. When a low-flying American helicopter tore a Shia religious flag off a radio tower, Ahmed immediately picked up on rumors, started by the Mahdi Army, that Americans were targeting Shia worshippers. His job required him to seek contact with members of Shiite militias, who sometimes reacted to him with suspicion. He once went to a council meeting near Sadr City that had been called to arrange a truce between the Americans and the Mahdi Army so that garbage could be cleared from the streets. A council member confronted Ahmed, demanding to know who he was. Ahmed responded, "I'm from a Korean organization. They sent me to find out what solution you guys come up with. Then we're ready to fund the cleanup." At another meeting, he identified himself as a correspondent from an Iraqi television network. No one outside his immediate family knew where he worked.

Ahmed took two taxis to the Green Zone, then walked the last few hundred yards, or drove a different route every day. He carried a decoy phone and hid his embassy phone in his car. He had always loved the idea of wearing a jacket and tie in an official job, but he had to keep them in his office at the embassy—it was impossible to drive to work dressed like that. Ahmed and the other Iraqis entered code names for friends and colleagues into their phones, in case they were kidnapped. Whenever they got a call in public from an American contact, they answered in Arabic and immediately hung up. They communicated mostly by text message. They never spoke English in front of their children. One Iraqi employee slept in his car in the Green Zone parking lot for several nights, because it was too dangerous to go home.

Baghdad, which has six million residents, at least provided the cover of anonymity. In a small Shia city in the south, no one knew that a twenty-six-year-old Shiite named Hussein was working for the Americans. "I lie and lie and lie," he said. He acted as a go-between, carrying information between the U.S. outpost, the local government, the Shia clergy, and the radical Sadrists. The Americans would send him to a meeting of clerics with a question, such as whether Iranian influence was fomenting violence. Instead of giving a direct answer, the clerics would demand to know why thousands of American soldiers were unable to protect Shia travelers on a ten-kilometer stretch of road. Hussein would take this back to the Americans and receive a "yes-slash-no kind of answer: We will take it up, we'll get back to them soon—the soon becomes never." In this way, he was privy to both sides of the deepening mutual disenchantment. The fact that he had no contact with Sunnis did not make Hussein feel any safer: by 2004, Shia militias were also targeting Iraqis who worked with Americans.

As a youth, Hussein was an overweight misfit obsessed with Second World War documentaries, and now he felt grateful to the Americans for freeing him from Saddam's tyranny. He also took a certain pride and pleasure in carrying off his risky job. "I'm James Bond, without the nice lady or the famous gadgets," he said. He worked out of a series of rented rooms, seldom going out in public, relying on his cell phone and his laptop, keeping a small "runaway bag" with him in case he needed to leave quickly (a neighbor once informed him that some strangers had asked who lived there, and Hussein moved out the same day). Every few days, he brought his laundry to his parents' house. He stopped seeing friends, and his life winnowed down to his work. "You have to live two separate lives, one visible and the other one invisible," Hussein told me when we spoke in Erbil. (He insisted on meeting in Kurdistan, because there was nowhere else in Iraq that he felt safe being seen with me.) "You have to always be aware of the car behind you. When you want to park, you make sure that the car passes you. You're always afraid of a person staring at you in an abnormal way."

He received three threats. The first was graffiti written across his door, the second a note left outside his house. Both said, "Leave your job or we'll kill you." The third came in December, after American soldiers killed a local militia leader who had been one of Hussein's most important contacts. A friend approached Hussein and conveyed an anonymous warning: "You better not have anything to do with this event. If you do, you'll have to take the consequences." Since Hussein was known to have interpreted for American soldiers at the start of the war, he said, his name had long been on the Mahdi Army's blacklist. It was not just frightening but also embarrassing to be a suspect in the militia leader's death; it undermined Hussein in the eyes of his carefully cultivated contacts. "The stamp that comes to you will never go—you will stay a spy," he said.

He informed his American supervisor, as he had after the previous two threats. And the reply was the same: lie low, take a leave with pay. Hussein had warm feelings for his supervisor, but he wanted a transfer to another country in the Middle East or a scholarship offer to the U.S.— some tangible sign that his safety mattered to them. None was forthcoming. Once, in April 2004, when the Mahdi Army had overrun coalition posts all over southern Iraq, he had asked to be evacuated along with the Americans and was refused; his pride wouldn't let him ask again. Soon after Hussein received his third threat, his supervisor left Iraq.

"You are now belonging to no side," Hussein said.

In June 2006, with kidnappings and sectarian killings out of control in Baghdad, the number of Iraqis working in the embassy's public affairs section dropped from nine to four; most of those who quit fled the country. The Americans began to replace them with Jordanians. The switch was deeply unpopular with the remaining Iraqis, who understood that it involved the fundamental issue of trust: Jordanians could be housed in the Green Zone without fear (Iraqis could secure temporary housing for only a limited time); Jordanians were issued badges that allowed them into the embassy without being searched; they weren't subject to threat and blackmail, because they lived inside the Green Zone. In every way, Jordanians were easier to deal with. But they also knew nothing about Iraq. One former embassy official, who considered the new policy absurd, lamented that a Jordanian couldn't possibly understand that the term "February 8th mustache," say, referred to the 1963 Baathist coup.

In the past year, the U.S. government has lost a quarter of its 206 Iraqi employees, and many have been replaced by Jordanians. Not long ago, the United States began training citizens of the Republic of Georgia to fill the jobs of Iraqis in Baghdad. "I don't know why it's better to have these people flown into Iraq and secure them in the Green Zone," a State Department official said. "Why wouldn't we bring Iraqis into the Green Zone and give them housing and secure them?" He added, "We're depriving people of jobs and we're getting them whacked. It's not a pretty picture."

On June 6, amid the exodus of Iraqis from the public affairs section, an embassy official sent a six-page cable to Washington whose subject line read "Public Affairs Staff Show Strains of Social Discord." The cable described the nightmarish lives of the section's Iraqi employees and the sectarian tensions rising among them. It was an astonishingly candid report, perhaps aimed at forcing the State Department to confront the growing disaster. The cable was leaked to *The Washington Post* and briefly became a political liability. One sentence has stuck in my mind: "A few staff members approached us to ask what provisions we would make for them if we evacuate."

I went to Baghdad in January partly because I wanted to find an answer to this question. Were there contingency plans for Iraqis, and if so, whom did they include, and would the Iraqis have to wait for a final American departure? Would any Iraqis be evacuated to the United States? No one at the embassy was willing to speak on the record about Iraqi staff, except an official spokesman, Lou Fintor, who read me a statement: "Like all residents of Baghdad, our local employees must attempt to maintain their daily routines despite the disruptions caused by terrorists, extremists, and criminals. The new Iraqi government is taking steps to improve the security situation and essential services in Baghdad. The Iraq security forces, in coordination with coalition forces, are now engaged in a wide-range effort to stabilize the security situation in Baghdad . . . President Bush strongly reaffirmed our commitment to work with the government of Iraq to answer the needs of all Iraqis."

I was granted an interview with two officials, who refused to be named. One of them consulted talking points that catalogued what the embassy had done for Iraqi employees: a Thanksgiving dinner, a recent 35 percent salary increase. Housing in the Green Zone could be made available for a week at a time in critical cases, I was told, though most Iraqis didn't want to be apart from their families. When I asked about contingency plans for evacuation, the second official refused to discuss it on security grounds, but he said, "If we reach that point and have people in danger, the ambassador would go to the secretary of state and ask that they be evacuated, and I think they would do it." The department was reviewing the possibility of issuing special immigrant visas.

To receive this briefing, I had passed through three security doors into the embassy's classified section, where there were no Iraqis and no natural light; it seemed as if every molecule of Baghdad air had been sealed off behind the last security door. The embassy officials struck me as decent, overworked people, yet I left the interview with a feeling of shame. The problem lay not with the individuals but with the institution and, beyond that, with the politics of the American project in Iraq, which from the beginning has been conducted under the illusion that controlling the message mattered more than the reality. A former official at the embassy told me, "When we say that the corridors of power are insulated, is it that the officials aren't receiving the information, or is it because the construct under which they're operating doesn't even allow them to absorb it?" To admit that Iraqis who work with Americans need to be evacuated would blow a hole in the administration's version of the war.

Several days after the interview at the embassy, I had a more frank conversation with an official there. "I don't know if it's fair to say, 'You work at an embassy of a foreign country, so that country has to evacuate you,'" he said. "Do the Australians have a plan? Do the Romanians? The Turks? The British?" He added, "If I worked at the Hungarian embassy in Washington, would the Hungarians evacuate me from the United States?"

When I mentioned these remarks to Othman, he asked, "Would the Americans behead an American working at the Hungarian embassy in Washington?"

The Hearts of Your Allies

In the summer of 2006, Iraqis were fleeing the country at the rate of forty thousand per month. The educated middle class of Baghdad was decamping to Jordan and Syria, taking with them the skills and the more secular ideas necessary for rebuilding a destroyed society, leaving the city to the religious militias—eastern Baghdad was controlled by the poor and increasingly radical Shia, the western districts dominated by Sunni insurgents. House by house, the capital was being ethnically cleansed.

By that time, Firas, Ali, and Ahmed had been working with the Americans for several years. Their commitment and loyalty were beyond doubt. Just going to work in the morning required an extraordinary ability to disregard danger. Panic, Firas realized, could trap you: when the threat came, you felt you were a dead man no matter where you turned, and your mind froze and you sat at home waiting for them to come for you. In order to function, Firas simply blocked out the fear. "My friends at work became the only friends I have," he said. "My entertainment is at work, my pleasure is at work, everything is at work." Firas and his friends never imagined that the decision to leave Iraq would be forced on them not by the violence beyond the Green Zone but from within the embassy itself.

After the bombing of the gold-domed Shia mosque in Samarra that February, Sadr City had become the base for the Mahdi Army's roving death squads. Ahmed's neighborhood fell under their complete control, and his drive to work took him through numerous unfriendly—and thorough—militia checkpoints. Strangers began to ask about him. A falafel vender in Sadr City whose stall was often surrounded by Mahdi Army *alaasa* warned Ahmed that his name had come up. On two occasions, people he scarcely knew approached him and expressed concern about his well-being. One evening, an American official named Oliver Moss, with whom Ahmed was close, walked him out of the embassy to the parking lot and said, "Ahmed, I know you work for us, but if something happens to you we won't be able to do anything for you." Ahmed asked for a cot in a Green Zone trailer and was given the yes/no answer—equal parts personal sympathy and bureaucratic delay—which sometimes felt worse than a flat refusal. The chaos in Baghdad had created a landgrab for Green Zone accommodations, and the Iraqi government was distributing coveted apartments to friends of the political parties while evicting Iraqis who worked with the Americans. The interpreters were distrusted and despised even by officials of the new government that the Americans had helped bring to power.

In April, a Shiite member of the parliament asked Ahmed to look into the status of a Mahdi Army member who had been detained by the Americans. Iraqis at the embassy sometimes used their office to do small favors for their compatriots; such gestures reminded them that they were serving Iraq as well as America. But Ahmed sent his inquiry through the wrong channel. His supervisor was on leave in the United States, and so he sent an e-mail to a reserve colonel in the political section. The colonel refused to provide him with any information, and a couple of weeks later, in May, Ahmed was summoned to talk to an agent from the regional security office.

To the Iraqis, a summons of this type was frightening. Ahmed and his friends had seen several colleagues report to the regional security office and never appear at their desks again, with no explanation; one had been turned over to the Iraqi police and was jailed for several weeks. "Don't go. They're going to arrest you," Ali told Ahmed. "Just quit. It's not worth it." Ahmed did not listen.

The agent, Barry Hale, who carried a Glock pistol, questioned Ahmed for an hour about his contacts with Sadrists. The notion that Ahmed's job required him to have contact with the Mahdi Army seemed foreign to Hale, as did the need to have well-informed Iraqis in the political section of the embassy. According to an American official close to the case, Hale had a general distrust of Iraqis and wanted to replace them with Jordanians. Another official spoke of a "paranoia partly founded on ignorance. If Ahmed wanted to hurt an American, he could have done it very easily in the three years he worked with us."

Robert Ford, the political counselor, spoke to top officials at the embassy to ensure that Ahmed—whom several Americans described as the best Iraqi employee they had worked with—would be "counseled" but not fired. Everyone assumed that the case was closed. But over the summer, after Ford's service in Baghdad ended, Hale started to pursue Ahmed again. "It was a witch hunt," one of the officials said. "They wanted to fire him and they were just looking for a reason. They decided he was a threat." The irony of his situation was not lost on Ahmed: he was suspected of giving information to a militia that would kill him instantly if they knew where he worked.

In late July, Hale summoned Ahmed again. On Hale's desk, Ahmed saw a thick file marked "Secret," next to a pair of steel handcuffs.

"Did you ever get a phone call from the Mahdi Army?" Hale asked.

"I'll be lucky if I get a phone call from them," Ahmed replied. "My supervisor will be very happy."

The interrogation came down to one point: Hale insisted that Ahmed had misled him by saying that the reserve colonel had "never answered" Ahmed's inquiry, when in fact the colonel had sent back an e-mail asking who had given Ahmed the detainee's name. Ahmed hadn't considered this an answer to his question about the detainee's status, and therefore hadn't mentioned it to Hale. This was his undoing.

When Ahmed returned to his desk, Firas and Ali embraced him and congratulated him on escaping detention. Meanwhile, lower-ranking embassy officials began frantically calling and e-mailing colleagues in Washington, some of whom tried to intervene on Ahmed's behalf. But by then it was too late. The new ambassador, Zalmay Khalilzad, and his deputy were out of the country, and the official in charge of the embassy was Ford's replacement, Margaret Scobey, a new arrival in Baghdad, who had no idea of Ahmed's value. Firas said of her, "She was really not into the Iraqis in the office." Some Americans and Iraqis described her as a note taker for the ambassador who sent oddly upbeat reports back to Washington. Two days after the second interrogation, Scobey signed off on Ahmed's termination and ordered a junior officer named Rebecca Fong to go down to Ahmed's office and, in front of his tearful American and Iraqi colleagues, fire him.

Ahmed later told an American official, "I think the U.S. is still in a war. I don't think you're going to win this war if you don't win the hearts of your allies." The State Department refused to discuss the case for reasons of privacy and security.

Ahmed's firing demoralized Americans and Iraqis alike. Fong transferred out of the political section. For Firas, it meant that no matter how long he worked with the Americans and how many risks he took, he, too, would ultimately be discarded. He began to tell himself, "My turn is coming, my turn is coming"—a perverse echo of his mantra before the fall of Saddam. The Iraqis now felt that, as Ali said, "heaven doesn't want us and hell doesn't want us. Where will we go?" If the Americans were turning against them, they had no friends at all.

Three days after Ahmed's departure, Scobey appeared in the Iraqis' office to say that she was sorry but there was nothing she could have done for Ahmed. Firas listened in disgust before bursting out, "All the sacrifices, all the work, all the devotion mean nothing to you. We are still terrorists in your eyes." When, a month later, Khalilzad met with a large group of Iraqi employees to hear their concerns, Firas attended reluctantly. After the Iraqis raised the possibility of immigrant visas to the United States, Khalilzad said, "We want the good Iraqi people to stay in the country." An Iraqi replied, "If we're still alive." Firas, speaking last, told the ambassador, "We are tense all the time, we don't know what we are doing, right or wrong. Some Iraqis are more afraid in the embassy than in the Red Zone"—that is, Baghdad. There was a ripple of laughter among the Iraqis, and Khalilzad couldn't suppress a smile.

At this point, Firas knew that he would leave Iraq. Through the efforts of Rebecca Fong and Oliver Moss—who pulled strings with counterparts in European embassies in Baghdad—Ahmed, Firas, and Ali obtained visas to Europe. By November, they were gone.

Johnson's List

On the morning of October 13, an Iraqi official with USAID named Yaghdan left his house in western Baghdad in search of fuel for his generator. He saw a scrap of paper lying by the garage door. It was a torn sheet of copybook paper—the kind that his agency distributed to schools around Iraq, with date and subject lines printed in English and Arabic. The paper bore a message, in Arabic: "We will cut off heads and throw them in the garbage." Nearby, against the garden fence, lay the severed upper half of a small dog.

Yaghdan (who wanted his real name used) was a mild, conscientious thirty-year-old from a family of struggling businessmen. Since taking a job with the Americans, in 2003, he had been so cautious that at first he couldn't imagine how his cover had been blown. Then he remembered: two weeks earlier, as he was showing his badge at the bridge offering entry into the Green Zone, Yaghdan had noticed a man from his neighborhood standing in the same line, watching him. The neighbor worked as a special guard with a Shia militia and must have been the *alaas* who betrayed him.

Yaghdan's request for a transfer to a post outside the country was never answered. Instead, USAID offered him a month's leave with pay or residence for six months in the agency compound in the Green Zone, which would have meant a long separation from his young wife. Yaghdan said, "I thought, I should not be selfish and put myself as a priority. It wasn't a happy decision." Within a week of the threat, Yaghdan and his wife flew to Dubai, in the United Arab Emirates.

Yaghdan sent his résumé to several companies in Dubai, highlighting his years of service with an American contractor and USAID. He got a call from a legal office that needed an administrative assistant. "Did you work in the United States?" the interviewer asked him. Yaghdan said that his work had been in Iraq. "Oh, in Iraq . . ." He could feel the interviewer pulling back. A man at another office said, "Oh, you worked against Saddam? You betrayed Saddam? The American people are stealing Iraq." Yaghdan, who is not given to bitterness, finally lost his cool: "No, the Arab people are stealing Iraq!" He didn't get the job. He was amazed—even in cosmopolitan Dubai, people loved Saddam, especially after his botched execution in late December. Yaghdan's résumé was an encumbrance. Iraqis were considered bad Arabs, and Iraqis who worked with the Americans were traitors. The slogans and illusions of Arab nationalism, which had seemed to collapse with the regime of Saddam, were being given a second life by the American failure in Iraq. What hurt Yaghdan most was the looks that said, "You trusted the Americans—and see what happened to you."

Yaghdan then contacted many American companies, thinking that they, at least, would look favorably on his service. He wasn't granted a single interview. The only work he could find was as a gofer in the office of a Dubai cleaning company.

Yaghdan's Emirates visa expired in mid-January, and he had to leave the country and renew the visa in Amman. I met him there. The Jordanians had been turning away young Iraqis at the border and the airport for several months, but they issued Yaghdan and his wife three-day visas, after which they had to pay a daily fine, on top of hotel bills. After a week's delay, the visas came through, but, upon returning to Dubai, Yaghdan learned that the Emirates would no longer extend the visas of Iraqis. A job offer as an administrative assistant came from a university in Qatar, but the Qataris wouldn't grant him a visa without a security clearance from the Iraqi Ministry of the Interior, which was in the hands of the Shia party whose militia had sent him the death threat. He couldn't even become a refugee, which would have given him some protection against deportation, because the United Nations High Commissioner for Refugees had closed its Emirates office years ago. Yaghdan had heard that the only way to get a U.S. visa was through a job offer—nearly impossible to obtain—or by marrying an American, so he didn't bother to try. He had reached the end of his legal options and would have to return to Iraq by April 1. "It's like taking the decision to commit suicide," he said.

While Yaghdan was in Dubai, news of his dilemma made its way through the USAID grapevine to Kirk Johnson, the young Arabic speaker who had asked to be transferred to Falluja. By then, Johnson's life had been turned upside down as well.

In Falluja, Johnson had supervised Iraqis who were clearing out blocked irrigation canals along the Euphrates River. His job was dangerous and seldom rewarding, but it gave him the sense of purpose that he had sought in Iraq. Determined to experience as much as possible, he went out several times a week in a Marine convoy to meet tribal sheikhs and local officials. As he rode through Falluja's lethal streets, Johnson eyed every bag of trash and parked car for hidden bombs and practiced swatting away imaginary grenades. After a local sniper shot several marines, Johnson's anxiety rose even higher.

In December 2005, after twelve exhausting months in Iraq, during which he lost forty pounds, Johnson went on leave and met his parents for a Christmas vacation in the Dominican Republic. In the middle of the night, Johnson rose unconscious from his hotel bed and climbed onto a ledge outside the second floor window. A night watchman noticed him staring at an unfinished concrete apartment complex across the road. The night before, the sight of the building had triggered his fear of the sniper, and he had instinctively dropped to the floor of his room. Standing on the ledge, he shouted something and then fell fifteen feet.

Johnson tore open his jaw and forehead and broke his nose, teeth, and wrists. He required numerous surgeries on his shattered face, and stayed in the hospital for several weeks. But it was much longer before he could accept that he would not rejoin the marines and Iraqis he had left in Falluja. There were rumors in Iraq that he had been drunk and was trying to avoid returning. Back home in Illinois, healing in his childhood bed, he dreamed every night that he was in Iraq, unable to save people, or else in mortal peril himself.

In January 2006, Paul Bremer came through Chicago to promote his book, *My Year in Iraq*. Johnson sat in one of the front rows, ready to challenge Bremer's upbeat version of the reconstruction, but during the question period Bremer avoided the young man with the bandaged face who was frantically waving his arms, which were still in casts.

Johnson moved to Boston, but he kept thinking about his failure to return to Iraq. One day, he heard the news about Yaghdan, whom he had known in Baghdad, and that night he barely slept. It suddenly occurred to him that this was an injustice he could address. He could send money; he could alert journalists and politicians. He wrote a detailed account of Yaghdan's situation and sent it to his congressman, Dennis Hastert. But Hastert's office, which was reeling from the Mark Foley scandal and the midterm elections, told Johnson that it could not help Yaghdan. Johnson wrote an op-ed article calling for asylum for Yaghdan and others like him, and on December 15 it ran in the *Los Angeles Times*. A USAID official in Baghdad sent it around to colleagues. Then Johnson began to hear from Iraqis.

First, it was people he knew—former colleagues in desperate circumstances like Yaghdan's. Iraqis forwarded his article to other Iraqis, and he started to compile a list of names; by January he was getting e-mails from strangers with subject lines like "Can you help me Please?" and "I want to be on the list." An Iraqi woman who had worked for the Coalition Provisional Authority attached a letter of recommendation written in 2003 by Bernard Kerik, then Iraq's acting minister of the interior. It proclaimed, "Your courage to support the Coalition forces has sent home an irrefutable message: that terror will not rule, that liberty will triumph, and that the seeds of freedom will be planted into the hearts of the great citizens of Iraq." The woman was now a refugee in Amman.

A former USAID procurement agent named Ibrahim wrote that he was stranded in Egypt after having paid traffickers twelve thousand dollars to smuggle him from Baghdad to Dubai to Mumbai to Alexandria, with the goal of reaching Europe. When the Egyptian police figured out the scheme, Ibrahim took shelter in a friend's flat in a Cairo slum. The Egyptians, wary of a popular backlash against rising Shia influence in the Middle East, were denying Iraqis legal status there. Ibrahim didn't know where to go next: in addition to his immigration troubles, he had an untreated brain tumor.

By the first week of February, Johnson's list had grown to more than a hundred names. Working tirelessly, he had found a way to channel his desire to do something for Iraq. He assembled the information on a spreadsheet, and on February 5 he took it with him on a bus to Washington—along with Yaghdan's threat letter and a picture of the severed dog.

Toward the end of January, I traveled to Damascus. Iraqis were tolerated by Syria, which opened its doors in the name of Arab brotherhood. Yet Syria offered them no prospect of earning a living: few Iraqis could get work permits.

About a million Iraqis were now in Syria. Every morning that I visited, there were long lines outside the United Nations High Commissioner for Refugees office in central Damascus. Forty-five thousand Iraqis had officially registered as refugees, and more were signing up every day, amid reports that the Syrian regime was about to tighten its visa policy and had begun turning people back at the border.

One chilly night, I went to Sayyida Zainab, a neighborhood centered around the shrine of the sister of Hussein, grandson of the Prophet and the central martyr of Shiism. This had become an Iraqi Shia district, and on the main street were butcher shops and kebab stands that reminded me of commercial streets in Baghdad. There were pictures of Shia martyrs, and also of Moqtada al-Sadr, outside the real estate offices, some of which, I was told, were fronts for brothels. (Large numbers of Iraqi women make their living in Syria as prostitutes.) Shortly before midnight, buses from Baghdad began to pull in to a parking lot where boys were still up, playing soccer. One bus had a shattered windshield from gunfire at the start of its journey. A minibus driver told me that the trip took fourteen hours, including a long wait at the border, and that the road through Iraq was menaced by insurgents, criminal gangs, and American patrols. And yet some Iraqis who had run out of money in Damascus hired the driver to take them back to Baghdad the same night. "No one is left there," he said. "Only those who are too poor to leave, and those with a bad omen on their heads, who will be killed in one of three ways—kidnapping, car bomb, or militias."

In another Damascus neighborhood, I met a family of four that had just arrived from Baghdad after receiving a warning from insurgents to abandon their house. They had settled in a three-room apartment and were huddled around a kerosene heater. They were middle-class people who had left almost everything behind—the mother had sold her gold and jewelry to pay for plane tickets to Damascus—and the son and daughter hadn't been able to finish school. The daughter, Zamzam, was seventeen, and in the past few months she had been seeing corpses in the streets on her way to school, some of them eaten by dogs because no one dared to take them away. On days when there was fighting in her neighborhood, Zamzam said, walking to school felt like a death wish. Her laptop computer had a picture of an American flag as its screen saver, but it also had recordings of insurgent ballads in praise of a famous Baghdad sniper. She was an energetic, ambitious girl, but her dark eyes had the haunted look of a much older woman.

I spent a couple of hours walking with the family around the souk and the grand Umayyad Mosque in the old city center. The parents strolled arm in arm—enjoying, they said, a ritual that had been impossible in Baghdad for the past two years. I left them outside a theater where a comedy featuring an all-Iraqi cast was playing to packed houses of refugees. The play was called *Homesick*.

In the past few months, Western and Arab governments announced that they would no longer honor Iraqi passports issued after the 2003 invasion, since the passport had been so shoddily produced that it was subject to widespread forgery. This was the first passport many Iraqis had ever owned, and it was now worthless. Iraqis with Saddam-era passports were also out of luck, because the Iraqi government had canceled them. A new series of passports was being printed, but the Ministry of the Interior had ordered only around twenty thousand copies, an Iraqi official told me, far too few to meet the need—which meant that obtaining a valid passport, like buying gas or heating oil, would become subject to black market influences. In Baghdad, Othman told me that a new passport would cost him six hundred dollars, paid to a fixer with connections at the passport offices. The Ministry of the Interior refused to allow Iraqi embassies to print the new series, so refugees outside Iraq who needed valid passports would have to return to the country they had fled or pay someone a thousand dollars to do it for them.

Between October 2005 and September 2006, the United States admitted 202 Iraqis as refugees, most of them from the years under Saddam. Last year, the Bush administration increased the allotment to 500. By the end of 2006, there were almost 2 million Iraqis living as refugees outside their country—most of them in Syria and Jordan. American policy held that these Iraqis were not refugees, that they would go back to their country as soon as it was stabilized. The U.S. embassies in Damascus and Amman continued to turn down almost all visa applications from Iraqis. So the fastest-growing refugee crisis in the world remained hidden, receiving little attention other than in a few reports from organizations like Human Rights Watch and Refugees International.

Then, in early January, UNHCR sent out an appeal for sixty million dollars for the support and eventual resettlement of Iraqi refugees. On January 16, the Senate Judiciary Committee's subcommittee on refugees, chaired by Senator Edward M. Kennedy of Massachusetts, held hearings on Iraqi refugees, with a special focus on Iraqis who had worked for the U.S. government. Pressure in Congress and the media began to build, and the administration scrambled to respond. When an Iraqi employee of the embassy was killed on January 11, and one from USAID on February 14, statements of condolence were sent out by Ambassador Khalilzad and the chief administrator of USAID—gestures that few could remember happening before.

In early February, the State Department announced the formation of a task force to deal with the problem of Iraqi refugees. A colleague of Kirk Johnson's at USAID, who had been skeptical that Johnson's efforts would achieve anything, wrote to him, "Interesting what a snowball rolled down a hill can cause. This is your baby. Good going." On February 14, at a press conference at the State Department, members of the task force declared a new policy: the United States would fund eighteen million dollars of the UNHCR appeal, and it would "plan to process expeditiously some seven thousand Iraqi refugee referrals," which meant that two or three thousand Iraqis might be admitted to the United States by the end of the fiscal year. Finally, the administration would seek legislation to create a special immigrant visa for Iraqis who had worked for the U.S. embassy.

During the briefing, Ellen Sauerbrey, the assistant secretary of state for population, refugees, and migration, insisted, "There was really nothing that was indicating there was any significant issue in terms of outflow until—I would say the first real indication began to reach us three or four months ago." Speaking of Iraqi employees, she added, "The numbers of those that have actually been seeking either movement out of the country or requesting assistance have been—our own embassy has said it is a very small number." Sauerbrey put it at less than fifty.

The excuses were unconvincing, but the stirrings of action were encouraging. When Johnson, wearing the only suit he owned, took his list to Washington and dropped it off at the State Department and the UNHCR office, the response was welcoming. But he pressed officials for details on the fates of specific individuals: Would Yaghdan be able to register as a refugee in Dubai, where there was no UNHCR office, before he was forced to go back to Iraq? How could Ibrahim, trapped in Egypt without legal travel documents, qualify for a visa before his brain tumor killed him? Would Iraqis who had paid ransom to kidnappers be barred entry under the "material support" clause of the Patriot Act? (One embassy employee already had been.) How would Iraqis who had no Kirk Johnson to help them—the military interpreters, the embassy staff, the contractors, the drivers—be able to sign up as refugees or candidates for special immigrant visas? Would the U.S. government seek them out? Would they have to flee the country and find a UNHCR office first?

Thanks in part to Johnson's list, Washington was paying attention. Privately, though, a former USAID colleague told Johnson that his actions would send the message "that it's game over" in Iraq, and America would end up with a million and a half asylum seekers. Johnson feared that the ingrained habit of giving yes/no answers might lower the pressure without solving the problem. His list kept growing after he had delivered it to the U.S. government, and the desperation of those already on it grew as well. By mid-March, Iraqis on the list still had no mechanism for applying to immigrate. According to the State Department, a humanitarian visa for Ibrahim would take up to six months. And Yaghdan's situation was just as dire now as it was when Johnson had written his op-ed. "No matter what is said by the administration, if Yaghdan isn't being helped, then the government is not responding," Johnson told me.

For him, it was a simple matter. "This is the brink right now, where our partners over there are running for their lives," he said. "I defy anyone to give me the counterargument for why we shouldn't let these people in." He quoted something that President Gerald Ford once said about his decision to admit a hundred and thirty thousand Vietnamese after the fall of Saigon: "To do less would have added moral shame to humiliation."

Evacuation

In 2005, Al Jazeera aired a typically heavy-handed piece about the American evacuation from Saigon, in April 1975, rebroadcasting the famous footage of children and old people being pushed back by marines from the embassy gates and kicked or punched as they tried to climb onto helicopters. The message for Iraqis working with Americans was clear, and when some of those who worked at USAID saw the program they were horrified. The next day at work, a small group of them met to talk about it. "Al Jazeera has their own propaganda. Don't believe it," said Ibrahim, the Iraqi who is now hiding out in Cairo.

Hussein, the go-between in southern Iraq, had also begun to think about Vietnam. He had heard that America had left the Vietnamese behind, but he couldn't believe that the same thing would happen in Iraq. "We might be given a good chance to leave with them," he said. "I think about that, because history is telling me that they always have a moral obligation." To Hussein, the obligation was mutual, because he still felt indebted to the Americans for his freedom. I asked him what he would do if he found himself abandoned. Hussein thought about it, then said, "If I reach this point, and I am still alive when I see moral obligation taking the incorrect course, I will say, 'I paid my debt. I am free.'"

At the end of the Vietnam War, Frank Snepp was the CIA's chief analyst at the American embassy in Saigon. His 1977 book about the last days of the Vietnam War, *Decent Interval*, describes how the willful ignorance and political illusions of top U.S. officials prevented any serious planning for an evacuation of America's Vietnamese allies. Thousands were left to the mercy of the Communists. The book contains a photograph of the author, thirty-one at the time, standing on the bridge of the USS *Denver* in the South China Sea, three days after being evacuated from Saigon by helicopter. He is leaning against the rail, his tan, handsome face drawn taut as he stares slightly downward. Recently, I asked Snepp what he had been thinking when the picture was taken.

"I was overwhelmed with guilt," he said. "I kept hearing the voices on the CIA radios of our agents in the field, our Vietnamese friends we wouldn't be able to rescue. And I had to understand how I had been made a party to this. I had been brought up in the Old South, in a chivalric tradition that comes out of the Civil War—you do not abandon your own. And that's exactly what I had done. It hasn't left me to this day."

No conquering enemy army is days away from taking Baghdad; the city is slowly breaking up into smaller, isolated enclaves, and America's Iraqi allies are being executed one by one. It's hard to imagine the American presence in Iraq ending with a dramatic helo lift from a Green Zone landing pad. But in some ways, the unlikelihood of a spectacularly conclusive finale makes the situation of the Iraqis more perilous than that of the South Vietnamese. It's easier for the U.S. government to leave them to their fate while telling itself that "the good Iraqis" are needed to build the new Iraq.

American institutions in Vietnam were just as unresponsive as they are in Iraq, but on an individual level, Americans did far more to evacuate their Vietnamese counterparts. In Saigon they had girlfriends, wives, friends, whereas Americans and Iraqis have established only work relationships, which end when the Americans rotate out after six months or a year. In the wide-open atmosphere of Saigon, many officials, including Snepp, broke rules or risked their lives to save people close to them. Americans in Baghdad don't have such discipline problems. A former embassy official pointed out that cell phones and e-mail connect officials in Iraq to their bosses there or in Washington around the clock. "When you can always connect, you can always pass the buck," he said. For all their technology, the Americans in Baghdad know far less about the Iraqis than those in Saigon knew about the Vietnamese. "Intelligence is the first key to empathy," Snepp said.

I asked Snepp what he would say to Americans in Iraq today. "If they want to keep their conscience clean, they better start making lists of people they must help," he said. "They should also not be cautious in questioning their superiors, and that's a very hard thing to do in a rigid environment."

Richard Armitage, who was deputy secretary of state under Colin Powell during the first years of the Iraq War, served as a naval officer in Vietnam. In the last days of that war, he returned as a civilian, on a mission to destroy military assets before they fell into North Vietnamese hands. He arrived too late, and instead turned his energy to the evacuation of South Vietnamese sailors and their families. Armitage led a convoy of barely seaworthy boats, carrying twenty thousand people, a thousand

miles across the South China Sea to Manila—the first stop on their journey to the United States.

When I met Armitage recently, at his office in Arlington, Virginia, he
was not confident that Iraqis would be similarly resettled. "I guarantee
you no one's thinking about it now, because it's so fatalistic and you'd be
considered sort of a traitor to the president's policy," he said. "I don't see
us taking them in this time, because, notwithstanding what we may owe
people, you're not going to bring in large numbers of Arabs to the United
States, given the fact that for the last six years the president has scared
the pants off the American public with fears of Islamic terrorism."

Even at this stage of the war, Armitage said, officials at the White
House retain an "agnosticism about the size of the problem." He added,
"The president believes so firmly that he is president for just this mission—and there's something religious about it—that it will succeed, and
that kind of permeates. I just take him at his word these days. I think it's
very improbable that he'll be successful."

I was in Baghdad when the administration announced its new security
plan—including an effort to stabilize Baghdad with a "surge" of twenty
thousand additional troops. I spent a day with Lt. Col. Steven Miska, who
commands a small American base surrounded by a large Iraqi one in the
old-line Shia district of Kadhimiya. Everywhere we went, Iraqi civilians
asked him when the surge would begin. Two dozen men hanging out at a
sidewalk tea shop seemed to have the new strategy confused with the
Iraq Study Group Report; I took the mix-up to mean that they were desperate for any possible solution. A Shia potentate named Sheikh Muhammad Baqr gave me his version of the new plan over lunch at his house: the
Americans were trying to separate the 10 percent of the population that
belonged to extremist militias—whether Shia or Sunni—from what he
called the "silent majority." If families evicted from mixed areas could be
convinced to return to their homes, and if unemployed young men could
be put to work, the plan had a chance of restoring confidence in the
Americans. The sheikh warned, "In six months you will have to see this
plan work, or else the Iraqi people will tell the Americans to find another
venue." The sheikh had even less faith in the government of Prime Minister Nuri al-Maliki, which he called a collection of "sectarian movements"

brought to power by American folly. "We don't need democracy," he said. "We need General Pinochet in Chile or General Franco in Spain. After they clear the country, we'll have elections."

Lieutenant Colonel Miska, for his part, described the security plan as an attempt to get Americans off the big bases and into Iraqi neighborhoods, where they would occupy small combat outposts on the fault lines of sectarian conflicts and, for the first time, make the protection of civilians a central goal. The new plan represented a repudiation of the strategy that the administration had pursued for the past two years—the handover of responsibility to Iraqi security forces as Americans pulled out of the cities. President Bush had chosen a new commander in Iraq, General David Petraeus, who recently oversaw the writing of the new Army and Marine Corps counterinsurgency manual. Petraeus has surrounded himself with a brain trust of counterinsurgency experts: Col. H. R. McMaster, who two years ago executed a nearly identical strategy in the northern city of Tal Afar; Col. Peter Mansoor; and David Kilcullen, an Australian strategist working at the State Department. Bush named Timothy Carney, a retired ambassador, to be his reconstruction czar in Iraq; Carney had left the Coalition Provisional Authority in disgust after seeing Bremer make mistake after mistake. After four years of displaying resolve while the war was being lost, the president has turned things over to a group of soldiers and civilians who have been steadfast critics of his strategy. It is almost certainly too late.

In Baghdad, among Iraqi civilians and American soldiers, it's impossible not to want to give the new strategy a try. The alternative, as Iraqis constantly point out, is a much greater catastrophe. "I'm still hoping Bush's new plan can do something," Othman told me. In the weeks after the surge was announced, there were anecdotal reports of Shia and Sunni families returning to their homes. But even if this tentative progress continues, three major obstacles remain. The first is the breakdown of U.S. ground forces, in manpower and equipment; it isn't clear that the strategy can be sustained for more than six months—nowhere near enough time to repair the physical and social destruction of Baghdad.

The second obstacle was described to me by an international official who has spent the past three years in Iraq. "The success of the American strategy is based on a premise that is fundamentally flawed," he said. "The premise is that the U.S. and Iraqi governments are working toward the same goal. It's simply not the case." Shia politicians, the official said, want "to hold on to their majority as long as they can." Their interest isn't democracy but power. Meanwhile, Sunni politicians want "to say no to everything," the official said; the insurgency is politically intractable.

Finally, there is the collapse of political support at home. Most Americans have lost faith in the leadership and conduct of the war, and they want to be rid of it. More important than all the maneuverings in Congress, at the White House, and among the presidential candidates is the fact that nobody wants to deal with Iraq anymore. The columnist Charles Krauthammer, the most ardent of neoconservative hawks, has found someone to blame for the war's failure: the Iraqis. He recently wrote, "We midwifed their freedom. They chose civil war." John Edwards, the Democratic presidential candidate, is also tired of Iraqis. "We've done our part, and now it's time for them to step up to the plate," he recently told this magazine. "When they're doing it to each other, and America's not there and not fomenting the situation, I think the odds are better of the place stabilizing." America is pulling away from Iraq in the fitful, irritable manner of someone trying to wake up from an unpleasant sleep. On my last day in Baghdad, I had lunch with an embassy official, and as we were leaving the restaurant he suddenly said, "Do you think this is all going to seem like a dream? Is it just going to be a fever dream that we'll wake up from and say, 'We got into this crazy war, but now it's over and we never have to think about Iraq again'?" If so, part of our legacy will be thousands of Iraqis who, because they joined the American effort, can no longer live in their own country.

Othman and Laith are still in Baghdad. Earlier this month, Othman spent more than two thousand dollars on passports for his mother, his two younger brothers, and himself. He is hoping to move the family to Syria. Laith wants to find a job in Kurdistan.

Firas, Ali, and Ahmed are now in Sweden. All three of them would have preferred to go to America. Ali had spent his childhood in the United States; Ahmed was fascinated with American politics; Firas never felt more at home than he had on their training trip, listening to jazz in Greenwich Village. Like all Iraqis who worked with Americans, they spoke in

American accents, using American idioms. Ahmed delighted in using phrases like "from the horse's mouth" and "hung out to dry."

I asked Firas why he hadn't tried to get a visa to the United States. "And what would I do with it?" he said.

"Ask for asylum."

"Do you think they would give me an asylum in the U.S.? Never."

"Why?"

"For the U.S. to give an asylum for an Iraqi, it means they have failed in Iraq."

This wasn't entirely true. Recently, Iraqis who made it to America have begun filing petitions for asylum, and, because they undoubtedly face a reasonable fear of harm back home, a few of them have been accepted. A much larger number of Iraqis are still waiting to learn their fates: USAID employees who jumped ship on training trips to Washington; Fulbright scholars who have been informed by the State Department that they have to go back to Iraq after their two- or three-year scholarships end, even if a job or another degree program is available to them in America. The U.S. government, for which Firas worked for three and a half years, had given him ample reason to believe that he could never become an American. Still, if he had somehow made it here, there is a chance that he could have stayed.

Instead, he is trying to become a Swede. I met him one recent winter morning in Malmö, a city of eighteenth-century storefronts and modern industrial decay at the southern tip of Sweden, just across the Öresund Strait from Copenhagen. He was waiting to hear the result of his asylum petition while living with Ahmed in a refugee apartment building that was rapidly filling up with Iraqis. Since the war began, nearly twenty thousand Iraqis had arrived in the country. Firas was granted asylum in February.

Sweden amazed Firas: the silence of passengers on trains; the intolerance for smoking; the motorists that wait for you to cross the street, as if they were trying to embarrass you with courtesy. When I joked that he would be bored living here, he laughed grimly and said, "Good. I want to be like other people—normal. How long before I can be afraid or shocked? There is nothing that makes me afraid or shocked anymore."

We walked from the train station to the Turning Torso, a new apartment tower, designed by Santiago Calatrava, that twists ninety degrees on its axis as it rises fifty-four stories into the slate-gray sky, and drank Swedish

Pilsners at the Torso Bar and Lounge. When the Americans came to Iraq, four years ago, Firas felt that he could finally begin his life. Now, at thirty-five, he was starting over yet again.

I asked him if he felt betrayed by America.

"I have this nature—I don't expect a lot from people," Firas said. "Not betrayed, no, not disappointed. I can never blame the Americans alone. It's the Iraqis who destroyed their country, with the help of the Americans, under the American eye." I was about to say that he deserved better, but Firas was lost in thought. "Until this moment," he said, "I dream about America."

Over Here

World Affairs, Winter 2008

One day in the summer of 2004, while I sat in the western Baghdad studio of Radio Dijla, Iraq's first all-talk station, listening to a deputy interior minister being interviewed, a man named Haithem called in. His story sounded garbled and frantic: late at night bandits had forced him off an unlit highway overpass, destroying his car, crushing his chest against the steering wheel, and shattering his leg. After twelve hours, American soldiers found him under the highway and called the Iraqi police, who stole his money and gun before loading him into an ambulance. The next day I went looking for Haithem in a modest neighborhood in eastern Baghdad. He lay sweating in a dark room, a radio and phone by the bed, sunlight burning around the window curtain. There was a towel wrapped around Haithem's waist, and his bandaged knee was held in traction by metal pins and a primitive sack of bricks, sand, and lead weights that hung from a wire over the bed frame. It looked as if torture, not healing, was going on in Haithem's room.

As it happened, the same leg had been fractured by Saddam's secret police in 1992. This latest injury seemed to have broken Haithem's will; he said that he'd attempted suicide by sticking his finger into the power strip on the floor. "I have no manhood right now, I can't feel my manhood. I'm asking you through the spirit of brotherhood to help me find compensation. I'm desperate—I have three children, how can I raise them, what can I do for them? I took money from my brother for cigarettes—it's killing me to say this. I don't want to go to charities as a beggar. I want to be a human being, and I want a human being in front of me who can give me my rights. I want any person to come and help me just like the Americans did—just for anyone to come here and help me as a human being."

As for the American soldiers, he was still marveling at their kindness. This was his second encounter with Americans; the first occurred a month earlier and did not go well. On that night, he had been careening down a side street at high speed when a Humvee emerged from the darkness. Unsurprisingly, Haithem ended up on the ground with soldiers screaming at him. But the Americans who heard his cries from under the highway were different; they offered him water and spent an hour dressing his wound. "This latest accident changed everything for me. I understood not everyone is the same. The soldier who treated me—the last thing he said as they put me in the ambulance was, 'Don't cry, you won't die,' and he wiped my tears. I never got the name of the soldier, and I'm sorry about that."

In Haithem's telling, the story became a parable of how some things had changed in Iraq while other, more fundamental truths had not. Ordinary Iraqis could now complain to a deputy interior minister on a call-in radio show, and the official might order his men to follow up; but the police were as corrupt as ever, the hospital care just as indifferent. Americans had humiliated Haithem and Americans had shown him humanity. But the Americans could not give Haithem the justice he craved. There would be no happy ending for him.

The Iraq War introduced entirely new kinds of cruelty to the world, so it's strange how many of my memories are of kindness. I often think of Abu Malik, a bearded, imposing man, his leather coat buttoned tight across his chest. Abu Malik would have been a frightening sight at a militia checkpoint in Sadr City, but whenever I came to stay with friends at the *New York Times* compound on the east bank of the Tigris, where he was chief of security, Abu Malik threw his arms around me, kissed my cheeks, and told me, in the openly tender way of Iraqi men, how much all the security guards had missed me. The last time I saw Abu Malik, a family I knew in Baghdad had just received a death threat and was trying to find a safe route out of their besieged neighborhood and then out of the country. Abu Malik, whose house was near the family's, got on the phone and offered these complete strangers safe passage to the airport.

I think of Muna, a social worker whose husband disappeared under Baath Party rule. In early 2004, she began a weekly therapy group in an abandoned building. Her patients had all been punished by the former regime and a judicial system that indelibly marked the bodies of army deserters, nonvoters, and those who spoke ill of the authorities. Some had their ears sliced off, their tongues cut out, their hands severed; others had their faces tattooed with derogatory symbols. They all called her "Mama" and she called them "my sons." "Even the child on the street looks at them and makes fun of them," Muna said. "This is a great humiliation for a human being. If he were dead it would be better. If his son asks him, 'What happened to your ear?' what is he supposed to say? If he wants to marry a girl, her family will say, 'We can't give you our daughter—you're a criminal.' For one and a half hours they talk and cry, until they get relief. Then they all laugh together."

Finally, I think of Steve Miska, an Army lieutenant colonel. On his second tour, as the surge got under way, Miska was in command of a small base in an old Shiite neighborhood in northern Baghdad. The area had fallen largely under the control of the Mahdi Army, and Miska's troops spent much of their time going house to house in search of fighters and weapons. But Miska also spent a lot of his time—more and more as his tour ground on—arranging passage out of the country for the unit's Iraqi interpreters. The interpreters constantly received death threats, and once the Americans were gone, they would be easy prey. Miska understood that their fate would, in a sense, be a verdict on the war, and he likened his effort, which involved running a gauntlet of Iraqi insurgents, Jordanian border officials, and American bureaucrats, to an "underground railroad." A few of the interpreters even managed to get visas to the United States.

In wartime Iraq, perhaps in most wars, viciousness and generosity were never far apart. The menace in the streets of Baghdad was always overwhelming—the suspicious piles of roadside garbage, the dark sedans casing other cars, the checkpoint that wasn't there thirty minutes ago, the hard stares in traffic, the hair trigger of American gunners, the heedless SUV convoys, and the explosions that always seemed to happen three streets away. In this national ruin, any act of kindness, even as small as offering someone a ride, created solidarity. You were always meeting someone who had run out of options, and someone else who would risk far more to help than he would in normal times. Perhaps it was part of their culture, and perhaps these were not normal times, but Iraqis lacked the sense of shame about heartfelt declarations and naked emotions that people in more secure, better functioning places possess naturally. All of this made them harsh and lovable, and it was possible to spend an hour with Haithem or Muna, or to see Abu Malik once every six months, and feel that more human business had been transacted than over a hundred New York lunches or dinners. The same was true of soldiers with whom I would have had nothing to discuss back at home. Without these connections, Iraq would have been unbearable.

I linger on these memories because they capture something elusive and hard to describe that was nonetheless a signature of the war. The American invasion of Iraq was, above all else, a revolution in the lives of Iraqis. Their institutions, their everyday routines, their futures, their sense of order were all turned upside down. This revolution, which is still ongoing and will play out for years to come, was the opening of a prison. When they staggered out into the light, most Iraqis didn't know where they were, what they wanted, even who they were, and the Americans who had so quickly and casually broken down the gate were standing around as if they had never even considered what to do next. The Americans were nominally in charge—the Iraqis expected them to be, and after the first few weeks of paralysis, the Americans flung themselves into a flurry of activities befitting an occupying power—but it was all illusion. No one was in charge. By the summer of 2003, when I first went to Iraq, it was clear that a void had opened up and the best-armed and most ruthless groups had moved in. Although it went through many phases and assumed a variety of forms, the process of mutual disenchantment between Iraqis and Americans began early. It was this process that interested me most about Iraq, because it went to the human heart of the matter: the experience of suffering, hope, illusion, need, violence, and disappointment that transformed both sides and made the war so painful for each.

These may be clichés for anyone who has spent much time in Iraq, or in any country at war. And yet here at home they have been almost impossible to convey. In the United States, the war is an abstraction that routinely shades into caricature. For all the television news coverage, Americans have the slimmest sense of what the war actually feels and looks like—crumbling deserts, blasted buildings, angry crowds, random firefights. The image of Iraq is flickering and formless. Each year of the war seems like the last, and the patrols and meetings with Iraqis that soldiers conduct every day don't make for good television ratings. With the exception of Falluja, there have been no memorable battles. The mundane character of counterinsurgency, the fact that journalists have become targets, and the media's sheer lack of imagination have combined to make this most covered of modern wars one of the least vivid. Iraq is more remote in our consciousness than Vietnam ever was. It has been strangely difficult for Americans even to picture the place. I've been asked more times than I can remember, "What does it look like over there?" If you think of World War II or Vietnam, a dozen photographs immediately come to mind. But Iraq has not been a photographer's war. What are its iconic images? Digital snapshots by military policemen in Abu Ghraib, footage of beheadings posted by jihadis on the Web. There was no shortage of superb photographers taking extraordinary risks in Iraq, and perhaps time will sort from their work a handful of images that will define this war in the same way that, for example, Robert Capa's photographs of Omaha Beach and Nick Ut's of children fleeing napalm defined earlier ones. But almost five years into this war, there is only blank space where America's picture of Iraq should be.

The problem here is not entirely visual. Iraq's remoteness also derives from the politics of the war, and from the political culture of contemporary America at war. The fighting only ever affected a tiny fraction of the public directly. The administration, which never leveled with the country about the potential costs and risks of the enterprise beforehand, tried to keep the war quiet by declaring victory prematurely, refusing to allow pictures of flag-draped caskets arriving at Dover Air Force Base, keeping silent when large numbers of soldiers were killed. The all-volunteer military bought the administration a year or two of goodwill before public opinion began to turn. The façade collapsed when the nation began to realize, around the time New Orleans was underwater, that the war was going badly. There was no reason to follow the president into the mouth of hell, and public support, which had always been thin, disintegrated almost overnight.

Unlike Vietnam, where the arguments became truly poisonous only after a few years of fighting, the Iraq War was born in dispute. The administration's deceptions, exaggerations, and always-evolving rationales provoked a counternarrative that mirrored the White House version of the war in its simplemindedness: the war was about nothing (except greed,

empire, and blind folly). Once, after a trip to Iraq, I attended a dinner
party in Los Angeles at which most of the other guests were movie types.
They wanted to know what it was like "over there." I began to describe a
Shiite doctor I'd gotten to know, who felt torn between gratitude and fear
that occupation and chaos were making Iraq less Islamic. A burst of in-
vective interrupted my sketch: none of it mattered—the only thing that
mattered was this immoral, criminal war. The guests had no interest in
hearing what it was like over there. They already knew.

So the lines were drawn from the start. To the pro-war side, criticism
was animated by partisanship and defeatism, if not treason. This view,
amplified on cable news, talk radio, and right-wing blogs, was tacitly encouraged by the White House. It kept a disastrous defense secretary in
office long after it was obvious that he was losing the war, ensured that no
senior officer was held accountable for military setbacks, and contributed
to the repetition of disastrous errors by the war's political architects.
Meanwhile, the fact that the best and brightest Iraqis were being slaughtered by a ruthless insurgency never aroused much interest or sympathy
among the war's opponents. The kind of people who would ordinarily inspire solidarity campaigns among Western progressives—trade unionists,
journalists, human rights advocates, women's rights activists, independent politicians, doctors, professors—were being systematically extermi-
nated. But since the war shouldn't have been fought in the first place,
what began badly must also end badly.

Each side picked and chose from its own catalogue of facts, and one's
opinion about everything from body armor to body counts was decided
accordingly. This exposed journalists covering the war to the never-ending
wrath of one side or the other. A friend who went in with the Marines
during the assault on Falluja in November 2004 paused one night in
an abandoned house, with mortars landing outside, and downloaded his
e-mail using a satellite modem. Pro-war readers had filled his in-box with
angry complaints that he was concealing the progress of the Marines—
the "mainstream media" was too lazy and unpatriotic to get off its ass and
go find the war. Conservative radio host Laura Ingraham accused journalists of missing all the good news because they never left their hotel rooms.
(Paul Wolfowitz said something similar; afterward, he issued his first and
only apology of the Iraq War.) Press critics on the left made essentially
the same charge from the opposite end: Michael Massing of *The New*

York Review of Books argued in 2004 that journalists echoed the official line because they were too frightened, linguistically incompetent, or incurious to go out and talk to Iraqis.

The Iraq War had its share of bad or indifferent journalism. But there was a huge distinction between the failure to expose the administration's falsehoods prior to the war and the effort to report the truth in Iraq once it began. The press redeemed in Baghdad what it had botched in Washington. If the names of the war's best reporters aren't widely known today and will never be recalled alongside their legendary predecessors in Vietnam, it's partly because the public—especially the portion of it that generates and consumes opinion on a regular basis—is less susceptible to the power of complex facts than it was in 1963.

The Iraq War coincided with a revolution in technology that allowed soldiers to disseminate digital images of missions within hours of completing them, a cable network to provide around-the-clock criticism of a rival network's war coverage, and reclusive twentysomethings to register their reactions every seventeen minutes on their blogs (and become influential commentators at the same time). The flood of information and commentary resulted in an intense, irritable, balkanized view of the war, but not a clearer view. The same combat that partisans waged over impeachment and the Florida recount found its latest battlefield in Iraq, where the American political debate was largely irrelevant and quickly became an impediment to understanding.

Two concurrent examples from the summer of 2007 offer case studies. First, a soldier on a base in Baghdad writes a pseudonymous dispatch for *The New Republic* that describes minor atrocities committed by him or others in his unit—mocking a disfigured woman in a dining hall, wearing a piece of a child's skull on his head, running over dogs while out on patrol. Pro-war journalists and bloggers deride the piece as fraudulent and antimilitary; officers in Iraq join them. The magazine reveals the identity of the soldier, provides a bit of corroborating evidence, and hunkers down. The pro-war side keeps firing away. The magazine eventually concedes; it cannot stand by the soldier's writings.

Second, two center-left think tank analysts return from a trip to Iraq and declare in an op-ed that the surge has produced military successes. Within minutes of being posted online, the op-ed appears in my e-mail in-box courtesy of a White House political strategist. By the next morning, antiwar journalists and bloggers are in full cry, deriding the piece as credulous, dishonest, and self-serving. Republican politicians, including the vice president, celebrate the op-ed; pro-war journalists and bloggers denounce the denouncers.

Readers who believed the first story refused to believe the second. Readers who believed the second refused to believe the first. In a sense, they believed or refused to believe each story before it was published, even before it occurred. There wasn't a moment's pause to digest information, much less to weigh facts dispassionately; objectivity wasn't even an aspiration. What mattered was whether the facts supported the theory or not. Throughout the opinion classes, the impulse to keep a little part of the brain open to inconvenient facts seemed to have been extinguished. In magazine offices, bloggers' bedrooms, Hollywood studios, and the White House, a fantasy war was under way, a demonstration of American virtue or a series of crimes against humanity—both of them self-serving fictions.

Anyone who bothered to read *The New Republic* or op-ed accounts knew that each probably contained a kernel of truth. War coarsens soldiers; almost two divisions' worth of combat power makes a difference. These claims are not extraordinary, except to highly educated people engaged in furious verbal combat eight thousand miles away. I find this even more depressing than the thought of Bradley Fighting Vehicles running over stray dogs.

Philip Carter, an Army captain whom I met in Baquba in 2006, wrote of *The New Republic*'s soldier-correspondent, "Anyone who finds Beauchamp's story incredible merely because it's upsetting has no idea what war can do." But Carter went on to say:

> The Beauchamp dispatches show the extent to which the discourse over Iraq has been poisoned and how quickly the left, the right, and the military were willing to go to the mat to defend their version of what is—or what they thought ought to be—true. No one cares anymore about the troops, the truth of their reports from Iraq, or the serious issues of professional journalism associated with a series of this type. The troops have become pawns in this debate; their stories a kind of Rorschach test that reveals more about how we view the war than its reality on the ground.

The tone of Carter's piece was revealing. It lacked the fury of the partisan arguments over Iraq. This was not a sign of his indifference—just the opposite. The noise of the polemics betrayed how little the polemicists had at stake.

The Iraq War has had only the slightest effect on American culture, including pop culture. No war anthems have caught on; neither "Ballad of the Green Berets" nor "I-Feel-Like-I'm-Fixin'-To-Die Rag" has been revised for Iraq. (Neil Young's record *Living with War* enjoyed a brief vogue, mostly among fans well beyond military age.) Iraq makes a short appearance in Ian McEwan's novel *Saturday*, when a father and daughter argue over an antiwar demonstration in London; Nicholson Baker's thin novel *Checkpoint* is an imagined dialogue in a Washington hotel room between two old friends, one of whom is obsessed with a shooting incident at an American checkpoint in Iraq and considers assassinating President Bush. In each novel, Iraq is only a distant rumor, quickly dispatched. *Saturday* doesn't pretend to be about the war; *Checkpoint*, which does, is an emission of toxic political gas, not an attempt at genuine engagement. As for movies, the best American works are two documentaries by filmmakers who, at considerable risk, spent a great deal of time among Iraqis and created intimate, subtle portraits against the backdrop of war: Laura Poitras's *My Country, My Country* and James Longley's *Iraq in Fragments*. Both films earned critical praise and prize nominations, but nothing resembling their visions appears in the more widely distributed feature films about Iraq.

Several films about the war have been released over the past year, all of them "based on actual events." *The Situation*, which didn't receive wide distribution, tells the story of a young American journalist who falls in love with an Iraqi photographer and attempts to untangle what happened when U.S. soldiers pushed two Iraqi suspects into the Tigris River. *In the Valley of Elah* is set entirely on the home front: the hard-bitten father of a soldier whose unit has just returned from Iraq learns that his son has gone AWOL and conducts his own investigation, which leads to shattering discoveries about the son, his son's buddies, and the war. And Brian de Palma's *Redacted* revolves around the most heinous incident of abuse by American soldiers in the war, the rape of an Iraqi girl and the murder of her and her family. The movie, which purports to tell the story "authentically" through a variety of verité camera lenses, indicts the media for its supposed complicity in war crimes. De Palma told a press conference at the Venice Film Festival that his intention was to end the war by showing images that, in his telling, no one in America sees. "The movie is an attempt to bring the reality of what is happening in Iraq to the American people," he declared. That reality turns out to be an aesthetically self-conscious snuff film that mixes fact with fiction and makes no attempt to get the details of Iraq right.

Two of these films do have merits—*In the Valley of Elah* features an affecting performance by Tommy Lee Jones, and *The Situation*, written by Wendell Steavenson, a British writer who spent over a year in occupied Iraq, contains two more or less recognizable Iraqi characters. But the films also present the war as incomprehensible mayhem, and they depict American soldiers as psychopaths who may as well be wearing SS uniforms. The GIs rape, burn, and mutilate corpses, torture detainees, accelerate a vehicle to run over a boy playing soccer, wantonly kill civilians and journalists in firefights, humiliate one another, and coolly record their own atrocities for entertainment. Have these things happened in Iraq? Many have. But in the cinematic version of the war, these are the only things that happen in Iraq. At a screening of *The Situation*, I was asked to discuss the film with its director, Philip Haas. Why had he portrayed the soldiers in cartoon fashion, I wondered. Why had he missed their humor, their fear, their tenderness for one another and even, every now and then, for Iraqis? Because, Haas said, he wanted to concentrate on humanizing his Iraqi characters instead.

It's curious that the Vietnam War, during which some Americans demonized soldiers, generated a number of movies that depict military personnel as thinking, feeling human beings, capable of committing terrible deeds but also possessed of insight, sorrow, and even redemption. Iraq, the war in which everyone loudly supports the troops, has produced a film genre that systematically dehumanizes them. I doubt these filmmakers truly regard American servicemen as moral degenerates. Instead, they treat soldiers as abstractions, empty canvases onto which the filmmakers can project their own fantasies about the war. And because filmmakers believe the war, with its shifting and mendacious rationales, its rabid politicization, and its extreme violence, to be about nothing, the soldiers in their movies must also be filled with nothing. The GIs don't find their belief in the mission undermined by incompetent leadership, their empathy for suffering Iraqis worn down by frustration, their best efforts gone to waste. They are killing machines that destroy and are destroyed.

A falsely justified and poorly waged war hardly deserves the excuse of good intentions. Iraq was a folly and a failure of the kind that happens once every few generations and leaves consequences for generations to come. The war swept up millions of lives, changing them in ways that were impossible for anyone to predict. In the summer of 2003, Iraq was volatile and fluid, and no one who knew anything knew what would come next. Some Iraqis spoke of a better future coming in six months or a year. Three years later, the better future had receded far into the distance: hunkered down in Baghdad or exiled in Damascus, Iraqis spoke of fifteen years.

By then the war was not about nothing. No war ever is. I don't know where Haithem and Muna and the others are today—some of them might well be among the Iraqis I know to be dead—but for them, the war had a meaning. It meant a chance to live a decent life, something that had never been remotely possible and remains a dream even today. The war began as folly; it became a tragedy when the hopes and lives of Iraqis and Americans began to be expended by the thousands.

"I can never blame the Americans alone," an Iraqi refugee named Firas told me in early 2007. "It's the Iraqis who destroyed their country, with the help of the Americans, under the American eye." To gain this wisdom, Firas had to lose almost everything. What would it take for Americans to understand what Firas already does? A recognition that Iraq was everyone's loss, whichever side you were on.

PART TWO

Trouble Spots

The Children of Freetown

The New Yorker, January 13, 2003

Every day, Americans are confronted with news of horrors throughout the world that seem both vividly intimate and impossibly distant; helpless outrage is a characteristic emotion of the global age. On an October afternoon three years ago, a New Yorker named Matthew Mirones was glancing through the *Times*'s "Week in Review" section when he came upon a photo essay on war amputees in Freetown, the capital of Sierra Leone, on the West African coast. A boy, his right arm gone to the shoulder, was being bathed by his mother. A man, missing both hands, was trying to write his name with the hook of an artificial arm. A teenage girl, also a double amputee, was lying at the water's edge with her stumps glistening in the surf. Mirones, who had never heard of this war—and had barely heard of Sierra Leone—felt the hair on his arms stand up.

Amputation has been the signature atrocity of Sierra Leone's civil war, which went on for eleven years and ended last January. The most credible estimates of the number of war amputees that I heard ranged from two thousand to four thousand, with perhaps twice that many dead from their wounds. (The Western press usually puts the number of war amputees at twenty thousand.) Whatever the number, reports and photographs of civilians—many of them children—missing ears, lips, legs, and hands finally drew international attention to the long-neglected war and played a role in bringing it to an end.

As Mirones read, he felt acute shame, and a rising excitement. Mirones is a prosthetist—he makes artificial limbs. "I said, 'This is my profession, and I'm not aware of this—that people are being disfigured?'" he told me recently. "Before I even finished the article, in my mind I said, 'I've got to try to do something here. I mean, I know I could help these people.'"

Mirones, a small man with a highly mobile face dominated by a black mustache, is a forty-six-year-old bachelor. Though he now lives on Staten Island, his speech and manner remain in Brooklyn, the borough where he was born, grew up, and has his main office, on a lively, seedy downtown street, next to a wig shop advertising 100% HUMAN HAIR.

Mirones's grandfather was a village cobbler on the Greek island of Chios. Mirones's father, Aristotle, immigrated to Brooklyn after the Second World War and set up a small prosthetics company called Arimed, below the apartment on Atlantic Avenue where Mirones spent his early years, three blocks from the firm's current headquarters. Mirones grew up in the business; by the age of seven, he was making deliveries around downtown Brooklyn, holding shopping bags at shoulder level to keep them from dragging on the pavement. When older kids surrounded him and tried to steal the leg braces and shoe inserts, he would talk his way out of trouble in the quick, ingratiating, street-smart manner that he still uses.

When Mirones speaks of his patients, a nervous physical empathy takes over, and his face and body get involved in the exaggerated way of a mime: his eyes narrow in pain, his mouth stretches out and down, his torso collapses against the desk as his whole arm up to the shoulder is pulled into a recycling machine; his ankle buckles and he slips into the jolting hobble of a diabetic who has lost sensation in his feet.

Mirones trained at New York University, and is an American board–certified prosthetist, a qualification that enabled him to greatly expand Arimed's operations and increase its sophistication. Yet he still can't help using the word "stump." "We call it a residual, not a stump," he corrects himself, for my benefit, but a minute later he uses the word again. "This is Mr. Montoya," he says, picking up the plaster model of a stump lying on a worktable in Arimed's second-floor lab. (Mr. Montoya's lower right leg was shot off by narcotics traffickers in the Medellín, Colombia, airport.) The lab looks like the studio of a sculptor in the grip of a macabre vision of the lower extremities.

It was not as a professional humanitarian with global ideas but as a small businessman, an outer-borough Republican, and a craftsman that Mirones decided to involve himself in an African calamity. His purpose, he said, was "to integrate the concept of life with disability over there, so that people will be more willing to accept their disability and work with what they have and use the devices to be self-sufficient." He decided that he would bring a small group of child amputees to New York, fit them with prostheses, train the children in using them, and then send them home to be "beacons of hope" to a desperate population.

Mirones approached several large nongovernmental organizations, or NGOs, such as the Red Cross, but found them unhelpful. "Everyone had to go through committee, and 'We'll bring it up at our annual or semi-annual or next quarter's meeting,'" he said. It affronted his can-do business sense and his idea of self-reliance. "I just felt that the more focused I stayed, the leaner and cleaner I stayed, the fewer people involved, I probably could be more effective."

But if he was going to bring a group of Sierra Leonean amputees to New York, Mirones would need help, and he looked for it in his own community. Staten Island University Hospital agreed to give free surgery and medical care. Local Rotary Clubs, led by a print shop owner named Joe Mandarino, agreed to organize food, housing, and transportation. The story of mutilated children seemed to render any objections moot. And as long as the children remained an abstraction, everyone who signed on to Mirones's idea wanted the same thing: to help.

Sierra Leone's civil war began in 1991, when a cashiered army corporal and itinerant photographer named Foday Sankoh brought a group of a hundred fighters, called the Revolutionary United Front, across the Liberian border and into the eastern jungles. The men had been trained in Libya, and the rebellion was backed by Charles Taylor, who was fighting his own war in Liberia. (He was elected president in 1997.) Sierra Leone's diamond mines fueled the RUF's operations—stones were smuggled out through Liberia, and weapons, mostly small arms, entered the same way—and the rebellion early on lost any claim to a purpose higher than organized crime.

Yet a number of people in Sierra Leone told me that they had initially welcomed the news of a rebellion. "All of us, we were waiting for this spark," Dennis Bright, a professor of French who works with street boys in Freetown, said. Three decades after independence from the British, the regime in power was hopelessly corrupt and utterly indifferent to the de-

spair of a generation of young people without prospects. The élite in Freetown sent their children out of the country; the economy was controlled,
almost entirely off the books, by an alliance of Western companies, Lebanese middlemen, and venal officials. "I describe this thing that has happened to us as a new kind of war," Bright said. It transcended any ethnic
or religious basis; it had no coherent ideology; it was largely a war of children and youth. "Somebody comes with some political thing and says the
thing is ready to happen," Bright went on. "But when it starts, the venom
itself surpasses whatever political thing might have sparked it. This is why
the vandalism, the unbridled terror, are just expressions of people being
left out. This is the injustice of the war. The perpetrators can get only
those they can reach. The poor people are doubly victims."

When the RUF began brutally targeting civilians, the rebellion lost
whatever chance of support it might have had among most Sierra Leoneans and the outside world. In 1996, in an election that was the freest
in the country's history, a United Nations official named Ahmad Tejan
Kabbah became president. His slogan, "The future is in your hands,"
prompted the first rash of amputations by the RUF, who told their victims
to ask the president for new hands. But the majority of the war's atrocities
took place in two campaigns of terror. The first, in early 1998, followed a
coup that temporarily overthrew Kabbah and replaced him with an alliance between elements of the armed forces and the RUF, who increasingly had come to resemble each other. (It's a common mistake to attribute
all the war's atrocities against civilians to the rebels; many of the worst
were committed by the Sierra Leone army.) When Nigerian-led peacekeeping troops drove the junta out of Freetown, in February 1998, and
restored the ineffectual Kabbah, soldiers and rebels in the north and east
went on a rampage. It was called Operation Pay Yourself. Whatever the
men with guns could get, they were entitled to keep.

Muctar Jalloh, a man in his early twenties, had come to the town of
Koidu, in the east, to dig for diamonds with his uncle. Jalloh had been a
student in the north, but his family needed money and he had to leave
high school and try to earn a living in the dangerous diamond business.
When Operation Pay Yourself hit the region, he, his uncle, his uncle's
wife, and their two children fled into the bush. There they stayed for two
months, foraging for food, hiding from rebels who sometimes passed within
twenty feet of them. The children's legs swelled for lack of salt. Jalloh had

been a Boy Scout, and he used his compass, water bottle, and knife to help the group survive, but eventually he got rid of his kit for fear of being caught and suspected of being a soldier. In a notebook, he recorded each day's activities: went east, southeast, searched for food, saw rebels and dashed. He called what he was writing "Struggle in the Bush."

Then Jalloh and his family heard that Nigerian troops had recaptured Koidu. On the morning of April 19, they decided to risk going home, but on the road they fell into a trap. About thirty rebel soldiers, mostly teenagers, were hiding behind trees. They burned Jalloh's possessions: his Scout ID, his school jacket, trousers, and tie, a paperback novel he'd taken from an abandoned village while searching for food, and "Struggle in the Bush." Then they hogtied him on a stick suspended between a tree and a rock. All afternoon, the rebels brought in more civilian prisoners. Jalloh watched as, one after another, six men were beheaded in front of him. He was told that he would be the seventh.

"I knew I'm going there," Jalloh recalled. "The way he was, I will be here soon." Jalloh thought about his mother and how he would die before he could help her. A Muslim, he prayed, "Oh, God, if this is the way, forgive my sins. Lord, this is the way you destined for my death. Okay, I thank you for that."

At some point, the commander, whose nom de guerre was Savage, sent a soldier off in the direction of a noise, with orders to bring back human hearts. The soldier returned with a sack of them, and others cooked and ate them. Jalloh found himself "trying to die."

Five hours later, the rebels untied Jalloh and took him to a felled mango tree. When he realized that they intended to cut off his hand, Jalloh laid his left arm on the tree and begged, "Please cut my left hand. I'm a student. My right hand is my future." A rebel hit his left hand with the back of a machete, and said, "This is not the hand I want. If you fail to put your right hand, I'm going to kill you." Jalloh was struck in the head with a gun butt and a machete. The rebels ordered his uncle to hold down Jalloh's right arm. Jalloh told his uncle that he wasn't to blame.

A sharp machete delivered the first hard blow. Jalloh got to his feet, thinking it was over, but his hand was still partially attached a few inches above the wrist. Rebels held his arm against a tree and began hacking, but now they were using a duller machete, and it required many blows to cut through the bone. Commander Savage fired a shot at the uncle's right hand and had it severed. Machetes hacked at Jalloh's thigh and shoulder, and then someone cut off his right ear. He lost consciousness.

When he came to, the rest of the family had scattered. (A year later, Jalloh learned that his uncle had managed to run off, but his wife and their two children had been abducted by the rebels. The wife became the possession of a young rebel; the four-year-old boy was conscripted as a porter; and the baby, when he wouldn't stop crying, was thrown into a latrine and died.) Jalloh staggered a few feet, until shooting started, and then he hid under a tree ("which the Lord used for my safety") as bullets showered around him. Darkness was falling, and it had begun to rain. "The rebels stayed awhile and went away, and I managed to walk and stay in a broken house," he recalled. There he spent a painful, sleepless night.

The next day, still bleeding, he walked five miles and finally met Nigerian troops, who bound his wounds. Two weeks later, his stump swollen and infested with maggots, he and a number of other wounded people were taken by armed convoy to Freetown for surgery, and were placed in refugee camps around the city. Jalloh was in despair. He told me, "I know what my hand did for me whenever I think of my writing, because I love writing. I love to take pen and write whatever I want, just write, write, write." He thought that no one would ever love him or want to marry him. "I was thinking how I was before and I shall never be that way again."

Then a group of amputees with no hands at all arrived at the camp. "I have my hand," he realized. "I saw that I'm better than that. It was after a year and a month that I finally accepted myself as I am."

The double amputees were victims of the second wave of terror, called Operation No Living Thing. It peaked on January 6, 1999, with a surprise attack on Freetown by rebel infiltrators and remnants of the army who called themselves the West Side Boys, because it made them sound like American gangsters. Thousands in the city were killed, and hundreds more were mutilated. Only a fierce counterattack by Nigerian-led troops kept the capital from falling to the rebels, but as the rebels retreated east they laid waste to miles of Freetown's poor, densely populated neighborhoods and suburbs. The violence was extraordinarily cruel and personal. Victims were raped, dismembered, or burned alive while the rebels taunted them; family members were forced to watch, and even to perform atrocities; boy conscripts returned to their old neighborhoods to settle scores. Commanders with names like Captain 2 Hands and Betty Cut Hands organized special amputation squads in neighborhoods from which the rebels were retreating. The grounds of Kissy Mental Hospital, where patients are chained to concrete floors, became a central mutilating zone.

A squad of nine rebels abducted a thirteen-year-old girl named Mariama Conteh, who was living with relatives, and five other teenagers. The girls were taken to the mental hospital and gang-raped, then were made to lie face down with their arms on some stones used for cooking. Mariama's left hand was nearly severed by an ax; the back of her right wrist sustained a deep cut, but she got up and ran away before the rebels could finish. She fell and broke her leg, got up and ran again, passed out, came to, and kept running till she reached home. Her aunt had fled. She asked her uncle for water; he said he couldn't help her and ran off with his grandchildren into the bush. Alone, naked, her left hand attached by nothing but flesh, Mariama went out again and finally found her aunt, who with a broken bottle completed the amputation of Mariama's left hand. For two days, Mariama hid among trees and in unfinished houses, her wounds untreated, and eventually got to a local hospital, but a doctor told her that rebels were lying in wait to amputate the other hand of people who came in with one hand still attached. Three days after the attack, Nigerian troops found her and took her to the city's main hospital. Her right hand was saved, but she had a bone infection in her leg for which she couldn't afford antibiotics. Mariama ended up with hundreds of others in a camp for amputees and war wounded run by Doctors Without Borders, in the western part of Freetown.

An American named Corinne Dufka lived around the corner from the camp. Dufka is the Human Rights Watch representative in Sierra Leone, and over the past four years she has meticulously recorded the atrocities. "Believe me, it's the thing of the future, this kind of rebellion," she told me. "Because of the frustrated youth—millions of frustrated youth sitting in slum areas looking at their role models doing nothing but stealing from them and exploiting them. It's all about survival. In conversations here, food is so important." Parents know that a certain number of their children will die—unless they can get what Dufka calls an "edge." She said, "A big part of life in Africa is getting an edge. For some, it's the military. For others, it's the RUF. And for others it's a foreigner."

• • •

Through the office of his congressman, Vito Fossella, Mirones was put in touch with an advocacy group called the Friends of Sierra Leone, made up of former Peace Corps volunteers and Sierra Leoneans living in the United States. He talked to a Sierra Leonean emigrée named Etta Touré, a tall, soft-spoken woman who works for a defense contractor in Arlington, Virginia. When I met her at the company's offices, she told me that the town where she grew up, in the north of Sierra Leone, had ceased to exist.

Of all the atrocities, Touré said, amputation was the worst. "The visual evidence that we have is going to be around us forever," she said. "The dead—after a while you forget, unless it's your own family. But this is something that's going to be permanent in our history, especially the children who will grow up and be like that always." Touré and the Friends of Sierra Leone had spent years trying to track down people uprooted by the war, and to get the attention of the United States government—without much success. In her company's photocopying room, a sign was posted to remind employees about the need for security. It said, "Countries Don't Have Friends—They Have Interests!" Every time she saw it, Touré thought about her country of birth. "It translates, 'Sierra Leone is not of interest,'" she said.

Mirones and Touré found what they were looking for in each other. Touré agreed with Mirones: they would approach the problem directly instead of trying to work through indifferent governments or sluggish international organizations. They wouldn't deal with the NGOs in Sierra Leone. Touré asked a cousin in Freetown, who sometimes visited the amputee camp with money or toys, to take snapshots of amputees with their stumps clearly visible. In the summer of 2000, a Federal Express envelope containing about twenty-five photographs arrived at the Arimed office.

Mirones waited until he was alone, at the end of the day, to look at the photographs. "I wanted maybe just to dwell on it, and enjoy the moment of having them actually in my hand—the actual people in my hand that I could help," he said.

It is a shock to see small bodies so damaged and deformed—an arm ending too soon in a scarred and ingrown fold of skin, a thigh sewn closed like a drawstring pouch. Most of the children stand against the background of a plastic sheet, dirty white with blue horizontal stripes—the international building material of refugee camps. Soaked in sunlight, they present themselves for view: an arm extended, a leg held up. There are no smiles, except for one girl who manages to turn up the ends of her mouth as she leans on a wooden crutch and displays her left thigh with her right hand: Bintu Amara, age eight. (The names and ages are written on the back of the photographs.) The children's eyes are flat, without expectation. They know why they're posing, what needs to be seen.

In each photograph, Mirones was looking at the length of the residual limb. The longer the limb, the better the outcome. The rebels were said to ask certain victims whether they wanted "short sleeve" or "long sleeve," meaning above or below the elbow. For prosthetic purposes, long sleeve was best. Mirones wanted a mixture of legs and arms, bilateral amputees as well as unilateral, boys and girls. Above all, he wanted children. "This may sound a little coarse, but I think that, to make it more compelling and more sensitive to the average person, seeing a child who's been hurt in such a way is much more powerful than an adult," he told me. It didn't take him long to make his choices. "It was pretty obvious who was going to be a good prosthetic candidate."

Mirones's original list included six girls ranging in age from eight to sixteen, including Mariama Conteh, and one four-year-old boy who didn't live at the camp but happened to be there on the day the photographs were taken. Etta Touré insisted that a four-year-old girl named Memunatu be included. Mirones had wanted to leave her out; her amputation was well above the elbow. But Memuna, as she is called, had become the poster child for the amputees: her picture had once hung at the United Nations. Sierra Leone's President Kabbah took her to Lomé, Togo, for the July 1999 signing of the peace accord that gave the rebels a share of power. (Within a year, the RUF had broken the accord.) At the ceremony, Foday Sankoh apologized for Memuna's suffering. But upon returning home from Lomé the president deposited her back in the amputee camp. Etta Touré believed that the little girl deserved medical care in the United States. So Memuna was added to the list.

Two bilateral amputees whom Mirones had selected, teenage girls, had gone to Guinea, acting on a rumor that amputees were receiving visas to the United States there (the rumor proved false); and so they missed their chance. But Mirones wanted at least one upper extremity bilateral— by far the most disabling amputation—and at the last minute a forty-seven-year-old man named Tommy Foday, who had been a driver for the ruling party until he lost both hands, was added to the list, along with Muctar Jalloh, whose English made him a likely spokesman for the group.

On September 21, 2000, almost a year after Mirones first learned of the devastation in Sierra Leone, two adult and six child amputees, along with two women acting as chaperones, arrived at Washington Dulles International Airport. *The Washington Post* and television news reporters covered the event. The next day, at a welcoming ceremony in an African church outside Washington, Mirones got his first look at his new patients. At one point, they were called to the front to sing Sierra Leone's national anthem in Krio, the country's lingua franca. They sang seated, but Tommy Foday eventually stood up and began to weep. He was wearing tinted glasses, and someone took them off to wipe his eyes.

The group testified before the House Subcommittee on Africa. Upon arrival in New York, they met the City Council and received a proclamation of welcome. They were taken to Staten Island, where Joe Mandarino and the Rotary Club arranged housing for them, eventually setting them up in a condominium near Staten Island University Hospital. Finally, a week after landing in the United States, the amputees arrived at Arimed's Brooklyn office. There Mirones and his staff put all other work on hold and began to make plaster casts of their stumps and fit them with prostheses.

The Sierra Leoneans were model patients. Two four-year-olds required revision surgery, because their bones were penciling—growing conically through the skin in sharp, painful points. Mariama, who had lost one hand and nearly lost the other, was so weakened by the bone infection that she might have died had she remained in the camp; she was put on a regimen of antibiotics. There were respiratory infections, evidence of exposure to tuberculosis and hepatitis, malnutrition, gynecological complications as a result of rape. And, of course, the patients needed to learn to use their new arms and legs. Mohammed, the four-year-old boy, whose left leg had been blown off just below the knee by bomb fragments and whose right leg had been rendered useless, was fitted with a limb and a brace and immediately began to walk, with the unbridled delight of a child who'd been crawling almost all his life. When he had arrived, he was nearly mute; walking made him garrulous. The girls, morbidly shy at first, put on the new devices and dedicated themselves to rehabilitation therapy. Dr. Jeffrey Weinberg, the chairman of rehabilitation medicine at Staten Island University Hospital, said, "After they were given prosthetics, they became totally different children."

Sierra Leoneans seldom say, "My hand was amputated." They say, "I was amputated." Erik Duret, a French psychologist treating amputees in Freetown, told me that when he sees his patients they continue to show him the stump. "Sometimes it's so present, so painful, that they are no longer anything but that," he said. "The amputated part takes the place of the whole." A stump moves as if of its own will, like something blind and mute that has attached itself to the body. The arm has lost its face and voice; especially in the case of a double amputee, it's as if he had been gagged as well as bound. When I first met the Sierra Leoneans, I kept imagining that the tongue had been cut off along with the hands.

"Think about it," Mirones told me, "the implications for your manhood. Not only can't you care for yourself—you can't touch a woman, your children. Christ, you can't even urinate. It's like castration."

Duret said, "The patient has to mourn this perfect body, to be able to admit afterward that, effectively, 'My body is no longer what it was, but, thanks to the prosthesis, I can do this, do that.'"

One afternoon while I was sitting in an Arimed examination room, I saw Tommy Foday, the driver who had lost both hands, take off his sweatshirt so that his prostheses could be adjusted. In five minutes of intense muscular activity, he dropped his torso as low as it would go, gripped the fabric behind his neck with his hooks, and, after several tries, pulled the sweatshirt over his head.

The Arimed prosthesis has a hard, laminated acrylic resin socket that conforms to every contour of the stump for the greatest muscular control. It's connected to a steel double hook, or terminal device, on one end, and a nylon harness fits over the shoulders; a cable runs from the harness to the terminal device, and the wearer controls the hook by hunching the shoulders. The first thing Foday had done when he received his prostheses was to go into the bathroom, unzip his fly without assistance, and urinate.

In the lobby on the way out, Foday tried to put on his sunglasses. He had the bridge in the pincer grip of his hook, but the balance was off; the glasses were askew on his face, and one of the hinges kept flopping. Finally, on the fifth or sixth try, he got them on straight.

Three months after the children arrived, Mirones's project began falling apart. The heart of the matter was this: What should become of the children? Mirones planned to send them back home after rehabilitation, to show Sierra Leone's other amputees that they could still lead independent lives. He had built room for growth into the prostheses and would send duplicate parts as needed, training one of the adults in maintenance. He would travel there at some unspecified time to expand his work—what he called Stage Two. But for the others involved in the project—especially Joe Mandarino and the Rotarians—it all sounded vague and impractical. Would the children be safe? Would their limbs be stolen? Would they really get the intensive follow-up care that prostheses—especially for children, who have to be refitted every eighteen months or so—require? Would they vanish back into the misery of Sierra Leone?

The amputees wanted to stay. Whenever the children misbehaved, the surest way to get them in line was to say that they'd be sent back to Freetown. Almost all the children had at least one living parent in Sierra Leone, but their parents were subsisting on rations in the amputee camp. The war seemed to be ending, but it had seemed that way before. One of the chaperones told me that the children seldom spoke of missing their parents. When I asked why, she answered, "Here they get everything they need, but there, even if they have parents, if they have no money the father gets angry, the mother gets angry. It's poverty." But they were not in the United States as asylum seekers; they had six-month humanitarian visas, renewable for up to two years. Promises had been made to both governments that the children would return home.

Something else was happening on Staten Island: a group of people in the tight community of the North Shore was falling in love with the children. Someone had to drive them to Our Lady Help of Christians School, where they were enrolled; someone had to give them phone cards so they could call Freetown. Nancy Passeri, a middle-aged woman with close-cropped hair who is the wife of Staten Island University Hospital's president, acted as a chauffeur on one occasion, and before long she was spending almost every free hour with the children, taking little Mohammed to have the stitches removed from his amputated leg and holding the boy in her arms as he broke into a sweat and screamed and kicked and pleaded, "Auntie Nancy!"

One day, as Passeri and I were driving to the small condominium where the group was housed, she said, "I'm not very into organized religion, but these kids are so profoundly—well, you've met them, you know. I have to believe there's more. They've made me more spiritual." She kept asking herself, "Is this a service or a disservice? How can they be sent back? How is this ever going to work? You show them hope and then you put them back, you show them heaven and then you take them back to hell." She concluded that, without losing their connection to home, the children should stay and be adopted. "I would like to go and meet the families," she said. "If I could sit with them and translate with them, and they could feel the love I have for their children, they wouldn't be so afraid."

Joe Mandarino, whom the children call Uncle Joe, is a combative man with salt-and-pepper hair and heavy black eyebrows over fatigued eyes. As I entered the cramped second-floor offices of his printing company one afternoon, he greeted me by saying, "I'm a negative person," and he began to assess Mirones's project. "Had it not been for Matthew, these kids would never have come here—that's the good side," he said. But Mirones had no follow-up plan for the children's return. "I'm Italian— when I feel someone's playing a game, I don't play along. He said, 'I feel the international community will get involved. It will blossom like a flower.' I said, 'Are you crazy? Just giving them a limb isn't enough. You have to give them yourself.' What he hasn't given is himself. His heart's not in it." Mandarino never intended to do more than arrange the children's housing. "But there's a beauty about the people of Sierra Leone that attracts you and catches you like a web. A beauty and a purity and an unconditional love. It's like Adam and Eve. It's like going back in time where the races don't matter. They hug you, they kiss you." He smiled. "If you ever feel a little down on yourself—market's not doing well, your business isn't good—you walk to their house and you feel like a million dollars."

In December 2000, Mandarino called a meeting on Staten Island between the Rotarians and the Friends of Sierra Leone. "We're going to give them all the advantages in America," Mandarino said. Etta Touré, who had come up from Washington, and the former Peace Corps volunteers countered that separating the children from their families and their culture would only deepen rifts caused by the war. "If you want to send them back," Mandarino told Touré, "take them now, back to D.C. with you. We're done with them." Instead, the Friends of Sierra Leone relented and turned the children's passports over to the Rotarians. Mandarino began applications for political asylum; at the same time, he and Nancy Passeri started looking for families to adopt the children. Mirones's original idea of inspiring large numbers of amputees in Sierra Leone gave way to saving the handful who were here.

"We're looking at the little picture," Mandarino said. "We're concerned not with the country but with a few people. Countries look at big issues that affect their national interest. That's why Sierra Leone never had an impact in this country. They could kill each other from here to eternity and we won't care. Unless a journalist writes a story—then we get angry. For a little while, we have a focus. But now we can't shut it off."

The rush to adoption struck some of the former Peace Corps volunteers as well-meaning American arrogance. Lynne Loomis-Price, who served in a village that has since been obliterated by the war, has daughters the same age as two of the children. "How can you amputate a girl from her mother?" she said. "'Do you want her to stay or not?' But what a rotten question to put to a woman who's already lost everything. 'We can raise your kids better than you, don't worry.'" No one involved in bringing the amputees from Sierra Leone had thought it through, she said. But Loomis-Price had no solution of her own. She concluded that the children shouldn't be sent back against their will. She said, "I don't know the happy ending here."

In order to strengthen the plea for asylum, the immigration lawyer who took down the children's stories tried to find cause for the cruelty in politics or in ethnicity or in religion. But the violence that the amputees had endured was both meaningless and indelible: the children of Sierra Leone had suffered for no reason at all. Such senselessness evoked a frenzy of emotion and action in the people of Staten Island: they arranged outings, held fund-raisers, and threw a sweet-sixteen party for Mariama, at the Staten Island Hotel with a hundred guests.

The children were being treated by a trauma specialist named Louise Abitbol, and when I went to see her at a child advocacy center, near the ferry terminal, she described the Staten Islanders' response to the children with the phrase "vicarious trauma." She said, "They've created their own little war zone." With the disputes over immigration and adoption, she continued, "They've taken on all the behaviors of these people." It was disrespectful to disregard the parents in Africa, she said—"very presumptuous to think that they're just going to give up their children." Abitbol credited the Staten Islanders for their devotion but said, "They're in over their heads, as far as I'm concerned. Culturally and politically."

One day at the advocacy center, Abitbol and Passeri were talking to the children about adoption. Each of the kids made up a "wish list" of what would be desirable in adoptive parents. But gradually the children became tense. Fatu, a ten-year-old, muttered, "No more Krio, only English," and in frustration she took a Magic Marker in her prosthetic hand and drew a line through the word "parents." The others did the same. Abitbol substituted "friends" for "parents." Bintu, nine, said, "I feel angry." Damba, eight, said, "I feel sad." In Passeri's car on the way home, the children were uncharacteristically silent. For days, the two women couldn't agree on what had happened. Passeri, who sees the children's future here, thought that they didn't like the word "friends," that they wanted those who adopted them to be "parents"; Abitbol, concerned about cultural sensitivity, thought the opposite. It turned out that the children were angry at Passeri: they had believed that she would adopt them and they would live in her house, and now they realized it wasn't to be.

It was hard to know the truth about the children's inner lives. Their backgrounds and stories were unclear; no one seemed to know whether Bintu's mother was alive, or exactly what had happened to Memuna and Mohammed. "What saved them was the ability to dissociate, to move outside their bodies," Abitbol said. "You see it on their faces, with this blank stare—nobody home."

The condominium where the Sierra Leoneans were living was a drab two-story affair, strewn with schoolbooks. The chaperones and the children lived downstairs, the two men—Muctar Jalloh and Tommy Foday—upstairs. One evening, as West African music played in the upstairs living room and the girls danced across the carpet, Damba talked about her mother, whose left hand had been cut off at the same time as her own. Damba was six when it happened, and in the hospital she asked her mother if her hand would grow back. Even now, Damba said, when she dreams about her mother they both have two hands. "When I wake up I didn't know if I have a hand," she said. "I look to see. But I didn't have my hand." The others chimed in, laughing. Bintu, who lost her leg to a gunshot, dreams of walking freely, and Mariama sees herself cooking and carrying water.

It was the hour for Muslim prayers. Upstairs, Jalloh and Foday laid out a towel in the corner of the room, where they were joined by a fifteen-year-old orphan named Sheku. When Sheku was eleven, his father was burned alive and his mother shot dead before his eyes; then rebels cut off both his hands. He was a late addition to the group: he had originally come over with four men, all double amputees, sponsored by a shopping mall developer who'd read another *Times* article about amputation. But after receiving prostheses from Mirones the five were sent back to the amputee camp in Freetown. When Nancy Passeri, who fantasizes about whole families immigrating from the camp, learned that a minor had been in the group, she bought Sheku a return ticket. Now, back in this country for the second time, he was getting ready to say his evening prayers on Staten Island.

Jalloh knelt in front, Foday and Sheku behind, facing east. They had taken off their prostheses. Jalloh had learned the Arabic verses in Koranic school, and he recited them in a glottal chant. He brought his left hand to his lips, passed it over his face, and raised it to heaven; Foday and Sheku were solemn. The refrigerator in the kitchen was humming, and the men rocked and prayed: "All praise and thanks are to Allah, the Lord of Mankind and all that exists. The most gracious, the most merciful, the only Owner and the only ruling judge of the day of Recompense. You alone we worship, and you alone we ask for help in everything."

Downstairs, the girls were watching a Nigerian video. It was a love story, and they were riveted. When it was over, Damba got up, went to a full-length mirror in the corner of the room, and stared at herself.

No one seemed to know what the children's parents wanted, and I decided to go to Sierra Leone to find out. My traveling companion was Matthew Mirones. He and the Rotarians were no longer speaking. His involvement with the children had waned. They were now just patients coming in every few weeks for follow-up care—with a frequency that made me wonder how his original plan of returning them to Africa could ever have worked.

Bringing the children to New York had transformed their lives, but not in the way Mirones had imagined. His project had been wrested away from him, and now he seemed determined to show that he was serious about wanting to help more than just eight people.

Mirones had never been to Africa, let alone to a ruined country like Sierra Leone, which a United Nations survey of human development had rated the worst place in the world. A ceasefire was holding, and the UN had seventeen thousand peacekeepers in the tiny country to oversee disarmament, but Mirones wondered if some rebel would say, "Oh, this is the wise guy who's going to help our people?" He didn't want to come back requiring his own company's services. Two nights before we were to leave New York, he telephoned me, and I thought he was going to back out. But he had just heard that there were Lebanese restaurants in Freetown. "I grew up with these guys on Atlantic Avenue," he said. "We'll have good food!"

Between long ocean beaches and a chain of lovely green hills, Freetown lay in a state of collapse. In African terms, it's an old city, settled at the end of the eighteenth century by freed slaves, and among its more extravagantly decayed buildings are nineteenth-century clapboard houses, the shutters slumping at the windows. It wasn't easy to tell which buildings had fallen into terminal neglect, which had never been finished, and which had been burned by the rebels. The war accelerated a process that had been going on for a long time. Tens of thousands of refugees had poured into the city, and the narrow potholed roads were clogged with vehicles and pedestrians, including the occasional amputee begging. Outside one shop, a sign announced, FREE HAIRCUT FOR ALL AMPUTEES.

Sierra Leone's misery has attracted more than a hundred and eighty NGOs, and their four-wheel-drive vehicles seemed to be the only new and functioning things in the landscape. Mirones made the rounds of the groups providing prostheses. An American woman named Kim Kargbo sat down with him in the sweltering conference room of World Hope International. She wore a blue denim jumper embroidered with pink flowers, and had a blond ponytail and the brisk manner of a daughter of missionaries. She had grown up here and was meeting a man whose project she had vehemently opposed. She said that she was shocked to see him.

"We're here on the ground pouring our blood, sweat, and tears in a war recovery situation," Kargbo said. "You did this as a sort of noncoordinated effort. Those kids were involved in a long-term rehab plan. All of a sudden they're gone, and none of us have even talked to you—that was kind of difficult."

Mirones explained his original idea of having the kids come back here as models.

"And that certainly has merits," Kargbo said. "But one problem is the kids are never coming back. So how does that fit in the mix?" The effect he'd had in Sierra Leone, Kargbo said, was to tear apart families, "which is what the war has been about," and to raise unreasonable hopes among the amputees who were left behind.

Mirones described how he'd tried to deflate the bubble of miraculous expectations among the kids in New York.

"But you can't burst the bubble," Kargbo told him. "It's too strong."

"I was glad she came clean with me," Mirones said on the way out. "Why beat around the bush?"

I asked if he now had any second thoughts.

"No. Look, you've seen what I've seen. She can talk, but I know our people got better care—medical, orthopedic, prosthetic. Look at this guy." An elderly man was sitting by the security gate with what looked like a boxing glove attached to metal rods that were strapped around his forearm without a socket. "Why should he have to wear a fucking arm like that?"

As we drove around the city, Mirones's mood rose and fell. "One minute I'm thinking, There's nothing I can do, it's out of my hands, and the next I'm thinking, How can we set up some kind of commissary to feed them?" The prosthetics labs were rudimentary by his standards, and they gave him an impression of profound idleness. Everywhere, people were sitting around with nothing to do, dozens of amputees were wearing no prostheses, and none of it made any sense. "That little girl needs a wheelchair," he muttered as we passed a child, crippled from polio in both legs, lurching along the road without crutches. "Where's the sense of urgency?" he kept asking. "I mean, get the show on the road, get on the phone, make a couple of calls, let's go!" The next minute, he would check himself: "Then again, we don't know all the circumstances, the obstacles."

The amputee camp on the western end of Freetown is a warren of plastic tents housing about three hundred amputees and twelve hundred relatives. There's a satellite dish by the entrance. Mirones's arrival drew a large group, who passed around my photographs of the children and ex-claimed over how much weight they'd gained. As we walked up a dirt road toward the camp's prosthetics lab, a man who was missing a hand shyly approached and said that he wondered if by some chance he would be the next one to be taken away. Mirones wasn't the only foreigner to have removed people from the camp. Groups with names like Feed My Lambs International and Christ End Timer Movement were regularly spiriting away amputees from under the noses of the NGOs that were supposedly providing prosthetics and therapy. Outsiders described the camp as "the national holocaust museum" and "a freak show" that ought to be shut down, but no one seemed prepared to take that step. The camp received attention, money, and consignments of goods that benefited the govern-ment, the NGOs, and the amputees. It attracted visitors like Madeleine Albright, Kofi Annan, and Matthew Mirones. A Dutch physical therapist who had worked in Sierra Leone sixteen years ago told me that he recog-nized a man in the camp who had lost part of his leg to diabetes long ago and was now presenting himself as an atrocity victim.

Another group, known as the War Wounded, had originally been sheltered with the amputees, but fights kept breaking out between the two groups over donations that were meant for amputees, and the War Wounded were moved to a camp about ten miles outside town. There they showed me deep machete gashes, bullet wounds in the face, and terrible burns. Two women said that they'd been shot in the vagina. A botched amputation had cost a man the use of both hands. But the War Wounded felt ignored by the world and envious of the amputees, who ranked higher on the scale of suffering. A joke was making the rounds in Freetown about how many fingers one would be willing to lose in order to go to America.

A woman and her husband, who was missing one arm and both ears, claimed a family relationship with Memuna, the poster child, but their claim was false. They said that a twelve-year-old rebel had chopped off the little girl's arm, but I discovered that it had been surgically amputated after being infected with fragments from the bullet that had killed her grandmother. One of the children on Staten Island had told me that she'd seen both her parents shot to death; I learned in Africa that her father had died of natural causes and her mother was still alive. The logic of survival, the need to be noticed, drove people to exaggerate already unspeakable horrors. The camp mocked Mirones's vision of self-sufficient amputees. I asked a double amputee who had received prostheses in New York and then been sent back why so few people in the camp wore their arms. "They want to win sympathy," he said. "In case someone like you comes to the camp." Amputation had given people an "edge," to use Corinne Dufka's word. Having lost everything else, the children's families were making what they could of it.

There is no Krio word for "adoption." In Sierra Leone, the concept doesn't exist. (The only people who used the word "adoption" were the rebels, insisting that they never abducted the boys and girls who became soldiers and servants.) But use of the Krio word *men*, meaning "to care for," is extremely widespread, as is the practice: a woman other than the biological parent will bring up a child because the parents can't, or because she is childless, or simply because she likes the child. Unlike adoption, there is no loss of legal rights, and it's expected that upon reaching adulthood the child will help support the biological parents. Of the children on Staten Island, three had been cared for by adults who were not their biological parents, and none lived with both parents. The families in the camp seemed to understand that a similar arrangement had been made for their children in America.

Each child had recorded a tape for her family. Fatu made one for her aging aunt: "I know very well that you're all suffering there. I want you to know I won't forget you. They're teaching us to cook. We go to church on Sunday. For now I can only send pictures. You need to see how happy I am. I've even forgotten that they amputated my hand. I can even write with the hand that was chopped off. That is the biggest thing that has happened to me. So I feel like a normal kid."

None of the families wanted the children to return. Bintu's aunt, who called herself the mother, said that the night after the girl went away she had a dream so frightening that it woke her up: Bintu was back, hobbling on her crutch. "You didn't go to America?" her aunt cried. "What happened?"

Damba's uncle, who called himself the father, said, "The problem that she had, the amputation, is a blessing in disguise. It was the will of God and the price she had to pay to go to America."

I tried to explain adoption in terms of the concrete rights that the parents would lose. Damba's mother, painfully thin from tuberculosis, began stroking her lip and then her forehead with her one hand, anxiety filling her eyes. Finally, the uncle, a small man in an embroidered Muslim gown and cap, spoke up. "I can't accept that, we don't do that," he said. "In our culture, when you get children the point is for us to prosper when she grows up. If you want to help us, *men* the child. Good. But if you want to take custody, that's out of the question."

Mariama's mother said, "I would prefer she lives there and comes to visit once in a while. I will never accept her being adopted, because she's my daughter and we were very close. I can't imagine that. My daughter will never accept it, either."

One by one, I spoke with each family, and they all said no.

When I thought about it later, it was difficult to know whether their fear was losing the child or losing the benefits. Perhaps one was inextricable from the other. What seemed clear was that the families had already made enough sacrifices. The children on Staten Island were all they had left.

Erik Duret, the French psychologist in Freetown, said of the children's situation, "For me, that's the worst of all—its absolute uprooting." The war, he said, was above all a story of broken bonds, which could be repaired only within the family, the community, the society. "These people, after the excitement of the beginning, after six months, a year, two years, are going to start asking themselves, 'What's become of my family? What's happening over there? Who am I?'"

I didn't disagree. But it occurred to me that the people who wanted the children sent back to Sierra Leone didn't have to live there. Sierra Leoneans themselves readily grasped the measures that the families had taken and the decision they had made.

One night at the hotel bar, Mirones said, "The easiest piece of the puzzle is the device. Considering all the other insurmountable obstacles they have to contend with, it seems that having an inferior prosthesis just adds to it. It's not brain surgery. It's pretty straightforward." He set down his Scotch. "Where do I fall on this now? Where do I put my emphasis? What do I advocate? Do I advocate supporting the mechanism that's in place? Come up with a new one? Who's got the time for that? Do I try to improve what they're doing? It's not political, technical, bureaucratic. It's a man-to-man, human-to-human issue. The hard part is to mobilize people to show the same passion they exhibited back home for the people here."

Mirones looked discouraged and slightly frantic. He had wanted to help people on a larger scale than the Rotarians envisioned, and in Sierra Leone itself; but a destroyed African country wasn't going to lend itself easily to the practical energies of a Brooklyn businessman. He had run up against the limits here: the very qualities that had worked so well back in New York— his single-mindedness, his refusal, as he often said, to "dwell on things" to the extent that action became impossible—left him at a loss about how to proceed in Freetown, among people who needed far more than limbs.

"Imagine not having a pair of hands!" he suddenly exclaimed. "It's part of what separates us from the animal kingdom, it's this beautiful ability to be dextrous and capable with the hands. And you lose that ability . . ." He stared at me, his mouth pulled down, his hands held out before him.

After a week in Africa, Mirones went home. A month later, in his Brooklyn office, he told me that he was eager to return and set up a facility to bring to Sierra Leone the kind of first-rate prosthetic care that the people there deserve. But as it turned out, that week in Freetown marked the end of his project; the amputees living new lives in America mark the extent of his contribution. They have all received political asylum, and though the families in the camp still have not given written consent for adoption, three of the children are now living with couples around the country, who are seeking legal guardianship, and Joe Mandarino and Nancy Passeri are looking for homes for the others. Last August, Sheku, the orphaned teenage boy, flew to Montana to meet a ranching couple who were interested in adopting some of the children. On the long drive from Billings to the ranch, he told me later, "It was dark, with mountains. Guess what? It give me the flashback. I remember when the men chop off my hands. I start suffering like I was a little boy. So I didn't like it." Sheku decided that a ranch in Montana would not be the best place for the children, who, more than two years after coming to the United States, were still living on Staten Island and awaiting new parents.

The man who brought them here no longer makes limbs. Last year, in a special election, Matthew Mirones ran as a Republican for an open seat in the New York State Assembly, and now serves his Staten Island constituents in Albany.

How Susie Bayer's T-Shirt
Ended Up on Yusuf Mama's Back

The New York Times Magazine, March 31, 2002

If you've ever left a bag of clothes outside the Salvation Army or given to a local church drive, chances are that you've dressed an African. All over Africa, people are wearing what Americans once wore and no longer want. Visit the continent and you'll find faded remnants of secondhand clothing in the strangest of places. The LET'S HELP MAKE PHILADELPHIA THE FASHION CAPITAL OF THE WORLD T-shirt on a Malawian laborer. The white bathrobe on a Liberian rebel boy with his wig and automatic rifle. And the muddy orange sweatshirt on the skeleton of a small child, lying on its side in a Rwandan classroom that has become a genocide memorial.

A long chain of charity and commerce binds the world's richest and poorest people in accidental intimacy. It's a curious feature of the global age that hardly anyone on either end knows it.

A few years ago, Susie Bayer bought a T-shirt for her workouts with the personal trainer who comes regularly to her apartment on East Sixty-fifth Street in Manhattan. It was a pale gray cotton shirt, size large, made in the U.S.A. by JanSport, with the red and black logo of the University of Pennsylvania on its front. Over time, it got a few stains on it, and Bayer, who is seventy-two, needed more drawer space, so last fall she decided to get rid of the shirt. She sent it, along with a few other T-shirts and a couple of silk nightgowns, to the thrift shop that she has been donating her clothes to for the past forty years.

Americans buy clothes in disposable quantities—$165 billion worth last year. Then, like Susie Bayer, we run out of storage space, or we put on weight, or we get tired of the way we look in them, and so we pack the clothes in garbage bags and lug them off to thrift shops.

When I told Susie Bayer that I was hoping to follow her T-shirt to Africa, she cried, "I know exactly what you're doing!" As a girl, her favorite movie at the Loews on West Eighty-third was *Tales of Manhattan*—the story of a coat that passes from Charles Boyer through a line of other people, including Charles Laughton and Edward G. Robinson, bringing tragedy or luck, before finally falling out of the sky with thousands of dollars in the pockets and landing on the dirt plot of a sharecropper played by Paul Robeson.

Bayer writes off about a thousand dollars a year in donations, and the idea that some of it ends up on the backs of Africans delights her. "Maybe our clothes change the lives of these people," she said. "This is Susie Bayer's statement. No one would agree with me, but maybe some of the vibrations are left over in the clothing. Maybe some of the good things about us can carry through." She went on: "I'd like us to be less selfish. Because we have been very greedy. Very greedy. Americans think they can buy happiness. They can't. The happiness comes in the giving, and that's why I love the thrift shop."

Twenty-four blocks north, up First Avenue, the Call Again Thrift Shop is run by two blunt-spoken women named Virginia Edelman and Marilyn Balk. They sit in their depressing back office, surrounded by malfunctioning TVs and used blenders and a rising sea of black garbage bags.

From a heap of clothing in front of her, Edelman extracts a baseball shirt that says "Yorkville" across its front. "Look at this. Who would want to buy something like this? It's just junk. Junky junky junk. This stuff bagged in a garbage bag, it's so wrinkled we don't even look at it. This is a Peter Pan costume or something—I don't know what the hell it is."

Edelman and Balk have been toiling at Call Again for two decades. Their dank little basement, crammed with last year's mildewing clothes, has no more space. The storage shed out back looks ready to explode. The women inspect every item that comes in, searching for any reason to get rid of it. Their shop space is limited, and their customers are relentlessly picky. This being the Upper East Side, the store displays a size 4 Kenneth Cole leather woman's suit, worn once or not at all, that retails for six hundred dollars but is selling here for two hundred.

Edelman and Balk sit neck-deep in the runoff of American prosperity, struggling to direct the flow and keep it from backing up and drowning them. "It's endless," Balk says. "Yesterday we got, I don't know, five donations. It's like seven maids and seven grooms trying to sweep the seas. Or Sisyphus, was it? Trying to roll the rock?"

One day a few years ago, relief came to them in the form of a young man named Eric Stubin, who runs Trans-Americas Trading Company, a textile recycling factory in Brooklyn. He said that he was willing to send a truck every Tuesday to haul away what the women didn't want and that he would pay them three cents a pound for it. "You never heard two people happier to hear from someone in your life," Edelman says. Now every month 1,200 or 1,300 pounds of rejected donations are trucked to Brooklyn, and every three months Call Again gets a check for a hundred dollars or so, money that goes to charity.

Edelman estimates that more than a third of the donations that Call Again receives ends up in Trans-Americas' recycling factory. Goodwill Industries, which handles more than a billion pounds a year in North America, puts its figure at 50 percent. Some sources estimate that of the 2.5 billion pounds of clothes that Americans donate each year, as much as 80 percent gets trucked off to places like Trans-Americas.

Though the proceeds go to charity programs, these numbers are not readily publicized. Susie Bayer isn't the typical donor. "Everybody who gives us things thinks that it's the best thing in the world," Edelman says. "They feel as if they're doing a wonderful thing for charity. And they do it for themselves—for the tax write-off. Unfortunately, I don't think people know what charity is anymore. They would be horrified if they thought that they bought a suit at Barneys or Bergdorf's for eleven hundred dollars and we chucked it for three cents a pound because of a torn lining."

Susie Bayer's T-shirt goes straight into the reject pile. "We have a thousand of them," Virginia Edelman says. "Get it out of here."

This is where the trail grows tricky, for what had been charitable suddenly crosses a line that tax law and moral convention think inviolable—it turns commercial, and no one likes to talk very much about what happens next. A whiff of secrecy and even shame still clings to the used clothing trade, left over from the days of shtetl Jews and Lower East Side rag dealers. The used clothing firms are mostly family-owned, and the general feeling seems to be that the less the public knows, the better.

The owners of Trans-Americas, Edward and Eric Stubin, father and son, are more open than most in the industry, though they wouldn't share their annual sales figures with me. In 2001, used clothing was one of

America's major exports to Africa, with $61.7 million in sales. Latin America and Asia have formidable trade barriers. Some African countries—Nigeria, Eritrea, South Africa—ban used clothing in order to protect their own domestic textile industries, which creates a thriving and quite open black market. For years, Africa has been Trans-Americas' leading overseas market for used clothing, absorbing two-thirds of its exports.

"There'll always be demand for secondhand clothing," says Eric Stubin, who reads widely about Africa, "because unfortunately the world is becoming a poorer and poorer place. Used clothing is the only affordable means for these people to put quality clothing on their body."

Edward Stubin agrees. "I have a quote: 'We can deliver a garment to Africa for less than the cost of a stamp.'"

Trans-Americas' five-story brick building stands a block from the East River wharves in Greenpoint, Brooklyn. Inside, sixty thousand pounds of clothes a day pour down the slides from the top floor, hurry along conveyor belts where Hispanic women stand and fling pieces into this bin or down that chute, fall through openings from floor to floor, and land in barrels and cages, where they are then pressure-packed into clear plastic four-foot-high bales and tied with metal strapping—but never washed. Whatever charming idiosyncrasy a pair of trousers might have once possessed is annihilated in the mass and crush. Not only does the clothing cease to be personal, it ceases to be clothing. Watching the process of sorting and grading feels a little like a visit to the slaughterhouse.

"We get the good, the bad, and the ugly," Eric Stubin tells me as we tour the factory. "Ripped sweaters, the occasional sweater with something disgusting on it, the pair of underwear you don't want to talk about. We're getting what the thrifts can't sell." There are more than three hundred export categories at the factory, but the four essential classifications are "Premium," "Africa A," "Africa B," and "Wiper Rag." "Premium" goes to Asia and Latin America. "Africa A"—a garment that has lost its brightness—goes to the better-off African countries like Kenya. "Africa B"—a stain or small hole—goes to the continent's disaster areas, its Congos and Angolas. By the time a shirt reaches Kisangani or Huambo, it has been discarded by its owner, rejected at the thrift shop, and graded two steps down by the recycler.

Standing in Trans-Americas' office, with wooden airplane propellers hanging next to photographs from Africa, Eric Stubin casts a professional eye on Susie Bayer's T-shirt. In a week, a fifty-four-thousand-pound container of used clothes will set sail on the steamship *Claudia*, destination Mombasa, Kenya. Stubin spots a pink stain on the belly of the T-shirt below the university logo and tosses the shirt aside. "Africa," he says.

But there are many Africas, and used clothing carries a different meaning in each of them. Christianity tenderized most of the continent for the foreign knife, but the societies of Muslim West Africa and Somalia are bits of gristle that have proved more resistant to Western clothes. In warlord-ridden, destitute Somalia, used clothing is called, rather contemptuously, *huudhaydh*—as in "Who died?" A woman in Kenya who once sold used dresses told me that not long ago Kenyans assumed the clothing was removed from dead people and washed it carefully to avoid skin diseases. In Togo, it is called "dead white man's clothing." In Sierra Leone, it's called "junks" and highly prized. In Rwanda, used clothing is known by the word for "choose," and in Uganda, it used to be called "Rwanda," which is where it came from illegally until Uganda opened its doors to what is now called *mivumba*.

At the vast Owino market in downtown Kampala, Uganda's capital, you can find every imaginable garment, all of it secondhand. Boys sit on hills of shoes, shining them to near-newness, hawkers shout prices, shoppers break a sweat bargaining, porters barge through with fresh bales on their heads. When the wire is cut and the bale bursts open like a piñata, a mob of retailers descends in a ferocious rugby scrum to fight over first pick. Between the humanity and the clothes there is hardly room to move. The used clothing market is the densest, most electric section of Owino— the only place where ordinary Africans can join the frenetic international ranks of consumers.

I knew what this thrice-rejected clothing had gone through to get here, but somehow "Africa" looks much better in Africa—the colors brighter, the shapes shapelier. A dress that moved along a Brooklyn conveyor belt like a gutted chicken becomes a dress again when it has been charcoal-ironed and hangs sunlit in a Kampala vendor's stall, and a customer holds it to her chest with all the frowning interest of a Call Again donor shopping at Bergdorf Goodman. Some of the stock looks so good that it gets passed off as new in the fashionable shops on Kampala Road. Government ministers, bodyguards in tow, are known to buy their suits at Owino. Once in Africa, the clothes undergo a transformation like inanimate objects coming to life in a fairy tale. Human effort and human desire work the necessary magic.

My guide through Owino is a radio talk show host named Anne Kizza, a sophisticated woman who knows what she wants in dance wear from reading South African fashion magazines. She always goes to the same vendors, whose merchandise and prices are to her liking; while I am with her, she buys a slim lime-green dress for the equivalent of sixty cents and a black skirt for thirty cents. Price tags are still stapled to some items— "Thrift Store, $3.99, All Sales Final"—but just as Americans don't know what happens beyond the thrift shop, Africans don't know the origin of the stuff. Most Ugandans assume that the clothes were sold by the American owner. When I explain to a retailer named Fred Tumushabe, who specializes in men's cotton shirts, that the process starts with a piece of clothing that has been given away, he finds the whole business a monstrous injustice. "Then why are they selling to us?" he asks.

The big importers have their shops on Nakivubo Road, which is a hairy ten-minute walk through traffic from Owino. Trans-Americas' buyer in Kampala is a Pakistani named Hussein Ali Merchant. He is forty, with a beard and a paunch and a sad, gentle manner. A diabetic cigarette smoker, he seems to expect to die any day and extends the same good-natured fatalism to his business. "It's a big chain," he says, and all the links beyond Merchant are forged on credit. "Sometimes the people disappear, sometimes they die. Each year I'm getting the loss of at least thirty thousand dollars. Last year a customer died of yellow fever. His whole body was yellow. He died in Jinja. The money is gone. Forget about it, heh-heh-heh."

We drink tea in his dark shop among unsold bales stacked twenty feet high. Five or six years ago, when there were only a few clothing shops on Nakivubo Road, his annual profit was about $75,000. Today, with more than fifty stores, his profits are much lower. Merchant is one of Africa's rootless Asian capitalists. Before coming to Uganda in 1995, he twice lost all his money to looting soldiers in Zaire. Between disasters he went to Australia and pumped gas for three months, but he fled back to Africa before his visa expired. "I've been sitting like this for twenty years here. In America you have to work hard, no money, things are very expensive.

Here, it's easy. I want to do hard work in America? For what?" Merchant
has a frightening vision of himself squeezing price tags onto convenience
store stock at midnight in Kentucky. As for Karachi, it terrifies him, and
he goes back only once a year to see his family, his doctor, and his tailor.
"I'm a prince here," he says. "I'm a king here in Africa."

Merchant's warehouse—"my go down," he calls it in local slang—is
in an industrial quarter of Kampala. On a Saturday afternoon in December, the truck carrying the Trans-Americas shipping container with Susie
Bayer's T-shirt pulls in after its long drive from the port of Mombasa on
the Kenyan coast. Seven customers—wholesalers from all over Uganda—
anxiously wait along with Merchant. Among them is a heavy woman in
her forties with a flapper's bob and a look of profound disgust on her fleshy
face. Her name is Proscovia Batwaula, but everyone calls her Mama Prossy.
As the bales start leaving the container on the heads of young porters,
Mama Prossy literally throws her weight around to claim the ones she wants.
Merchant, standing back from the flurry, murmurs that a week before, she
bloodied another woman's nose in a scuffle over a bale of Canadian cotton skirts.

Eric Stubin has stenciled my initials on the bale containing Susie
Bayer's T-shirt. But I never imagined five hundred and forty bales coming
off the truck at a frantic clip, turned at all angles on young men's heads,
amid the chaos of bellowing wholesalers in the glare of the afternoon sun.
Finding the T-shirt suddenly seems impossible. When I try to explain my
purpose to Mama Prossy, she answers without taking her eyes off the precious merchandise leaving the truck: "What gain will I have? Why should
I accommodate you?" She scoffs at the idea of publicity benefits in New
York, and as bales disappear into wholesalers' trucks, I start getting a bit
desperate.

Then Mama Prossy learns that I teach in American universities. She
badly wants her son to attend one; for the first time she takes an interest
in me. Moments later, more good luck. Merchant spots my bale coming
off the truck, the initials "GP" all of three inches high.

Mama Prossy insists on the right to tear it open and have a look. The
used clothing trade in Africa is fraught with suspicion and rumor and fear of
bad bales. Wholesalers bribe the importers' laborers to give them first crack
at the most promising stock, based on the look of things through clear
plastic. But what Mama Prossy extracts from the top of my bale makes her

lip curl in ever-deepening disgust. It is a pink woman's T-shirt. Women's clothes are not supposed to be mixed in with men's. "I will lose money," she announces, and pulls out another piece. "Is this for a fat child? Where are they in Africa? We don't have fat children here in Uganda."

She is angling for a price cut from Merchant, who reminds her that she still owes him fifty thousand Ugandan shillings (thirty dollars) from last week. She starts calling him "boss." After all, he is higher on the chain, and she needs him more than he needs her. They settle on the equivalent of sixty dollars for the bale, a price that amounts to nineteen cents a shirt. Merchant has paid Trans-Americas around thirteen cents each, excluding freight charges; he will have little or no profit on the bale, which was graded "mixed," Africa A and B.

Mama Prossy turns to me. "You say this bale is best quality, better than the others?" It wasn't what I'd said, but I keep my mouth shut. "I doubt," says Mama Prossy, looking me over with quite naked contempt. "We shall see."

A Kampala journalist named Michael Wakabi told me that Kampala has become "a used culture." The cars are used—they arrive from Japan with broken power windows and air conditioners, so Ugandan drivers bake in the sun. Used furniture from Europe lines the streets in Kampala. The Ugandan army occupies part of neighboring Congo with used tanks and aircraft from Ukraine. And the traditional Ugandan dress made from local cotton, called *gomesi*, is as rare as the mountain gorilla. To dress African, Ugandans have to have money.

Twenty years ago, when I was a Peace Corps volunteer in Togo, all the village women wore printed cloth, and many of the men wore embroidered shirts of the same material. The village had at least half a dozen tailors. The mother of eight who lived next door dreamed of making clothes in her own market stall and asked me to help her buy a hand-cranked sewing machine. Used clothes were sold in limited and fairly expensive supply; a villager wore the same piece every day as it disintegrated on his body.

Then the floodgates opened. With the liberalization in Africa of the rules governing used clothing imports in the past ten years, Africans, who keep getting poorer, can now afford to wear better than rags. Many told me that without used clothes they would go naked, which, as one pointed out, is not in their traditional culture. And yet they know that something precious has been lost.

"These secondhand clothes are a problem," a young driver named Robert Ssebunya told me. "Ugandan culture will be dead in ten years, because we are all looking to these Western things. Ugandan culture is dying even now. It is dead. Dead and buried." The ocean of used clothes that now covers the continent plays its part in telling Africans that their own things are worthless, that Africans can do nothing for themselves.

But the intensity of the used clothing section in every market I entered suggests that if something called "Ugandan culture" is dying, something else is taking its place. The used clothes create a new culture here, one of furious commercial enterprise and local interpretation of foreign styles, cut-rate and imitative and vibrant.

For all this, Uganda is quite capable of mass-producing its own clothes. On the banks of the White Nile, at its source in Jinja on Lake Victoria, a textile company called Southern Range Nyanza uses local cotton, considered the second-best in the world after Egyptian, to manufacture thirteen million yards of fabric a year. With the Africa Growth and Opportunity Act of 2000 opening the American market, Southern Range has begun exporting men's cotton shirts to New York—so shirts that begin in Uganda might make a double crossing of the ocean and end there as well.

Viren Thakkar, Southern Range's Indian managing director, insists that he can sell the same shirts in Uganda for three dollars—less than twice the cost of a used shirt—but the dumping of foreign clothes makes it impossible for him to break into the market. "The country has to decide what they want to do," he says, "whether they want to use secondhand clothes continually, or whether they want to bring industry and grow the economy." Globalization has helped to destroy Uganda's textile industry, but Ugandans simply don't believe that their own factory could make clothes as durable and stylish as the stuff that comes in bales from overseas.

In Jinja's market, Mama Prossy sits like a queen on her wooden storage bin and watches the morning trade. At her feet, half a dozen retailers poke through the innards of the Trans-Americas bale. "You see how you are picking very, very old material," she scolds me. "And you are mixing ladies'. My friend, why are you mixing ladies'? And too much is white."

"I told you," I say, "I don't work for them."

"But you put your initials on it."

She will lose money on my bale, Mama Prossy insists; she will never buy Trans-Americas again. But the entries she makes in her ledger book show a profit of ninety-eight dollars—more than 150 percent.

Her retailers sort the T-shirts by their own three-tier grading system. Susie Bayer's is rated second-class and goes for sixty cents to a slender, grave young man in slightly tattered maroon trousers who seems intimidated by the queen on her throne. His name is Philip Nandala, and he is the next-to-last link in the chain. Philip is an itinerant peddler of used clothes, the closest thing in Uganda to the nineteenth-century rag dealer with his horse-drawn cart—except that Philip transports his fifty-pound bag from market to market by minibus or on his own head, five days a week on the road. "If I stay at home," he says, "I can die of poverty."

His weekly odyssey begins in Kamu, a trading center on a plateau high above the plains that stretch north all the way to Sudan. I follow Philip and his bag of clothes through the market, watching him dive into one scrum after another as bales burst open. Out comes children's rummage, and Philip fights off several women for a handful of little T-shirts that go into his bag: MS. Y'S GOOFY GOOF TROOP, 2 BUSY + 2 SMART FOR TOBACCO 4H, and FUTURE HARVARD FRESHMAN.

The sun beats down, and Scovia Kuloba, the woman who introduced Philip to the trade, sits under an umbrella among mounds of clothes. Her barker scolds at the market crowd: "People leave the clothes to buy fish! They let their children go naked! This white man brought the clothes with him—don't you want to buy?"

When I explain to Scovia Kuloba that her goods come from American charities, she stares in disbelief. "Sure? I thought maybe we Africans are the only ones who suffer. The people from there—I thought they were well off. I think they don't even work."

Her teenage daughter, Susan, whose braids and clothes look straight out of Brooklyn, adds: "I don't want to be poor, you just cry all the time. I hate the sun. I hate Africans." She'll only marry a *mzungu*, she says, because she knows from movies like *Titanic* and *Why Do Fools Fall in Love?* that white men are always faithful, unlike Africans.

Slowly, I become aware of the sound of amplified American voices nearby, along with gunshots and screeching tires. Next to the used clothing market, an action flick plays on video, with speakers hooked up outside to attract customers. In a dark little room, two dozen adults and children, who have paid six cents apiece, sit riveted to *Storm Catcher*, starring Dolph Lundgren.

The end of the road is a small hilltop town, green and windswept, called Kapchorwa, about 110 miles northeast of Mama Prossy's stall in downtown Jinja. Clouds hide fourteen-thousand-foot Mount Elgon and, beyond it, Kenya. Philip spreads his wares on a plastic sheet at the foot of a brick wall and works hard all day, a tape measure around his neck. Poor rural Ugandans, the chain's last links, crowd close, arguing and pleading, but Philip is now the one with power, and he barely stirs from his asking price. One young man comes back half a dozen times to try on the same gray hooded coat. It fits perfectly, and it has arrived just in time for the chilly season that is blowing in. But Philip wants $4.70, and the customer has only $1.75.

"This coat is as thick as fish soup," Philip says. "The material lasts twenty years."

"You are killing me," the customer says. "The money is killing me."

"I am not killing you. I bought it at a high price, I ask a high price."

The customer finally walks away, and Philip returns the coat to his pile. The thrift shop's price tag is still stapled to the back: "$1." At the sight of it, I suddenly feel sad. I think of Virginia Edelman and Marilyn Balk back on the Upper East Side, tossing out truckloads of the stuff, desperate to get rid of it. I remember the torrent pouring down the chutes at Trans-Americas' factory in Brooklyn. On balance, in spite of its problems, I have become a convert to used clothing. Africans want it. It gives them dignity and choice. But now that I have seen them prize so highly, and with such profound effects, what we throw away without a thought, the trail of Susie Bayer's T-shirt only seems to tell one story, a very old one, about the unfairness of the world as it is.

The T-shirt is buried deep in Philip's pile. My flight back to New York is leaving in four days, and I am concerned about missing it. So I reach into the pile, wanting to position the T-shirt more advantageously. As soon as I touch it, the shirt flies out of my hand. An old man in an embroidered Muslim cap and djellaba, who is missing his lower front teeth, holds it up for inspection. Tracing with his finger, he puzzles out the words printed in red and black around an academic insignia: "University Pennsylvania," he says. He dances away, brandishing the shirt in his fist. Ninety cents is his first offer, but Philip won't budge from $1.20. Eventually, the old man pays. Yusuf Mama, seventy-one, husband of four, father of thirty-two, has found what he wants.

I ask him why, of all the shirts in the pile, he has chosen this one. "It can help me," he says vaguely. "I have only one shirt."

Later, when I tell the story to people back in Kampala, they shake their heads. Yusuf Mama wanted Susie Bayer's T-shirt, they say, because a *mzungu* had touched it.

The Images in Our Heads

The New York Times Magazine, April 21, 2002 (under the title "When Here Sees There")

An Arab intellectual named Abdel Monem Said recently surveyed the massive anti-Israel and anti-American protests by Egyptian students and said: "They are galvanized by the images that they see on television. They want to be like the rock throwers." By now everyone knows that satellite TV has helped deepen divisions in the Middle East. But it's worth remembering that it wasn't supposed to be this way.

The globalization of the media was supposed to knit the world together. The more information we receive about one another, the thinking went, the more international understanding will prevail. An injustice in Thailand will be instantly known and ultimately remedied by people in London or San Francisco. The father of worldwide television, Ted Turner, once said, "My main concern is to be a benefit to the world, to build up a global communications system that helps humanity come together." These days we are living with the results—a young man in Somalia watches the attack on the South Tower live, while Americans can hear more, and sooner, about Kandahar or Ramallah than the county next to theirs.

But this technological togetherness has not created the human bonds that were promised. In some ways, global satellite TV and Internet access have actually made the world a less understanding, less tolerant place. What the media provide is superficial familiarity—images without context, indignation without remedy. The problem isn't just the content of the media, but the fact that while images become international, people's lives remain parochial—in the Arab world and everywhere else, including here.

"I think what's best about my country is not exportable," says Frank

Holliwell, the American anthropologist in *A Flag for Sunrise*, Robert Stone's 1981 novel about Central America. The line kept playing in my mind recently as I traveled through Africa and watched, on television screens from Butare, Rwanda, to Burao, Somalia, CNN's coverage of the war on terrorism, which was shown like a miniseries, complete with the ominous score. Three months after the World Trade Center attacks, I found myself sitting in a hotel lobby by Lake Victoria watching Larry King preside over a special commemoration with a montage of grief-stricken American faces and flags while Melissa Etheridge sang "Heal Me." Back home, I would have had the requisite tears in my eyes. But I was in Africa, and I wanted us to stop talking about ourselves in front of strangers. Worse, the Ugandans watching with me seemed to expect to hear nothing else. Like a dinner guest who realizes he has been the subject of all the talk, I wanted to turn to one of them: "But enough about me—anything momentous happening to you?" In CNN's global village, everyone has to overhear one family's conversation.

What America exports to poor countries through the ubiquitous media—pictures of glittering abundance and national self-absorption—enrages those whom it doesn't depress. In Sierra Leone, a teenage rebel in a disarmament camp tried to explain to me why he had joined one of the modern world's most brutal insurgencies: "I see on television you have motorbikes, cars. I see some of your children on TV this high"—he held his hand up to his waist—"they have bikes for themselves, but we in Sierra Leone have nothing." Unable to possess what he saw in images beamed from halfway around the world, the teenager picked up an automatic rifle and turned his anger on his countrymen. On generator-powered VCRs in rebel jungle camps, the fantasies of such boy fighters were stoked with Rambo movies. To most of the world, America looks like a cross between a heavily armed action hero and a Lexus ad.

Meanwhile, in this country the aperture for news from elsewhere has widened considerably since September 11. And how does the world look to Americans? Like a nonstop series of human outrages. Just as what's best about America can't be exported, our imports in the global-image trade hardly represent the best from other countries either. Of course, the world *is* a nonstop series of human outrages, and you can argue that it's a good thing for Americans, with all our power, to know. But what interests me is the psychological effect of knowing. One day, you read that six hundred Nigerians have been killed in a munitions explosion at an army barracks. The next day, you read that the number has risen to a thousand. The next day, you read nothing. The story has disappeared—except something remains, a thousand dead Nigerians are lodged in some dim region of the mind, where they exact a toll. You've been exposed to one corner of human misery, but you've done nothing about it. Nor will you. You feel—perhaps without being conscious of it—an impotent guilt, and your helplessness makes you irritated and resentful, almost as if it's the fault of those thousand Nigerians for becoming your burden. We carry around the mental residue of millions of suffering human beings for whom we've done nothing.

It is possible, of course, for media attention to galvanize action. Because of a newspaper photo, ordinary citizens send checks or pick up rocks. On the whole, knowing is better than not knowing; in any case, there's no going back. But at this halfway point between mutual ignorance and true understanding, the "global village" actually resembles a real one—in my experience, not the utopian community promised by the boosters of globalization, but a parochial place of manifold suspicions, rumors, resentments, and half-truths. If the world seems to be growing more, rather than less, nasty these days, it might have something to do with the images all of us now carry around in our heads.

Gangsta War

The New Yorker, November 3, 2003

From my balcony on the eighth floor of the Hotel Ivoire, I could see downtown Abidjan across the lagoon in the mist. Skyscrapers rose along the waterfront, a blue neon sign blinked NISSAN, and the plate glass of the commercial banks reflected the silver afternoon light. At this distance, it was easy to pretend that these skyscrapers weren't emptying out; that the African Development Bank hadn't abandoned the city; that the shipping traffic at the port, on which all West Africa depended for an economic pulse, hadn't dropped by 50 percent. From the balcony, it still looked like the glamorous capital of twenty years ago, before decline and civil war, when young men and women from all over French-speaking Africa came to Abidjan to seek their future in the city of success.

I was living in a small village in Togo then, two countries east of Ivory Coast; in the evenings, I would listen to the mother of the family in my compound describe the time she had spent in Abidjan as a kind of dream. There was abundant work in Ivory Coast, and foreigners like her were thrilled to find themselves in a truly cosmopolitan city, one where everyone spoke the same Abidjanaise French. The ambitious students in the village school where I taught knew that, short of Paris, Abidjan was the best place to be. An African privileged class of bureaucrats and professionals ate in fine restaurants downtown and kept the nightclubs open till all hours. A robust economy based on coffee and cocoa exports employed several million African immigrants to do the manual labor and forty thousand French expatriates to run businesses and advise the government. The French, some of them third or fourth generation, enjoyed a slightly updated version of the colonial life. In the eighties, a French teenager in Abidjan could celebrate his birthday by racing his moped around town and then jumping off a bridge into the lagoon, to the cheers of an Ivorian crowd. The French who have remained in Abidjan now call that time *la belle époque*.

In Togo, I was a Peace Corps volunteer, living in a village without electricity, and one detail I learned about Abidjan struck me as miraculous. The Hotel Ivoire, I was told, had a large skating rink with ice that kept a perfectly glazed surface even when the temperature outside topped a hundred degrees. The capital also had world-class golf courses, because President Félix Houphouët-Boigny, the relatively benign dictator who had led Ivory Coast since its nominal independence from France in 1960, considered the sport to be a mark of civilization. He had turned his home village of Yamoussoukro, 125 miles north of Abidjan, into a grand political capital of wide boulevards lined with street lamps. He built a Catholic basilica there that rises out of the palm forests like a hallucination of St. Peter's, of which it is an actual-size replica. He also erected a vast presidential palace, and surrounded it with man-made lakes that were filled with crocodiles. (Houphouët-Boigny, who died in 1993, is buried in a mausoleum near the cathedral.) While the rest of the region was becoming mired in coups and wars and deepening poverty, social scientists talked about the "Ivorian miracle." The country was one of the most prosperous in Africa, and Ivorians weren't killing one another. The residents of Abidjan said that their country was "blessed by the gods."

As soon as I went down to the hotel's lobby, my vision of old Abidjan began to fade. The skating rink, on the grounds behind the hotel, was closed. An artificial lake that once was dotted with paddleboats had been drained because of chronic scum, and blue paint was peeling off its concrete walls. In the restaurant, a Liberian lounge singer was belting out "Yesterday" and the theme from *Fame* for a handful of lonely white mercenaries and West African peacekeepers and their prostitutes; she had the desperate brio of a resort performer in the off-season. I hailed a taxi, and as I sat in back, listening to my driver—who was garrulous with rage, like most men in Abidjan—complain about the traffic, the heat, the economy, the government death squads, and the ongoing civil war, it was hard to believe that the ovens of the Patisserie Abidjanaise, across the Charles de Gaulle Bridge, were still disgorging sheets of warm, perfect baguettes. But so they were.

Abidjan valiantly clings to the idea that it remains the refined city it was twenty years ago. The University of Abidjan, once an impressive institution, now decrepit, continues to turn out thousands of graduates every term for government jobs or foreign scholarships that no longer exist. In the nineties, the French began to restrict immigration and opportunities to study abroad, just after a catastrophic drop in commodity prices plunged Ivory Coast, the world's largest cocoa producer, into deep debt. Today, Abidjan is populated with educated young men and women who have no outlet for their ambitions. "All the generations until 1985 found work— state work, private work," Ousmane Dembele, a social geographer at the university, told me. "All goals were satisfied. But after '85, '90, '95, all these generations of youth in Abidjan could find nothing. Nothing."

These days, Abidjan looks less like Paris and more like a decaying Third World city. Residents encounter symptoms of decline on every street, from collapsing infrastructure to violent crime. "It's not Lagos yet," the financial manager of an architecture firm told me. "But we're headed straight there."

The northern part of Ivory Coast is largely Muslim, and poorer than the mostly Christian south, with its cocoa plantations and Abidjan. On September 19, 2002, rebel soldiers from the north mutinied against the government. The civil war has regional, religious, and economic dimensions, but its basic cause is political. The mutiny was a violent reaction to several years of anti-northern and anti-immigrant policies pursued by the series of southern presidents who succeeded Houphouët-Boigny. During the 2000 election, the presidential candidate from the north, a former International Monetary Fund official named Alassane Ouattara, was disqualified on the dubious ground that he was not of Ivorian parentage. The winner, a history professor named Laurent Gbagbo, from the cocoa region, took office amid riots, during which his supporters killed hundreds of Ouattara's primarily Muslim followers. Since the civil war broke out, at least three thousand people have been killed and more than a million have been displaced from their homes. Throughout the conflict, one of the government's favored weapons has been the rhetoric of xenophobia.

The taxi was taking me to a rally of Ivory Coast's Young Patriots, a coterie of young men paid by the government to stir up nationalistic feelings against the rebels, who, soon after starting the civil war, occupied the north of the country. The Young Patriots railed with equal intensity against immigrants, blaming them for the country's soaring unemployment rate.

At the Young Patriots' rally, I wanted to get a glimpse of their leader, Charles Blé Goudé. The drive to the rally took me near the Place de la République, a public square of cracked concrete, where, in late January, Blé Goudé had spoken to tens of thousands, denouncing the French government for failing to rescue Ivory Coast from the rebels. (France, refusing to take sides, had pushed Gbagbo's government to reconcile with the insurgent forces.) The iconography of those demonstrations was remarkable. It was virulently anti-French and desperately pro-American. U.S.A. WE NEED YOU AGAINST THE "OLD EUROPE," one sign pleaded, just a few days after Donald Rumsfeld coined the term. Blé Goudé waved an American flag and delighted the crowd by refusing to speak French. "Are you ready for English?" he yelled, and the crowd roared as he spoke a few clumsy sentences in the tongue of the superpower, which, in Ivory Coast, is the language of youthful resistance. The January demonstrations had led to anti-French riots, and thousands of French expatriates fled the country while young Ivorians spat upon them, attacked their businesses and schools, and tried to block the departure of Air France jets from the airport.

The rally this afternoon was in a slum called Port-Bouët, on a waterfront strip near the airport. My driver got lost in Port-Bouët's labyrinthine streets, which were choked with the blue taxis known as *woro-woro*. About fifteen years ago, the city government of Paris sent Abidjan a fleet of used green-and-white municipal buses, which grew filthy, broke down, and were never replaced or repaired, even as the city's population exploded. The *woro-woro* run local routes to fill in the gaps, but their drivers are notoriously reckless. We passed clogged roads, shantytowns, and entire neighborhoods without decent water, power, or sewage systems.

The taxi turned a corner, and suddenly there were hundreds of people crowding around the perimeter of a dirt rectangle the size of a football field. This was Place Laurent Gbagbo.

Port-Bouët is a government stronghold. High-rise housing projects in advanced states of decay ringed the field, and residents hung out from the windows, their arms dangling beside their laundry. A young m.c. was warming up the crowd with a call-and-response that always ended in the word *bête*, or "stupid." The rebels who held the northern half of the country were *bête*. The neighboring countries suspected of arming them, Burkina Faso and Liberia, were *bête*. The immigrants in Abidjan with Muslim names, who supposedly sympathized and even conspired with the rebels, were *bête*. And the French, who had failed to defend their Ivorian brothers and sisters in the hour of crisis—the French were more *bête* than anyone.

For all the hostility in the slogans, the crowd was cheerful, like spectators awaiting the main act of a show they'd seen before. Almost everyone in the crowd was young; most of them clearly had nothing better to do. Boy vendors were selling hats in the national colors, orange and green, with the warning DON'T TOUCH OUR COUNTRY and T-shirts declaring XENO-PHOBE—SO WHAT?

In the front row of a tented seating area were the Young Patriot leaders, local stars in their twenties who were dressed like American hip-hop singers: gold chains, tracksuits, floppy hats. Their scowling bodyguards sat behind them, wearing muscle shirts and mirror glasses; a few were armed with Kalashnikov rifles. Sitting quietly and pathetically in the back rows were the neighborhood elders. In the traditional hierarchy of African villages, the old are elaborately deferred to by the young. Here the elders had no role other than to applaud while the Young Patriots took turns swaggering and jigging out on the speaker's platform and the loudspeakers blasted reggae or *zouglou*, the homegrown pop music of the movement. A favorite anthem, by a *zouglou* group called the Bastards, was "Sacrificed Generation":

> *They say students make too much trouble*
> *They say students go on strike too much*
> *At the start they took away our scholarships*
> *They made us pay for rooms and meal tickets*
> *Students are poor . . .*
> *When we present our demands*
> *They answer us with tear gas . . .*
> *The big brothers are angry*
> *The old fathers don't want to get out of the way!*

Each speaker tried to outdo the last in scabrous wit and extremist views, before boogying back to the tent to touch fists with the others, like an NBA star returning to the bench. At another Young Patriot event, I had heard a heavyset demagogue pronounce the true "axis of evil" to be Liberia, Burkina Faso, and France, and then declare, with malicious irony, "Yeah, I'm Jean-Marie Le Pen!" Meanwhile, at night, immigrants were being hounded from their homes under the pretext that they were supporting the rebels, entire shantytowns had been bulldozed, and the corpses of opposition politicians were turning up at dawn in remote corners of the city. Everyone knew that paramilitary death squads were at work, though no one could prove the rumor that they were directed by the president's wife, Simone, an evangelical Christian with a taste for inflammatory rhetoric against Muslims, immigrants, and whites.

This spring, President Gbagbo, under pressure from France, agreed to include rebel ministers in a new cabinet. In July, the civil war was declared to be over. But late last month, rebels started boycotting meetings of the unity government, and threatened to resume the war. This was fine with the leaders of the Young Patriots, who had thrived during the civil war, making regular appearances on television; many had become national celebrities. These young men have no desire to return to the ranks of the eternal students and the jobless street-corner orators.

Blé Goudé arrived very late, in a convoy. "They're coming! They're coming! I see Charles!" the m.c. informed the crowd. By the time Blé Goudé, his figure lean and tense, made his way with an armed bodyguard to the tent, and then out across the open dirt to the speaker's stand, the moon was rising over Port-Bouët.

Blé Goudé, the son of a peasant from President Gbagbo's region, rose to prominence in the nineties, when he became a leader of the national student movement. The group clashed frequently with police during the chaotic years following Houphouët-Boigny's death, and Blé Goudé was sent to prison many times. At the end of that decade, when the student movement split into two factions, the university campus became the scene of a small war. Blé Goudé, whose side won, earned the nickname Machete. (He never received a degree, however, though for years he pretended that he had.) The leader of the losing side was Guillaume Soro, an overweight, soft-spoken student from the north. Soro is now the political leader of a major rebel group, the Patriotic Movement of Ivory Coast. The country's destiny is being shaped by former students who have never held a job.

Blé Goudé took the speaker's platform. He was wearing baggy green army pants, a tank top, an Adidas pullover tied around his waist, and a black baseball cap with the bill turned up—the imitation-gangsta style of the Young Patriots. But he didn't strut; his hungry, liquid eyes and knowing smile projected the self-containment of a leader. As he spoke, darkness fell, and gradually he became a disembodied voice. He didn't shout, unlike the others; his was a deep, calm voice.

Blé Goudé denied press reports that he was getting rich off his leadership of the Young Patriot movement. "They don't understand that some people fight for their beliefs," he said. "They think everyone can be bought. They say my belly is getting bigger." Shrieks of laughter rose from the crowd as he patted his flat stomach. "All this stuff about xenophobia and exclusion is just a cover," he said. "The Ivorian youth is showing the whole world its attachment to democratic principles. I'm not just talking about the Ivory Coast of today. I'm talking about the generation that will rule Ivory Coast. Because the little kids of ten or eight all say France is no good."

Other Young Patriots had been funnier and nastier. But when Blé Goudé finished speaking and the music started up, the crowd swarmed around him. For a moment, he had actually made them feel that the future was theirs.

The Young Patriots represent a new kind of African success story. They're celebrated by many young people in Abidjan for beating and cheating a system gone rancid. With the corrupt "old fathers" refusing to get out of the way, and with all the old channels to success—emigration, foreign study, state employment, family connections—blocked, the new hero is a young trickster with a talent for self-promotion. The model is no longer the formal bureaucratic style of the French colonizer; it's the loud, unrestrained style that everyone in Ivory Coast calls American.

When Blé Goudé drives around Abidjan in his armed two-car convoy—Renault in front, four-by-four behind—he's saluted as "the General of the Youth." According to one well-connected Frenchman I spoke with, the government, at the height of the demonstrations in January, was giv-

ing Blé Goudé eighty thousand dollars a week to distribute to his fellow
Young Patriots and their crowds of followers. I was told by a Western diplomat that he runs a Mob-style racket in the campus dorms, taking a cut
off the illegal lodging of students, who sleep two to a cot or on the floor.
Blé Goudé has become a sort of urban warlord.

He hasn't completely grown into his success, however. When I sat
down to talk with him over lunch, it was in his mother's underfurnished
cinder-block house, across a rutted dirt road from a small shantytown. Blé
Goudé was wearing gray socks monogrammed with his initials, CBG (a
friend had made him ten pairs), and, along with half a dozen hangers-on,
he was eating the peasant dish of rice and sauce.

"Our elders deceived us," he told me. "Our predecessors, the political
leaders and others, have shown us clearly that our future doesn't matter.
That's why I've organized the Ivorian youth. To give it a political arm."

Blé Goudé says he is thirty-one; others claim he is older. In his mother's living room, without the charmer's smile I had seen in Port-Bouët, he
looked hard-featured and edgy. He said that he was tired from his work,
but he mustered the energy to urge an American intervention in his country along the lines of the Iraq invasion—a request that his followers had
presented to an American official outside the U.S. embassy. Blé Goudé
hoped to exploit the Franco-American rift over Iraq, and he explained
that Ivory Coast's struggle was the same as America's: for democracy and
against terrorism. The rebellion of September 19, 2002, splintered Ivory
Coast, and to him the connection with 9/11 was obvious. "There's only
eight days' difference," he pointed out.

"And a year."

"And a year. That's all. It's the same thing. Only it wasn't helicopters
here, that's all. It wasn't the World Trade Center, that's all. So, voilà—the
connection."

I asked whether he thought Americans even knew what was going on
in Ivory Coast. He didn't respond, but it was clear that the youth of Ivory
Coast thought they knew what was going on in America.

"Even if the United States didn't colonize our country, they should
come to our assistance," he said. "Ivory Coast is a land to be taken. Above
all, the generation today has been educated in the American spirit. The
American spirit is freedom. The American spirit is integrity in action." Blé
Goudé extended his arm in front of him. "When the United States says

what they'll do, they do it. They don't say one thing at night and the opposite the next day, like the French." It was just as true, he said, of the
American celebrities worshipped in Ivory Coast, like Mike Tyson and
Jay-Z. "Boxing has no tricks in it. When someone hits you, he hits you.
Basketball—it's all straight up and down. Rap comes out of the ghetto, to
convey the suffering of the young people there. When they sing, you listen, and the message comes straight at you."

In the eyes of Blé Goudé and the Young Patriots, Amadou Guindo is the
enemy. Guindo, an immigrant's son, lives in Koumassi, another Abidjan
slum, separated from Port-Bouët by a land bridge across the lagoon. It
smells of oranges and sewage. Because there is a high concentration of
northerners and foreigners in Koumassi, the government regards it as a
hotbed of rebel sympathy. One morning, a month after the war began,
several gendarmes stormed down an alleyway, entered a cinder-block compound where the landlady was washing clothes, and broke down Guindo's
door. (He happened to be out.) The landlady convinced the gendarmes
that it was a case of mistaken identity, but not before they had rifled
through all his belongings.

Guindo, thirty-three years old and unemployed, is known as Cool B,
for Cool Boy. On the wall above his bed hung a large American flag; overhead, taped to the low ceiling panels, were posters for B movies like *War
Dog* and *The Arrival*. A Richard Wright novel was on his bedside table,
next to CDs by Stevie Wonder and R. Kelly. Outdoors, when he cruised
the crowded dirt roads of the neighborhood he calls *mon ghetto*, where
someone yelled out his name every few yards and the teenage prostitutes
approached to flirt and the guys sitting in doorways exchanged fist-to-
chest salutations with him, Cool B, his head shaved and his eyes concealed behind a pair of Ray-Bans, carried himself in a manner that he
called "the American style." It bore a close resemblance to the style of the
young men on the other side of the conflict. Cool B told me that 90 percent of the young people in Abidjan imitate the American style, which he
defined as "total independence. Liberty to express yourself. Economic
independence, too. A way of talking and walking." And he demonstrated
by sauntering up the road with a novel combination of the pimp roll and
the keep-on-truckin' stride.

Though he has spent his entire life in Ivory Coast, Cool B is technically a citizen of Mali, to the north, where his father comes from. This
is how he acquired Malian citizenship: One night in 1996, Cool B was
walking through his ghetto in the company of his German girlfriend,
Petra, when a group of policemen approached and demanded his papers.
He produced his Ivorian identity card (his father had had him naturalized
when he was sixteen), but this only enraged the police. "Amadou Guindo,"
one of them said, seeing that the name was foreign. "What name is that?"

"It's my name."

The police pocketed Cool B's card and told him to come with them
to the station. When he asked why, they fell on him and handcuffed
him. His white girlfriend's presence seemed to provoke them to ridicule,
Cool B recalled. "I said, 'It's because of my name you arrest me, you humiliate me. Okay, you don't have to be Ivorian to be happy in life. Go shit
with my card, I don't give a fuck. From now on, I'll keep the nationality of
my parents.'" Instead of going to the police station to ask for his card back
and suffer more abuse, he took citizenship from the Malian embassy. "I'm
proud of it," he said. "I know nothing of Mali. But if I try to get Ivorian
nationality, they'll humiliate me every time."

Cool B speaks with a slight stutter, and as he told me this story, in the
privacy of his sweltering ten-foot-square room, the stutter grew more
pronounced, his crossed leg jiggled, and the lines deepened in his face,
which, with the Ray-Bans off, looked older than his years. Stripped of the
American style, he seemed vulnerable, as if he were trying to ward off
disappointment.

In 1996, the same year Cool B became a "foreigner," a new word
emerged on the political scene in Abidjan: *ivoirité*. The English equivalent that best captures the word's absurdity might be "Ivoryness." In practice, *ivoirité* meant that immigrants were subjected to harassment and
shakedowns and restrictive new laws. Ivorians from the north, who tend
to share family names and the Muslim faith with immigrants from Mali,
Guinea, and Burkina Faso, came in for similar treatment. If a single word
can be said to have started a war, *ivoirité* started Ivory Coast's.

Cool B's father worked as a nurse in Abidjan for thirty years before
retiring and returning to Mali, in 1991. Cool B didn't go beyond high
school—instead, he pursued an early career in what he calls *voyousie*, or
the hoodlum life. The scale of his activities was small, but he made it a

habit to insult pretty much everyone who crossed his path. "The trouble-maker doesn't know why he makes trouble," he said. "He's just proud of himself. He has a certain pride." One day in 1990, when Cool B was in high school, a Frenchman came to his drawing class and asked the students to do illustrations showing the proper use of condoms. Cool B found the assignment foolish, and at the end of the class he stood in the doorway to block the Frenchman's exit.

"You're going around the world showing people pictures of how to use condoms?" Cool B asked mockingly. "I'll show you what to do." He snatched away the man's prospectus and, reading from the text, improvised an anti-AIDS rap on the spot in the manner of LL Cool J.

The Frenchman was impressed. Within a couple of days, he had arranged for Cool B to record the rap at a downtown nightclub, and the song made him a momentary celebrity among Abidjan youth. It also began his long association with white people—among them Petra, his girlfriend, who eventually went back to Germany, and Éliane de Latour, a French filmmaker who employed him for a while as a researcher on a feature about Abidjan youth. Cool B keeps pictures of them on his wall, and he tries to figure out why, in spite of these connections, he remains stuck in Koumassi. He spends his ample free time and his limited funds at a local Internet café, surfing international dating sites and chat rooms where people he knows have found marriage opportunities that got them out of Africa. Or he visits a green card lottery website. His ambition, short of leaving Africa, is to open his own Internet café.

"I don't understand my situation," he said. "I'm still blocked. I want to get out of my problems one day. I don't have the totality of independence." Cool B's residence permit expired last year, making him an illegal alien in the only country in which he has ever lived.

When the room grew too hot for us to stay inside, even with a fan blowing, we went around the corner to pay a visit to Cool B's gang. A dozen young men were seated on facing benches under a ramshackle tin roof; they spent twelve hours a day there, like a conclave of village elders, except that Cool B was the oldest person in the group. The others regarded him with respect and sought his advice. They were all immigrants or northerners, keeping an eye out for the police. They wore gold chains, tank tops, and Nike caps. When I asked what kind of work they did, most of them replied, "Tent rental," which began to seem like a euphemism for unemployment, though some of them had part-time work fencing stolen goods.

At noon, a communal basin of rice and sauce appeared, and the young men plunged their right hands into it. The gang argot of Abidjan, which combines French, profane English, and the language of Ivory Coast's north, is called Nushi, or "mustache," a reference to the way bad guys look in Hollywood movies. The inferior type of rice that Cool B and his friends had to eat is derisively referred to in Nushi as *deni kasha*, or "lots of children." The young men all came from poor and enormous polygamous families in which there were as many as thirty-five siblings. "That's what spoiled our future," a surly fellow with a shaved head told me. "When our parents worked, they didn't think of us first. In Europe, they set up an account to help the kids when they grow up, right?"

This was the story they all told: fathers who did nothing for their sons, extended families that might have made sense in a rural village but crushed the life out of them here in the city. Cool B's closest friend in the group was a rangy twenty-five-year-old, wearing wire-rim glasses, who introduced himself as McKenzie. He'd taken the name from a character in an action movie. Growing up in a northern town called Odienne, McKenzie (whose real name is Morifere Bamba) used to watch American Westerns on a communal TV. John Wayne made a particularly strong impression. These movies lit a desire to live in his "dream country," which remains McKenzie's sole ambition.

At twelve, he quit school—his mother was dead, his father too poor to support him—and the next year, 1990, he came alone to Abidjan. I asked how he had imagined the city then. "It was the city of success," McKenzie said. "The city that would give me the ability to realize my dream." Abidjan was a way station on his escape route to America. This, I thought, was the difference between Cool B's gang and the Young Patriots: they all copied the American style, but the Young Patriots had found a way to make it work for them in Abidjan.

After a few years in the city of success, McKenzie realized that he was entirely alone. "Succeed how?" he said. "You have to have lots of connections and acquaintances. Guys go into banditry to realize their success." McKenzie joined a gang, began smoking cocaine, fought, stole, and saw a friend die at the hands of the police. Movies like *Menace II Society*, which seemed to glamorize the gangster life, finally convinced him that it was a dead end. McKenzie left the gang and learned the electrician's trade, at which he worked irregularly, trying to save money for the trip to America, until the war started and jobs disappeared altogether.

• • •

The war was out there somewhere. In Abidjan, a ten-o'clock curfew enforced by gendarmes at roadblocks had shut down nightlife, but the city
was no longer a conflict zone. It was hard to believe that a couple of hundred miles away, in the interior, teenage militias were machine-gunning
children and cutting old men's throats. Like so many African wars, Ivory
Coast's had degenerated into looting and massacres by bands of loosely
controlled, generally underage fighters; it became part of a larger conflict
that had been spreading through the region for years—ever since the outbreak of Liberia's civil war, in 1989—producing hundreds of thousands of
corpses and millions of refugees.

Seen from a distance, Africa's man-made disasters look senseless.
But to the participants, who tend to be young and poor, these wars have
meaning. The war in Ivory Coast began as a struggle over identity—over
the question that haunted Cool B, the question of who gets to be considered Ivorian. The country's decline made identity a political issue, but it
also extends to the larger, almost existential question of what it means to
be a young African living in the modern world.

After a week in Abidjan, I drove north, to Bouaké, Ivory Coast's
second-largest city and the main rebel command center. Behind the
cease-fire line patrolled by French and West African peacekeeping troops,
the town hadn't seen fighting in months. At rebel headquarters, in a
former nursing school, a polite, bored young official was doing a Yahoo!
search for Uzis and grenades. Out on the half-empty streets, every civilian vehicle had been commandeered, license plates had been removed,
doors had been ripped off, and young rebels had painted the sides of
the vehicles with Spider-Man logos and self-styled unit names: Delta
Force, Highway of Death. Without a war to fight, they were turning into
gangsters.

At the hospital, the staff of Doctors Without Borders reported that
the most serious injuries were sustained by the young rebels who routinely
smashed up cars or accidentally shot themselves in the foot. One night
while I was in Bouaké, a notoriously violent young commander named
Wattao threw himself a lavish birthday party, with a fawning m.c., cam-
eramen, hundreds of guests who watched themselves live on video screens,
and gate-crashers who ended up exchanging gunfire.

The rebel military leadership, which had maintained fairly good discipline since the outbreak of hostilities, was turning to a local priest called
Abbé Moïse to rehabilitate the restless underage recruits. "They haven't
killed a lot," the Abbé told me. "They're recoverable here. The children of
Bouaké aren't as traumatized as those in the west."

That was where the real war was taking place. In November 2002,
two new rebel groups had suddenly appeared near the Liberian border.
The western groups claimed an alliance with the northern rebels, but
they had no clear political motivation, and their rebellion quickly took on
the violent, anarchic quality of Liberia's and Sierra Leone's civil wars. In
fact, some experts have concluded that the western rebellion was the inspiration of Liberia's president, Charles Taylor, who has had a hand in all
the region's murderous and intertwined wars, organizing and arming rebels in Sierra Leone and Guinea as well as terrorizing his own country for
a decade and a half, until his forced departure this past August. Although
Taylor is out of power, the widespread instability he fomented won't dis-
sipate in West Africa anytime soon. The region is now populated with
young fighters who float from country to country, looking for war.

The conflict in the west was a catastrophe. Both the rebels and the
government were recruiting Liberian mercenaries to do their fighting.
The Ivory Coast government also used MI-24 helicopter gunships with
Eastern European or South African mercenary crews; the rebels used the
feared Sierra Leonean warlord Sam (Mosquito) Bockarie and his battle-
hardened teenage fighters. (Bockarie was killed in Liberia in early May,
most likely on the orders of Taylor, against whom he might have testified
at the war crimes court in Sierra Leone, which had indicted him in March.)
Hundreds of civilians were being slaughtered in western Ivory Coast, and
entire villages had been looted and left empty. It was in the west that the
"Ivorian miracle" met its final demise and Ivory Coast became just another West African nightmare.

Before the civil war broke out, the journey from Bouaké to Man, the
biggest town in the west, took eight or nine hours. It took me two days,
because I had to pass through at least fifty roadblocks. In some places,
there was a roadblock every quarter mile. They were makeshift affairs: a
tree limb, pieces of junked machinery, concrete blocks. The boys on guard
roused themselves from the shade of a tree. When they noticed a white
face in the car, they put on angry expressions and went back to grab their

AK-47s. Glowering behind sunglasses, they stalked over to the car, fingers on triggers. Around their necks hung leather thongs with polished wooden or stone amulets, which they believed made them bulletproof. Carved fetish figurines stood guard alongside the roadblock. The boys ordered me to open the trunk, they pretended to search inside, they demanded to see my travel permit. A standoff: everything was in order, but they hadn't given the signal to go, and they had the guns. This last detail made all the difference, yet I found it hard to accept the obvious power relation. Most of them looked the age of the middle-school village boys I had taught twenty years ago in Togo. Those boys had called me Monsieur and left presents of papaya at my door. It was as if I had come back to the region to find all my students armed and snarling, ordering me to get out of the car.

I tried to talk my way through the roadblocks in the old jokey Peace Corps way. And it usually worked: the boys' faces softened, the barked orders turned into requests for cigarettes or money or aspirin, which were only half serious and then even a bit sheepish, and, as the car started rolling forward, we exchanged a thumbs-up, and a boy began giving me breezy compliments—"If you Americans were here, we'd already be in Abidjan!"—as if the guns had just been props and everything were friendly between us.

The farther west I drove—past the ripe anacard-fruit trees that no one was tending and the storehouses of cotton that couldn't be sold and the carcasses of vehicles that the rebels had wrecked and abandoned—the less useful my Peace Corps skills became. In Man itself, picturesquely nestled in a ring of steep green mountains with waterfalls, the boys at the roadblocks, drunk or high, muttered about stealing the car. Pickup trucks bristling with Liberians carrying rocket-propelled grenade launchers slalomed wildly through the rebel army's obstacle courses. The walls of government buildings were bullet-riddled, and the freshly turned mass graves gave off a sharp smell. It was hard to tell who was in charge of Man—the rebel commanders or their underage Ivorian and Liberian recruits, who, according to townspeople, were becoming indistinguishable.

In the middle of town, the young rebels hung out at a *maquis*, or open-air eatery, called the Tirbo, which smelled of porcupine stew. The youngest I saw, toting his AK-47, was no more than nine. I ordered a plate of rice and looked around. A boy with a red checked kaffiyeh on his head was staring straight ahead, filled with some private rage. Draped around the necks of other boys were leather clubs or sheathed knives or bandoliers. There was no one over thirty in sight.

At midday, a group of four Liberians arrived and sat down at a table. The young men, who propped their weapons between their legs, began making their way through a bottle of Mangoustan's rum. Their names were Sha, Shala, Johnson, and Romeo. Shala wore an American flag bandanna, Rambo style. Sha, the most intoxicated of the group, lifted his shirt to show me his wounds.

I asked how much he was paid for his services to the rebels.

"The cause is much more important than pay," Sha said. "I don't appreciate pay."

What was the cause?

"Peace and unity in Africa," he said.

After the war, Sha said, he wanted to go to New York and become an American marine and learn to fly helicopters and use heavy weapons. "I love America," he slurred, making an effort to lean forward. "America is my culture." He waved his glass at the others. "All of them love America."

Romeo's glass fell to the floor and shattered. He stared at the fragments without moving. Johnson told the waitress that they would pay for it. Romeo slouched, sunk in a dark mood.

A few months earlier, a recruiter had come to a refugee camp along the Liberian border and persuaded Romeo to join the rebels. There was no better offer on the horizon. "I want something because I don't want to be suffering, I don't have nowhere to go," he said. "Someone say, 'Take money, go to war. You will not go there? You will go.'" He turned his dead-eyed stare on me. "If you can't pay the young stuff, the war will go all over the world. The war will enter America—let me tell you today. Because you don't give them money. The man we want to see is bin Laden. We want to see him, to join him. Because he can pay revolutionaries. You think you can get pay for this?" Romeo held up his left calf to show me a bullet wound. "You can't. Bin Laden can pay it."

I had seen bin Laden's face painted on the side of a rebel vehicle. Some fighters wore T-shirts with bin Laden's face and Bush's face side by side. In this part of the world, there was no ideological contradiction. Both men stood for power.

At a hospital in a town not far from Man, an Italian doctor named Albert Brizio described the imagery of this war as "a perverse effect of globalization," adding, "It's what I call the Liberianization of war." Brizio had seen the effect in other African countries: young fighters styling themselves after performances, often brutal ones, that they'd seen on TV or in movies. "It allows people to see events or situations they would never have thought of, and they imitate them. These situations have always been contagious, but then you had contagion by contact. Now you have contagion by media."

But contagion by media can go in both directions, as I discovered when I met a young woman in Man named Jeannette Badouel. She was moving around town in the company of rebels, but unlike the handful of girl recruits in their ranks, she carried herself with an air of blithe authority and pop stylishness. Jeannette was impossible to miss, decked out in sparkly gold jeans labeled "Pussy" and rolled to the calf, six-inch platform shoes, and a pink frilly blouse; her hair was dyed blond and done in short braids. She shopped for her Liberian-made American-style T-shirts and shoes at Saturday markets along the border, which was one of the most dangerous places on earth. She was born in a village twenty miles south of Man but had been living with her French husband and their children in Rennes, where she directed a nonprofit group called Association Métissage, whose website says that it "realizes projects favoring cultural diversity and solidarity among peoples." When the western rebellion broke out, just as Jeannette was visiting her parents in Man, she refused the French government's offer of evacuation and decided to set up a rebel television station, using the digital equipment she happened to have brought. Though she claimed to operate free of political interference, it was clear that TV Grand Ouest served up pro-rebel propaganda to the region, if anyone was watching.

I sat in the station's bug-filled studio with Jeannette and watched programming. There was a traditional dance, performed to express villagers' happiness with rebel rule, the voice-over explained. There were Eddie Murphy movies. And there was footage of the aftermath of a recent massacre by government and Liberian forces—the hacked and bullet-ridden bodies of peasants lying in houses and on roads just south of Man—with Jeannette conducting breathless interviews.

I had trouble figuring Jeannette out. She loved fashion and reading

Paris Match, yet rebel-held Man seemed to suit her fine. The rebellion looked to her like a wonderful example of cultural diversity and solidarity among peoples. It was almost like America. "For me, it's democracy," she gushed. "Everyone is here—the Liberians are everywhere. You'll see a lot on the way to the border. Guineans, Malians. For me, it's the people."

Twenty years ago, V. S. Naipaul published an essay in *The New Yorker* called "The Crocodiles of Yamoussoukro," an account of life in Ivory Coast at the height of the "miracle" under Houphouët-Boigny. Toward the end of the piece, Naipaul has a dream: the bridge on which he is standing starts to melt away. The concrete and steel of Abidjan turn out to be perishable. "The new world existed in the minds of other men," he writes. "Remove those men, and their ideas—which, after all, had no finality—would disappear."

Naipaul's prophecy that Ivory Coast would slip back into a primordial past seemed comforting compared with the new reality that was taking hold. Cool B and his gang, and the Young Patriots, and the rebels in the north and the west are severed irrevocably from the traditional sources of meaning—the village, the elders, the extended family—that I found in West Africa two decades ago. Their heroes are American celebrities, local warlords, gangsters, and demagogues. In the cities and the ragtag armies, they live in a society consisting of only the young. Tempted and tormented by images and words from elsewhere, trapped in a money economy with nothing to sell, they have no ready way of realizing their desires. But they can't go back. To some hardheaded observers in the West, they are "loose molecules," mindless forces of anarchy or a new primitivism. In fact, the opposite is true: the struggle in Ivory Coast, and perhaps in other parts of Africa, is recognizable as the unlovely effort of individuals to find an identity and a place in a world that has no use for them.

In Abidjan, I spoke with Ruth Marshall-Fratani, a researcher with the French journal *Politique Africaine*. "The gap between aspirations and possibilities—I think that gap has widened incredibly in the last fifteen years," she said. "Access to global images has increased it amazingly." The phrase she borrowed to describe the situation of the young Africans I had met was *lèche-vitrines*—window-licking. "It isn't window-shopping," she explained. "That means you can go in and buy. This is just licking the window. And, basically, that's this generation's experience." She went on, "Everybody wants to get a part of the action. They have these aspirations and they're not prepared to give them up. Politics is one way. Religion is another. And war is another."

On one of my last days in Ivory Coast, I went back to Koumassi to see Cool B. He wanted to introduce me to two young men he knew. Madness and Yul, twenty-six and twenty-three, had both done time in prison and had the razor scars to prove it. Madness, whose real name is Mohamed Bamba, had been on the street since the age of twelve, working as a petty thief and drug dealer. His eyelids were heavy and his voice slow from years of smoking heroin. Yul, born Issouf Traore, hustled stolen pharmaceuticals. Both of them were trying to go straight as barkers at a *woro-woro* station, snagging passengers for local runs. Cool B, Madness, Yul, and I sat in a *maquis* and drank Guinness. Madness was stoic; Yul, whose nickname came from his shaved head, grew frantic as he talked. It was the same story I'd heard from the others—a father who hadn't taken care of him. "He told me, 'If you come back here I'll put you in prison again.' I said, 'You're my father, you put me in the world.'" What agitated Yul to distraction was the fact that his father had gone back to Mali and died and been buried before they could reconcile. "He died when it still wasn't okay with us. He spoke to me, but I don't know what was at the bottom of his heart."

From his trouser pocket Yul withdrew a piece of folded officialdom. It wasn't proof of citizenship—his father had failed to naturalize him. Nor did Yul have Malian papers. But when his girlfriend gave birth, Yul, who never attended school, needed to establish himself as the legal father. He bribed the police to give him a document stating, falsely, that he had lost his identity card. The document was called a "Certificate of Declaration of Loss." It wasn't sufficient to confer his last name on his son, but it was the sum of Yul's identity in Ivory Coast.

"A man has to have a father at his side to help him. If he doesn't—" Yul stared at me a bit wildly, his toothy mouth open. "Who's going to help me? Who? I don't see."

Madness said calmly, "If you talk to a thousand youths, there isn't one who will tell you it's going okay for him."

I asked Madness and Yul what they imagined Americans thought of them.

"They've forgotten us," Yul said.

"They don't know what we're living here in Africa," Madness said. "Africa is misery. Africa—really—it's hard, hard, hard. People of goodwill are interested in us. But there are others, with means, who aren't interested at all. Because Africa—it's a continent of hell."

The Moderate Martyr

The New Yorker, September 11, 2006

In 1967, a law student at the University of Khartoum named Abdullahi Ahmed an-Naim was looking for a way to spend a summer evening in his home town, a railway junction on the banks of the Nile in northern Sudan. No good movies were showing at the local cinemas, so he went with a friend to hear a public lecture by Mahmoud Muhammad Taha, an unorthodox Sudanese mystic with a small but ardent following. Taha's subject, "An Islamic Constitution: Yes and No," tantalized Naim. In the years after Sudan became independent, in 1956, the role of Islam in the state was fiercely debated by traditional Sufists, secular Marxists, and the increasingly powerful Islamists of the Muslim Brotherhood, who, at the time, were led in Sudan by Hasan al-Turabi, a legal scholar. Politically, Naim was drifting toward the left, but his upbringing in a conservative Muslim home had formed him. "I was very torn," Naim recently recalled. "I am a Muslim, but I couldn't accept sharia"—Islamic law. "I studied sharia and I knew what it said. I couldn't see how Sudan could be viable without women being full citizens and without non-Muslims being full citizens. I'm a Muslim, but I couldn't live with this view of Islam."

Naim's quandary over Islam was an intensely personal conflict—he called it a "deadlock." What he heard at Taha's lecture resolved it. Taha said that the Sudanese constitution needed to be reformed, in order to reconcile "the individual's need for absolute freedom with the community's need for total social justice." This political ideal, he argued, could be best achieved not through Marxism or liberalism but through Islam—that is, Islam in its original, uncorrupted form, in which women and people of other faiths were accorded equal status. As Naim listened, a profound sense of peace washed over him; he joined Taha's movement, which came to be known as the Republican Brothers, and the night that had begun so idly changed his life.

It is a revelation story, and some version of it is surprisingly easy to hear in the Islamic world, especially among educated middle-class Muslims in the generation that came after the failures of nationalism and socialism. During a recent trip to Sudan, I visited the University of Khartoum, which is housed in a collection of mostly colonial era, earth-colored brick buildings in the city center, where I met a woman named Suhair Osman, who was doing graduate work in statistics. In 1993, at the age of eighteen, she spent the year between high school and college in her parents' house on the Blue Nile, south of Khartoum, asking herself theological questions. As a schoolgirl, she had been taught that sinners would be eternally tormented after death; she couldn't help feeling sorry for them, but she didn't dare speak about it in class. Would all of creation simply end either in fire or in paradise? Was her worth as a woman really no more than a quarter that of a man, as she felt Islamic law implied by granting men the right to take four wives? Did believers really have a duty to kill infidels? One day, Osman took a book by Taha off her father's shelf, *The Koran, Mustapha Mahmoud, and Modern Understanding*, published in 1970. By the time she finished it, she was weeping. For the first time, she felt that religion had accorded her fully equal status. "Inside this thinking, I'm a human being," she said. "Outside this thinking, I'm not." It was as if she had been asleep all her life and had suddenly woken up: the air, the taste of water, food, even the smell of things changed. She felt as if she were walking a little off the ground.

The quest for spiritual meaning is typically a personal matter in the West. In the Islamic world, it often leads the seeker into some kind of collective action, informed by utopian aspiration, that admits no distinction between proselytizing, social reform, and politics. The Islamic revival of the past several decades is the history of millions of revelation stories. Far from being idiosyncratic or marginal, they have combined into a tremendous surge that is now a full-time concern of the West. Renewal and reform—in Arabic, *tajdid* and *islah*—have an ambiguous and contested meaning in the Islamic world. They signify a stripping away of accumulated misreadings and wrong or lapsed practices, as in the Protestant

Reformation, and a return to the founding texts of the Koran and the Sunna—guidelines based on the recorded words and deeds of the Prophet. But beyond that, what is the nature of the reform? The father of one modern revelation story is Sayyid Qutb, the Egyptian religious thinker who, after advocating jihad and the overthrow of secular Arab regimes, was hanged by Gamal Abdel Nasser in 1966. Qutb's prison writings reject modernity, with its unholy secularism, and call on adherents of Islam to return to a radically purified version of the religion, which was established in the seventh century. Among the idealistic young believers who found in his books a guide to worldwide Islamization were Ayman al-Zawahiri and Osama bin Laden. With the newest generation of jihadis—Qutb's spiritual grandchildren—the ideas of the master have been construed as a justification for killing just about anyone in the name of reviving the days of the Prophet; earlier this year, several Baghdad falafel vendors were killed by Islamists because falafel did not exist in the seventh century.

Mahmoud Muhammad Taha is the anti-Qutb. Taha, like Qutb, was hanged by an Arab dictatorship; he was executed in 1985 for sedition and apostasy, after protesting the imposition of sharia in Sudan by President Jaafar al-Nimeiri. In death, Taha became something rare in contemporary Islam: a moderate martyr. His method of reconciling Muslim belief with twentieth-century values was, in its way, every bit as revolutionary as the contrary vision of Qutb. It is one sign of the current state of the struggle over Islam that in the five years since September 11, millions of people around the world have learned the name Sayyid Qutb, while Mahmoud Muhammad Taha's is virtually unknown. Islamism has taken on the frightening and faceless aspect of the masked jihadi, the full-length veil, the religious militia, the blurred figure in a security video, the messianic head of state, the anti-American mob. At Islam's core, in the countries of the Middle East from Egypt to Iran, *tajdid* and *islah* have helped push societies toward extremes of fervor, repression, and violence. But on the periphery, from Senegal to Indonesia—where the vast majority of Muslims live—Islamic reform comes in more varieties than most Westerners imagine. At the edges, the influence of American policy and the Israeli-Palestinian siege is less overwhelming, and it is easier to see that the real drama in Islam is the essential dilemma addressed by Taha: how to revive ancient sacred texts in a way that allows one to live in the modern world.

• • •

Taha was born sometime early in the twentieth century—scholars say 1909 or 1911—in a town on the eastern bank of the Blue Nile, two hours south of Khartoum, called Rufaa. It is a somnolent, heat-drenched town, one of those silent places—they stretch from one harsh end to the other of the North African region known as the Sahel—where mystical movements often begin. In the years before Sudan's independence, Taha was educated as a civil engineer in a British-run university, and after working briefly for Sudan Railways he started his own engineering business. He absorbed modern political and social ideas by reading widely, if incompletely, the works of Marx, Lenin, Russell, Shaw, and Wells. In 1945, he founded an antimonarchical political group, the Republican Party, and was twice imprisoned by the British authorities: first for writing pro-independence pamphlets, and then for leading an uprising in Rufaa against the arrest of a local woman who had subjected her daughter to a particularly severe form of female circumcision. (Taha opposed the practice but believed that the colonial edict banning it would only make it more widespread.) His second imprisonment lasted two years, and when he was released, in 1948, he entered a period of seclusion, prayer, and fasting in a small mud building in the courtyard next to his in-laws' house. By the time I visited Rufaa, in July, the hut had been torn down and replaced, and the house was occupied by a family of southern Sudanese.

While in seclusion, Taha spoke to few people; one man described him as having long, unruly hair and bloodshot eyes. His wife brought him plates of simple food—her family urged her to divorce this formerly successful professional, who some people thought had gone mad, but she refused—and he left the hut only to take swims in the Nile, a short walk away. During this period, which lasted three years, Taha developed his radically new vision of the meaning of the Koran. After emerging from seclusion, in 1951, he dedicated the rest of his life to teaching it.

For any Muslim who believes in universal human rights, tolerance, equality, freedom, and democracy, the Koran presents an apparently insoluble problem. Some of its verses carry commands that violate a modern person's sense of morality. The Koran accepts slavery. The Koran appoints men to be "the protectors and maintainers of women," to whom women owe obedience; if disobeyed, men have the duty first to warn them, then to deny them sex, and finally to "beat them (lightly)." The Koran orders believers to wait until the holy months are finished, and then to "fight and slay the Pagans wherever you find them, and seize them, beleaguer them, and lie in wait for them in every stratagem [of war]." These and other verses present God's purpose in clear, unmistakable terms, and they have become some of the favorite passages in the sermons, fatwas, and Internet postings of present-day fundamentalists to justify violence and jihad. An enormous industry of reform-minded interpreters has arisen in recent years to explain them away, contextualize them, downplay them, or simply ignore them, often quoting the well-known verse that says there is "no compulsion in religion." Not long ago, I received one such lecture from a Shiite cleric in Baghdad, who cited the "no compulsion" verse while sitting under a portrait of Ayatollah Khomeini. In confronting the troublesome verses head-on, Taha showed more intellectual honesty than all the Islamic scholars, community leaders, and world statesmen who think that they have solved the problem by flatly declaring Islam to be a religion of peace.

The Koran was revealed to Muhammad in two phases—first in Mecca, where for thirteen years he and his followers were a besieged minority, and then in Medina, where the Prophet established Islamic rule in a city filled with Jews and pagans. The Meccan verses are addressed, through Muhammad, to humanity in general, and are suffused with a spirit of freedom and equality; according to Taha, they present Islam in its perfect form, as the Prophet lived it, through exhortation rather than threat. In Taha's most important book, a slender volume called *The Second Message of Islam* (published in 1967, with the dedication "To humanity!"), he writes that the lives of the "early Muslims" in Mecca "were the supreme expression of their religion and consisted of sincere worship, kindness, and peaceful coexistence with all other people." Abdullahi an-Naim, who is now a law professor at Emory University, translated the book into English; in his introduction, he writes, "Islam, being the final and universal religion according to Muslim belief, was offered first in tolerant and egalitarian terms in Mecca, where the Prophet preached equality and individual responsibility between all men and women without distinction on grounds of race, sex, or social origin. As that message was rejected in practice, and the Prophet and his few followers were persecuted and forced to migrate to Medina, some aspects of the message changed."

As Taha puts it in *The Second Message of Islam*, whereas Muhammad propagated "verses of peaceful persuasion" during his Meccan period, in Medina "the verses of compulsion by the sword prevailed." The Medinan verses are full of rules, coercion, and threats, including the orders for jihad, and in Taha's view they were a historical adaptation to the reality of life in a seventh-century Islamic city-state, in which "there was no law except the sword." At one point, Taha writes that two modest decrees of the Meccan verses—"You are only a reminder, you have no dominion over them"—were appended with a harsh Medinan edict: "Except he who shuns and disbelieves, on whom God shall inflict the greatest suffering." In his distinctive rhetorical style, which combines dense exegesis with humanistic uplift, Taha observed, "It is as if God had said, 'We have granted you, Muhammad, dominion over anyone who shuns and disbelieves, so that God shall subject him to minor suffering at your hands through fighting, then God shall also subject him to the greatest suffering in hell.' . . . Thus the first two verses were abrogated or repealed by the two second verses."

The Medinan verses, directed not to Muhammad alone but to the community of early believers, became the basis for sharia as it was developed by legal scholars over the next few centuries—what Taha calls the "first message of Islam." In Taha's revisionist reading, the elevation of the Medinan verses was only a historical postponement—the Meccan verses, representing the ideal religion, would be revived when humanity had reached a stage of development capable of accepting them, ushering in a renewed Islam based on freedom and equality. Taha quoted a hadith, or saying of the Prophet, that declared, "Islam started as a stranger, and it shall return as a stranger in the same way it started." This "second message of Islam" is higher and better than the first, delivered by a messenger who came to seventh-century Arabia, in a sense, from the future. And in the twentieth century, the time had come for Muslims finally to receive it. Taha offered a hermeneutical way out of the modern crisis of Islam, allowing Muslims to affirm their faith without having to live by an inhumane code.

Taha's reputation and importance far exceeded his actual following, which never amounted to more than a few thousand intensely devoted Sudanese: the stories of overwhelming personal transformation that I heard from Naim, Osman, and other Republican Brothers were apparently common among his adherents. (Taha adapted the name of his old political party for his new spiritual movement; he was wary of substituting Islamist slogans for critical thinking.) He received visitors at his house in Omdurman, northwest of Khartoum, at all hours, engaging in a kind of continuous seminar in which he was unmistakably the instructor—Republican Brothers still call him Ustazh, or "revered teacher"—but one who welcomed argument. "He would listen with utmost respect," a follower named Omer el-Garrai told me. "I never saw him frustrated, I never saw him angry, I never heard him shout." Naim recalled, "Taha could not transmit his religious enlightenment to us by talking about it. We would see the fruit of it by his personal lifestyle, in his attitudes. His honesty, his intellectual vigor, his serenity, his charisma—those are the things that we can observe, and from them I understood that this is someone who had a transformative religious experience." Taha lived simply, urging his followers to do the same, and even today Republican Brothers are known for their lack of show in dress and in wedding ceremonies. An aura of saintliness hangs over stories I heard about Taha in Sudan, and, as with Gandhi, to whom he is sometimes compared, there's an unappealingly remote quality to his moral example. A man named Anour Hassan recalled that when Taha's twelve-year-old son vanished in the Blue Nile, in 1954, Taha calmly told people who wanted to continue looking for the boy, "No, he's gone to a kinder father than I am."

Perhaps the twentieth century was too soon for the second message of Islam. Taha was condemned for apostasy by Sudanese and Egyptian clerics, his movement was under constant attack from the fundamentalist Muslim Brotherhood, and his public appearances were banned by the government. Various rumors began to circulate: that Taha and his followers believed him to be a new prophet, or even a divinity; that Taha didn't pray; that he was insane. His legacy became controversial even among liberal-minded Sudanese. One evening in July, I spoke with the moderate politician and intellectual Sadiq al-Mahdi on the terrace overlooking the garden of his palatial home in Omdurman. Mahdi, who twice served as prime minister of Sudan and was twice ousted, in 1967 and 1989, is an imposing man: he was wearing the traditional white djellaba and turban, and his beard was hennaed. He spoke respectfully of Taha but found him theologically unsound. "Amongst the Islamists, there are those who jump into the future and those who jump into the past," Mahdi said, comparing Taha with Qutb. "Taha is amongst those who jump into the future. He definitely is for radical Islamic reform. But he based it on arguments that are not legitimate." Mahdi, like many other modern Muslim thinkers, believes that the Koran already offers the basis for affirming democratic values; there is no need, as he put it, to perform "these somersaults."

What's truly remarkable about Taha is that he existed at all. In the midst of a gathering storm of Islamist extremism, he articulated a message of liberal reform that was rigorous, coherent, and courageous. His vision asked Muslims to abandon fourteen hundred years of accepted dogma in favor of a radical and demanding new methodology that would set them free from the burdens of traditional jurisprudence. Islamic law, with its harsh punishments and its repression of free thought, was, Taha argued, a human interpretation of the Medinan verses and the recorded words and deeds of the Prophet in Medina; developed in the early centuries after Muhammad, it was then closed off to critical revision for a millennium. When Taha spoke of "sharia," he meant the enlightened message of the Meccan verses, which is universal and eternal. To Muslims like Mahdi, this vision seemed to declare that part of the holy book was a mistake. Taha's message requires of Muslims such an intellectual leap that those who actually made it—as opposed to those who merely admired Taha or were interested in him—took on the quality of cult members, with their white garments, street-corner sermons, and egalitarian marriage contracts. Small wonder that Taha failed to create a durable mass movement. In *Quest for Divinity*, a new and generally sympathetic study of Taha, to be published this fall, Professor Mohamed A. Mahmoud, of Tufts University, writes, "The outcome of this culture of guardianship and total intellectual dependency was a movement with impoverished inner intellectual and spiritual resources, intrinsically incapable of surviving Taha's death."

Why did the Sudanese state, the religious establishment, and the Islamist hard-liners consider the leader of such a small movement worth killing? Perhaps because, as Khalid el-Haj, a retired school administrator in Rufaa, who first met Taha in the early sixties, told me, "They are afraid of the ideas, not the numbers. They know that the ideas are from inside Islam and they cannot face it."

Eventually, Taha's teaching collided with Islamist power politics. Sudan's military dictator, Jaafar al-Nimeiri, who had seized control of the country in 1969, was an opportunistic tyrant who had exhausted one model after another to justify his rule: Marxism, Arab nationalism, pro-Americanism. By the early eighties, Nimeiri's hold on power was loosening, and he felt particularly threatened by one of his advisers: Hasan al-Turabi, the legal scholar, who had an increasingly energetic Islamist following. Turabi, a brilliant politician with a British and French education, was an authoritarian ideologue, more in the mold of a Bolshevik than a hidebound cleric. One of Turabi's prime intellectual enemies was Taha, whose interpretation of the Koran he considered illegitimate. Taha, for his part, once dismissed Turabi as "clever but not insightful"—and many Sudanese believe that Turabi never forgot the slight.

In 1983, Nimeiri, aiming to counter Turabi's growing popularity, decided to make his own Islamic claim. He hastily pushed through laws that imposed a severe version of sharia on Sudan, including its Christian and animist south. Within eighteen months, more than fifty suspected thieves had their hands chopped off. A Coptic Christian was hanged for possessing foreign currency; poor women were flogged for selling local beer. It was exactly the kind of brutal, divisive, politically motivated sharia that Taha had long warned against, and southerners intensified a decades-long civil war against Khartoum. Taha and other Republican Brothers, including Naim, had been jailed in advance by Nimeiri to prevent them from leading protests; their imprisonment lasted a year and a half.

Soon after Taha was released, he distributed a leaflet, on Christmas Day 1984, titled "Either This or the Flood." "It is futile for anyone to claim that a Christian person is not adversely affected by the implementation of sharia," he wrote. "It is not enough for a citizen today merely to enjoy freedom of worship. He is entitled to the full rights of a citizen in total equality with all other citizens. The rights of southern citizens in their country are not provided for in sharia but rather in Islam at the level of fundamental Koranic revelation."

Taha, who was now in his mid-seventies, had been preparing half his life for this moment. It was central to his vision that Islamic law in its historical form, rather than in what he considered its original, authentic meaning, would be a monstrous injustice in modern society. His opposition was brave and absolute, and yet his statement reveals the limits of a

philosophy that he hoped to make universal. Taha opposed secularism—
he once declared that the secular West "is not a civilization because its
values are confused"—and he could not conceive of rights outside the
framework of Islam and the Koran. At the very moment that he was defending nonbelievers from the second-class status enshrined in Islamic
law, he was extending their equal rights through a higher, better sharia.

Abdullahi an-Naim defends Taha's approach, saying that in the Islamic world a Turkish-style secularism will always be self-defeating. "It is
an illusion to think you can sustain constitutionalism, democratization,
without addressing its Islamic foundation," he said. "Because for Muslims you cannot say, 'I'm a Muslim, but—' That 'but' does not work. What
unites Muslims is an idea. It is Islam as an idea. And therefore contesting
that idea, I think, is going to be permanent." Whenever secular intellectuals in Muslim countries try to bypass the question of sharia, Naim
said, "they leave the high moral ground to the fundamentalists, and they
lose." Invoking Islam as the highest authority for universal rights was not
simply a matter of belief; it meant that Taha and his movement could stay
in the game.

Soon after Taha's Christmas statement was released, he was arrested
again. This time, the government pressed charges amounting to apostasy,
which carried the death penalty. Taha refused to recognize the legitimacy
of the court under sharia, refused to repent, and in a matter of hours was
condemned to death. The hanging was scheduled for the morning of January 18, 1985. Among the hundreds of spectators in the vast courtyard of
Kober Prison, in Khartoum North, was Judith Miller, then a *Times* reporter, disguised in a white cloak and head scarf. In the opening of her
1996 book, *God Has Ninety-nine Names*, Miller described the scene:

> Shortly before the appointed time, Mahmoud Muhammad Taha
> was led into the courtyard. The condemned man, his hands tied
> behind him, was smaller than I expected him to be, and from
> where I sat, as his guards hustled him along, he looked younger
> than his seventy-six years. He held his head high and stared si-
> lently into the crowd. When they saw him, many in the crowd
> leaped to their feet, jeering and shaking their fists at him. A few
> waved their Korans in the air.
>
> I managed to catch only a glimpse of Taha's face before the

executioner placed an oatmeal-colored sack over his head and body, but I shall never forget his expression: His eyes were defiant; his mouth firm. He showed no hint of fear.

In the instant that the trapdoor opened and Taha's body fell through, the crowd began to scream, *"Allahu Akbar! Allahu Akbar! Islam huwa al-hall!"*—"God is great! Islam is the solution!"—the slogan of the Muslim Brotherhood.

Some of Taha's followers could not accept that he was dead—they had actually come to believe in Taha's divinity—and they spent several days by one of the bridges spanning the Nile, waiting for him to appear. When he didn't (his body was flown by helicopter to an unknown location in the desert for a hasty burial), the Republican Brotherhood essentially died. Some members, including Naim, went abroad; others stayed in Sudan but ceased any public activity. The regime forced a number of imprisoned Republican Brothers to repudiate Taha's ideas in order to avoid his fate. His books were burned in public bonfires.

The execution appalled large numbers of Sudanese, who were unused to political violence, and it helped precipitate the downfall of Nimeiri, four months later, when a popular uprising restored democratic rule. January 18 became Arab Human Rights Day. In 2000, a Sudanese reporter asked Nimeiri about the death of Taha. Nimeiri expressed regret over the killing, then made a startling claim: Taha's execution had been secretly engineered by Hasan al-Turabi.

"I didn't want him killed," Nimeiri said of Taha. "Turabi told me that Mahmoud Muhammad Taha wanted to side with the left against me and that the Republican Brothers are a force not to be underestimated, and that if he united with the left I am definitely doomed. Turabi brought me the order to execute him and asked me to sign off on it . . . I decided to postpone my decision for two days, and on the third day I went to Taha, dressed in civilian clothes. I told him, 'Your death would sadden me. Just back down on your decision.' But he spoke to me in a way that at the time I felt was blustering but now I see it was honorable, considering the situation. He told me, 'You back down on your decision. As for me, I know that I'm going to be killed. If I'm not killed in court, the Muslim Brotherhood will kill me in secret. So leave and let me be. I know that I am going to die.'"

I asked a number of people in Khartoum about the role that Turabi might have played in Taha's death. "Turabi killed him" was the blunt verdict of Hyder Ibrahim Ali, a sociologist and the director of the Sudanese Studies Center. "I think Turabi was behind all this. Taha was a real rival for Turabi. At that time, the only people at the University of Khartoum as strong as the Muslim Brotherhood were the Republican Brothers." Others echoed this view: even if Turabi hadn't played a direct role in Taha's death, Taha's reform-minded movement had offered the most serious theological challenge to Turabi's severe Islamism.

In the decade after Taha's death, Turabi and his hard-line politics flourished. In 1989, he was the prime strategist of the Islamist revolution that followed the military overthrow of Prime Minister Sadiq al-Mahdi. He became the intellectual architect of the new regime, led by Omar al-Bashir, and presided over its reign of terror in the nineties. He was the impresario who attracted just about every leading jihadi terrorist to Sudan; journalists started calling him "the Khomeini of the Sunnis" and "the pope of terrorism." In 1999, however, Turabi's fortunes abruptly changed: he lost a power struggle with Bashir, who fired him.

This spring, Turabi, in a striking return to Sudanese politics, said some astonishing things about Islam. Though he had always been more supportive of women's rights than other hard-liners, he was now declaring that women and men are equal, that women can lead Islamic prayers, that covering the hair is not obligatory, that apostasy should not be a crime. He said that Muslim women can marry Christians or Jews. Quotations in the Arab press made him sound like a liberal reformer. In Khartoum, people marveled that he sounded exactly like Taha. Suhair Osman, the young woman I met at the University of Khartoum, informed me, with a wan smile, "It is said in the daily papers and in the discussion centers here in the university that Turabi killed Ustazh Mahmoud and now he's stealing his ideas."

In the next few decades, several Arab countries—Iraq, Palestine, perhaps Egypt and Algeria—may well come under some form of Islamist rule, either by election or by force. If so, they would do well to study the example of Sudan. A whole generation in Sudan has grown up under the hard-line ideology that was imposed by Turabi and his colleagues after 1989. "We are the wounded surgeons, we have had the plague," Sadiq al-Mahdi told me. "We have been the guinea pig of this whole exercise, and you should listen to us."

Islam is as diverse as Muslims themselves, but Islamism, thus far in its short history, tends to look the same wherever it appears. The Sudanese version was not a genuine revolution like the Iranian one; it was more of an élite project that never gained legitimacy outside of student, intellectual, and military circles. Still, Sudan's hard-line party, the National Islamic Front, marched the country through familiar paces. Suliman Baldo, the director of the Africa program at the International Crisis Group, who lived through the years of Islamization in Khartoum and published a report documenting the return of slavery in Sudan, said of the government, "They came with a social engineering project—they were very open about this." Education became a form of indoctrination: small children learned jihadist chants; school uniforms were replaced with combat fatigues; students engaged in paramilitary drills and memorized the Koran; teachers overhauled the curriculum to focus on the glory of Arab and Islamic culture. Khartoum had been a socially relaxed city that celebrated Christmas, but now the morals police ensured that women were veiled, especially in government offices and universities. The security agencies were taken over by Islamists, and torture chambers known as "ghost houses" proliferated in what had been a tolerant political culture. (Some torturers were reportedly trained by Iranian Revolutionary Guards.) Young men were conscripted into the new People's Defense Force and sent to fight in the jihad against the infidels of the south, thousands of them crying *"Allahu Akbar!"* as they went to their deaths. Turabi declared that the jihadis would ascend directly to paradise. Actors simulated "weddings" between martyrs and heavenly virgins on state television. Turabi gave asylum and assistance to terrorists, including bin Laden and other Al Qaeda members, and Sudan soon made enemies of every one of its many neighbors, along with the United States. And so an ethnically and religiously mixed African country, with an egalitarian brand of Sufism as its dominant form of Islam, was mobilized by intellectuals and soldiers to create a militaristic, ideologically extreme state whose main achievements were civil war, slavery, famine, and mass death.

Sometime in the late nineties, Turabi realized that his grand enterprise was a failure. Sudan had come under United Nations sanctions for sponsoring a 1995 assassination attempt on President Hosni Mubarak of Egypt. The country was internationally isolated; the civil war was killing millions. And the Islamist project was bankrupt. As in Iran, it had produced an increasingly wealthy and corrupt ruling class of ideologues and security officers, while young Sudanese, including many of Turabi's followers, left the country or turned inward.

It was at this low point that Omar al-Bashir expelled Turabi from the government. Until last year, Turabi found himself in and out of jail, and he began to rethink his politics. He declared that the war in the south had not been a jihad after all but, rather, a meaningless waste. In prison, he began to write about where the Islamists had gone wrong. The problem, he decided, was a failure to adhere to principles of democracy and human rights. This spring, Turabi began attracting attention with his liberal statements about women and Islam. He welcomed the deployment of a United Nations force to the Darfur region, where the government had launched a campaign of ethnic cleansing, and he mocked bin Laden for threatening to mount a jihad against the peacekeepers. (Some analysts believe that Turabi had a hand in the rebellion that preceded the mass killings in the region, but no one has been able to prove it.) His remarks were so radical that they earned him charges of apostasy by clerics in Sudan and Saudi Arabia. The Saudi edition of the Sudanese newspaper that quoted his proclamations had the offending lines torn out of every copy.

In Khartoum, people used the same phrase over and over: there had been "a hundred-and-eighty-degree turn" in Turabi's views. I heard several explanations. Sadiq al-Mahdi, the former prime minister, believed that Turabi was trying to atone for the damage he had inflicted on Sudan. Others saw old opportunism under new slogans: Turabi realized that thanks to Islamist misrule, democracy would be the next wave in Sudan, and he wanted to get out in front of it. There was also the possibility that he couldn't bear to be ignored.

One day in late July, during a hard Sahara windstorm that obscured the merciless sun and left sand in my molars, Turabi received me in his office on the outskirts of Khartoum, beyond the airport. I found him sitting behind a vast desk, which was almost bare; so were the bookcases next to it, as if he were waiting for someone to refurnish the trappings of power. Turabi is now seventy-four years old. He has a trim white beard and bright eyes framed by elegant wire-rim glasses; he wore a white djel-

laba and turban, white patent leather loafers, and flower-patterned poly-
ester socks. He has a resonant voice, which, when the topic turns serious,
often breaks into a disconcerting giggle, accompanied by a bucktoothed
grin. Turabi is inexhaustible: before I arrived, he had spoken for three
days to members of his breakaway political party, but he required scarcely
any prompting to carry on a nearly three-hour monologue with me. It was
like trying to follow the flight path of a mosquito: he would leave sentences unfinished, switch subjects in the span of a clause, swallow the
point in a laugh, then suddenly alight somewhere—on hidebound Saudi
clerics, clueless Algerian Islamists, pigheaded Sudanese soldiers, shortsighted American politicians—and draw blood.

Turabi presented himself as older but wiser, free now to be the one
independent thinker in a world of ideologues, an emissary for both sides
in the war between Islam and the West, unafraid of uttering any truth,
including truths about his own mistakes—but whenever I tried to pin
him down on one he blamed someone else and claimed that his role was
exaggerated. "Oh, Turabi, he's the 'pope of terrorism,' of fundamentalism,
the *pope noir du terrorisme!*" he mocked. The Bush administration's war
on terror, he said, was a gigantic misunderstanding based on a failure to
communicate. As for the Islamic revival, it held no dangers for the West.
"Oh, no, it's positive!" he said. "What is our economic model? It's not the
Soviet model. It's not the old capitalist model, or the feudal model. It's
your model! What is our political model? It's your model! Almost the same
model! Okay?"

Toward the end of his discourse, I mentioned that a number of Sudanese had heard echoes of Mahmoud Muhammad Taha in his recent statements. For the first time, Turabi lost his good humor. "Ooh," he groaned.
He called Taha "an apostate" who was "not normal," and he insisted that,
far from being behind Taha's death, he had argued with Nimeiri for his
life: "I said, 'Why do you jail this man? He won't hurt you, he's not against
this regime. He thinks he's the impersonation of Jesus Christ!'" Turabi
laughed dismissively. "I said, 'Let him go and advocate his message. He
will persuade a few people for some time. He's not harmful to you.'" He
said of Taha, "From early days, I don't read his books, I don't mention his
name. Even if people ask me questions, I try to evade, because in every
society, in America, you have had these cult people—everyone has to
drink the killing material! Jim Jones!"

Turabi giggled and stood up to say goodbye.

When I had asked Abdullahi an-Naim about Turabi's recent statements on women, minorities, and Islam, he had scoffed, "He has no methodology." It was true: Turabi threw out opinions like handfuls of seed. But, as Taha had said, the one constant in his long career has been cleverness. Turabi seemed to recognize that in the ruins of his own making in Sudan, his countrymen required a new notion of Islam and government. Great turns in history seldom come because someone writes a manifesto or proposes a theory. Instead, concrete experience, usually in the form of catastrophic failure, forces people to search for new ideas, many of which have been lying around for quite a while. Naim, who had fled the country after the 1989 coup, went back to Sudan in 2003 to find that "people were totally disillusioned about the Islamist project. They could see that it was corrupting and corrupt." In reaction, a small but growing number of Sudanese have come under the influence of Saudi Wahhabism—turning to an even more extreme theology as the pure Islam. Others, such as Osman Mirghani, a newspaper columnist and a former follower of Turabi, have concluded that the problem in Sudan has less to do with religion than with its civic culture. Mirghani has formed a new citizens' movement, Sudan Forum, waging its first campaign against corruption in high places.

Taha's solution to the modern Muslim dilemma hovers over the conversations of Sudanese who are too young to have any memory of him. In a dingy office in downtown Khartoum, I met a man named Hussein and a woman named Buthina, two social activists who are just the kind of idealists that the Islamists used to attract. In 1989, as a teenager, Hussein had at first welcomed the new government. He soon realized that its promises of Islamic justice were false, and he was traumatized by the year he spent as a conscript in the jihad against the south. "In my view, this regime is a great shame in the history of Islam," he said. "It's pushed people away from Islam. Their mentality has changed. They are no longer abiding by Islamic regulations." He mentioned prostitution, drinking, and corruption. For all Hussein's disillusionment, he still believed in sharia—in flogging for fornication, stoning for adultery, and beheading for apostasy—but he wanted it to be applied under a democratic government grounded in human rights. Buthina shook her head; Islamist rule had turned her toward secularism. "This is a very, very sensitive issue," she said. "When you design your regulations and constitution, you have to accept that all the people look at this constitution and see themselves in it. Otherwise, they will not implement it. If we design the constitution and the law of the country on Islam, this will create a problem."

When I described Hussein to Naim, he said, "He sees the corruption of the current regime, and he sees the unworkability of an Islamic state, but he has no alternative. That is the point about Taha. Taha provides an alternative. As the crisis intensifies, the receptivity to something like Taha's ideas will grow." The misrule of Turabi and the Sudanese Islamists, Naim said, had done more to advance the project of reforming sharia than Taha's followers could ever have achieved. At the same time, he admitted that most people in Sudan today have never heard of Taha. All that is left of his movement is a few hundred followers, some of whom gather in the evenings at a house in Omdurman. I was invited to join them there one night: the men sat in chairs on one side of the courtyard, the women on the other, but they mixed more than the religious Muslims at most gatherings. All dressed in white, they chanted traditional Sufi songs and a mournful hymn about their martyred leader.

The hollowness at the core of Sudan, and the widespread cynicism about Islamist rule, with its enforced ideology and rituals, is reminiscent of Eastern Europe in the years before the fall of the Berlin Wall. But if you spend time in an Islamic country you soon realize that the Communism analogy runs dry. For Islam, unlike Marxism, is deeply rooted and still present in everyday life in profound ways. As such, it is an irresistible mobilizing tool for politicians: an Islamist leader in Morocco, Nadia Yassin, once said, "If I go into the streets and I call people to come with me to a demonstration, and I talk to them about Che Guevara and Lenin, nobody will go out. But if I start talking about Muhammad and Ali and Aisha and all the prophets of Islam, they will follow me." Islam remains the system of values by which Muslims live; it is strong enough to survive Islamism. Perhaps, in time, the religion's centrality will subside, but for the foreseeable future, the Islamic enlightenment in which so many Western thinkers have placed their hopes—that is, secularism—will not sweep the Muslim world. The Islamic revival, and its attendant struggles and ills, is less like the eighteenth century in Europe than like the sixteenth, the age of Luther, when the most sensitive and ambitious Englishmen, French-men, and Germans devoted their efforts to finding in the words of the Bible a meaning for which they were prepared to live and die.

On the wall of Naim's office at Emory University, just above a picture of his parents, there is a black-and-white portrait of Taha in old age, seated, with the folds of a white robe draped over his shoulders and the Sudanese turban wrapped around his head; his gaze is both direct and abstracted, taking in something far beyond the camera. Ever since the night Naim attended Taha's lecture as a young law student, he has be-lieved that Muslims must find a way out of the predicament in which their own history has placed them—if not by accepting Taha's vision, then by working toward another.

"I don't really have high hopes for change in the Arab region, because it is too self-absorbed in its own sense of superiority and victimhood," he said. His hope lies in the periphery—West Africa, the Sahel, Central and Southeast Asia: "They are not noticed, but that's where the hope is." The damage done to Muslim lives under the slogan "Islam is the solution," and Islamism's failure to solve their daily problems and answer people's deepest needs, has forced younger Muslims in countries like Indonesia, Turkey, and Morocco to approach religion and politics in a more sophisti-cated way. Naim's newest project, which he calls a work of advocacy more than of scholarship, is a manuscript called "The Future of Sharia." Even before its English publication, he has begun to post it on the Web, trans-lated into Persian, Urdu, Bengali, Turkish, Arabic, and Bahasa Indonesia. Its theme is more radical than anything he has written before; although it is based on his long devotion to Taha's ideas, it goes beyond them and, according to some of Taha's followers, leaves them behind. "The Future of Sharia" amounts to a kind of secularism: it proposes not a rigid separa-tion of politics and religion, as in Turkey, but rather a scheme in which Islam informs political life but cannot be introduced into law by an ap-peal to any religious authority. Otherwise, Muslims would not be free. "I need a secular state to be a Muslim," Naim said. "If I don't have the free-dom to disbelieve, I cannot believe."

Two days after we spoke, Naim flew to Nigeria to give a series of lectures, based on the new book, in the northern states that have imposed a particularly harsh form of sharia. He plans to travel next year to Indone-sia and, if possible, to Iran. Two years ago, when he lectured in northern

Nigeria, a quarter of his audience of eight hundred people walked out on him, and he had to slip away through a side door. He acknowledged that violence, even murder, might be the response this time. But Naim believes that, despite the evidence of the headlines, Islamic history is moving in his direction.

"In Sudan this simplistic answer failed," Naim said. "In Iran it failed. In northern Nigeria it failed. In Pakistan it failed. As these experiences fail, people are going to realize that there is no shortcut—that you have to confront the hard questions." His message to Muslims on his travels will be this: "I have been that way and I've seen the street is closed and I came back. And I see someone rushing and I tell him, this street is deadlocked, and he will not take my word and go all the way and discover that it is deadlocked and come back." He will tell them, "Listen, you don't have to do this, you don't have to go down this dead-end street. There is an Arabic expression: 'The fortunate ones will learn from the mistakes of others, the unfortunate ones will learn from their own mistakes.'"

By taking his message to the Muslim public and risking his own life, Naim is, perhaps unconsciously, following the example of one of the intellectual heroes of modern Islam. The first years of the twenty-first century hardly seem hospitable to Mahmoud Muhammad Taha's humane vision, but his words are there for young Muslims to discover once they get to the end of the street and need a way to turn around.

The Megacity

The New Yorker, November 13, 2006

The Third Mainland Bridge is a looping ribbon of concrete that connects Lagos Island to the continent of Africa. It was built in the 1970s, part of a vast network of bridges, cloverleafs, and expressways intended to transform the districts and islands of this Nigerian city—then comprising three million people—into an efficient modern metropolis. As the bridge snakes over sunken piers just above the waters of Lagos Lagoon, it passes a floating slum: thousands of wooden houses, perched on stilts a few feet above their own bobbing refuse, with rust-colored iron roofs wreathed in the haze from thousands of cooking fires. Fishermen and market women paddle dugout canoes on water as black and viscous as an oil slick. The bridge then passes the sawmill district, where rain-forest logs—sent across from the far shore, thirty miles to the east—form a floating mass by the piers.

Smoldering hills of sawdust landfill send white smoke across the bridge, which mixes with diesel exhaust from the traffic. Beyond the sawmills, the old waterfront markets, the fishermen's shanties, the blackened façades of high-rise housing projects, and the half-abandoned skyscrapers of downtown Lagos Island loom under a low, dirty sky. Around the city, garbage dumps steam with the combustion of natural gases, and auto yards glow with fires from fuel spills. All of Lagos seems to be burning.

The bridge descends into Lagos Island and a pandemonium of vendors' stalls crammed with spare parts, locks, hard hats, chains, screws, charcoal, detergent, and DVDs. On a recent afternoon, car horns, shouting voices, and radio music mingled with the snarling engines of motorcycle

taxis stalled in traffic and the roar of an air compressor in an oily tire repair yard. Two months earlier, a huge cast-iron water main suspended
beneath the bridge had broken free of its rusted clip, crushing a vacant
scrap market below and cutting off clean water from tens of thousands of
the fifteen million people who now live in Lagos.

In the absence of piped water, wealthier residents of the waterfront
slum at the end of the bridge, called Isale Eko, pay private contractors to
sink boreholes sixty feet deep. All day and night, residents line up at the
boreholes to pay five cents and fill their plastic buckets with contami-
nated water, which some of them drink anyway. Isale Eko is the oldest
and densest part of Lagos Island. Every square foot is claimed by someone—for selling, for washing, even for sleeping—and there is almost
no privacy. Many residents sleep outdoors. A young man sitting in an
alley pointed to some concrete ledges three feet above a gutter. "These
are beds," he said.

In the newer slums on the mainland, such as Mushin, rectangular
concrete-block houses squeeze seven or eight people into a single,
mosquito-infested room—in bunks or on the floor—along a narrow corridor of opposing chambers. This arrangement is known as "face me I
face you." One compound can contain eighty people. In Mushin, Muslim
Hausas from the north of Nigeria coexist uneasily with mostly Christian
Yorubas from the south. Armed gangs represent the interests of both groups.
On the night of February 2, 2002, a witness told me, a Hausa youth saw
a Yoruba youth squatting over a gutter on the street and demanded, "Why
are you shitting there?" In a city where only 0.4 percent of the inhabitants
have a toilet connected to a sewer system, it was more of a provocation
than a serious question. The incident that night led to a brawl. Almost
immediately, the surrounding compounds emptied out, and the streets
filled with Yorubas and Hausas armed with machetes and guns. The fighting lasted four days and was ended only by the military occupation of
Mushin. By then, more than a hundred residents had been killed, thousands had fled the area, and hundreds of houses had burned down.

Newcomers to the city are not greeted with the words "Welcome to Lagos." They are told "This is Lagos"—an ominous statement of fact. Olisa
Izeobi, a worker in one of the sawmills along the lagoon, said, "We under-

stand this as 'Nobody will care for you, and you have to struggle to survive.'" It is the singular truth awaiting the six hundred thousand people who pour into Lagos from West Africa every year. Their lungs will burn with smoke and exhaust; their eyes will sting; their skin will turn charcoal gray. And hardly any of them will ever leave.

Immigrants come to Lagos with the thinnest margin of support, dependent on a local relative or contact whose assistance usually lasts less than twenty-four hours. A girl from the Ibo country, in the southeast, said that she had been told by a woman in her hometown that she would get restaurant work in Lagos. Upon arrival, she discovered that she owed the woman more than two hundred dollars for transport and that the restaurant job didn't exist. The girl, her hair combed straight back and her soft face fixed in a faraway stare, told me that she was eighteen, but she looked fifteen. She is now a prostitute in a small hotel called Happiness. Working seven nights a week, with each customer spending three and a half dollars and staying five minutes, she had paid off her debt after seven months. She has no friends except the other girls in the hotel. In her room, on the third floor, the words "I am covered by the blood of Jesus. Amen" are chalked on a wall three times.

A woman named Safrat Yinusa left behind her husband and two of her children in Ilorin, north of the city, and found work in one of Lagos's huge markets as a porter, carrying loads of produce on her head. She was nursing a baby boy, whom she carried as she worked. She paid twenty cents a night for sleeping space on the floor of a room with forty other women porters. In two months, she had saved less than four dollars. Considering that the price of rice in Lagos is thirty-three cents per pound, it is hard to understand how people like Yinusa stay alive. The paradox has been called the "wage puzzle."

When Michael Chinedu, an Ibo, arrived in Lagos, he knew no one. On his first day, he saw a man smoking marijuana—in Lagos, it's called India hemp—and, being a smoker as well, introduced himself. On this slim connection, Chinedu asked the man if he knew of any jobs, and he was taken to the sawmill, where he began at once, working long days amid the scream of the ripsaw and burning clouds of sawdust, sleeping outside at night on a stack of hardwood planks. After three months, he had saved enough for a room. "If you sit down, you will die of hunger," he said.

The hustle never stops in Lagos. Informal transactions make up at least 60 percent of economic activity; at stoplights and on highways, crowds of boys as young as eight hawk everything from cell phones to fire extinguishers. Begging is rare. In many African cities, there is an oppressive atmosphere of people lying about in the middle of the day, of idleness sinking into despair. In Lagos, everyone is a striver. I once saw a woman navigating across several lanes of traffic with her small boy in tow, and the expression on her face was one I came to think of as typically Lagosian: a look hard, closed, and unsmiling, yet quick and shrewd, taking in everything, ready to ward off an obstacle or seize a chance.

In 1950, fewer than three hundred thousand people lived in Lagos. In the second half of the twentieth century, the city grew at a rate of more than 6 percent annually. It is currently the sixth-largest city in the world, and it is growing faster than any of the world's other megacities (the term used by the United Nations Center for Human Settlements for "urban agglomerations" with more than ten million people). By 2015, it is projected, Lagos will rank third, behind Tokyo and Mumbai, with twenty-three million inhabitants.

When I first went to Lagos, in 1983, it already had a fearsome reputation among Westerners and Africans alike. Many potential visitors were kept away simply by the prospect of getting through the airport, with its official shakedowns and swarming touts. Once you made it into the city, a gauntlet of armed robbers, con men, corrupt policemen, and homicidal bus drivers awaited you.

Recently, Lagos has begun to acquire a new image. In the early years of the twenty-first century, the Third World's megacities have become the focus of intense scholarly interest, in books such as Mike Davis's *Planet of Slums*, Suketu Mehta's *Maximum City*, and Robert Neuwirth's *Shadow Cities*. Neuwirth, having lived for two years in slum neighborhoods of Rio de Janeiro, Nairobi, and other cities, came to see the world's urban squatters as pioneers and patriots, creating solid communities without official approval from the state or the market. "Today, the world's squatters are demonstrating a new way forward in the fight to create a more equitable globe," he wrote. What squatters need most of all, he argued, is the right to stay where they are: "Without any laws to support them, they are making their improper, illegal communities grow and prosper."

Stewart Brand, the founder of the *Whole Earth Catalog* and a business strategist based in Marin County, California, goes even further. "Squatter cities are vibrant," he writes in a recent article on megacities. "Each narrow street is one long bustling market." He sees in the explosive growth of "aspirational shantytowns" a cure for Third World poverty and an extraordinary profit-making opportunity. "How does all this relate to businesspeople in the developed world?" Brand asks. "One-fourth of humanity trying new things in new cities is a lot of potential customers, collaborators, and competitors."

In the dirty gray light of Lagos, however, Neuwirth's portrait of heroic builders of the cities of tomorrow seems a bit romantic, and Brand's vision of a global city of interconnected entrepreneurs seems perverse. The vibrancy of the squatters in Lagos is the furious activity of people who live in a globalized economy and have no safety net and virtually no hope of moving upward.

Around a billion people—almost half of the developing world's urban population—live in slums. The United Nations Human Settlements Program, in a 2003 report titled *The Challenge of the Slums*, declared, "The urban poor are trapped in an informal and 'illegal' world—in slums that are not reflected on maps, where waste is not collected, where taxes are not paid, and where public services are not provided. Officially, they do not exist." According to the report, "Over the course of the next two decades, the global urban population will double, from 2.5 to 5 billion. Almost all of this increase will be in developing countries."

In 2000, the United Nations established the Millennium Development Goals. One of them is to improve the lives of a hundred million slum dwellers by 2020, in terms of shelter, water, sewers, jobs, and governance. This will require enormous expenditures of money and effort, but even if the goal is achieved, nearly a quarter of the world's population—more than two billion people—will still be living in conditions like those in Lagos.

To some Western intellectuals, Lagos has become the archetype of the megacity—perhaps because its growth has been so explosive, and perhaps because its cityscape has become so apocalyptic. It has attracted the attention of leading writers and artists, who have mounted international exhibitions in London and Berlin. All this interest has somehow transformed Lagos into a hip icon of the latest global trends, the much-studied megalopolis of the future, like London and Paris in the nineteenth century or New York and Tokyo in the twentieth. For several years, the Dutch architect

and urban theorist Rem Koolhaas has been working with his students at
the Harvard Graduate School of Design on a project to study the future
of cities; he has gone to Lagos four times and produced several articles as
well as a book to be published early next year, *Lagos: How It Works*. Koolhaas once described Lagos to an interviewer as a protean organism that
creatively defies constrictive Western ideas of urban order. "What is now
fascinating is how, with some level of self-organization, there is a strange
combination of extreme underdevelopment and development," he said.
"And what particularly amazes me is how the kinds of infrastructure of
modernity in the city trigger off all sorts of unpredictable improvised conditions, so that there is a kind of mutual dependency that I've never seen
anywhere else." With its massive traffic jams creating instant markets on
roads and highways, Lagos is not "a kind of backward situation," Koolhaas
said, but, rather, "an announcement of the future."

As a picture of the urban future, Lagos is fascinating only if you're
able to leave it. After just a few days in the city's slums, it is hard to maintain Koolhaas's intellectual excitement. What he calls "self-organization"
is simply collective adaptation to extreme hardship. Traffic pileups lead to
"improvised conditions" because there is no other way for most people in
Lagos to scratch out a living than to sell on the street. It would be preferable to have some respite from buying and selling, some separation between private and public life. It would be preferable not to have five-hour
"go-slows"—traffic jams—that force many workers to get up well before
dawn and spend almost no waking hours at home. And it would be preferable not to have an economy in which millions of people have to invent
marginal forms of employment because there are so few jobs.

I asked Paul Okunlola, an editor at the Nigerian newspaper the
Guardian, why people kept coming to Lagos when there seemed so little
chance of getting ahead. "They never believe there's no chance," he said.
Okunlola described the largest market in Lagos: the Mile 12, on the highway heading north out of town, where foodstuff coming into the city is
bought and sold wholesale. It is a muddy area—much of Lagos is reclaimed
swampland—and workers with buckets of water earn seven cents washing the feet of market women. "That is the kind of entrepreneurship that
keeps a lot of people in Lagos," Okunlola said. "If you took that to my
hometown, who would wash feet—and who would pay money for it, anyway? That is what drives Lagos."

Folarin Gbadebo-Smith, the chairman of a district on Lagos Island, said that globalization, in the form of mass media, attracts Nigerians to Lagos as a substitute for New York or London. A distorted picture then flows back to the village. "Come Christmas, everybody in Lagos—the successful and the unsuccessful—packs their bags and goes off to the rural areas to show off what they have achieved," Gbadebo-Smith said. "Some achievements are real, for some it's just a mirage, but everybody's there showing off. So the young people in the villages very quickly come to the conclusion that 'Hey, I've got to go to Lagos, make enough to be able to come back here, and to show off.'" In this way, the West African countryside is being rapidly depopulated.

Adegoke Taylor, a skinny, solemn thirty-two-year-old itinerant trader with anxious eyes, shares an eight-by-ten-foot room with three other young men, on an alley in Isale Eko several hundred feet from the Third Mainland Bridge. In 1999, Taylor came to Lagos from Ile-Oluji, a Yoruba town a hundred and thirty miles to the northeast. He had a degree in mining from a polytechnic school and the goal of establishing a professional career. Upon arriving in the city, he went to a club that played *juju*—pop music infused with Yoruba rhythms—and stayed out until two in the morning. "This experience alone makes me believe I have a new life living now," he said, in English, the lingua franca of Lagos. "All the time, you see crowds everywhere. I was motivated by that. In the village, you're not free at all, and whatever you're going to do today you'll do tomorrow." Taylor soon found that none of the few mining positions being advertised in Lagos newspapers were open to him. "If you are not connected, it's not easy, because there are many more applications than jobs," he said. "The moment you don't have a recognized person saying, 'This is my boy, give him a job,' it's very hard. In this country, if you don't belong to the élite"— he pronounced it "e-light"—"you will find things very, very hard."

Taylor fell into a series of odd jobs: changing money, peddling stationery and hair plaits, and moving heavy loads in a warehouse for a daily wage of four hundred naira—about three dollars. Occasionally, he worked for West African traders who came to the markets near the port and needed middlemen to locate goods. At first, he stayed with the sister of a childhood friend in Mushin, then found cheap lodging there in a shared room for seven dollars a month, until the building was burned down during the ethnic riots. Taylor lost everything. He decided to move to Lagos Island, where he pays a higher rent, twenty dollars a month.

Taylor had tried to leave Africa but was turned down for a visa by the American and British embassies. At times, he longed for the calm of his hometown, but there was never any question of returning to Ile-Oluji, with its early nights and monotonous days and the prospect of a lifetime of manual labor. His future was in Lagos, and he kept trying various small-business plans, none of which had worked out, for a simple reason. "There's no capital to start," he said. For this, he blamed the Nigerian government. "Most of the people who lead us embezzle instead of using that money to create factories," he said. "Our parents' generation was okay. But this generation is a wasted generation—unless God comes to the aid. Because we know there is money in Nigeria." In fact, oil export revenue exceeded fifty billion dollars in 2005.

Taylor escorted me along the alley to my car, which was in the shadow of the bridge. We slipped past a menacing group of "area boys," who act as parking attendants and shake down anyone who drives onto their turf.

"There's no escape, except to make it," Taylor said.

Stephen Omojoro, a fifty-two-year-old taxi driver and father of four with broad horizontal and vertical tribal scars carved into both cheeks, took me around Lagos in an aging Mercedes. In his version of the arrival story, Omojoro came to Lagos when he was seventeen, in the early seventies, after his father's death forced him to quit school. He spent the first night with a relative, who gave him enough money for one dinner. After that, he was on his own. The following morning, having heard about the sawmills, he showed up and was given a job carrying planks and logs. At night, he slept outside. Many people in Lagos sleep where they work—in markets under flyovers, in truck cabs parked in truck yards, inside tiny shops, on the handlebars of their motorcycle taxis.

As we drove around the megacity, Omojoro described his recent history in a harsh, hoarse voice that seemed to have been seared by the polluted air. In his view, Lagos has been deteriorating since shortly after his arrival, owing to a general moral collapse brought on by the oil boom of the seventies. What he remembered as a city of enterprising family men like himself is now overrun with corrupt soldiers, politicians, and police, and with a mass of young people willing to do anything for money except honest work. He believes in order, and he disdainfully pointed out planned residential neighborhoods that are now overgrown with roadside markets, and "temporary" settlements that have survived for decades. (Omojoro once got into a shouting match with a woman in Mushin who had put out a display of wigs on a stretch of roadside pavement that theoretically belonged to traffic, not commerce.) He also condemned the heedless, often lethal driving of young men who, fortified at dawn by palm-wine gin or India hemp, make their living behind the wheel of the ubiquitous yellow passenger minibuses known as *danfo*. Omojoro described such drivers as "irresponsible somebodies—they don't care for nobody, nobody cares for them." (The wooden-backed pickup trucks used to carry produce and other goods are called *bole kaja*, which means "get down and let's fight.")

What is missing from Omojoro's declinist account is the effect of national and international economic policies on the city. There was once a master plan for Lagos. One day, Oyesanya Oyelola, the director of the regional and master plan department in the state government, spread a faded map across his desk. The plan, jointly drawn up in the seventies by the firm of Wilbur Smith and Associates, the United Nations Development Program, and the Lagos state government, was intended to guide the growth of the city in the last two decades of the twentieth century. There were to be thirty-five self-sufficient district centers, represented on the map by clusters of dots, each with commercial, industrial, and residential zones, to prevent congestion on Lagos Island. A fourth mainland bridge would connect the Lekki peninsula, extending east from Victoria Island along the coast, to the towns popping up on the north shore of the lagoon, which would disperse traffic heading into the city. There was to be a light rail and ferry system bringing commuters to the major business centers on the mainland and across to Lagos Island. To the east and west of the city, wetlands, forest, and agricultural land were reserved.

On New Year's Eve 1983, a bloodless coup overthrew civilian rule, and for the next sixteen years a series of military dictators from northern Nigeria treated Lagos, the country's center of democratic activism, as a source of personal enrichment. While the military rulers cut themselves in on the city's commercial action, the master plan "was abandoned," Oyelola said, along with any thought of investing in the infrastructure necessary to absorb millions of new arrivals. He showed me the result, unfurling a second map of Lagos, as it is today: a sea of yellow spreading out across the mainland. "Most of the green land has been eaten up by the flow of people—it has become residential," he said. On the master plan, there were forty-two areas identified as "blighted" and scheduled for improvement; now there are fifty-four.

Shina Loremikan, who runs an anticorruption organization, lives in Ajegunle, Lagos's biggest and most dangerous slum, across a canal from the port. The drainage ditches of Ajegunle are frequently blocked, and during the rainy season they overflow into houses and across streets, which fill up with sludge, sacks, scraps of clothing, and plastic bags, so that some of Ajegunle's streets seem to be wholly composed of trash. I asked Loremikan to show me the slum areas on a map of Lagos. With his finger, he drew a line from the southeast corner all the way to the northwest. "From here to here, they are all slums," Loremikan said flatly. "Refuse is everywhere, either in Victoria Island or Ikoyi"—Lagos's two relatively upscale districts—"or in Agege or Mushin. Black water is everywhere. They are all slums."

Other megacities, such as Mumbai, Dhaka, Manila, and São Paulo, have spawned entire satellite cities that house migrants and the destitute, who lead lives that often have nothing to do with the urban center to which they were originally drawn. Lagos expanded differently: there is no distinct area where a million people squat in flimsy hovels. The whole city suffers from misuse. Planned residential areas—such as Surulere, built for civil servants on the mainland—are gradually taken over by the commercial activity that springs up everywhere in Lagos like fungus after the rains. Areas reclaimed from swamps give rise to economic clusters whose nature depends on location: for example, Mushin became one of the city's central spare parts yards when the Apapa-Oshodi Expressway was built near it, in the seventies. "Everywhere is market," Stephen Omojoro said as we drove around. "There's no dull area at all." It's hard to decide if the extravagant ugliness of the cityscape is a sign of vigor or of disease—a life force or an impending apocalypse.

Although new developments spring up in every possible direction—west toward the Benin border, north to the boundary of Lagos state, east toward the oil delta—most of them are unaffordable to the urban poor or too far from practical employment. Instead, Lagos packs its millions into existing concrete-block housing, in ever larger numbers. There was a building spree of public housing projects in the years before the 1983 coup—the complexes are still called Jakande estates, after the Lagos state governor who led the effort—but today the clusters of eight- or ten-story high-rises have a leprous aspect, as if some blackening disease were creeping across their façades. Most of them are being sold off to private developers, who resell them at market rates.

In the mid-eighties, under the dictatorship of General Ibrahim Babangida, Nigeria submitted to austerity measures prescribed by the World Bank and the International Monetary Fund, in order to reduce a thirty-billion-dollar debt. Over time, the country shut down or sold off inefficient state-run enterprises, including construction industries, port facilities, oil refineries, and textile and steel mills; electricity, water, and telephone services were privatized. With these structural adjustments, civil service jobs, the mainstay of the middle class in districts like Surulere, disappeared; meanwhile, privatization often occurred at fire-sale prices, with the profits benefiting politicians or soldiers and their cronies. The remaining savings were devoured by the corrupt military regimes. (An official report released after the fall of Babangida, in 1994, could not account for twelve billion dollars.)

The effect of these policies in Nigeria has been to concentrate enormous wealth in a few hands while leaving the vast majority of people poorer every year. The rare job that still awaits young men and women who come to Lagos pays less than it did a quarter century ago; it is also less likely to be salaried and more likely to be menial. At the same time, the cost of rent, food, and fuel has soared. If there is an element of American frontier capitalism in the unregulated informal economy of Lagos, there is much less opportunity to make hard work pay off. And if the teeming slums of Lagos recall the "darkness, dirt, pestilence, obscenity, misery and early death" that Dickens described in an essay about Victorian London, there is no industrial base to offer the poor masses at least the possibility of regular employment.

One morning, on the entrance ramp to a highway, a Peugeot in front of Omojoro's car braked in heavy traffic. Between us, a sinewy old man was pulling a two-wheeled cart loaded down with so much rusty machinery that he couldn't keep it under control. It's common in Lagos to see work-ers performing savagely hard labor out of the pre-industrial age. When the old man tried to stop, the cart's right wheel sank into a pothole; then the cart lurched forward, its wooden handle breaking the glass of the Peugeot's taillight. The driver checked his rearview mirror and moved as if to get out, but before he could open his door two teenagers who were sitting on the guardrail stood up and waved him to go on, then walked over and began negotiating with the old man, who was already reaching into his trouser pocket with a kind of humble resignation. The incident happened so fast that afterward Omojoro had to explain to me what had been immediately understood by all the participants. The teenagers were area boys, and since this block was under their control, the money that the old man owed the driver for his taillight would, according to the city's peculiar logic, go to them instead.

What looks like anarchic activity in Lagos is actually governed by a set of informal but ironclad rules. Although the vast majority of people in the city are small-time entrepreneurs, almost no one works for himself. Everyone occupies a place in an economic hierarchy and owes fealty, as well as cash, to the person above him—known as an *oga*, or master—who, in turn, provides help or protection. Every group of workers—even at the stolen-goods market in the Ijora district—has a union that amounts to an extortion racket. The teenager hawking sunglasses in traffic receives the merchandise from a wholesaler, to whom he turns over 90 percent of his earnings; if he tries to cheat or cut out, his guarantor—an authority figure such as a relative or a man from his hometown, known to the ven-dor and the wholesaler alike—has to make up the loss, then hunt down his wayward charge. The patronage system helps the megacity absorb the continual influx of newcomers for whom the formal economy has no use. Wealth accrues not to the most imaginative or industrious but to those who rise up through the chain of patronage. It amounts to a predatory system of obligation, set down in no laws, enforced by implied threat.

Omojoro's Mercedes was creeping through the dense market streets of Ajegunle one day when he started to make a left turn into a narrow road. Suddenly, a young man came out of the crowd, yelling that Omojoro had made an illegal turn. He was an *agbero*—a member of the transport workers' union, whose official job is to act as an intermediary between bus drivers and their passengers. The *agberos* of the state transport union, who wore yellow-and-maroon reflector vests, were in open warfare with the *agberos* of the federal union, who wore white vests and black berets. This man wasn't wearing a vest, but his swagger implied that the corner was under his personal control. He wanted money, on the pretext of helping Omojoro bribe the traffic police—he would keep part of it for himself, and the rest would go to his branch of the union local, one of fifty-seven in Lagos state. The *agberos* of a given zone have to generate a minimum of, say, thirty-five dollars a day for their local branch and the police. All this activity is technically illegal.

"Go to hell, I won't deal with you," Omojoro almost spat out the window. "You're an *agbero*."

The man glared and pointed. "You called me *agbero* because you don't know me."

"I don't want to know you," Omojoro said. "I respect the man in uniform."

A traffic cop had come over to investigate the dispute. "I thank you for that statement," he told Omojoro. "I am ready to settle with you." They negotiated a fine down from fourteen dollars to three-fifty. Most people would have cooperated with the *agbero*, who always has a network of area boys in the vicinity, to vandalize the car until the driver pays up. Omojoro called the *agbero*'s bluff, having seen the traffic cop, who was forced to intervene, in order not to be reported up his chain of command for failing to take a bribe himself.

A sign near the headquarters of Shell Oil on Victoria Island says, DID YOU GO TO SCHOOL, COLLEGE, UNIVERSITY, POLYTECHNIC, AND YOU STILL THROW REFUSE OUT OF YOUR CAR OR FROM THE BUS? DUMP GARBAGE BAGS ON THE ROAD MEDIANS OR IN DRAINS? BUILD YOUR HOUSE/SHOP ON DRAINS? URINATE OR DEFECATE IN PUBLIC PLACES? THEN WHY DID YOU BOTHER TO GET AN EDUCATION? THINK ABOUT IT!

The sign is part of a government-led campaign for beautification and order in Lagos. Such efforts appeal to the middle-class public-spiritedness of older Lagosians like Stephen Omojoro. But the megacity doesn't encourage social responsibility and collective action to improve public life. The very scale of it is atomizing. The absence of government services in most neighborhoods rarely leads to protest; instead, it forces slum dwellers to become self-sufficient through illegal activity. They tap into electrical lines, causing blackouts and fires; they pay off local gangs to provide security, which means that justice in the slums is vigilante justice. In Mushin, several members of the Oodua People's Congress, a Yoruba gang, displayed for me a suspected motorcycle thief whom they had caught the night before and were holding in a dingy back room of their clubhouse: he was chained at the hands and feet, and bleeding from the head. His captors hadn't decided whether to turn him over to the police or simply kill him. Alongside the Badagry Expressway, I saw the charred remains of a corpse, recognizably human only from the buttocks and thighs, which had been burned and left to rot. No one I asked knew what it was doing there, and no one seemed particularly surprised.

In *Lagos: A City at Work*, a new book of photographs and essays published by a local bookshop, David Aradeon, a professor of architecture at the University of Lagos, writes, "The people who use public space in the city and those who are supposed to regulate its use are constantly reasserting their personal interests above and beyond the common interest, and that is really what the city is about. That is the story of Lagos. And how do we go about changing this?" I asked Paul Okunlola, of the *Guardian*, why there is no organization or political party representing the millions of poor people in Lagos. He explained that Nigeria has never seen the kind of mass movements that have flourished elsewhere in Africa; in Lagos, the spirit of individualism overwhelms the idea of solidarity. "Everybody believes that his lot can and will be better," he said. "They see themselves in the mold of these more affluent people. In South Africa, they say, 'Yes, I am living in a slum,' and they will pull themselves together and fight on that basis. In Nigeria, the moment you call it a 'slum dwellers' association' you will not find anybody who is ready to join." The animating principle among the poor is the inevitability of the *oga*: no salvation without patronage. "You find people who think, It's more worth my while to associate with this man who doles out some money to me from time to time rather than congregate with like-minded, like-situationed people who are not that well-to-do."

The most famous shantytown in Lagos, called Maroko, rose up on prime oceanfront property along the southern shore of Victoria Island. In the eighties, the Lagos business district began to move to Victoria from Lagos Island, and the land became valuable. In July 1990, the military government sent bulldozers and soldiers into Maroko, and within a few hours a quarter of a million people had been made homeless. A few miles down the coast from the site, in a concrete public housing apartment whose ceiling was caving in, I found Prince S. A. Aiyeyemi, a sixty-eight-year-old retired postal authority worker and the leader of the Maroko Evictees Committee. From his desk, he brought out a letter that he wanted me to give to Bola Tinubu, the Lagos governor. The letter demanded compensation for the loss of the houses owned by committee members and for resettlement to equivalent property. In the meantime, Aiyeyemi was allowing the apartment to which he'd been removed to disintegrate around him. He was slight and frail from a stroke that had left half his face paralyzed. "We shall continue to live till we get justice," he said, slurring his words. "And if we, the elderly, die, our children are ready to continue. This is our own contribution to the social engineering of Nigeria." When I asked him whether it was fair for ten people to have to live in a single room, he said, "Well, there's nothing we can do about that. We don't take that so much as a social injustice. That is their economic limitations. It's only when those ten people are tampered with by government, thrown out into the open air—that is social injustice."

I had never heard anyone else in Lagos speak this way. This indignant old man was going to die waiting for something called justice, while everyone else in the city struggled.

Beneath the relentlessly commercial surface of Lagos lies a kind of moral unease. In many conversations, the physical blight of the city was described in ethical terms, as a general failure of character originating in the leaders and spreading down through the population. "The work ethic was destroyed by the military," Folarin Gbadebo-Smith said. "It was substituted by a lottery mentality. You were going to make it, not because you put in all this work but because you were lucky. You knew someone, or your ticket came in." Even the Pentecostal fervor that has swept across West Africa takes the form of personal striving in Lagos. Abandoned warehouses and factories on the Apapa-Oshodi Expressway have been converted into huge churches with signs that promise, THE LORD SHALL ADD, and on Sundays they fill up with adherents of what is known as "the gospel of prosperity." "They pray to be rich," Omojoro said. "Whether they go to heaven or to hell, they could care less. Because Nigeria is a hell already."

One afternoon, near the edge of Lagos Lagoon, I met a young man named Tosin Owolabi. He was barefoot, small, and solidly built, in rolled-up jeans and a dirty singlet, with the perpetually aggrieved scowl of a street urchin. He had been kicked out of school in his teens and now, at twenty-three, he was in constant motion at a variety of odd jobs at a nearby construction site: parking cars; running errands for his *oga*, who had set him up here; and loading concrete blocks and sand, which was retrieved by the bucketful from the bottom of the polluted lagoon by young men who dived forty feet without air. Owolabi spent his nights at the construction site and in the morning begged for water at a community borehole to wash himself in the bush. He smelled as if he'd missed a few days. Every Sunday, he went to church.

I asked Owolabi if he had a girlfriend. He sneered and burst out in rough, rapid English: "Lonely. Because when you have a girlfriend . . . I make a dollar and a half yesterday. To make it will be hard. Lonely. I have only me. I don't waste my money. If I don't eat, nobody will know. If I don't give her seventy-five cents, she will not trust me. I trust myself, okay?"

Occasionally, he went on, he paid a girl a dollar or a dollar fifty to sleep with him, but if she called him later on his cell phone he always said, "Bye-bye, safe journey." Instead, he had saved his money—five hundred and seventy dollars, he said—and had paid a recording studio to produce his songs. They were traditional religious songs, and he sang one for me, in a high, sweet, but unremarkable voice:

> *God take my thanks*
> *I am ready to praise you*
> *Continue to do*
> *As you are doing for me.*

The studio scammed Owolabi and left him with a recording of terrible quality. Nevertheless, he was determined to try again, and had already saved more than a hundred dollars. He refused to accept that his hard-earned money could go to a likelier enterprise. Getting started as a dealer in building materials would cost him more than two thousand dollars. He was going to make it as a singer. He had put all his faith in God and himself. As we talked, he kept working, filling a customer's bag with sand, scowling and arguing about the amount. "If you want to be a big some-body in this Nigeria, you need money," he said.

Nigerians have become notorious for their Internet scams, such as e-mails with a bogus request to move funds to an offshore bank, which ask for the recipient's account number in exchange for lucrative profit. The con, which originated in Lagos, represents the perversion of talent and initiative in a society where normal paths of opportunity are closed to all but the well-connected. Corruption is intrinsic to getting anything done in Lagos: while stalled in traffic, Omojoro was often on the phone with his twenty-four-year-old daughter, who had recently taken her college board exams and was trying to negotiate a price to obtain the results. (He ended up paying thirty-five dollars.) Even morgues demand bribes for the release of corpses. The shorthand for financial crimes is "419," from the relevant chapter in the Nigerian criminal code. The words THIS HOUSE IS NOT FOR SALE: BEWARE OF 419 are painted across the exterior walls of dilapidated houses all over the city—a warning to potential buyers not to be taken in by someone falsely claiming to be the owner.

The night before I left Lagos, Adegoke Taylor, the unemployed mining engineer in Isale Eko, sat down with me in the lobby of my hotel and laid out an offer. On a recent visit to his home village, he said, a high school friend who had been the housekeeper of one of Nigeria's military dictators revealed that he had stolen a million and a half pounds sterling from the dictator's house after his death, in 1998. The money, Taylor said, was buried in a hole on a cacao farm, and the friend wanted to transfer it to Lagos and exchange it for naira. "'It is too risky,'" Taylor said that he told his friend. "'You can't bring that much money to Lagos.'" Hesitantly, circuitously, Taylor arrived at his offer—a bank-to-bank transfer to my account. I had seen it coming and gently suggested that this was a dirty, dangerous business that neither of us would want any part of. Taylor backed off. "Wisdom is more important than money," he announced as I escorted him out. Still, a business opportunity in the form of an American had come his way, and he would have been regarded locally as a fool if he hadn't tried to exploit it. We said goodbye amicably, but he avoided my eyes.

The government that came to power in the democratic elections of 1999 has begun to revive the old master plan for Lagos. "We hope that in the new plan there will be a program for the poor people, to get affordable housing for them," Oyesanya Oyelola, the state planning official, said. Conditions in Lagos have marginally improved since the restoration of civilian rule. The traffic jams have eased slightly with new roads, and trash removal has increased. One Saturday each month, the city shuts down and every homeowner or business owner is responsible for cleaning his property; the results are startling, for a few hours, anyway.

Bola Tinubu, the city's governor, told me that when he was elected, in 1999, the scale of the task overwhelmed him. "Sky-high refuse!" he said. "It was a disaster area. It's like a hurricane has just gone through Lagos state, on a daily basis." He went on, "Now, compared to a serious civilization, Lagos state is dirty, very dirty. But to an average Lagosian, it's clean compared to what they faced before."

I met the governor in his large, gilt-trimmed flat on New Cavendish Street, in central London. Heavy-lidded and barefoot, wearing jeans and a striped T-shirt and sunk into an overstuffed sofa, Tinubu seemed to be temporarily convalescing from the job. I gave him the letter from the Maroko Evictees Committee; he cited his achievements in employment and housing creation, on an annual budget of three-quarters of a billion dollars, and he blamed the federal government—which is based in Abuja, two hundred and fifty miles to the northeast, and has long had a hostile relationship with Lagos—for politically motivated financial neglect. "I need ten times what I'm having today," Tinubu said. "The money that Lagos state is having is not enough to maintain a county hospital in New York." The governor, who once worked for Mobil Oil and for Deloitte, the accounting firm, brought out the report of a consultant hired to draw up a new master plan. It was much the same as the old, neglected one. The key, Tinubu said, is "to arrest the unplanned growth in different directions, the octopus of unplanned and uncontrolled building." In London, the governor sounded optimistic. He presented Lagos, with its phenomenal annual growth rate, as a victim of its own success.

Folarin Gbadebo-Smith, the local government chairman, was less sanguine. His district, eastern Lagos Island, includes extremes of wealth and poverty. A big man with a deep, self-confident voice, he is the son of middle-class Lagosians, and a dentist by trade. He spent years working hard and falling farther behind as the naira lost its value and the city descended into the corruption of military rule. Finally, after the restoration of democracy, he decided that it was time to stop complaining and do something. He ran for office in 2003 and now manages a district of seventy thousand people, installing public toilets and bus shelters, rebuilding primary schools, cleaning up streets, juggling the "diametrically opposed" interests of his rich and poor constituents, and, as he put it, "trying to maintain some sense of order." He compared Lagos unfavorably with Rio de Janeiro, where, he said, "in the city center there is strict law enforcement. Here, the problem is everything is happening everywhere."

We drove in his Land Rover to a parking lot next to a filthy police barracks, under an overpass leading to Victoria Island. Gbadebo-Smith had a plan to turn the lot into a nighttime market for vendors and motorcycle taxi drivers.

The owner of the lot, Jacob Wood, joined us for a walk around it. "Security should be very tough," he said. He seemed eager to cooperate but skeptical of the plan.

"It will be tough," Gbadebo-Smith agreed. He promised that the night market, with food stalls and music, would close at midnight. The real purpose of the project was to clear out the helter-skelter buying and selling in a neighborhood that was, by Lagos standards, upscale. "Get people off the street and give them something more organized," Gbadebo-Smith said. "The first thing is to control who comes, because we can't have the whole town coming here. We'd have to give sellers a license, so I can detect anyone who isn't a resident of this place. I will aggressively pursue anyone selling on the street, and if necessary put them in jail."

Gbadebo-Smith's plan is part of the Kick Against Indiscipline, a citywide effort to rationalize Lagos—for example, to clear out the informal markets clogging nearly every street, with mobile courts issuing fines. The sawmills, whose smoke smothers traffic on the Third Mainland Bridge, are slated for removal to a site on the far side of the lagoon; the floating slum by the bridge is to be demolished and its fishermen residents sent to new residences on the north shore; the scrap yards and stolen-goods markets in Ijora are to be relocated westward. Government officials talk of providing housing and job training to the displaced, to keep them anchored to their new neighborhoods. But I found it hard to imagine Gbadebo-Smith ever bringing order to his district. The hawkers would inevitably return to the traffic circles, for the same reason that hundreds of thousands of people continue to come to Lagos year after year. The concentration of humanity brings work, which further intensifies the concentration. When I mentioned the Kick Against Indiscipline to Paul Okunlola, of the *Guardian*, he said, "It will never work. This is the only way people can make ends meet. Wherever there's a traffic jam, you will see vendors there. They're like sprouts. You can't get rid of them."

The most widely available commodity in Lagos is garbage. It is an engine of growth in the underworld of the city's informal economy, a vast sector with an astonishing volume of supply.

Babatunde Ilufoye, an Ibo in his early forties, was brought to Lagos at the age of eighteen by a German man whose flat tire Ilufoye had fixed one day in his village, and who decided to teach the young man the import-export business. Today, Ilufoye lives near the sawmills, in the shabby-genteel district of Ebute-Meta, where there are many three-story colonial-era buildings in various stages of neglect. He is a polite, neatly dressed, hardworking man, whose wife owns a dry goods shop next to the house; in a European city, Ilufoye would be a successful entrepreneur. In 2004, after visiting a Lagos friend who dealt in cow horns and hooves, he went to an Internet café and typed those words into Google. Nothing useful appeared, but when he entered "plastic scraps," thousands of links came up.

Ilufoye is now a full-time exporter of recycled hard plastics, selling the ground-up fragments to Indian and South African companies for a minimum of a hundred dollars a ton. In choosing plastics, Ilufoye tapped into a growth market, but Nigeria's international reputation as a breeding ground for online scam artists makes it difficult for him to find customers, and he can't move the product fast enough to become profitable. "Do you expect me to commit a crime at this age and be locked up?" he e-mailed one wary Pakistani buyer. "If I'm not a fool at twenty-one or thirty, how can I be a fool now?"

Ilufoye's grinder is Andrew Okolie, a gloomy man who operates two crushing machines in a gloomy concrete building under an expressway. The narrow rooms are filled to the ceilings with dirty plastic kitchenware, pails, milk cartons, empty bottles of shampoo, car-wash fluid, cosmetic gels, all pouring out of open doorways in little landslides. When I visited, the power had been out for days and Okolie sat idle in the front room, chewing hard on a piece of gum. Like Ilufoye, he is frustrated by structural limitations: he could handle a capacity of one ton a day, but he can't afford a generator to keep his machines running during the frequent outages. Unless you are rich and connected, the banks charge as much as 30 percent interest on loans, he said. To upgrade his business, Okolie needed someone to invest twenty thousand dollars, which he said he would be able to pay back in two years—because plastic is "in vogue these days." The business was poised to take off, and Ilufoye and Okolie could put many youths to work. But nobody would help them realize their plan.

In the recycling business, Okolie said, most of the suppliers are "dropouts, miscreants"—scavenger boys who scour the gutters and streets and municipal dumps, filling up sacks or carts, and sell what they collect to their *oga*, who has twenty or so boys working for him, in a kind of dependency that resembles that of Fagin and the pickpockets of *Oliver Twist*. The *oga*, in turn, sells the refuse to Okolie, who then sells the ground bits to Ilufoye, who exports them. The scavengers, who are called pickers, can collect two or three hundred pounds of plastic a week, for which they are paid six cents per pound. They spend most of their cash, according to Okolie, on marijuana or glue.

Half a dozen miles north of Andrew Okolie's plastics grinding shop, along the expressway, is the largest municipal dump in Lagos. The first time I visited, a line of trucks stretched from the dumping area to the highway. One badly overloaded truck had tipped over on the entrance road and taken down another, and the mound of garbage left by the spill made it difficult for other trucks to move past. On the entrance road, I met a young plastics picker named Ayo Adio, who had arrived by standing on the back of a garbage truck. He carried a nylon sack, into which he was dropping scraps of plastic from the roadside with a piece of steel rebar bent into a hook. Adio's expression was grim, and he had smeared white lotion across his face, which made him look like a mournful clown. I noticed that other pickers wore plastic masks or face cloths. At the approach to the dump site, the smell of burning rot became overpowering.

Hundreds of pickers were trudging across an undulating landscape of garbage. Every minute, another dump truck backed in and released its load, with a tremendous sliding noise culminating in a crash that shook the trash underfoot. As a bulldozer pushed the fresh garbage up into a wave that crested and broke across the older landfill, the pickers rushed over it, swarming dangerously close to the vehicles. Bent under their sacks, they worked quickly and with focus, knowing what they were looking for. Some pickers wanted only copper; others specialized in printer cartridges. One man inspected a wheel axle for half a minute before tossing it aside. A girl sold water from a bucket on her head. Most of the scavengers had closed shoes and some kind of headwear, but only a few wore rubber boots and gloves. They all clawed at the trash with bent rebar, sharpened with use to a shiny point.

A fifty-year-old man with squinting red eyes named Moshood Babatunde, who was wearing a baseball cap and an impossibly clean white shirt, paused to talk with me. He had been working at this dump for fifteen years, collecting wire. On a good day, he said, he made two and a half or three dollars. But because of the soaring rents in Lagos, he had to commute by train and bus to the dump site from a neighboring state, which cost him almost two dollars a day. He supported five children, three of them in school. "If you don't find some help, you have to help yourself," he said. "I thank God, I will never regret this opportunity."

The dump—a hole gouged out of the earth—is as broad as a small town, and surrounded on all sides by fifty-foot cliffs composed of laterite and garbage. We were standing at the edge of one such cliff, and the pickers took turns pushing their full sacks over the edge, sending them bouncing down to the bottom and then scurrying after them. Across the floor of the pit are hundreds of hovels, a sizable shantytown of dwellings made of plastic sheeting and scrap metal bound together with baling wire. A thousand pickers live down in the pit, among flocks of white cowbirds, and middlemen come to buy their stock. The pickers have built a mosque and a church, and at Christmas they celebrate by decorating their shacks.

"It is somewhere between the law of the jungle and civilization," Aremu Hakeem, a municipal worker with a master's degree, who escorted me across the dump site, said. "They have an organization, a chairman, rules and regulations. But the physically stronger prevail when the trucks come." Hakeem spoke excitedly about recent improvements to the dump, including the opening of the entrance road. He had read books about landfills and checked out garbage-related websites. He was extremely proud of the dump, which he called a "reference point" for all of Nigeria. Then he gazed out over the site and grew quiet. "Someday I would like to come to your country and use what I have here," he said, pointing to his head. "Here we are not using it very much."

In an essay called "Fragments of a Lecture on Lagos," Rem Koolhaas described how his team, on their first visit to the city, was too intimidated to leave their car. Eventually, the group rented the Nigerian president's helicopter and was granted a more reassuring view:

> From the air, the apparently burning garbage heap turned out to be, in fact, a village, an urban phenomenon with a highly organized community living on its crust . . . What seemed, on ground level, an accumulation of dysfunctional movements, seemed from above an impressive performance, evidence of how well Lagos might perform if it were the third largest city in the world.

The impulse to look at an "apparently burning garbage heap" and see an "urban phenomenon," and then make it the raw material of an elaborate aesthetic construct, is not so different from the more common impulse not to look at all. And that reaction is understandable, for the human misery of Lagos not only overwhelms one's senses and sympathy but also seems irreversible. Koolhaas's words reminded me of something that Gbadebo-Smith told me. "You're aware of the 'megacity' thing," he said. "Lagosians sometimes talk about it as a trophy. As far as I'm concerned, it's an impending disaster." The vision of twenty-three million people squeezed together and trying to survive, like creatures in a mad demographer's experiment gone badly wrong, fills Gbadebo-Smith with foreboding. "We have a massive growth in population with a stagnant or shrinking economy," he said. "Picture this city ten, twenty years from now. This is not the urban poor—this is the new urban destitute." He expressed surprise that the level of crime and ethnic violence in Lagos, let alone civil insurrection, is still relatively contained. "We're sitting on a powder keg here," he said. "If we don't address this question of economic growth, and I mean vigorously, there is no doubt as to what's going to happen here eventually. It's just going to boil over." He added, "And guess what? If all this fails, the world will feel the weight of Lagos not working out."

There is an even darker possibility: that the world won't feel the weight of it much at all. The really disturbing thing about Lagos's pickers and vendors is that their lives have essentially nothing to do with ours. They scavenge an existence beyond the margins of macroeconomics. They are, in the harsh terms of globalization, superfluous.

Drowning

The New Yorker, August 25, 2008

When night falls in Rangoon, the city's spectacular decay—patches of black mold devouring the yellowed walls of colonial buildings, trees growing wildly into crumbling third-story terraces—nearly disappears from view. The tea shops fill up, locals crowd the bookstalls on Pansodan Road, and the city, which seems furtive and depressed by day, becomes a communal stage. In the Chinatown district, two men in an alley crank out schoolbooks with a hand-operated printing press. At a sidewalk fish market, women sell shrimp, scallops, and squid by candlelight, while two teenagers nearby strum guitars. Further east, along the Rangoon River, in the old residential quarter of Pazundaung, the wooden houses are open to the street, like storefronts, revealing an old woman sitting on a couch, a living-room shrine strewn with votive candles, and two men laughing as they listen to a radio.

One such evening in June, I had dinner at an outdoor restaurant north of downtown with a young man I'll call Myat Min. He grew up in a working-class township on the outskirts of Rangoon, the son of a mechanic and a woman who sold spices from Thailand. His father had been trained by British Air Force officers, and in the years after the 1962 coup, which gave control of the country to the Burmese military, he kept the family radio tuned to the BBC. Each evening, he ate fried noodles, listened to the news in English, and cursed the dictatorship.

Over the decades, the Burmese government has subjected its citizens to epic misrule, systematically destroying every institution of society except the army, whose leaders have made staying in power their overriding goal. The streets of Rangoon and Mandalay are monitored by the secret police and by a group of armed thugs known as Swan Arr Shin—the Masters of Force. Dissidents are routinely tortured. The generals' irrational economic policies have reduced one of Asia's richest countries, once the world's leading exporter of rice, to penury. Burma's gross domestic product per capita is now less than half that of its neighbor Cambodia. Economic sanctions—a form of protest against the government's human rights abuses—have made the country even poorer.

Myat Min was not quite thirty when we met, with a dark, high-cheekboned face, but he had the manner of a much older, eccentric man who had seen too much of life and was too vital to be self-effacing, even if his repressive society demanded it. He had an unusually loud voice by Burmese standards, which drew looks in public, and a laugh that often couldn't stop. The American expatriates in Rangoon called him Mr. Intensity. He wore only *longyis*, the Burmese sarong; he didn't own any pants. "I hate modern life," he said.

In 1995, when he was sixteen, Myat Min noticed a collection of stories by W. Somerset Maugham in a bookstall on Pansodan Road. He rented it (few Burmese can afford to buy books) and read the stories with such strong identification that he began calling himself Somerset. He moved on to Dickens, learning not just to read English but to speak it, sometimes with oddly Victorian cadences. I asked him why these British writers appealed to him. "All of the characters are me," he said, with a boisterous laugh. "Neither a British nor an American young man living in the twenty-first century can understand a Dickens as well as I can! I am living in a Dickensian atmosphere. Our country is at least one or two centuries behind the Western world. My neighborhood—bleak, poor, with small domestic industries, children playing in the street, parents fighting with each other, some with great debt, everyone dirty—that is Dickens. I am more equipped to understand Dickens than modern novels. I don't know what is air-conditioning, what is subway, what is fingerprint exam."

In 1988, when Myat Min was ten, Rangoon and other Burmese cities filled with millions of demonstrators calling for an end to military rule. It was a revolutionary moment, and by far the most serious challenge to the reign of the generals; the protest led by monks last September is the only event that comes close. Myat Min's older brothers disappeared from home for several months to join the uprising, and his father went looking for them every day. At the height of the demonstrations, Myat Min sneaked out of his house. He saw a mob of people, some of whom were carrying spikes on which the severed heads of informers—burned charcoal black—had been impaled. "Democracy!" the people shouted.

"I became interested in politics because of those scenes," Myat Min told me. At home, his father said, "Aung San Suu Kyi is the new leader of our country. American troops will come liberate us." But Suu Kyi—the daughter of the general who led Burma to independence in 1948, and who became an accidental heroine to the protesters in 1988—was soon placed under house arrest, on the shore of Inya Lake, in the middle of the city. She has for the most part remained there ever since, in an isolation as profound as her country's.

Myat Min decided to pursue his passion for English literature at Rangoon University; he dreamed of a life immersed in ideas, "like walking through the forest in the dead of night." But by 1996, the year he enrolled, the university had almost ceased to exist. To prevent students from gathering in protest, the government repeatedly closed the main campus and began busing undergraduates to makeshift campuses outside the capital. The semester dwindled to ten days in the classroom, with assignments and exams handled through the mail. In order to maintain the illusion of a successful system, the government continued to pass large numbers of students, even though their base of knowledge was shrinking precipitately. Higher education in Burma, once the training ground of a skilled civil service, was destroyed.

Myat Min found himself at a miserable campus in the satellite township of Dagon. "I met no like-minded students and teachers," he said. "I wanted a library with good books—there was none." A few months into his first year, after more antigovernment protests, the university was closed indefinitely. In August 1998, the government suddenly announced that students would sit for exams in the very classes that had been terminated two years earlier. Students began to demonstrate, but this time their initial demands were modest, with slogans like "Postpone exams" and "Provide distance students with hostels."

Myat Min decided to protest his farcical education. "No student at exams was as furious as I was," he said. "I was angry at everyone. I would kick a dog, even." He brought the autobiography of Thomas Jefferson to class, hoping to be punished. "But the teachers were okay with it," he said. "I was very angry with that okay." In his Burmese literature class, he didn't bother reading the professor's exam questions, and wrote an anti-government essay instead. Still nothing happened. The next day, he sat down in English class and ripped his exam book to pieces. Everyone in the room was terrified. A teacher approached his chair, told Myat Min that he had to complete the test, and gave him a new exam book. He tore it up as well. Then he wrote on the shredded paper, in English, "Down with the regime" and "I'm a nonconformist." Only fifteen minutes had gone by, but Myat Min had nothing more to say. He left the classroom and went out into the street, where he started distributing antigovernment pamphlets. Two weeks later, military intelligence officers came to his house.

During his interrogation, Myat Min was kicked and beaten. He was sent to Burma's most notorious prison, Insein, north of Rangoon, near the airport. He showed me a short account he later wrote of the months before his "trial": "Sometimes I ate cooked rice with a strong bad smell, and the curry was a blend of green roots, a spoonful of saffron powder, and a good amount of water. After two or three months of living on such food, my tongue and stomach started wriggling in a search for their usual stimuli, so much so that I sometimes felt like chewing my own thigh."

In January 1999, Myat Min and several friends were tried and sentenced en masse by a judge who refused to allow any of them to speak. Myat Min received twenty-one years—seven for illegal printing, seven for distributing the pamphlets, and seven for antigovernment activities. He was twenty years old.

In Burma's military intelligence lockups, political detainees are given repeated beatings, placed in stress positions, and made to stand in water for days on end. In Insein, the torture takes a different form: extreme isolation, no sunlight, inedible food, no writing materials. (I was told that a political prisoner found with a pen was punished more severely than a prisoner hiding a knife.) When Myat Min was there, prisoners had to wear cotton hoods with cutout eyeholes anytime they left their cell, in order to prevent communication between inmates. A friend of Myat Min's was caught trying to teach himself Chinese characters by writing on a piece of plastic with a nail; his ankles were shackled together for two weeks.

Reading was banned at Insein until 1999, when the International Committee of the Red Cross was allowed to make prison visits. After that, the regime gave inmates access to Buddhist writings, then to government newspapers, Burmese magazines, and finally English books. In the early years, Myat Min used a piece of red brick to write the names of novels and novelists on his cell floor. With a nail or shard of iron, he inscribed on plastic bags stories that he remembered, including dialogue, and passed them to his friends, who read the texts against the light. He retold the story of Ted Kaczynski, the Unabomber, whom he had read about in *Time* and found fascinating because of his hatred of modernity. After government newspapers were permitted, he followed the *New Light of Myanmar*'s critical coverage of the U.S.-led invasion of Iraq in 2003. Reading between the lines, he predicted, to his own delight, the rapid fall of Saddam's regime, charting the Americans' progress with elaborate maps.

Myat Min was freed from prison on July 6, 2005. He spoke of his seven years in a cell with unsettling equanimity. "The years I spent in prison were by far the most efficient and productive time of my life," he said. "Outside, we waste so many hours, so many days, yet we are not satisfied with how we spend our time. In prison, I feel I have complete control of my life."

On a quiet street near downtown Rangoon, in a neighborhood of elegantly faded colonial buildings, is a gated compound that is known as the American Center—a cultural outpost of the State Department. The James Baldwin Library and the Ella Fitzgerald Auditorium are open to any Burmese citizen willing to brave the police spies who haunt the area. Across the street, a security camera on the wall of a school is pointed at the center's front gate. No one seems to know if it actually works.

When I visited the Baldwin Library, which has twenty-two thousand members and thirteen thousand volumes, young Burmese were sitting on every available piece of furniture. For all their isolation and lack of analytical training, the citizens of Burma are stupendous readers. The bulletin board at the American Center library was covered with notes requesting books: biographies of Churchill, Margaret Atwood's *The Handmaid's Tale*, Naomi Klein's *The Shock Doctrine*. One note said, "Thank you very much for new books of Berryman, Papa, and Donald Hall. I'd like to request more books of Samuel Beckett and Hermann Hesse."

Three years ago, a thirty-six-year-old American named Thomas Pierce arrived in Rangoon to take charge of the American Center. Working with another official, Kim Penland, Pierce bought thousands of new books, tripled library membership, and started an English class for monks, a political discussion class, a training workshop for journalists, and a literature book club. Another group composed a Burmese Wikipedia entry about the country. A debate club attracted surprisingly animated audiences for subversive propositions like "Democracy is the best form of government."

The American Center brought together Burmese of different ages and backgrounds in a way that leveled their society's normally rigid hierarchies. Former political prisoners from the 1988 demonstrations—the '88 Generation—discussed Machiavelli with twentysomething hip-hop fans. Politicos from Aung San Suu Kyi's party and respectable businessmen sat down with members of ethnic minorities from the provinces. Senior monks learned English verbs alongside junior monks. Political activists attended seminars on human rights and on strategic communications. Pierce and Penland encouraged the students who were reading Montesquieu and Havel to make connections with their own political predicament. In a country where the law forbids unauthorized meetings of more than five people, none of this could have happened anywhere outside the gates of the center.

Dozens of political prisoners were released in 2005. Finding themselves unemployable and shunned by friends, many found their way to the center. They were welcomed with offers of scholarship classes. One of the former prisoners was Myat Min.

"I came out of prison not with plans but with dreams," he said. "One dream was to become a reporter." He worked as an intern at a Rangoon weekly, but his colleagues were nervous about having a former political prisoner in their midst, and he left. Barred from pursuing a degree in a Burmese university, he enrolled in courses at the American Center, including an Internet-based program with an American university, studying Latin to better understand Shakespeare and early English literature.

Myat Min still had an excitable demeanor, but he had emerged from prison with a more philosophical view, rooted in Buddhism, about the possibilities of politics in Burma. "I started soul-searching," he said. "I shouldn't have been angry that much. Freedom of expression became less important to me than freedom from anger, freedom from destruction, freedom from repentance, freedom from dilemmas. I wanted a peaceful and strong state of mind. As long as my mind is weak, I cannot do anything. I found values more important than any political ideology."

Myat Min and many other activists in his generation began to reconsider the wisdom of a head-on confrontation with a ruthless regime. But they wanted to stay in Burma, and so they began to think about changing their country in a more indirect way, beginning with their own lives—with the simple daily struggle not to abandon thought and passion, even in the face of a government that tried to smother its people. That struggle took many forms, some as apparently banal as producing a play or working to help poor children. The American Center became the focal point of these desires, and when two events in the past year shook the country—the monks' demonstrations, in September, and the devastation of Cyclone Nargis, in May—young Burmese responded in ways that, in the long term, may pose a serious threat to the rule of the generals.

In 1987, I backpacked through Burma on a one-week visa, the maximum time allowed. I had never seen a place so untouched by the West; even Pepsi was illegal. The country was ruled by General Ne Win, who had led the 1962 coup and subsequently imposed on Burma an isolation nearly as extreme and self-destructive as North Korea's. He governed through force, paranoia, and superstition: a few weeks before my visit, Ne Win, advised by his astrologer that the number nine was auspicious, abolished all Burmese banknotes of twenty-five, thirty-five, and seventy-five kyats, replacing them with two new denominations—forty-five and ninety—that are divisible by nine and whose numerals add up to nine. Countless Burmese lost their life savings. Yet there were no major protests. In the ancient Buddhist city of Pagan, on the Upper Irrawaddy River, the manager of a guesthouse where I stayed quietly grumbled that the government didn't care if its people were ruined. My guide around Rangoon invited me to lunch at his house and he made the same muted complaint. I left agreeing with a common observation about Burma: its people were, perhaps, too gentle to rebel.

The next year, after months of small student-led demonstrations and arrests, at eight minutes past eight o'clock on the morning of August 8, 1988—numerology also holds sway over the regime's opponents—Burmese of all backgrounds took to the streets to protest the military dictatorship. As many as three thousand people were killed before the army imposed order. Ne Win was replaced by a new group of generals, who named their junta the State Law and Order Restoration Council. The SLORC held elections in 1990; Aung San Suu Kyi's opposition party won overwhelmingly, but the junta ignored the results and continued to rule as before.

Some things changed. In 1989, Burma became Myanmar and Rangoon became Yangon, and the junta is now called the State Peace and Development Council, led by Senior General Than Shwe. Luxury hotels have gone up in downtown Rangoon; there's a new terminal at the airport; and in Mandalay, Chinese-built shopping centers have replaced entire neighborhoods. Over the past few years—at an estimated cost thus far of four billion dollars, and with the use of forced child labor—the regime has constructed a new capital, Naypyidaw, in the hot flatlands in the country's center. But since 1988, or even 1962, Burma has remained remarkably static, while its neighbors China, India, and Thailand have raced ahead.

Even its opposition politics seems frozen in time. The monks' demonstrations last September, and the violent repression by armed troops, looked like a small-scale version of the 1988 uprising, in the same rainwashed streets. Suu Kyi—"the Lady," in the almost universal indirect address—remains the country's iconic dissident figure, and her party is paralyzed as it awaits her endlessly deferred release. In its lassitude, Burma seems to be under a magic spell that only some external force can break.

During the two crises of the past year, Burmese listened to foreign news on shortwave radios and wondered if the world was about to come to their rescue. After the cyclone, the USS *Essex* and other Navy ships, which had been conducting joint exercises with the Thai military, floated offshore in the Andaman Sea while American officials tried to negotiate the unloading of vital relief equipment, such as heavy-lift helicopters and water purification machines. Reports of the ships' proximity gave a lot of people in the devastated Irrawaddy Delta the hope that an armed intervention was at hand. In the end, the regime refused to allow the *Essex* to unload its cargo.

One night in Rangoon, I had beers with a famous artist whose work is banned by the regime. He told the story of a friend in Mandalay who became pregnant and developed a serious case of swollen feet. She was taken to the hospital, where a doctor kept bringing in medical students to examine her, without ever telling her what could be done. "When the UN comes here, someone always wants to see me," the artist said. "They tell me they're sorry about the situation, to be patient." These visits, he said, had begun to feel like the examination of his pregnant friend. He suddenly declared, "The only solution is for the U.S. to drop a bomb on Naypyidaw. That's the only way! Ninety percent of Burmese would tell you the same thing. The world is very angry at America because of Iraq. If you use one percent of the money and one percent of the bombs here, the world will see you in a better way." It's a commonly expressed wish in Rangoon: I met a man who had hand-delivered a letter to the American embassy, where the United States keeps a low-level diplomatic presence, petitioning President George W. Bush to "bombard Burma." No one at the embassy would accept the letter, and when I advised the man not to expect an American invasion, he looked crushed. "Why?" he pleaded.

In recent years, millions of Burmese have responded to the country's seemingly incurable condition by fleeing. The poor escape to Thailand, which has up to two million migrant workers from Burma, many employed in conditions of semislavery; those with some means move to Singapore, London, or America. The authorities have recently made it easier to get a passport, which has only encouraged the hemorrhaging of the talented and disgruntled, so that potential threats leave the country, the competition for spoils inside is eased, and those who remain are increasingly supported by remittances from abroad. The endgame seems to be a regime virtually without citizens.

It's not clear why the junta has such an unshakable hold on power. There is no personality cult in Burma; I saw only one publicly displayed picture of Than Shwe, in the front hall of the run-down and nearly deserted National Museum. Nor does the state justify itself with relentless propaganda. Under Ne Win, the country's official ideology was a virulently nativist philosophy known as the Burmese Way to Socialism, which led to the expulsion of hundreds of thousands of Indian merchants after 1962 and anti-Chinese riots in 1967, and a disastrous economic policy of sweeping nationalization and closed borders. After Ne Win's fall, the junta adopted

Chinese-style authoritarian capitalism, but Burma never achieved economic growth—in part because of foreign sanctions, but also because the generals insist on a cut of any new business. (According to Transparency International, Burma is the second most corrupt country in the world, after Somalia.)

Most of Burma's top government posts are held by military officers, many of whom have a frighteningly weak grasp of governance. After a senior general went to Singapore and heard that all schools there had access to the Internet, he announced that Burmese schools would also be wired—never mind that most classrooms lacked books and paper. A Rangoon school was quickly fitted with computers and modems; the general visited, attended by the state media, and the next day everything was removed. During a dam opening attended by important officials, the river failed to flow, and Burmese upstream were ordered to gather buckets and pour in additional water.

Civil servants survive by protecting senior leaders from bad news. In an end-of-mission report, Charles Petrie, who was the chief United Nations official in Rangoon until November, called this system of denial "mutually strategic ignorance" and blamed it for "a number of disastrous economic and social policies." Following September's demonstrations, Petrie delivered remarks urging the regime to heed the monks' protest and address the growing poverty. Ten days later, Petrie and other foreign officials were summoned to Naypyidaw. The minister of planning, a hard-liner named Soe Tha, gave a long speech that attempted to rebut Petrie's remarks, using the UN's own statistics. "Some of it was really funny," Petrie recalls. "He said, for example, 'The UN states that a third of the children under five are malnourished. That's absolutely not true. The real figure is 31.2 percent. The UN states that three-quarters of an average family's income is used on food. That's actually not true. It's 68.7 percent.' He was using our statistics to say there was no poverty—that everything was fine." After the speech, Petrie was handed a letter informing him of his expulsion.

When I asked a Burmese journalist to describe the regime's philosophy, he suggested the word *sit-padaytharit*, or "military feudalism." The generals regard the population as unruly children incapable of taking responsibility for themselves; they believe that they alone can prevent Burma from dissolving. Since independence, Burma has contended with various ideological and ethnic insurgencies. At first, the chief threat to the state came from the Communist Party, which collapsed in 1989. But regional wars fought by the central government against armies of the Karen, Shan, Kachin, and other minorities raged on, largely out of international view, creating hundreds of thousands of refugees along Burma's borders and destroying thousands of hill villages. Mass killings, rapes, and forced labor have been widely documented by Human Rights Watch. Most senior members of the junta are veterans of these wars.

In recent years, the regime has signed cease-fire agreements with most of its antagonists, allowing ethnic leaders to exploit resources such as timber, opium, and gems. The truces are the regime's one notable achievement, but the political grievances that inspired the fighting have not been resolved, and the regime remains psychologically at war. Thant Myint-U, a former UN official who is the grandson of the UN secretary general U Thant, frequently travels to Burma, and he has met with senior government officials there. (He is also the author of *The River of Lost Footsteps*, a recent history of modern Burma.) He told me, "For the army leadership, the country is essentially a huge counterinsurgency battlefield." When a rural school is built, he said, the purpose is not to educate local children but to win the loyalty of people in the area, in the manner of a military hearts-and-minds campaign.

National unity and the threat from foreign and domestic agents of instability are the dominant themes of Burma's official literature. Next to my hotel in Rangoon, there was a hulking brick colonial railroad building that now garrisons a detachment of undernourished-looking soldiers. Under a banyan tree, in one corner of the grounds, at the intersection of two major streets, stood a red and white billboard that announced, in English, PEOPLE'S DESIRE: OPPOSE THOSE RELYING ON EXTERNAL ELEMENTS, ACTING AS STOOGES, HOLDING NEGATIVE VIEWS. OPPOSE THOSE TRYING TO JEOPARDIZE STABILITY OF THE STATE AND PROGRESS OF THE NATION. OPPOSE FOREIGN NATIONS INTERFERING IN INTERNAL AFFAIRS OF THE STATE. CRUSH ALL INTERNAL AND EXTERNAL DESTRUCTIVE ELEMENTS AS THE COMMON ENEMY. The sign was blown down in May by Cyclone Nargis, and no one bothered to put it back up. Its exhortation seemed to lack conviction. The Burmese regime has somehow preserved the mechanics of totalitarianism—the censorship board, the secret police, the armed civilian thugs, the concentration of vast wealth in a few corrupt hands, the official xenophobia, the atmosphere of distrust—without the ideological vigor.

Analysts of the regime say that Than Shwe, who is seventy-five and thought to be ill, believes himself to be the reincarnation of a Burmese king. This may explain why he named the new capital Naypyidaw—"Home of Kings." In 2005, Than Shwe announced a three-year plan to replace its forty thousand barrels of daily oil imports with homegrown biodiesel produced from the jatropha plant. (Many Burmese believe that Than Shwe hoped that growing jatropha would mystically undermine the opposition, because the Burmese name for the plant sounds like "Suu Kyi" in reverse.) Seven million acres of farmland were to be converted into jatropha plantations. Families were encouraged to grow the plant in their fields. Farmers were forced to abandon other crops, such as rice, which contributed to fears of food shortages after the cyclone. The jatropha frenzy left the country with unharvested fields, plants growing wild, and children rushed to the hospital after eating the plant, which is toxic.

Some experts explain the durability of the military regime by citing Theravada Buddhism, which is practiced by most Burmese, and which emphasizes individual salvation. Christina Fink, the author of *Living Silence: Burma Under Military Rule*, told me, "There are certain cultural practices that help maintain the regime. Burmese society is a hierarchical society, where obedience to authority is taught in the family, in religious institutions, in educational institutions." Fink pointed out that education in Burma was based on rote memorization, and she had found that "if you ask Burmese students to paraphrase something they cannot do it." Kit Young, an American musician who lived for many years in Rangoon, and who founded a music school there, told me that the Burmese word for deference is *anade*, which involves an unwillingness to make people feel uncomfortable. "You skirt, you go around things," she said.

I once asked a teacher in Rangoon, a woman whose refined manners did not conceal her hatred of the regime, why attempts to destabilize the government through targeted attacks were so rare. "We can blame the religion, and we can blame the live-and-let-live attitude of the Burmese," she said. "Even people like me, unless we go out of the country from time to time to refresh our minds, we become conditioned to the suppression. We are fearful without knowing we are fearful, and we are submissive without knowing we are submissive."

Perhaps the most convincing explanation for the persistence of the junta was given by a Burmese economics professor to a local journalist I met. "Other regimes are interdependent with the people," the professor said. "Here the government isn't dependent on the people, and the people aren't dependent on the government. When there's no electricity or water, you get it yourself." In other words, the regime has endured because it is not distracted by an effort to provide good government. Myat Min told me that this is why I saw so few security men on the streets of Rangoon: crushing the life out of the population is their only task, and so they have learned to do it with supreme efficiency.

Even in a country of small people, Thar Gyi, as I'll call him, was a wisp of a man, with sleek eyeglasses, tousled hair, and wrists the size of an American third grader's. One day in February, we sat at a table on the grounds of the American Center, under an umbrella that shielded us from the tropical sun. In a calm voice that barely rose above a whisper, Thar Gyi told me about his passion—contemporary theater, which is practically nonexistent in Burma.

In 1998, when he was twenty, he was arrested for participating in a student demonstration on behalf of Aung San Suu Kyi's party. The next year, he received a seven-year sentence. Confined to Insein prison, Thar Gyi fell into despair when he met dissidents who had been incarcerated multiple times. "I meet some people, older people. They're just telling their old stories, the political history of our country, and I feel sorry for them," he said. "They want to help their community, but they only sit in their cell, telling the old stories. I got a new idea from them. My idea is that I want to do something outside prison, so I can help other people. Maybe I'm a results-oriented person, and in prison we don't get results. That's labor lost."

Thar Gyi's sentence was reduced, and he was released in 2002. (He called himself lucky.) He came out of prison with two strong desires: not to end up back in prison or in exile, like so many other activists, and to teach the arts to young people. With the help of an English teacher at the American Center named Phillip Howse, he worked on a series of theatrical productions. He stage-managed a performance of *Romeo and Juliet* at a nightclub that later burned down. In 2006, he helped direct a production of the musical *Rent* at the American Center. The show's portrait of New York during the AIDS crisis still felt current in Rangoon, where the disease is rampant. To underscore this connection, Thar Gyi handed out twenty free tickets to Burmese youths infected with HIV.

On his own, he staged a production of Sartre's *No Exit*. He had borrowed a copy of the play from the American Center. "The title caught my attention," he said. "Sometimes my brain is blocked by something, and I can't get through that block and find the answer. That is a human theme." One afternoon, *No Exit* was performed, in English, in a cramped and sweltering apartment; the windows were covered to block out the sunlight. The state requires all group events to be vetted and cleared by the authorities—not only to stop the flow of unsanctioned ideas but also to prevent people from gathering in one place. Thar Gyi told the neighborhood authorities that English language classes were being held at the apartment.

No Exit was embraced by its audience, and there were several additional performances. Thar Gyi's production had highlighted the similarities between Sartre's claustrophobic scenario, with characters trapped by forces beyond their control, and the suffocated existence of the average young Burmese growing up in a tiny Rangoon apartment.

Through theater, Thar Gyi hoped to encourage young Burmese to develop their talents and transcend inertia and helplessness. He no longer wanted to focus on displacing the regime, and he even found the American Center's more political activities misguided. "American people say that political changes will change the conditions in our country," Thar Gyi said. "That's true. But I think we need to develop our own capacities. We are not ready for democracy. We don't have any good platform, good foundation, to get those changes." He spoke of the garbage that often blocked the drains, flooding the streets of Rangoon. Residents complained that the city was dirty, he said. "Where does that garbage come from? People throw it recklessly. When there was a flood, people said that is the responsibility of Yangon City Development Committee. It was their fault!" Thar Gyi's whisper gave his voice a strange urgency. "But you can't just say, 'You should take the responsibility!' That's why I want to use the arts. I want to teach people critical thinking."

The tradition of reading groups in Burma goes back to the 1920s, when the Burma Book Club was established by a British anthropologist named

John S. Furnivall. Under Burma's successive dictatorships, these clubs have met in secret, serving as forums for political discussion among groups of trusted friends. Ideas tend to reach Burma piecemeal twenty or thirty years after they've had their moment elsewhere. After the protests of 1988, intellectuals turned away from Marxism and embraced the existentialism of Camus and Sartre, Orwell's antitotalitarian fictions, and Kafka. Recently, fragments from Jacques Derrida and the post-structuralists have begun to be championed in Rangoon as the latest model for the dismantling of tyranny.

In early 2007, a book club began meeting on Saturday afternoons at the American Center. The group's leaders were in their thirties and forties; many had become acquainted in prison. Each of them brought into the club one or two Burmese in their twenties who had no political experience. At its height, the club had forty members. Its purpose was to reach across the gap between the '88 Generation, which had been locked away for so many years, and younger people, for whom, as one woman in the club put it, the events of 1988 were "a fairy tale."

Over time, about ten of the younger students dropped out, after intelligence officers spoke to them and their university teachers. The leaders assumed that the club had been infiltrated by at least one government spy, and so they reserved the most sensitive topics—about Burmese politics and opposition strategy—for conversations outside the classroom.

One of the leaders was a writer in her late thirties, who asked to be identified as Hnin Se. "We didn't expect that much from these young people," she told me in Rangoon. "But the topics they raised were surprising. Some raised the question 'Why is this nation different from the rest of the world?' They knew the answer. They asked the question because they couldn't control their feelings." One of the students' favorite books was *Heroes Without Capes*, a Burmese collection of profiles of ordinary people who, in small ways, defied the authorities in order to improve the world immediately around them.

Hnin Se is tall and slender, with black hair flowing down her back; she cuts it short during times of crisis. She maintains the outward calm that is typical of the Burmese, but once, when I asked how the rule of the generals could ever end, she hissed, "Kill them all." She grew up in a fishing village in the Irrawaddy Delta. Her mother was a teacher and her father owned an ice factory; he took to drink and left the family, but not before encouraging his daughter's artistic temperament. By the age of six, Hnin Se had read *Gone with the Wind* in Burmese. At fourteen, she was sent to Rangoon to continue her education, and for years she picked up dried fish and rice sent by her mother to the Rangoon jetty and sold them in Aung San Market to support the family. She was in her third year at Rangoon University, and just beginning to write fiction, when the events of August 1988 took place. She saw police driving students into Inya Lake—where many drowned—and beating and shooting others who tried to escape. "As a nineteen-year-old girl, I might not have any knowledge about democracy," she said, "but I had the sense to distinguish right from wrong." In 1991, she distributed poems protesting the government's refusal to let Aung San Suu Kyi, who had won the Nobel Peace Prize, travel to Oslo. Hnin Se was arrested and sent to Insein. When she first laid eyes on the prison, she smiled. "I was already a writer, and I thought this would be a new experience," she said.

For the crime of opening her cell window, Hnin Se spent her early imprisonment on death row, in a block with condemned women. They had to remain silent during the day, but at night they talked through six-inch holes in their cell doors and sang Burmese popular songs. The women developed a deep solidarity, and Hnin Se made several close friends in prison, two of whom later joined the book club.

She was released in a general amnesty in 1992, and spent the next several years on the run, sometimes forced to sell dried fish and rice again. It was also the most prolific period of her life, and she became noted for her short stories. But the novel that she really wanted to write—about the political evolution of a Burmese girl—eluded her. She married, had two children, and moved into a narrow two-story house of wood and brick in eastern Rangoon, filled with books: Katharine Graham's *Personal History*; André Maurois's *The Art of Living*, translated into English; and Burmese translations of Mahfouz and García Márquez. Instead of resuming political activity, she threw herself into work on behalf of the Burmese poor. It was a way for her to engage in social change without risking a return to Insein.

On a hazy Sunday morning in February, at the beginning of the hot season, we drove out of Rangoon, across the wide, sluggish Hlaing River, into a marshy landscape dotted with low-slung industrial buildings. Just off the highway, down a dirt road lined with banana trees and palm groves, was a village of five hundred families. Next to a muddy lily pond stood a monastery—two stories, with a rusted metal pagoda-style roof and walls of reclaimed boards and woven thatch. In these cramped quarters, monks ran a school for three hundred students, including sixty orphans. Hnin Se and four friends from her book club were helping to support the school, and had raised about a thousand dollars.

The junior monks and novices slept on planks on the lower level, in a sort of glorified crawl space. Upstairs, children were scattered across the floor, learning lessons. At lunchtime, young monks served rice, beans, and fish paste from huge cooking pots. The abbot received us on the floor of his little office, which was also his bedroom; piles of red-brown robes had been neatly folded before a golden Buddha. Hnin Se knelt before the abbot, brought her hands together, and bowed her head to the floor. The abbot was forty-six years old and from central Burma, the heartland of the *sangha*, or monkhood.

Hnin Se and the abbot spoke to me about the challenges of funding the school. "It's very difficult to feed everyone in this compound," she said. "So we pool the money from donations in a bank and get some interest."

"We need at least fifty dollars a day," the abbot said. This paid for two meatless meals daily. Ordinarily, monks live off alms, which they collect as they walk in a line through local neighborhoods, their begging bowls held out. But poverty has grown so deep and food prices so high that people can't spare enough to feed the monks; many Burmese eat only once a day. At the same time, with fees for government schools out of reach, families increasingly bring their children to monasteries for a free education. The *sangha* is Burma's safety net, but every year the monks have to do more with less.

The abbot was locked in a struggle with local authorities who were conspiring to sell the monastery's land to factory owners across the highway. (Three hundred families from the village had already been displaced.) Every day, it seemed, there was a confrontation between the monks and the authorities. There was nothing passively transcendent about the monks I met in Burma. Their bare shoulders and biceps revealing robust physiques, they often reminded me of labor organizers or political strategists. When a company man showed up one morning to measure a piece of the land, a young monk came out to meet him, quarreled, and punched him in the jaw.

"They want us to smile, we have to smile," the abbot said of the government. "They want us to cry, we have to cry. We are living with our body but with their soul." I asked him about the attitude of soldiers, most of whom are Buddhists, toward monks. "They're from another planet," he said. "They fear their commanders more than they fear punishment in the next life."

A visitor arrived: a matronly woman from Rangoon with oversized glasses had come to pray, as she did every Sunday. Seeing us, she bowed obsequiously. The abbot told me that she was a member of the regime's civilian mass movement, and that she was sent to keep an eye on him.

As Hnin Se and I left the monastery, four men in green *longyis* stood by and watched us. Something as small as a group of friends taking on a charitable project was irregular enough to arouse suspicion, and a foreigner meant nothing but trouble. We drove away without looking back.

The leaders of the '88 Generation who were released from prison in 2004 and 2005 waited a year or more before attempting any public actions. They then made the kind of simple, earnest gestures that give the Burmese democratic opposition its air of moral depth and political naïveté. There was the Open Heart Campaign, in which citizens wrote letters to Than Shwe describing their hardships. Then, there were White Sundays, when activists dressed in the color of purity and visited the families of political prisoners still behind bars. None of the '88 leaders seemed to have a long-term vision, but the formal opposition party, the National League for Democracy, was moribund—waiting patiently for Suu Kyi to release statements—and someone had to fill the void.

Last August, the regime abruptly announced that fuel subsidies would be eliminated, thereby doubling the price of bus fare in Rangoon. In spite of Burma's nearly three billion dollars in annual natural gas sales, the national budget had critical shortfalls. The policy change forced thousands of people to walk instead of taking the bus. On August 19, ten members of the '88 Generation held an emergency meeting and decided to test the junta. Their goal was to force a dialogue between the government and Suu Kyi. (An activist who attended the meeting told me, "Asking for regime change isn't very practical.") Later that day, a small group of activists entered the streets of Rangoon and, in solidarity with the working

poor, began to walk—no signs, no chanting, no colors. Even so, the regime pounced. On August 21, a dozen leaders of the new movement were
arrested. (They are once again serving long sentences in Insein, often in
solitary confinement.) The rest went into hiding. The moment of protest,
now leaderless, appeared to be over.

Then, on September 5, in the town of Pakokku, twenty miles up the
Irrawaddy River from the magnificent medieval temples of Pagan, several
hundred monks took to the streets chanting the *metta sutta*, the Buddhist
scripture that urges a universal extension of kindness:

> *As a mother would risk her life*
> *To protect her child, her only child,*
> *Even so should one cultivate a limitless heart*
> *With regard to all beings.*

It was clearly a continuation of the aborted August movement.

Monks have been politicized throughout modern Burmese history.
The *sangha* led demonstrations against British rule and has played a part
in every eruption of protest since 1962. "When Burmese people suffer,
normally they don't dare to speak out," a monk who later fled to the Thai
border town of Mae Sot said. "So we express their suffering for them."
Thousands of townspeople in Pakokku cheered the monks, until the security forces moved in, firing over the monks' heads and tying some of
them to utility poles and beating them with rifles. News of this violence—
shocking in a country where monks are revered—spread quickly.

On September 9, in Mandalay, half a dozen leaders from the most
activist monasteries gathered in secret. They communicated in code, by
mobile phone. ("Let's meet where we had tea together the last time.") At
the meeting, they formed the All Burma Monks Alliance, an illegal act—
monks, like all Burmese, are forbidden to form nonsanctioned organizations. The alliance made four demands of the regime: apologize for the
incident in Pakokku; lower commodity prices; release all political prisoners, including Suu Kyi; begin a dialogue with the opposition. The regime
had nine days, until September 18, to respond. The monk in Mae Sot, who
attended the meeting, recalls, "I said, 'September 18 is good,' because the
military took back power that day in 1988." He also pointed out the
numerological significance of a deadline nine days after September 9:

9+9+2+0+0+7=27. "The generals are superstitious. I knew they would go through these calculations."

The monks were aware that their demands would not be met—certainly, an apology from the generals was unimaginable. The list was strategic: the regime would look intransigent, allowing the monks to ratchet up the pressure. In general, the monks I interviewed were far more unsentimental in their political calculations than students and artists were; they thought like dedicated organizers who understood just how long and hard the battle would be. The monk in Mae Sot, who had the handshake of a stevedore, seemed to suggest even that the monks knew that lethal force was inevitable, and could work to their advantage. When I asked him whether he had studied the experiences of Gandhi and King, he smiled. "There was a movement earlier than them," he said. "And that is the teachings of Buddha."

September 18 came, with no response from the government. The monks began making peaceful marches to holy sites in Rangoon and Mandalay, with Burmese and foreign journalists contacted in advance to document the protests. (According to the monk in Mae Sot, there was a high-level meeting after each day's demonstration focusing on next-day planning and media outreach.) At first, the alliance barred lay people from joining the demonstrations, in order to preserve the spiritual character of the movement, but the entreaties of the public eventually compelled the monks to let them participate, in the form of human chains, lining either side of the monks' single-file columns. On September 21, the demonstrations were formally opened to all. The next day, a group of monks in Rangoon walked down University Avenue, along Inya Lake, and cowed the police who stood at the barricades on the road to Aung San Suu Kyi's house. The Lady herself was at the front gate, with tears in her eyes. Pictures and news of the encounter were transmitted by local journalists to international outlets and to publications run by Burmese in exile; these stories were soon posted on websites accessible to people inside Burma. The effect of this media boomerang was to send tens of thousands more Burmese into the streets.

Among them were members of Hnin Se's book group and other students from the American Center. Hnin Se was out of the country at the time, but she learned, with pride, that four of her students, while protesting, had raised the flag of the banned All Burma Student Union, which depicted a fighting peacock. They called themselves the 2007 Student Union.

Throughout the uprising, the American Center was a crucial point of contact, where monks, youths, and '88ers could exchange messages that were otherwise too dangerous to transmit. Monks and students who had never encountered the might of the state got on the phone with veteran '88ers and received tactical advice.

The September protests were led by a core of monks, but in downtown Rangoon the swelling crowds were essentially leaderless. A thirty-year-old blogger in Rangoon explained to me that this "decentralized" movement stood a better chance of surviving than the '88 version. "The brain of this government cannot understand postmodernism," he said. "In September, the trend of the demonstration was just like postmodernism, because it started everywhere. There's no main direction. When the government tried to arrest the leader of the demonstration, they could not find him or her."

Yet the September protests ended up conforming to the narrative structure of all the others. On September 25 and 26, the soldiers of the 66th and 77th Light Infantry Divisions arrived in Rangoon and began shooting monks and unarmed civilians. A lanky, guitar-loving sixteen-year-old boy was swept up in the protests and found himself outside a high school in the district of Tamwe. There he saw soldiers and militiamen shoot a monk in the head and drive an army truck into a group of students carrying the peacock flag. The prospect of killing monks made some members of the regime pause. In Mandalay, it is widely believed, the regional commander cut a deal with the monks' leaders; no shots were fired. Burma's ruling council of ten generals was reportedly divided on whether to use force. Those in favor of violence won out, seven to three.

Two days into the crackdown, in which unknown numbers were killed—Burmese I spoke with claimed several dozen—the protests fizzled out. Thousands of people were arrested, monasteries were raided, and student leaders were rounded up. Among Hnin Se's students, three were jailed (one with a head injury so severe that he still hasn't recovered) and a fourth escaped to Thailand.

The American Center was one of the government's main targets. Most of the book group's leaders were arrested. The debate club stopped meeting, and the political discussion class was disbanded.

On December 3, at the Ministry of Information in Naypyidaw, Khin Yi, the head of the Burmese police force, spoke at a press conference and presented the regime's version of the September events—the speech was headlined "Myanmar Government Really Desires Democracy." By then, enough arrested activists had been tortured, revealing the names of other participants, and a coherent story could be assembled. The government's facts were at least partly true: money had come from foreign organizations (George Soros's Open Society Institute, which has given almost forty million dollars to the Burmese democracy movement since 1994, was named several times); training had been provided in Rangoon at the American Center, as well as in Mae Sot; monks and students who had met in prison had become the leaders of a new wave of opposition whose ultimate goal was regime change. These facts were filtered through an outraged paranoia that could name names but had no grasp of motives. The police chief maintained that "bogus monks" and other subversives had been directed from abroad to act "under the pretext of the increase of fuel prices" and "disrupt law and order, and destabilize the peace and tranquility of the State."

Thar Gyi, the theater director, did not join the September protests. "I analyze that situation," he said five months later. "I'm not a professor of political science, but I have some experience, and I look at things and say, 'This is not an endgame.'"

Myat Min joined the marchers, and, although they were largely peaceful, he was disturbed by what he saw. "Many people were in a state of rage, hysteria—throwing bottles. Very few people realize the power of silence. Silence is harder to crush. We were expecting a few leaders who, like Gandhi, can meet their death very calmly. We didn't see that, and we were very disappointed." A friend of his from prison said, "The only one like that is Aung San Suu Kyi," and he added that the September events "had a very good form, but less content." The monks, they said, had chanted the *metta sutta* without genuine loving-kindness. There was still anger in their hearts. I told Myat Min and his friend that they had come out of prison with extremely high standards for politics. They didn't deny it.

For the past two decades, American policy toward Burma has been to isolate the regime through sanctions. This policy has been pursued as a moral response to a deplorable government, without much regard for its effectiveness. In Washington, Burma is an afterthought: a handful of senators pay attention to the issue, and a handful of advocates have their ear. A Western diplomat in Rangoon told me, "American foreign policy has been outsourced to the exiles and their patrons on the Hill. There's a lack of interest at the State Department in Burma." The diplomat added, "Sanctions are a joke—they're just a pressure release. The generals don't care what the rest of the world thinks about them, because they don't think about the rest of the world. What they care about is their financial and physical security."

Win Min, an analyst of the Burmese military who lives in Thailand, told me, "Burmese military officers say that they have three cards to play in the international community: China, India, and ASEAN"—the Association of Southeast Asian Nations. "They say they don't need to worry as long as they have these cards." China and India have been competing for contracts to explore offshore oil and gas, and to build a gas pipeline across Burma. Thailand, a member of ASEAN, buys most of Burma's gas and other commodities.

These economic relationships have always trumped moral concerns. Last September, after the world saw pictures of monks and civilians being shot in Rangoon, China, which sells arms to the regime, issued the mildest expression of concern, then tried to prevent the UN Security Council from even discussing Burma. India said nothing, and at the height of the crackdown its petroleum minister signed a gas contract in Naypyidaw. ASEAN, which admitted Burma as a member in 1997, officially deplored the violence. Two months later, Ibrahim Gambari of Nigeria, the UN envoy to Burma, was scheduled to give a briefing at an ASEAN meeting in Singapore on the prospect of talks between the Burmese government and Aung San Suu Kyi. At a dinner two nights earlier, the Burmese prime minister, Thein Sein, announced to his ASEAN counterparts that Burma would walk out if Gambari was allowed to speak. The briefing was canceled.

Burma is one of those countries, like Zimbabwe and Sudan, whose brutal rulers have successfully defied Washington and managed to make America seem impotent in its self-righteousness. The occupation of Iraq has been a boon to the Burmese generals. The idea, popular in the 1990s, that the world may intervene in countries whose governments show no regard for human life is now seen as reflecting Western arrogance; China's approach of tolerating human rights abuses in the name of stability and noninterference has become the standard. While the West stays out of Burma, Chinese businessmen are making huge investments in Mandalay, pulling the country's economy toward the Chinese border. Rather than being a throwback to a more benighted age, Burma might be a picture of the geopolitical future.

The American policy of isolating Burma is largely considered a failure. But, if reforming the regime is the goal, the alternative policy—economic engagement, along the lines of Burma's neighbors—has also failed. Every year, the junta grows stronger while the country sinks deeper into poverty. A Burmese journalist explained, "The regime here, unlike regimes elsewhere, is trying to prevent the formation of a middle class." Sean Turnell, an economist and a Burma expert at Macquarie University, in Sydney, said, "The biggest sanction on Burma is the regime: no investment, no property law, no rule of law, restrictions on exports and imports, corruption off the dial." He pointed out that Burma's sale of natural gas is recorded at the official exchange rate of six Burmese kyats per dollar, whereas the real rate is more like twelve hundred kyats. These clandestine profits are sent offshore or hoarded in Naypyidaw. "It's like a spouse not declaring his income and making the family starve, even though he's earning a Wall Street salary," Turnell said. According to Thiha Saw, the editor of a business magazine in Rangoon, there has been no public budget in Burma since 2000.

The hope—and it isn't much more than that—of critics of American policy is that a new generation of military officers will come to power with the understanding that government by plunder has hit diminishing returns. Thant Myint-U said that the pragmatists among Burma's leaders-in-waiting will be helped if international pressure eases. "If there's one thing that's fueled Burma's many problems over the last half century, it's been its isolation. If outside economic relationships are reduced to a few oil companies, Chinese logging companies, and twelve UN agencies, it's easy for the generals to play games. If we're talking about thousands of individual business relationships, even if it leads to a certain amount of corruption, you'll have a much more open political space." But Win Min argues that only a combination of international pressure and engagement can bring about reform. "In the history of the Burmese military, pragmatists have never got the upper hand," he said.

Even the staunchest opponents of the regime—such as Maureen Aung-Thwin of the Open Society Institute's Burma project, which funds civic and political activities inside and outside Burma—acknowledge that the military will have to play a role in any transition to democracy. Having strangled civil society, hollowed out the bureaucracy, and locked up the political opposition, the army can rightly claim to be the only institution capable of running things. The junta held a referendum in May on a new constitution that mandates elections in 2010 and a central role for the military in future governments. (The referendum passed; open criticism of the plan was punishable by twenty years in prison.) The opposition is deeply divided on whether or not to go along with this "road map." In general, I found dissidents inside the country more willing than the political opposition in exile to accept the inevitable compromises through which they might escape a life under the generals' cruel delusions. They don't want foreigners to boycott Burma; they long for contact with the world. At the same time, they are less likely than outsiders to be gulled by the regime's feints toward openness. "In historical terms, fifty years is not a long period," a journalist in Rangoon said. "So we may not get to enjoy democracy in our lifetimes. But my son or grandson—I'm sure of that."

On April 29, the Burmese government announced that rain showers, with winds of forty-five miles an hour, were approaching the southern coast, from the Bay of Bengal. The population never learned what was coming until Nargis, a Category 4 cyclone, made landfall on May 2, with winds three times as strong. Nargis raged all night, and the storm surge drowned much of the Irrawaddy Delta in twelve feet of water. Whole villages vanished. Families tried to survive by climbing palm trees in the darkness and holding on until the morning; afterward, the corpses of parents and children were found with their wrists lashed to one another. At least a hundred and thirty thousand people died, making Nargis the worst natural disaster in Burma's history.

In Rangoon, a computer programmer watched the storm from the seventh floor of a building in Chinatown that swayed in the wind. Satellite dishes and water tanks flew off rooftops; boats blew back and forth across the river. In the morning, he went out with his son and found a city that had lost most of its great old trees. For the next two or three days, there was scarcely any government presence on the streets. Citizens were trying to remove the trees blocking the roads with handsaws. No news was coming in from the devastated delta. It was as if the government had ceased to exist.

"I realized we must do this ourselves," the programmer said. His cell phone was still working, and he called friends in Upper Burma, asking them to send down bags of rice. By the fifth day, he and his friends in Rangoon had organized themselves into an emergency relief team, bringing supplies to refugees who had gathered in makeshift camps at schools and monasteries. At one site, the first evidence of civil authority appeared in the form of two policemen, who demanded to know what the programmer and his friends were doing. A monk shouted at the officers, "This is the job you should be doing!" The policemen backed away before the refugees could turn into a mob.

The night of the storm, a wave of water entered Hnin Se's small house and destroyed her books. She had written in an essay that she let herself cry only when she was outside the country. This time, she could not contain her despair.

The next morning, she ventured out and met people who had lost their entire houses. "I realized their situation was worse than mine," she said. "And I wanted to help." A friend from the delta arrived to tell her that he had lost eight nephews and nieces. A week after the storm, Hnin Se and her husband managed to reach the delta. She saw fifteen corpses—floating in rivers, sprawled on the banks, flung into flooded rice paddies. Somehow, being amid the destruction made her feel strong again, because at least she was doing something.

I returned to Burma a month after the storm. Rangoon looked emptier and far less green, as if the ravenous urban decay had consumed whole buildings and trees. In the park around Shwedagon Pagoda, trunks and branches had been cut and stacked like firewood; the root systems, torn out of the earth, were too massive to move, and lay in agonized poses. But the Burmese had a feverish sense of purpose. Everyone I had met on my first trip was collecting relief supplies for the delta, with no thought of returning to normal routine. They barely had time to sleep, and many of them fell ill after taking arduous trips south, amid monsoon rains. Hnin Se was leading a group of friends to the delta twice a week. The students at Kit Young's music school were running convoys of trucks to the delta; in one refugee center, children had drawn pictures of the night when the world seemed to be ending. Thar Gyi was living in the delta town of Labutta, organizing theater games for cyclone orphans who were numb—except when it rained and they were terrified.

Myat Min and two friends from prison also made trips to the delta, then realized that there were refugees around Rangoon who were getting no help. In an e-mail, Myat Min wrote an account of one visit to refugees in Hlaing Tharyar, across the river from the city. "We really wanted to buy them bamboos and plastic sheets," he said. "But we did not do that, believing many of them who are eager to start small businesses would resell those materials at a lower price." Instead, Myat Min and his friends donated food and clothing, including a hundred dresses. He went on, "Before we left, we made some secret cash donations."

A Burmese journalist, speaking of the students, told me, "The American Center opened their eyes." Then, he said, Nargis set them in motion. Several years ago, foreign aid workers debated whether, after four decades of dictatorship, anything like civil society still existed in Burma. The question was answered by Nargis. When I arrived, the government was harassing the volunteer convoys and throwing bureaucratic obstacles in front of foreign aid workers. The World Food Program was haggling with the authorities to bring in ten helicopters scavenged from places like Uganda and Ukraine. American and French warships were idling offshore with relief equipment while the government tried to figure out if they were preparing to invade. Nothing was working except the artists' associations, the small businesses, the hiking clubs, the student groups, and the networks of friends that are barely allowed to exist in Burma.

"They have become a movement," Thiha Saw, the magazine editor, said. "They are writers, comedians, engineers, doctors, small groups—but they become like activists."

It was only a matter of time before the junta recognized the emerging threat. In June, the government arrested seven members of a group that was collecting rotting corpses around the delta and giving them proper burials. During my visit, a famous comedian named Zaganar was arrested after trying to send footage from the delta to the exile media. (I had tried to interview Zaganar on my first trip, but I arrived early at the restaurant where we were to meet and caught the cleaning staff wiretapping the room; our lunch had to be canceled.)

• • •

One morning in mid-June, I drove east of Rangoon with Myat Min and his friends to visit a refugee encampment. After we crossed the Bago River, a group of three policemen stopped us at a roadside checkpoint and demanded that we turn around. "Insurgent area," one of the officers explained cheerfully. Myat Min had a hard time suppressing a laugh. "They don't want foreign eyes in the affected areas," he said.

We then drove to another camp, on the west side of Rangoon, near the monastery that Hnin Se helped support. In a drenching rain, we found forty-seven families living along a muddy path under blue tarps donated by the Red Cross. The husbands were away at jobs in a dye factory; the wives crouched on bamboo slats with their children, who appeared ill and listless. One woman laughed when I asked if they had enough to eat.

"Regime change can happen in many ways besides mass revolution," Myat Min said later. He said that after the September events and the cyclone, Burmese society was unraveling. "We will see more chaos than organized struggle against the regime," he said. "But I also sense the end of the regime is getting nearer and nearer."

Six weeks after the storm, the Burmese government and international aid groups were still negotiating the rules under which relief workers could operate in the delta. On the whiteboard at the Save the Children office in Rangoon, a chart that tracked travel requests noted in numerous cases "Lost in DSW!"—the Department of Social Welfare. An aid official, fuming, said to me, "We're trying to uphold pure humanitarian standards—that's a concept the generals don't recognize. We're always trying to control the idiocy of their actions, because it always gets interpreted negatively outside and has a major impact on people's willingness to help."

After the storm, senior American military officers tried to persuade their Burmese counterparts to allow them to unload relief supplies. Admiral Timothy J. Keating, of the U.S. Pacific Command, met Vice Admiral Soe Thein, the chief of the Burmese navy, at the old Rangoon airport terminal. According to a Burmese man who attended the meeting, Soe Thein said to Keating, the commander of all American forces in the Pacific, "Everything is okay. You're just a little late." This was on May 12, when most survivors in the delta had not yet received any help. Keating proposed that a Burmese officer ride along on American helicopter relief flights, but Soe Thein brushed away the offer. When an American civilian pressed him about the condition of refugees, he gathered his maps and said, "This meeting is over."

Hnin Se, whose hair was now cut short, had made ten trips to the delta, bringing rice and clothing to remote villages that had received almost no help. She was suffering from exhaustion. The authorities were telling groups like hers to hand over their supplies. Unauthorized foreigners were being sent back to Rangoon and, in a few cases, expelled from the country, but Hnin Se offered to take me to the delta.

We left Rangoon in a predawn rain. Hnin Se, wearing jeans and a head scarf, had somehow commandeered what seemed to be a rusted-out city bus. Inside were eighteen young Burmese, of whom she was the clear leader—two booksellers, a goldsmith, a photocopy attendant, a former soldier, a graduate student reading *Colonial Policy and Practice*, by John S. Furnivall, the founder of the Burma Book Club. The bus rattled and bounced through mud and rain down to the delta, with a hundred fifty-kilo sacks of rice ballasting the rear. We hit a police checkpoint, and Hnin Se gestured for me to disappear under the hood of my windbreaker. But it was early Sunday morning, the search was cursory, and we were waved on after being given a flyer that said, essentially, "Do Not Feed the Cyclone Victims."

At midmorning, we arrived in a town called Kun Chan Kone and boarded a fifty-foot boat—home to a fishing family who had lost their house in the storm. As we sailed down the Toe River, a mile-wide branch of the Irrawaddy, Hnin Se's friends gazed at the palm-lined shore, where there had once been village after village. There appeared to be nothing left.

The Irrawaddy Delta is a labyrinth of waterways that wind toward the Bay of Bengal; many are almost impossible to navigate. For hours, we drifted slowly in fog and drizzle along narrow channels, the overhanging branches of damaged trees scraping the deck. On either side of us, paddies were flooded, and although the monsoon rice season was nearing its height, there was little sign of planting or plowing. The bones of drowned water buffalo gleamed as white as the storks in the tall grass, and twice we saw human remains on the riverbank.

At noon, we reached the first village, at the bend of a stream. Dozens of villagers gathered at the little jetty, the women and girls wearing on their cheeks and foreheads *thanaka*—a yellow powder that is both a sunscreen and a cosmetic. As we disembarked, a village leader with a megaphone called men and boys to come offload sixty-four bags of rice. Almost two hundred villagers had died. Most of the fourteen hundred survivors were living in makeshift hovels, with families doubled up.

Hnin Se led the way along a path to the monastery, a collapsed ruin of century-and-a-half-old timber. The abbot received us in his pagoda. This was how the supplies were distributed—not through the local authorities, whom no one trusted, but through the monks. The government's contribution to the village thus far consisted of thirty-five blankets, fifteen bags of rice, and five tarps. Here and throughout the delta, the private effort was keeping people fed.

We sat on the floor of the monks' quarters and were given a lunch that seemed, in these circumstances, much too grand. One of the women who served us was a thirty-year-old whose house had been out in the fields, and so she and her family had been mercilessly exposed when the wall of water came. She had clung to a tree for a day and a night while, one after another, her husband and four of her children were carried away. A two-year-old daughter who had been staying with the woman's sister was all that was left of her family. "We didn't suffer alone," she said. "All of us, together, suffered. That's how we can survive."

By the time we returned to the pagoda, the rain was coming down in torrents. The world beyond the village had disappeared. Hnin Se had told me that through her relief work in the delta, she had learned how few of her countrymen knew that they had any rights, even the right to complain. The Burmese people were even further from being free than she had imagined. But at least one thing was achieved. Beyond Rangoon, the violence of the September events had been only a rumor among the vast numbers of poor people; the criminal aftermath of the cyclone was something that they saw for themselves. "When I was younger, I hoped and waited for outside help to come to our country and liberate it," she said. "Now I realize that we have to rely on ourselves."

A crowd of women and children had gathered outside the pagoda, clutching plastic bags. Two men in Hnin Se's group opened the sacks of rice and poured their contents onto a sheltered walkway outside the pagoda, making a great white mound. A young monk stood with a megaphone and called out the name of each of the 385 surviving families. There were far too many people to take cover beneath the shelter, and the villagers stood in the rain, shivering under umbrellas, pieces of plastic, and straw hats, waiting for their turn to step forward and receive three scoops of rice and a piece of clothing from Hnin Se.

PART THREE

Writers at War

V. S. Naipaul's Pursuit of Happiness

Dissent, Summer 2002

In October 1953, V. S. Naipaul's father died in Port of Spain, Trinidad. He died in disappointment and misery. He had been waiting to see his son, who was finishing a degree at Oxford, and waiting for his own book of stories to find a publisher. All his life he had struggled to be more than a journalist for the Trinidad *Guardian*—to be a writer. V. S. Naipaul had not so much been handed this ambition as become its living extension. "I had always looked upon my life as a continuation of his—a continuation which, I hoped, would also be a fulfillment." To read the letters published recently in *Between Father and Son* is to see where Naipaul got the spareness of his style, right down to the semicolons.

Naipaul's mother and older sister pleaded with him to come home to Trinidad and take up his family duty. Before his death, his father had asked the same thing, and Naipaul had written from Oxford: "If I did so, I shall die from intellectual starvation." With his father dead, the pressure to return became intense. "Our family was in distress. I should have done something for them, gone back to them. But, without having become a writer, I couldn't go back." And so for three years Naipaul put his family off. He was living in London, writing occasional scripts for the BBC Caribbean Service, and trying to complete the book that would make him a writer and lift his family out of debt.

Years later, Naipaul would come across a de Chirico painting to which Guillaume Apollinaire had given the title *The Enigma of Arrival*. In his book of the same title, Naipaul wrote, "I felt that in an indirect, poetical way the title referred to something in my own experience." It gave him the idea for a story:

My narrator . . . would arrive—for a reason I had yet to work out—at that classical port with the walls and gateways like cut-outs. He would walk past that muffled figure on the quayside. He would move from that silence and desolation, that blankness, to a gateway or door. He would enter there and be swallowed by the life and noise of a crowded city. (I imagined something like an Indian bazaar scene.) The mission he had come on—family business, study, religious initiation—would give him encounters and adventures. He would enter interiors, of houses and temples. Gradually there would come to him a feeling that he was getting nowhere; he would lose his sense of mission; he would begin to know only that he was lost. His feeling of adventure would give way to panic. He would want to escape, to get back to the quayside and his ship. But he wouldn't know how. I imagined some religious ritual in which, led on by kindly people, he would unwittingly take part and find himself the intended victim. At the moment of crisis he would come upon a door, open it, and find himself back on the quayside of arrival. He has been saved; the world is as he remembered it. Only one thing is missing now. Above the cutout walls and buildings there is no mast, no sail. The antique ship has gone. The traveler has lived out his life.

Put this unwritten fantasy alongside the moment when Naipaul chose his vocation over the expectations of his family. It required an immense leap of faith for a young Indian in the grip of "a panic about failing to be what I should be" not to lose his own sense of mission. His letters home, often filled with shame, also display an astonishing assurance: "Look, I am going to be a success as a writer. I know that. I have gambled all my future on that possibility. Do you want to throw your lot with me or don't you?" And yet all his life the enigma of arrival has haunted Naipaul—the sense of living out his life, like the traveler in the unwritten tale, without having achieved his purpose.

The bet paid off. At the end of 1955, he sold his first novel, *The Mystic Masseur*. Half a century and two dozen books later, Naipaul at last has his Nobel Prize.

When the announcement came last fall—after years of rumors, short lists, and steadily avowed indifference from Naipaul himself—an article in *Le Monde diplomatique* compared the selection to Henry Kissinger's receiving the Nobel Peace Prize. According to Pascale Casanova, Naipaul "disavows his past; he sees himself as an English writer . . . [He] is contemptuous of the peoples of the South, and he is a mouthpiece for extreme conservative and nationalist views." And, as if that weren't bad enough, "His favorite novelist is Balzac."

Through much of his career, Naipaul has been denounced from the left, especially by partisans of Third World countries and cultures, those societies that he's called "half-made." Derek Walcott, a fellow West Indian Nobelist, attacked the author of *The Enigma of Arrival* as racist. And as his rejection by the left grew, Naipaul became something of a hero to the right, the one dark-skinned writer who could be counted on to tell the Third World what it didn't want to hear about itself. The embrace culminated in this country a decade ago with an invitation for Naipaul to speak before the conservative Manhattan Institute. Last fall, when the World Trade Center attacks and Naipaul's Nobel followed each other in rapid succession, the address to the Manhattan Institute circulated on the Internet.

Its title is "Our Universal Civilization," and in an unspoken way, it takes one back to the crucial period when Naipaul defied his family's wishes and stayed in London to become a writer. Naipaul turns seventy this summer, in the same month that his latest work, a collection of his essays called *The Writer and the World*, including the Manhattan Institute address, is to be published. He appears to have reached the end of his career. His most recent novel, *Half a Life*, turning over much-plowed ground, is barely half a book. V. S. Naipaul seems to have said what he has to say. Seen from this vantage point, the course of his work follows an internal logic that was not at all clear before. The decision not to return to Trinidad, the pivotal moment of his literary career, also holds the key to the vision that receives its most explicit expression in "Our Universal Civilization." And Naipaul himself turns out not to be what his shallower critics and admirers imagined.

His writing life falls into three phases. First there was an early, comic phase. Working alarmingly hard, he produced four books while still in his twenties, books about Trinidadian Indians and their marginal lives and strivings and futilities, culminating in the great portrait of his father, *A House for Mr. Biswas*. Trinidad hasn't yet become one of the "half-made societies." Naipaul is recording what he knows from childhood, and everything—

even the epic-length *Biswas*—comes across as a dense miniature, befitting the scale of the insular world where he would have faced intellectual starvation. The speed of composition betrays what Naipaul would call "a fear of extinction."

Then, knowing that he had come to the end of his childhood material, and riding the confidence of having written a masterpiece, in the early 1960s Naipaul began to travel. The travel began his middle phase, a severe and tragic phase, for the places he traveled to, repeatedly, even obsessively (back to the West Indies where racial revolution was stirring; then to his ancestral India; and finally to newly independent Africa) brought out a new kind of panic in Naipaul. This wasn't the merely personal raw nerves of a young colonial becoming a writer in the imperial center. His travels put politics in his writing, and his panic became a political panic:

> The new politics, the curious reliance of men on institutions they were yet working to undermine, the simplicity of beliefs and the hideous simplicity of actions, the corruption of causes, half-made societies that seemed doomed to remain half-made: these were the things that began to preoccupy me. They were not things from which I could detach myself.

Instead of suppressing this political panic in order to write, he wrote directly out of it—beginning with *The Mimic Men* (1967), a lesser-known novel that marks the start of the new phase, and then in the novels from the 1970s that made him an international writer: *In a Free State*, *Guerrillas*, and *A Bend in the River*.

The violence that characterizes these books, physical and emotional, confirms that Naipaul could not easily "detach himself." He had nowhere to go, no position from which to view the world's disorders with equanimity. The Europeans in these books appear to have a free ride in the Third World countries where they seek personal or political fulfillment, dabbling in Caribbean revolution or African authenticity, only to find out in brutal, sometimes fatal ways that the late colonial world has turned back on them in nihilistic rage. A group of expatriates in *A Bend in the River*, set in a thinly disguised Zaire under Mobutu, sit in a room listening to Joan Baez songs, and only the narrator, an Indian from the east coast of Africa, entranced though he is by the sound of the voice, knows that it was make-believe . . . You couldn't listen to sweet songs about injustice unless you expected justice and received it much of the time. You couldn't sing songs about the end of the world unless— like the other people in that room, so beautiful with such simple things: African mats on the floor and African hangings on the wall and spears and masks—you felt that the world was going on and you were safe in it. How easy it was, in that room, to make those assumptions!

The narrator's own credo, set down in the opening sentence, is that of a man who lives outside the room, without the luxury of indulgent fantasies: "The world is what it is; men who are nothing, who allow themselves to become nothing, have no place in it."

And so Naipaul's great novels from the middle phase gave him the reputation of a conservative. Not only that: a traitor as well, for a writer with brown skin was not supposed to point out the shams and illusions of Third World politics. In fact, there's no use pretending that Naipaul's political panic made him a sympathetic or even fair interpreter of the postcolonial world. Under his scrutiny, Africa in particular is prone to dissolving in a singularly powerful mood of menace, fear, and disgust. Naipaul never tells you what country is inducing these feelings; it is, indiscriminately, "Africa." After picking up a couple of African hitchhikers, one of the English expatriates driving through Africa in *In a Free State* (1971), for which Naipaul won the Booker Prize, comments on the "smell of Africa . . . It is a smell of rotting vegetation and Africans. One is very much like the other."

Guerrillas (1975), about racial disturbance on a Caribbean island, is even uglier. It ends with a scene in which a mixed-race man of revolutionary delusions sodomizes a white Englishwoman who's taken a passing sexual and political interest in him. Just before leading her out to be slaughtered by machete,

He said, very softly, "You are rotten meat."

It was his tone, rather than the words, that alarmed her. When she turned over to look at him she saw that his eyes were very bright and appeared sightless, the pupils mere points of glitter. He was still erect and looked very big.

He put his hand lightly on her shoulder and said, "You look frightened, Jane."

"I'm thinking I have to go back."

She swung her legs over the edge of the bed, he allowed his hand to slip off her shoulder, and she stood up.

"But I haven't come, Jane."

This is the Naipaul most people think they know. The ruthlessness of observation is matched by the precision of language, as if Naipaul can only represent the source of panic with the utmost syntactical control. "The greatest writing is a disturbing vision offered from a position of strength," he once said. "Aspire to that." But the idea of a supreme and coldhearted detachment is an illusion. Naipaul couldn't enter the experience of his blighted characters as deeply as he does, even in a novel like *Guerrillas*, if he were not writing about rage and despair from the inside.

It was these novels, from the middle phase, that introduced me to Naipaul. I read him before I knew not to like him. I had come back from living in Africa in my early twenties, I was trying to write about it, and Naipaul's ability to evoke the anxiety and disorientation I was feeling presented a model from which a young writer could learn. I couldn't feel close to him as I did to other writers—the ugliness was too much—and I was fairly sure that if I met him I wouldn't like him (Saul Bellow once said that after spending an hour with Naipaul he could skip Yom Kippur that year). But as a master of literary craft and a writer fearlessly dedicated to a vision, Naipaul inspired, and still does. It didn't matter that his vision of Africa was different from mine and in some ways repelled me. It was the intensity of his commitment that mattered.

A Bend in the River is Naipaul's masterpiece, and also the last novel of the middle phase. Its imaginative range is broader than anything before it. Indians, Europeans, and Africans are all portrayed as individuals caught in the swell of history, trying to realize themselves against their own and the world's limitations. In the middle of the novel there is an extraordinary passage, a monologue filling fifteen pages. Indar, a childhood friend of the narrator—both Indians from the east coast of Africa, meeting again as adults in Mobutu's Zaire—tells the story of how he went down from Oxford to London in search of a career. In the story, he presents himself at India House as a candidate for the Indian diplomatic service and is humiliated by a series of lackeys and time servers. He leaves in a daze of rage and starts walking along the Thames, playing with a fantasy of going back to his old village life. Then he begins to notice the wrought-iron dolphins on lamp standards along the Embankment, the wrought-iron camels acting as bench supports. And he has an insight:

> I understood that London wasn't simply a place that was there, as people say of mountains, but that it had been made by men, that men had given attention to details as minute as those camels.
>
> I began to understand at the same time that my anguish about being a man adrift was false, that for me that dream of home and security was nothing more than a dream of isolation, anachronistic and stupid and very feeble. I belonged to myself alone. I was going to surrender my manhood to nobody. For someone like me there was only one civilization and one place—London, or a place like it. Every other kind of life was make-believe. Home—what for? To hide? To bow to our great men? For people in our situation, led into slavery, that is the biggest trap of all. We have nothing. We solace ourselves with that idea of the great men of our tribe, the Gandhi and the Nehru, and we castrate ourselves.
>
> "Here, take my manhood and invest it for me. Take my manhood and be a greater man yourself, for my sake!" No! I want to be a man myself.

In the middle of his great novel about Africa, Naipaul is suddenly writing the central story of his own life, of his younger self—of that moment when he decided not to return to Trinidad after his father's death. And this would become the constant subject of his third, late phase—an autobiographical phase, an obsessive and, finally, exhausted return to his origins as a writer, in books like *Finding the Center* (1984), *The Enigma of Arrival* (1987), *A Way in the World* (1994), and last year's *Half a Life*. The anxiety has subsided. The fiction has turned inward, and the nonfiction (for Naipaul has been an equally obsessive traveler, writing journalism about the troubled corners of the world well into his seventh decade) has grown more generous—his portraits of static and decaying societies are no less harsh, but individuals trapped within those societies emerge as the true voices of these books.

Then what are we to make of the charge that Naipaul has repudiated his background, that he identifies with the oppressor and despises the oppressed? The truth is that Naipaul has no easily identifiable political views. The great ideological struggle of his writing life, the Cold War, is totally ignored in his work. He hasn't chosen sides in competing visions of how modern societies should be organized. He is profoundly skeptical of every ideology. What interests him is the individual, and his fiercest passion has always been for the individual to be free from the dead hand of the given. The closest he's come to expressing something like a vision of the good society is the Manhattan Institute talk. In it, he tells the story of a young Indonesian whom he met years ago, and who was thwarted in his desire to become a poet. Naipaul then describes the "universal civilization" that made room for him, a young Indian from Trinidad, when he was trying to become a writer.

> I would say that it is the civilization that both gave the prompting and the idea of the literary vocation; and also gave the means to fulfill that prompting; the civilization that enables me to make that journey from the periphery to the center; the civilization that links me not only to this audience but also that now not-so-young man in Java whose background was as ritualized as my own, and on whom—as on me—the outer world had worked, and given the ambition to write.

It sounds like utter hubris and the worst sort of solipsism: the "universal civilization" is the one that made room for Naipaul to become a writer. And yet, in one form or another, this is the longing of millions of people the world over—those oppressed and nameless masses whom Naipaul is supposed to despise. It is an idea that his critics take entirely for granted. Looking back over the half century of his writing life, one can now see that his purpose all along was to give value to that longing. At the end of his talk to the Manhattan Institute, Naipaul suddenly mentions the phrase "the pursuit of happiness." He says: "So much is contained in it: the idea of the individual, responsibility, choice, the life of the intellect, the idea of vocation and perfectibility and achievement. It is an immense human idea." Naipaul, often accused of making himself over as an Englishman, turns out to be an American.

With Friends Like These

Dissent, Winter 1999

These revenges dressed up as memoirs* are untrustworthy, not necessarily in the facts presented, but in the sense Orwell meant when he wrote, "Autobiography is only to be trusted when it reveals something disgraceful." They suffer from the problems of tone and meaning that arise when books claim to be doing something other, and higher, than what they're really doing. They present themselves as dispassionately truthful remembrances. In fact, the spirit of rancor is so corrosive that it strips the glamor off the back of the most stubbornly glamorous literary fantasies: the writer as traveler and exile, the circle of New York Intellectuals. Nonetheless, it would be wrong to speak of betrayal in the ordinary sense. Because these two books call into question the very notion that literary friendship is itself possible, the real betrayal here is not of the subject-targets but the self.

Paul Theroux's account of his three decades as V. S. Naipaul's protégé has been made out to be a worse book than it actually is, and Theroux himself is to blame for this. He did himself a disservice by allowing *The New Yorker* to run a version before the book appeared that squeezed together the choicest slices of incriminating detail: Naipaul's contempt for Africans and white "infies," his cruel treatment of his long-suffering wife, Pat, his affairs, his monumental prickliness, his cheapness, his second marriage to a domineering Pakistani woman—who apparently prevailed on

---

*Sir Vidia's Shadow: A Friendship Across Five Continents by Paul Theroux (Houghton Mifflin, 1998), and *Ex-Friends: Falling Out with Allen Ginsberg, Lionel and Diana Trilling, Lillian Hellman, Hannah Arendt, and Norman Mailer* by Norman Podhoretz (The Free Press, 1999).

him to cut Theroux off. *The New Yorker* beckoned and Theroux obliged with his nastiest gossip fodder. In doing so he violated one of his teacher's most important maxims: "The man must never precede the book!" In punishment, the book became the object of venom and rebuttal before it had even come out. And Theroux compounded the damage postpublication, in an exercise of blunt self-justification, by writing more Naipaulia for *The New York Times Book Review*, like a machine that can't be turned off.

But the first hundred pages of *Sir Vidia's Shadow* have some good descriptions of East African travel and of expatriate life in Uganda, where Theroux, age twenty-four, and Naipaul, a very old thirty-four, met at the university in Kampala in 1966. For Theroux, at the start of his career, encountering in that unlikely place this uncompromising, "almost unlovable," yet curious and intimate man, who encouraged him and then pronounced him a writer, was one of the "miracles" that Naipaul told him sometimes happen. These pages are vivid with the rush of youthful good luck, guileless ambition, and libido, in a landscape at once seductive and menacing.

Naipaul was free with literary advice of a grimly bracing sort, and his wintry aphorisms are perhaps the most valuable thing in the book. "Aim high. Tell the truth." "Don't use words for effect." "Every good book suggests that the writer, however painful its subject, has arrived at some inward peace about it, some inner resolution, even of anger and despair, even though this peace and resolution is purely temporary. So that you know where a man stands." "This faith [that you will be all right in the end] your friends cannot give you: it is something you have to discover in yourself." "The only consolation of the writing profession is that it is fair." "The greatest writing is a disturbing vision offered from a position of strength—aspire to that."

Naipaul leaves Africa, and eventually Theroux does too. There are letters exchanged across continents, reunions over dinner in London, and Theroux marries and has children and begins to publish his work, prolifically enough for Naipaul to cease giving advice and start expressing envy, and the two become neighbors again in the English countryside, and Naipaul's behavior grows insufferable, and Theroux spends three decades listening with a smile on his face, and something goes wrong with this book. Scene after scene—so much improbably remembered dialogue—with no apparent purpose. What started fresh has become dull, a transcription bent on exposure, like the Starr Report. The form of faithful recollection is more and more undermined by a tone of unacknowledged hostility in the choice of incidents. Theroux does not reflect on his material, because he cannot let himself reflect. If he were to reflect, he would have to admit something like this: "I am recording these scenes because for three decades I said nothing while this man reduced his wife to tears or insulted the waiter or spoke ill of children. I let him stick me with an expensive dinner bill and went home to my son without the story book I'd promised to buy him. To stay in this man's good graces I flattered and lied. Even my obituary for his wife was dishonest. I was content to be Sir Vidia's shadow because his approval meant the world to me. And now that he has cut me off, I want revenge for the lifelong mark my teeth have left in my tongue."

The last few pages finally say as much. "Challenge him and he was an enemy; treat him handsomely and there was a chance he would be kind. Cherish him and he was yours. Hadn't I cherished him? So we had never quarreled." What a high price for this nettled attention. Once Theroux is "freed"—rejected, but not for having challenged Naipaul, for he never did—the resentment flows. Naipaul's later works, his whole literary project, his very soul, now come in for harsh review. "It is not virtue at all to be cruel in this way. It only implied a mean heart." Theroux is fifty-seven. It seems late for these recognitions. In a way it is late for Theroux the writer as well, for his own books owe something of their strain of sourness to the teacher's example (without the teacher's brilliant vision). Perhaps this literary style is as much a self-betrayal as sitting by while Naipaul condescended to Mrs. Theroux.

Over and over, with the ardor of a lover, Theroux speaks of Naipaul as his friend. "He is my friend, I thought. I have a friend. I was a part of his writing life now, and he was certainly part of mine." "This friendship I now realized was as strong as love. He was my friend, he had shown me what was good in my writing, he had drawn a line through anything that was false. I was inspired by his work and his conviction. I wanted always to be his friend." "By now we knew each other well and had arrived at that point at which friends realize they cannot know each other any better. His friendship was a pleasure and a relief." For three decades Theroux lived for Naipaul's praise, or even his presence, and received more of both than almost anyone; Naipaul in return enjoyed many favors done and was made to feel like a master. Both men made out well, and the end should have prompted profits counting and not debt collecting. Naipaul and Theroux were never friends.

Friendship between writers is inherently unstable: the basis of friendship is also the source of rivalry. Writers make friends with other writers because they are writers, and immediately they are in competition. The strength of one diminishes the other. You see this in *Sir Vidia's Shadow*: Naipaul wanes whenever Theroux waxes. And literary friendship is sometimes a pretty phrase for what amounts to mutual use—so that when friends become ex-friends it is generally because the use has been used up.

Norman Podhoretz's new book provides an inadvertent guide to the pathology of literary relationships. As a sequel to *Making It* and *Breaking Ranks* (from which it exhumes long passages), *Ex-Friends* ought to have been called *Settling Scores*. Even more than Theroux, who buries his spite in the raw clay of narrative, Podhoretz's writing suffers from the clash of ostensible and true motives. This clash produces a characteristic tone, with its own roundabout syntax, a tone of high-minded insult, as when Podhoretz ("after a long debate with myself") turns down an invitation to Norman Mailer's seventy-fifth birthday party: "I had no wish to put myself in the false position of participating in the celebration of a career that had so bitterly disappointed my literary expectations."

With its bald confession of success worship, *Making It* brought down the contempt of almost everyone he admired on Podhoretz's head when it appeared in 1967. But revisited three decades on, and compared to *Ex-Friends*, it reads a little like the early passages in *Sir Vidia's Shadow*—almost winning in its frank hungers (maybe the problem with literary friendships is that writers get older). At one point in *Making It*, Podhoretz drew a nice distinction between pre-Freudian hypocrisy, which took the form of nobility—"the ascription of purer motives to oneself than one was actually acting upon"—and the Freudian kind, which took the form of honesty—"ascribing baser motives to oneself than one is in fact being driven by."

Between *Making It* and *Ex-Friends* Podhoretz has reverted from Freudian to pre-Freudian hypocrisy. We are supposed to believe that the new book examines "why it is so hard for friends who disagree about large and apparently impersonal subjects like politics or literature to remain friends." In other words, this is an account of friendships that ended over principle. Podhoretz says that he lost his famous friends—Ginsberg, the Trillings, Arendt, Hellman, and Mailer—because he lost his radical faith. Most of these were friends in the Naipaulian way, and in the case of the one exception, cause and effect seem more appropriately reversed: Podhoretz lost his radical faith because he lost his friend.

Ex-Friends gets the last self-justifying word into arguments with half a dozen people, all but one dead. Its lack of generosity and wisdom is almost astonishing. Allen Ginsberg, former Columbia literary pal, toward the end of his life tried to end their decades of mutual hatred, but Podhoretz rebuffed him in life and "still could not bring myself to forgive *him*, not even now that he was dead" for promoting drug use and sexual promiscuity. With Lillian Hellman, Podhoretz lied for several years about his opinion of her writing and kept silent about his opinion of her politics so that he wouldn't lose his purchase on "the glamour and the glitter to which she offered easy access." Now, he says, "I remain proud of the part I went on to take in the fight against the political ideas and attitudes in whose service she corrupted her work and brought, as I now see it, lasting dishonor upon her name."

Diana Trilling was tolerated only because she was Lionel's wife. A footnote explaining how she called Podhoretz a liar for claiming in *Breaking Ranks* that Trilling had warned him not to publish *Making It* gives you an idea of the airless, joyless atmosphere of this third autobiography:

> One reason my wife was so angry was that she recalled a conversation during our trip together to Germany—a conversation at which Diana had been present and in the course of which Lionel repeated what he had previously told me *tête-à-tête* about publishing *Making It*. If my wife's memory was accurate, then Diana was simply lying, and not fantasizing when she accused *me* of lying about Lionel's advice. But I continued to give Diana the benefit of the doubt on this matter, because although I did remember a difficult conversation the four of us had in Germany about *Making It*, I did not recall Lionel's repeating his advice not to publish it. Which does not prove, I hasten to add, that my wife's memory was faulty.

Podhoretz is one of the last survivors of what he calls the Family. Conceivably this is the last memoir we shall have of a blood member. If

so, all the fierce battles of the New York Intellectuals, from Stalinism and
the Pound Award to Eichmann and Vietnam, shall have ended in this
byzantine footnote. We shall be left with the Trillings and the Podho-
retzes quarreling in Germany over a book, and then quarreling in another
book over the first book, and then still quarreling over the second book in
yet another book. If a book had a face, *Ex-Friends* would be thick-featured
with dull wary eyes, its mouth ajar over some old wrong, the last idiot
child of too much Family inbreeding.

But why did Podhoretz write it? After all, the material in *Ex-Friends* is
not fresh. Some of it is as stale as hardtack. There is a quality of exhausted
ideas, even intellectual deterioration, in its prose. Long passages quote or
closely paraphrase without attribution Podhoretz's previous books (this
was also the case with *Breaking Ranks*; and Theroux cannibalizes old articles in *Sir Vidia's Shadow*). Thus, in *Ex-Friends*:

> All [Trilling] ever did was allow me to publish one of the lectures
> he delivered at Harvard that were subsequently brought together
> in his book *Sincerity and Authenticity*. I featured it as a lead arti-
> cle even though it disappointed me in being so muffled in its at-
> tack on the idea of insanity as a species of rebellion against the
> spiritual oppressions of middle-class society. This idea had been
> from the beginning—in Allen Ginsberg's declaration that "the
> best minds" of his generation had been driven mad and in Nor-
> man Mailer's celebration of the psychopath (about which more
> later)—a central element of the new radicalism. It also still fig-
> ured in the work of serious thinkers like psychologist R. D. Laing
> and in more popular form in a novel like Ken Kesey's *One Flew
> Over the Cuckoo's Nest*, which, as a measure of its by then mass
> appeal, was turned into a very successful movie. And it was, fi-
> nally, an idea profoundly repugnant to Lionel. Yet he could only
> bring himself to an expression of this repugnance by a route so
> convoluted and difficult to follow that many readers were at a loss
> to figure out what he was trying to say.

And in *Breaking Ranks*:

> He allowed me to publish a section of *Sincerity and Authenticity*
> which I featured even though I found it characteristically muffled

in its attack on the idea of insanity as a species of rebellion against the spiritual oppressions of middle-class society. This idea had been from the beginning (in Allen Ginsberg's declaration that the "best minds" of his generation had gone mad and in Norman Mailer's celebration of the psychopath) a central element of the new radicalism, and it still figured in the work of serious thinkers like the psychologist R. D. Laing and in more popular form in the novel like Ken Kesey's *One Flew Over the Cuckoo's Nest* which, as measure of its by-then mass appeal, was subsequently turned into a very successful movie. It was also an idea profoundly repugnant to Trilling, and yet, as is the case of his Jefferson Lecture, he could only bring himself to an expression of this repugnance by a route so convoluted and difficult to follow that many readers were lost on the way.

The slight changes are baffling. *Making It* is similarly pilfered—with a twist. Near the end of the 1967 book this passage appears:

> Like most famous writers, [Mailer] was surrounded by courtiers and sycophants, but with this difference: he allowed them into his life not to flatter but to give his radically egalitarian imagination a constant workout. He had the true novelist's curiosity about people unlike himself—you could see him getting hooked ten times a night by strangers at a party—and his respect for modes of life other than his own was so great that it often led him into romanticizing people and things that might legitimately have been dismissed as uninteresting or mediocre. He would look into the empty eyes of some vapid upper-class girl and announce to her that she could be the madam of a Mexican whorehouse . . .

Thirty years later, here is what's become of the passage in *Ex-Friends*:

> Like many famous people, Mailer liked to surround himself with a crowd of courtiers, many of whom had nothing to recommend them that I could see other than their worshipful attitude toward him. A few of them I grew to like well enough . . . But even in the company of these, Mailer was always at his worst, and with the

other hangers-on, who came and went and sometimes stayed, he could be positively intolerable—posing, showing off, bumping heads (another of his favorite sports), bullying, ordering about, and, underneath it all, flattering.

The flattering was especially in evidence with women, not only or even primarily as a means of seduction but mainly a way of romanticizing and thereby inflating the significance of everything that came into his life. He would inform some perfectly ordinary and uninteresting girl that she could have been a great madam running the best whorehouse in town . . .

If you're going to change your mind about a friend, at least you could find new prose for the occasion. To depend on an earlier passage for phrasing and observation while making small changes that give it, unacknowledged, an entirely different coloring, strikes me as deeply dishonest. It throws every other observation and interpretation into doubt. But this self-plagiarism also gives the writer away. Here we see contrasted as vividly as possible the generous, excitable, somewhat sycophantic Norman Podhoretz of 1967 and the dismissive, soured man he became. Decades of political combat have not had an elevating effect on the temperament of this former literary critic. And his change of mind about Mailer gives us a clue to why he would choose, nearing old age, to turn back and declare himself well rid of the friends of his youth.

Mailer is in many ways this book's exception, and its key. He is still alive; and unlike the other ex-friends, the quality of the other Norman's relationship with him appears to have been a real friendship. Lillian Hellman gave access to glamor and fun; Hannah Arendt's company lent intellectual distinction; Ginsberg was a rival and enemy almost from the start; Lionel Trilling was the teacher; Diana Trilling was the teacher's wearisome wife. They were all primarily useful, whereas the "existentialist" Mailer of the late fifties and sixties, with his radical ideas about sex and success, caught Podhoretz's imagination in an uncalculated way. Norman P., seven years younger, wanted to be more like Norman M. Knowing that he couldn't, he enjoyed Mailer's high-voltage companionship enormously.

Until 1967—when *Making It* appeared to denunciations from the Family, and Mailer, having expressed private approval to Podhoretz, wrote a good-tempered but ultimately critical review of the book for *Partisan Review*. Podhoretz felt betrayed—not in the lofty contest of ideas, but in the most humiliatingly personal way possible, kicked by a friend when he was down. And that was the beginning of the end for the Normans. Perhaps coincidentally, Podhoretz can't summon much admiration for any of Mailer's books since *The Armies of the Night*—which appeared around the same time as the piece in *Partisan Review*—and as for Mailer's criticism of *Making It*, Podhoretz elaborated a theory in *Breaking Ranks*, recycled in *Ex-Friends*, that Mailer couldn't bring himself to defy the verdict of the literary establishment (Trilling's disapproval of the book is given essentially the same account: he didn't have the stomach to fight the increasingly radical New York Intellectuals).

"I am reasonably sure," Podhoretz writes, in the syntax of pre-Freudian hypocrisy, "after conscientiously probing the region surrounding the lower depths of critical integrity, that not even a minor contribution has been made to my harsh judgment of [Mailer's] later work by a lingering resentment over his article on *Making It*." Maybe not—but it is clear that after the hurtful experience of 1967–68, Podhoretz's cherished entry to Family gatherings lost a good deal of its pleasure. He did not become a neoconservative because *Making It* was rejected by his friends, but their rejection made the move less wrenching than it might have been. Nonetheless, it was a loss. His post-sixties politics made Podhoretz a pariah in the literary circles to which he had coveted admittance. As Ford Madox Ford said of his own divorce, it hurt him in his dinner invitations. No one should underestimate the price this exacted from the author of *Making It*. One would like to honor Podhoretz for what was, after all, a principled sacrifice, though this is made difficult by the fact that his sense of humor was lost along with his friends. And here perhaps we arrive at the real motive for digging up these old quarrels in *Ex-Friends*: Podhoretz wants to convince himself that the losses were worth it.

Just as Theroux's real feelings, shame and anger, erupt in the closing pages of his book, as Podhoretz says his last goodbye to his ex-friends the tone of high-minded insult collapses and he comes clean. "Conceivably, there are lively parties today to which I am not invited that are similar to the ones I used to go to and give," he speculates. "But if similar parties are being held today, I think rumors of them would have reached me, and so I can only conclude that they are as much a thing of the past as the intel-

lectual life out of which they originally emerged." It's a comfort to think
so, anyway. And yet remembering Mailer et al. has left him unexpectedly
nostalgic. He summoned these ghosts to get in the last word and ends up
missing them. His posthumous wins have begun to seem hollow. By the
last sentences the conflict between ostensible and true motives is utterly,
almost movingly, apparent:

> I owe my ex-friends a perverse debt. I was who I was in some part
> because of my friendship with them, and I am who I am in larger
> part because we ceased being friends. In all truth, I much pre-
> fer who I am to who I was. Nevertheless, I cannot help feeling
> nostalgic about the "old days" when I was, in Norman Mailer's
> estimation, so much "merrier" than I am now, and I cannot help
> missing the people I admired, liked, enjoyed, and even (in a few
> cases) loved when I was young and they, though not so young,
> were all at their best and still in their prime.

Or in the words of Joseph Conrad: "The pity of it is that there comes
a time when *all* the fun of one's life must be looked for in the past."

These words are quoted in *Joseph Conrad, A Personal Remembrance*
by Ford Madox Ford. The book is his *Sir Vidia's Shadow*; and *Portraits
from Life* is his *Ex-Friends*. Ford collaborated with Conrad on three novels
before falling out; he fell out with some of the subjects of his *Portraits*,
including D. H. Lawrence, whom he had discovered. Yet the two books
are suffused with a kind of critical warmth that makes every well-made
sentence glow. Ford did not write out of a grievance; self-justification was
not his motive. He knew what our memoirists have forgotten: justice demands that some things be omitted. He omitted the whole account of
their rift from his book on Conrad. Quoting a letter in which Lawrence
gives his first impression of Ford—"fairish, fat, about forty"—he omitted
the next phrase: "and the kindest man on earth." Read his literary memoirs and you will see that age can bring generosity; that writers might not
be able to remain good friends but in remembering can at least remain
good writers; that outliving friends-turned-enemies gives you, along with
the last word, a burden of trustworthy portraiture.

Graham Greene and the New Quiet Americans

The Boston Globe, February 2, 2003 (under the title "Innocents Abroad?")

Graham Greene, whose 1955 novel *The Quiet American* foresaw the U.S. disaster in Vietnam and has been made into a new film, was the literary voice of anti-Americanism. For that reason alone, his sardonic ghost seems to hover in the air these days as the United States marches off into another war of avowed high purpose while the world howls in protest.

But unlike most of the people in the streets of London, Berlin, Cairo, and Karachi, Greene didn't object to America simply for its power and its policies. He would have brushed aside the cliché about opposing the government but not the people. Greene's anti-Americanism went to the philosophical core. His was the deep contempt of a man whose lifelong obsession was the loss of faith; it hardly mattered whether the faith was Catholicism or Communism, though in his case it was both. In America he saw nothing but dangerous innocence, shallow materialism, and a spiritual emptiness that left Americans unable to reach the transcendent levels of Communism or Catholicism, let alone to fall from them.

"The weight of this consumer society oppresses me," Greene once told an interviewer, and he agreed with a reviewer of *The Quiet American* who wrote that Greene's attack could have come from either the right or the left, "since what I truly detested was American liberalism."

These days, there is no shortage of skeptics warning of another Vietnam-style quagmire in Iraq. The Bush administration's vision of sweeping democratic transformation in the Arab world bears more than a passing resemblance to the high-minded arrogance of American policymakers during the Cold War who couldn't be troubled to find out what exactly was happening on the ground. There's even a new domino theory in play, one that imagines Middle East dictatorships collapsing one on top of another. In Philip Noyce's new film of *The Quiet American*, words spoken by the American idealist Alden Pyle (and not found in the novel) seem to be taken straight from today's front pages: "We're not colonialists. We're here to help people. The French aren't going to stop the Communists. They haven't got the brains and they haven't got the guts."

Greene famously got Vietnam right. He spent four winters there during the early 1950s, reporting for the London Sunday *Times* on the French defeat at the hands of the Vietminh and watching the growing involvement of the Americans in the next phase of the war. He kept going back because Indochina suited his temperament completely—the decadence of the late French empire, the rising power of the ardent Communists, the sensuality of smells and fabrics, the opium dens. Greene's Vietnam is a place where a French policeman whiles away a hot Saigon night by reading Pascal.

Vietnam at the end of the French war was beginning to draw a type of American that Greene immediately nailed down: the naïve evangelist of that superficial creed called liberal democracy. Greene once shared a long car ride with an American who probably worked for the CIA, and who lectured Greene the entire time on the need to find a democratic "third force" between the French and the Communists. By the time they reached Saigon, Greene had the idea for *The Quiet American*.

"My companion bore no resemblance at all to Pyle, the quiet American of my story," he later wrote in his memoir *Ways of Escape*. "He was a man of greater intelligence and less innocence." In fact, Alden Pyle, the undercover CIA agent with a shelf full of books on *The Challenge to Democracy* and *The Role of the West* (and also *The Physiology of Marriage*), is a character of such blind faith in his own good intentions that much of his dialogue becomes unintentionally funny as Greene's satire turns crude. It's no coincidence that Greene has Pyle hail from Boston, the capital of Protestant rectitude. At one point, Greene imagines Pyle "walking back across the Common in Boston, his arms full of the books he had been reading in advance on the Far East and the problems of China."

In the new film—whose release was delayed by Miramax for a year after September 11, 2001, out of fears of being called unpatriotic—the actor Brendan Fraser redeems Pyle a bit with the edge of toughness that a man in his position would have to possess. Nonetheless, the emotional story of both the novel and the film is almost formulaically simple. The narrator is an aging, worldly British journalist named Fowler (played by Michael Caine) whose policy in Vietnam is one of ruthless noninvolvement. Fowler's Catholic wife back in London won't give him a divorce so that he can marry his Vietnamese mistress, Phuong (Do Thi Hai Yen), who spends her evenings lighting Fowler's opium pipe and paging through picture books on the British royal family while dreaming of life as Mrs. Fowler in London.

Enter the blundering American, who steals Phuong away from Fowler—and, at the same time, manages to get a lot of innocent people killed by channeling explosives to a "third force" that turns out to be not very democratic after all.

Greene's plot is a variation on the theme of decayed European sophistication meeting exuberant American innocence; in this case, innocence is ultimately far more culpable. Greene shares the notion expressed by T. S. Eliot in his famous essay on Baudelaire: "The worst that can be said of us is that we are not men enough to be damned."

Greene has a savage nose for the antiseptic smell of American virtue, which extends from foreign affairs to affairs of the flesh and often seems to produce corpses. Just before a CIA-financed car bomb goes off in central Saigon, tearing bystanders limb from limb, Fowler's eye settles on two young American women who have been tipped off and are leaving the scene: "It was impossible to conceive either of them a prey to untidy passion: they did not belong to rumpled sheets and the sweat of sex. Did they take deodorants to bed with them? I found myself for a moment envying them their sterilized world."

This is the one complicating factor in *The Quiet American*: Fowler, a man of weak flesh and lost convictions, can't help wanting Pyle's strength and sureness. After all, he knows that Pyle has more to offer Phuong than he does, and he is self-hating enough to feel the attractive power of Pyle's innocent belief. When the loss of his mistress forces Fowler to confront the prospect of his own decline and death, he's finally moved to action, self-servingly—and he's the type who won't spare himself the unappealing truth about his own conduct. In the end, what Greene asks of his characters is not that they refrain from sin, but that they recognize it when they see it.

Reviewing an earlier Greene novel, *The Heart of the Matter*, in 1948, George Orwell took aim at what he called "this cult of the sanctified sinner": "It is impossible not to feel a sort of snobbishness in Mr. Greene's attitude," he wrote. "He appears to share the idea, which has been floating around ever since Baudelaire, that there is something rather distingué in being damned; Hell is a sort of high-class night club, entry to which is reserved for Catholics only, since the others, the non-Catholics, are too ignorant to be held guilty." In fact, the first time that Greene smoked opium—in the company of a French official in a backstreet apartment in Haiphong—he lay back and recited Baudelaire's poem "Invitation au voyage," with its sensuous evocation of "luxe, calme et volupté." Pyle, of course, never smokes.

The Quiet American is better journalism than fiction. For all its character improbabilities and moral simplifications, Greene hit upon a truth very early in the American experience in Vietnam, perhaps earlier than anyone else, and exaggerated it. He saw the blind spot in the American mission—that its capacity for mistakes and crime was exactly proportionate to its self-righteousness.

In his 1958 film version of the novel, director Joseph Mankiewicz apparently couldn't tolerate this prophecy and changed the ending to vindicate Pyle. Noyce has at last undone the insult to the book and made a faithful version that honors Greene's prescience (to the discomfort of the film's distributor). At the end of the Noyce film, a series of mock-up newspaper articles by Fowler is superimposed alongside familiar images of the American war that followed. The point doesn't need such heavy-handed iteration—everyone knows how that story turned out.

If Greene got Vietnam right, he also got America wrong. Like so much cultural (as opposed to merely political) anti-Americanism, of the left as well as the right, his attitude did amount to snobbishness.

One sees the same prejudice, for example, in the condescending criticism of the United States after September 11 by the Indian novelist Arundhati Roy and the British playwright Harold Pinter. Beneath the political arguments, it seems, lies an indignant sense that America—this vast commercial culture that dumps its fast food and its soulless movies on ancient civilizations—doesn't deserve to be the world power; its spiritual and intellectual deficiencies ought to disqualify it. The masses of demonstrators in the streets of European and Arab-Muslim cities these days resent America's outsized power, but it's more highbrow to despise America for its mediocrity.

This prejudice was Greene's blind spot, and it kept him from understanding the modern world. The very qualities of America that repelled him appeal to millions of people around the world who can't afford his brand of sophistication: the openness, the fluidity, the freedom from those entanglements of faith and inherited identity that filled Greene, the lapsed believer, with nostalgia and longing. To many, America represents modernity; it promises a vast improvement in the lives of most human beings. The failure of critics like Greene to see this keeps them from grasping America's power of attraction.

Perhaps the United States is about to make a colossal mistake in Iraq. Or perhaps a war will bring some measure of relief and freedom to long-suffering Iraqis who, whatever their resentments against America, see their own predicament more realistically than we do. Perhaps neither World War II nor Vietnam is the precedent for what's going to happen in the Middle East; perhaps we will all have to think up a new way to understand America's role in the world. The trouble is, America's strength is also its weakness—and at the same time, what the rest of the world resents it also admires. To understand the times in which we live, we need to keep that entire thought in our heads. Graham Greene was able to hold only half of it, which makes him worth listening to as a cautionary voice—but not as a prophet.

The Spanish Prisoner

The New Yorker, October 31, 2005

There was a moment, in April 1937, when the Lost Generation of 1920s Paris reunited in Madrid. The occasion was the Spanish Civil War, already in its ninth month, but the regular shelling of the Hotel Florida and other privations of the Fascist siege didn't prevent Ernest Hemingway, John Dos Passos, Josephine Herbst, and Hemingway's latest distraction from the thought of suicide, Martha Gellhorn, from living well. Though the Hotel Florida wasn't the Café des Amateurs, Hemingway managed to procure, thanks in part to impeccable connections with the Spanish government and the Russian general staff, the best food and brandy in the city. Every morning, the other guests woke up to the smell of eggs, bacon, and coffee being prepared by a Hemingway flunky in room 108, courtesy of the Communist International. The moveable feast had crashed the Red decade.

Hemingway was an unlikely recruit to the Spanish cause. He had long since made his separate peace with the war of his youth and focused his talent on the terse eloquence of the nobly wounded, the faithfully adrift, the stoically defeated; the Hemingway antihero, withdrawn from all causes, became a type of such popular influence that a whole crop of movies, novels, and actual lives grew laconic in imitation. But, in the 1930s, the literary infatuation with Communism returned to American prose the kind of lofty, romantic language that Hemingway had condemned at the end of *A Farewell to Arms*:

> There were many words that you could not stand to hear and finally only the names of places had dignity. Certain numbers were the

same way and certain dates and these with the names of places were all you could say and have them mean anything. Abstract words such as glory, honor, courage, or hallow were obscene beside the concrete names of villages, the numbers of roads, the names of rivers, the numbers of regiments and the dates.

For Hemingway, the 1930s had nothing to do with coal strikes and the Scottsboro trial, and everything to do with bullfighting, marlin fishing, big game hunting, and staving off the decline of his literary powers. By 1936, a decade past being very poor and very happy, he had become his own chief imitator—an international celebrity without a published novel in seven years and with a bad one (*To Have and Have Not*) in manuscript. He had grown bored with his second marriage, to the wealthy, adoring, and shallow Pauline—ruthlessly portrayed in one of his last great stories, "The Snows of Kilimanjaro," as the desperately cheerful wife of a writer dying of gangrene and soul rot on an East African game reserve. With an animal instinct of impending doom, Hemingway, at the age of thirty-seven, sought out two familiar escape routes: violence and sex.

In February 1936, Spanish voters elected by a narrow plurality a center-left coalition government of Anarchists, Socialists, Communists, and Republicans. It was the third democratic election in five years in a country that had not yet shed its feudal and clerical past. Some factions in the elected government had revolutionary goals, with those on the far left calling for "democracy of a new type," meaning a prelude to the dictatorship of the proletariat; after five months of chaos, two of the Spanish institutions that had long exercised repressive power under the old monarchy—the military and the Church—were ready to overthrow the Republic. The civil war began on July 17, when General Francisco Franco launched a rebellion from Spanish Morocco that quickly cut Spain in half. The Western democracies imposed an arms embargo on both sides, but Nazi Germany and Fascist Italy began giving troops and matériel to Franco's rebels almost immediately, even as the Soviet Union advised and armed the Republic.

In late September, Hemingway wrote his editor at Scribners, Maxwell Perkins, "I hate to have missed the Spanish thing worse than anything in the world but have to have this book finished first." The civil war, which most people assumed would last a few months, accommodated Hemingway's writing schedule; it would go on for another two and a half years. He finished a draft of *To Have and Have Not* and immediately contracted to write a series of newspaper dispatches from the Madrid front. In short order, he also fell in love with Gellhorn, a beautiful and well-connected younger journalist who sailed into his marooned life on Key West just before she was scheduled to depart for Spain herself, on assignment for *Collier's*. In Madrid, he offered literary advice and patronage; she educated him in Popular Front propaganda while accommodating him sexually to the extent, according to one biographer, of undergoing a widening procedure known as vaginoplasty.

John Dos Passos was traveling to Spain as well. He was Hemingway's friend from their days in Paris, and he had met his wife through him. Hemingway, near the end of his life, portrayed Dos Passos in the nasty last pages of *A Moveable Feast* as a treacherous little "pilot fish" who had led Pauline and her rich friends into Hemingway's youthful domestic bliss in the twenties and lured him into breaking up his first marriage. But Hemingway's friendship with Dos Passos was already strained by the publication, in 1936, of *The Big Money*, the third novel of Dos Passos's *U.S.A.* trilogy, to general acclaim and a *Time* cover story the week that fighting began in Spain. For a brief moment, Dos Passos was as big as the big man of American letters. It's hard now to remember that several generations ago, the trio of great novelists born around the turn of the century—Hemingway, Fitzgerald, Faulkner—was a quartet, with the fourth chair occupied by Dos Passos. *U.S.A.*, which tells an alternative, submerged history of the first three decades of the American century, has become one of the great neglected achievements of literary modernism, with its nervy, jarring formal juxtapositions—newspaper headlines, popular songs, autobiographical fragments, short biographies of the famous—punctuating deceptively flat sagas of ordinary fictional types on the margins of great events, driven by the blind force of history across blighted human landscapes.

Dos Passos was, to the core, a political writer, whose radical vision was crystallized the night of Sacco and Vanzetti's electrocution, in 1927. "America our nation has been beaten by strangers who have turned our language inside out who have taken the clean words our fathers spoke and made them slimy and foul . . . all right we are two nations," he declaimed in a prose poem about the incident near the end of *The Big Money*. Though Dos Passos's characters had some resemblance to the downtrodden figures of the proletarian novel of the thirties, his technical brio belonged to the defiant, avant-garde twenties, when radicalism had more to do with art than with politics. Dos Passos never managed or even tried to depict a fully realized inner life, and his experimentalism, his technique of narrating characters externally in the vernacular of their own voices, prevented him from achieving the tragic effects of Dreiser's clumsier, more earthbound realism, though the picture of American dreaming is just as dark. "You yourself seem to enjoy life more than most people and are by way of being a brilliant talker; but you tend to make your characters talk clichés, and they always get a bad egg for breakfast," Edmund Wilson—who was also made by the twenties but took a keen interest in the revolutionary movements of the thirties—observed in a letter to him. "I sometimes think you consider this a duty of some kind." Dos Passos whose single greatest burst of prose describes the burial of the Unknown Soldier after the First World War, culminating in the words, "Woodrow Wilson brought a bouquet of poppies," will always have a tenuous hold on popularity.

Dos Passos went to Spain in order to work on a documentary about the war, *The Spanish Earth*, to be shot by a brilliant young Dutch filmmaker named Joris Ivens, under the auspices of a group of New York writers led by Archibald MacLeish. The project's purpose was to galvanize American support for the beleaguered Spanish government and to encourage President Roosevelt to lift the arms embargo. Dos Passos, already growing disenchanted with the American left, was encumbered with all the luggage of his embattled political ideals. There was a lot he didn't know about what he had signed on for: Ivens was a hireling of the Comintern; the whole undertaking was a piece of propaganda controlled by Moscow; and Dos Passos himself, always an independent radical, was officially out of favor with the Communist Party, having been denounced at the 1934 Soviet Writers Congress, where the party line on art turned from modernism to socialist realism. Moscow meant to use Dos Passos to lure the biggest fish of all to lend his name to the film. Hemingway, indifferent to left-wing politics until he met Martha Gellhorn, was happy to oblige.

What happened between Hemingway and Dos Passos in Spain is the subject of Stephen Koch's new book, *The Breaking Point: Hemingway, Dos Passos, and the Murder of José Robles*. Koch's story illustrates, among other things, the danger of writers plunging into politics and war, and it offers an unlovely portrait of the engagé artist as useful idiot. Its small drama leads directly to all the big questions about the nature of the Spanish Civil War which have recently generated controversy among historians. The Spaniard of Koch's subtitle was Dos Passos's close friend from youthful wanderings in Spain. José Robles was a left-wing aristocrat, a political exile and a professor at Johns Hopkins during the rule of the Spanish monarchy, who was vacationing in Spain at the time of Franco's rebellion. But Robles maintained enough independence of mind to raise an alarm among pro-Communist Spanish authorities and the Soviet intelligence agents who, by early 1937, were bringing the government increasingly under Stalin's control. Dos Passos was counting on Robles to serve as his main Spanish contact on the film; but by the time the two American novelists reached Madrid, separately, Robles had disappeared. It was Hemingway who learned first—from the Greenwich Village journalist Josephine Herbst, herself on a tour of the war zone very likely sponsored by the Comintern—that Robles had been arrested and shot as a Fascist spy. To this day, the manner and motive of Robles's death remain a mystery; he was almost certainly a victim of the Stalinist purges that began around the same time in Spain.

Dos Passos, concerned for his friend's wife and children, made the rounds of Spanish officials, only to encounter an unctuous series of bureaucratic lies and brushoffs—now that they had Hemingway, they didn't even need to be polite to Dos Passos. Still, Dos Passos's response to his friend's disappearance reflected his sense that progressive politics without human decency is a sham. Hemingway, in a thinly disguised magazine article about the episode published in a short-lived *Esquire* spinoff called *Ken*, described these scruples as "the good-hearted naïveté of a typical American liberal attitude." Bookish, balding, tall and ungainly, sunny in temperament, too trusting of others' goodwill: Dos Passos was the sort of man who aroused Hemingway's sadistic appetite. "White as the under half of an unsold flounder at 11 o'clock in the morning just before the fish market shuts" was one of Hemingway's fictionalized descriptions of his old friend. Hemingway seems to have needed to destroy a friendship or a marriage every few years just to keep functioning. In Madrid he did both.

He and Gellhorn received Dos Passos coldly when he arrived emptyhanded at their well-provisioned suite; they were embarrassed by all the questions he was asking around town. "If it's your professor bloke's disap-

pearance, think nothing of it," Hemingway sneers, in Stephen Koch's re-
telling. "People disappear every day." This was war, and there was a way to
behave during a war, and Dos Passos was failing the code. "Dos was not
good in war, Hem claimed, because he was not a hunter," Koch writes,
paraphrasing Herbst's own observations in her book *Spanish Journal*. "He
didn't know how to take care of himself in the wild. That's what made him
show up with no food. Dos had no balls; Dos had no understanding of war."
At one key moment in *The Breaking Point*, Dos Passos tells Hemingway,
"The question I keep putting to myself is what's the use of fighting a war
for civil liberties, if you destroy civil liberties in the process?" Hemingway
shoots back, "Civil liberties, shit. Are you with us or are you against us?"

Hemingway never embraced the ideological dogma of the Communists, though he admired their hard-boiled stance, and he regarded the
revolutionary fervor of the Anarchists as a joke. If chance had placed him
in the Fascist sector, he would have been attracted to the steely nerve of
Franco's lieutenants. The reasons for Hemingway's partisanship were entirely personal and literary. The imperative to hold the purity of his line
through the maximum of exposure, which in 1931 made him an aficio-
nado of bullfighting and in 1934 a crack shot in Kenya, in 1937 turned
Hemingway into a willing tool of Stalin's secret police. It was a rough
brand of radical chic that also created a new type: the war correspondent
as habitué of a particularly exclusive nightclub, who knows how and how
not to act under shelling, where to get the best whiskey, what tone to use
when drinking with killers. He's drawn to violence and power for their
own sake; war and the politics of war simply provide the stage for his own
display of sangfroid. The influence of this type helped to mar the work of
successive generations of war writers up to our own.

The falseness of Hemingway's period in Spain can be felt in the novel
that he eventually got out of the civil war. *For Whom the Bell Tolls* was a
wild success with the American left and with Hollywood (as was the film
The Spanish Earth, a masterly piece of cinematic propaganda narrated by
Hemingway, who also toured with it around the country; Dos Passos was
entirely cut out). Hemingway's hero Robert Jordan, an American volunteer in the International Brigade, carries himself through revolution and
war with all the stylized, self-conscious poise of a lonely matador in the
ring. The Spanish critic Arturo Barea, himself a target of the secret police,
wrote after the novel's publication, in 1940, "I find myself awkwardly

alone in the conviction that, as a novel about Spaniards and their war, it is unreal and, in the last analysis, deeply untruthful."

As for Dos Passos, Spain seems to have killed something in him. He had gone there to see what he had given up on seeing in America—workers and peasants struggling to create a more just society—not to drink *anis* with Russian commissars in range of enemy artillery. The betrayals he experienced in Spain, personal and political, were so devastating that he could not bring himself to write an account of what happened to his murdered friend José Robles and his former friend Ernest Hemingway. (Hemingway, meanwhile, was spreading the news back home, in person and in print, that Dos Passos was a coward and a traitor to *la causa*.) But in 1938, when Dos Passos was still trying to sort out the meaning of Robles's death, he published a novel (lambasted by fellow-traveling critics such as Malcolm Cowley) about a disillusioned young radical who goes to fight in Spain and dies there. No one today has heard of *Adventures of a Young Man*, while *For Whom the Bell Tolls* is still taught in high schools. Hemingway's romantic fable is in almost every way more compelling. But Dos Passos, in his dispirited and unblinking realism, was the one to convey what it meant to be alive in the 1930s.

Koch, who is also the author of *Double Lives*, a study of the Comintern's exploitation of intellectuals in the thirties, as well as two novels, has structured his book as a series of vividly rendered scenes connected by intelligent commentary, with the extensive dialogue largely drawn from the many pieces and books—some fictional—that his main characters devoted to Spain. In the trade-off between the pleasurable and the verifiable, though, Koch has a bias toward the former, and not all of the dramatic specificity of *The Breaking Point* can be sustained by its sources. (The rude welcome given by Hemingway and Gellhorn to Dos Passos on his arrival at the Hotel Florida is drawn entirely from a scene in *Century's Ebb*, a novel written by Dos Passos almost forty years later, at the end of his life.) Without these liberties, of course, the book would be far less readable. But some flourishes aren't necessary: when Koch tries to amplify a tale that requires none with his own one-sentence-paragraph interjections ("Hadn't noticed him?"), he puts his thumb on the scales. We already know where the author's sympathies lie.

• • •

What are we now to think about the Spanish Civil War? Though Koch focuses on the theme of friendship and betrayal, the larger historical question hovers over all the action of *The Breaking Point*. Spain was where the twentieth century's great lie, the totalitarian lie, flowered. And yet for decades the Popular Front line that the war was a simple black-and-white struggle between democracy and fascism remained one of the century's most stubborn myths. In 1984, when I was in my early twenties, I saw a documentary, narrated by Studs Terkel, called *The Good Fight*, a direct descendant of *The Spanish Earth*; and the heroic testimony of those aging survivors of the Abraham Lincoln Brigade, sitting on neatly made cots in narrow furnished rooms, overwhelmed me. I knew that most of them were Communists, under party discipline, and I knew (having read *Homage to Catalonia* earlier that year) that Moscow-backed agents had engineered the violent betrayal of the independent worker movement in Barcelona in May 1937, just after Dos Passos left the country. Somehow none of this mattered in the face of a struggle in which neutrality seemed impossible. The whole point of Spain to several generations of left-wing intellectuals was the need for people ordinarily disposed toward equivocation to take sides. Auden, who contributed a statement to a pamphlet on Spain called "Authors Take Sides," expressed the reluctant longing in "Spain," the poem that he wrote just before the street fighting broke out in Barcelona, and later repudiated:

> *What's your proposal? To build the Just City? I will,*
> *I agree. Or is it the suicide pact, the romantic*
> *Death? Very well, I accept, for*
> *I am your choice, your decision: yes, I am Spain.*

Since the fall of the Soviet Union and the opening of state archives in Moscow, scholarship has considerably darkened the view of the Communist role in Republican Spain. Moscow's subversion of the Spanish government, especially after May 1937, when the pro-Communist Juan Negrín became prime minister, turns out to have been more extensive than most of the Republic's defenders ever knew, and more Machiavellian. The historian Stanley G. Payne's *The Spanish Civil War, the Soviet Union, and Communism*, published last year, portrays a Spanish government that was in no serious sense democratic: though elected by a small plurality, it was composed largely of revolutionary parties that showed no willingness to allow the right wing a political future in Spain, and it was extremely brutal in its treatment of clerics, landowners, and suspected Fascists. In other words, Payne suggests, the elected Spanish government was probably headed toward Soviet-style totalitarianism before Franco ever launched his rebellion. Nor, according to recent scholarship, was the Republic forced to turn to the dubious embrace of the Soviet Union only after the Western democracies imposed their embargo; Stalin was among the Spanish government's first arms suppliers of choice. Such discoveries have been enough to persuade some writers on Spain that the right side won.

In military and political terms, the civil war didn't resemble the coming world war; from the start, it was an internal struggle between revolutionary and counterrevolutionary forces. But many revisionists have replaced one set of simplifications with another. The failure of the democracies to defend the Spanish Republic convinced Hitler and Mussolini that fascist takeovers elsewhere in Europe would go unchecked; Soviet interference was inevitable given the weakness of the Republic and the maneuverings of Germany and Italy. If it was acceptable for Winston Churchill, now the darling of the anti-appeasement lobby in Washington, to enter into an alliance with Stalin ("If Hitler invaded hell," Churchill explained, "I would make at least a favorable reference to the devil in the House of Commons"), it's difficult to see why the same calculation, when made by Spaniards in 1936 in circumstances at least as desperate as Britain's in 1941, should disqualify the entire struggle. When Heinrich Himmler visited Spain in 1940, the year after Franco's protracted victory, he was shocked by the brutality of the Falangist repression. Whether or not democracy was on one side, fascism was clearly on the other.

Intellectuals can hardly keep away from politics any more than other citizens, and probably less, especially in decades like the 1930s (or this one, for that matter). But because they typically bring to it an unstable mix of abstraction and narcissism, their judgments tend to be absolute, when nothing in politics ever is. This is why a writer as devoted to the visible, concrete world as Hemingway could nonetheless stumble so badly during his time in Spain: he lacked a sense of politics. The writer forever in search of one true sentence ended up accepting a whole raft of lies. Dos Passos, for his part, lacked the inner toughness to recover from the blow his idealism was dealt by José Robles's murder and Hemingway's betrayal. Dos Passos, of course, never wrote another book that came anywhere near the brilliance of *U.S.A.* At the same time, as if his literary flame required the fuel of radical politics to keep burning, after Spain he began a rightward drift, which by the 1964 election had become so extreme that Edmund Wilson wrote him, "I feel obliged to tell you that your article about the San Francisco convention sounded like a teenager squealing over the Beatles. What on earth has happened to you? How can you take Goldwater seriously?" (Even during his Goldwater phase, though, Dos Passos never repudiated his belief in the Spanish Republican cause.) When war, politics, and writers mix, the results are seldom inspiring.

Toward the end of *The Breaking Point*, Dos Passos, reeling from these revelations and on his way out of the country, walks into a Barcelona hotel lobby and is accosted by a lanky, battered-looking Englishman who is on leave after months at the front and has been waiting to meet him. "Things I've heard lead me to believe that you are one of the few who understand what's going on," George Orwell tells John Dos Passos. His appearance in the story amounts to a cameo, but because he was better cut out for Spain and politics than either Hemingway or Dos Passos, Orwell kept his bearings, neither turning the war into a stage for his own psychodrama nor wilting under the pressure of ambiguous reality. Almost seventy years after its publication, his *Homage to Catalonia* holds up against all the recent revelations and controversies about the Spanish Civil War. Orwell was always able to sustain two ideas about it: one of betrayal, the other of hope. His encounter with reality in Spain was steady enough that these didn't have to cancel each other out. "What I saw in Spain did not make me cynical," he wrote to a friend just after returning to England, "but it does make me think that the future is pretty grim." Summing up the war several years after it ended, Orwell still hadn't followed Dos Passos to the right. "In essence it was a class war," he wrote. "That was the real issue; all else was froth on its surface."

Because we live in the age after the age of class war, when no idea has taken the place of socialism to carry the human aspiration for equality, the historiographical debate over the nature of the Spanish Civil War has a blind spot when it comes to the human heart of the matter. The files of the Soviet secret police have exploded forever the fiction of good versus evil in Spain. But in the early scenes of *Homage to Catalonia*, and in the photographs of Robert Capa from Barcelona and Madrid, and in Arturo Barea's memoir, one keeps encountering a certain expression on the human face. Octavio Paz, who, though he fought in Spain, was not a writer given to illusion, described it years later in *The Labyrinth of Solitude*: "In those faces—obtuse and obstinate, gross and brutal, like those the great Spanish painters, without the least touch of complacency and with an almost flesh-and-blood realism, have left us—there was something like a desperate hopefulness, something very concrete and at the same time universal. Since then I have never seen the same expression on any face . . . The memory will never leave me. Anyone who has looked Hope in the face will never forget it. He will search for it everywhere he goes."

PART FOUR

End of an Era

The Choice

The New Yorker, January 28, 2008

In the fall of 1971, a Yale Law School student named Greg Craig sublet his apartment, on Edgewood Avenue in New Haven, to his classmate Hillary Rodham and her boyfriend, Bill Clinton, for seventy-five dollars a month. Over the following decades, Craig and the Clintons continued to cross paths. Craig, who became a partner at the blue-chip law firm Williams & Connolly in Washington, D.C., received regular invitations to White House Christmas parties, where Hillary always remembered to ask about his five children. In the fall of 1998, President Clinton asked him to lead the defense team that the White House was assembling for the impeachment battle. On a bookshelf in Craig's large corner office are several photographs of him with one or both Clintons, including a snapshot of the president and his lawyers—their arms folded victoriously across their chests—taken after Craig's successful presentation during the Senate trial. An inscription reads, "To Greg. We struck the right pose—and you struck the right chords! Thanks—Bill Clinton, 2/99."

Despite his long history with the Clintons, Craig is an adviser to Barack Obama's campaign. "Ninety-five percent of it is because of my enthusiasm for Obama," he said last month, at his law office. "I really regard him as a fresh and exciting voice in American politics that has not been in my life since Robert Kennedy." In 1968, Craig, who is sixty-two, was campaigning for Eugene McCarthy when he heard a Bobby Kennedy speech at the University of Nebraska and became a believer on the spot. Since then, Craig has not been inspired by any American president. As for the prospect of another Clinton presidency, he said, "I don't discount the possibility of her being able to inspire me. But she hasn't in the past, and Obama has."

Inspiration is an underexamined part of political life and presidential leadership. In its lowest, most common form, inspiration is simple charisma that becomes magnified by the media, as with Ronald Reagan or Bill Clinton. On rare occasions, however, a leader can become the object of an intensely personal, almost spiritual desire for cleansing, community, renewal—for what Hillary, in a 1969 commencement speech at Wellesley, called "more immediate, ecstatic, and penetrating modes of living." Somewhere between the merely great communicators and the secular saints are the exceptional politicians who, as Hillary put it then, "practice politics as the art of making what appears to be impossible possible."

Robert B. Reich, the secretary of labor in Clinton's first term, who now teaches at Berkeley, told me that he believes political inspiration to be "the legitimizing of social movements and social change, the empowering of all sorts of people and groups to act as remarkable change agents." Reich was once a close friend of both Clintons—he met Hillary when they were undergraduates and began a Rhodes scholarship the same year as Bill—but he has not endorsed a candidate, and he seems drawn to Obama, for the same reasons that attracted Craig. "Obama is to me very analogous to Robert Kennedy," Reich said. "The closer you got to him, the more you realized that his magic lay in his effect on others rather than in any specific policies. But he became a very important vehicle. He got young people very excited. He was transformative in the sense of just who he was. And a few things he said about social justice licensed people. Obama does all that, almost effortlessly."

The alternatives facing Democratic voters have been characterized variously as a choice between experience and change, between an insider and an outsider, and between two firsts—a woman and a black man. But perhaps the most important difference between these two politicians—whose policy views, after all, are almost indistinguishable—lies in their rival conceptions of the presidency. Obama offers himself as a catalyst by which disenchanted Americans can overcome two decades of vicious partisanship, energize our democracy, and restore faith in government. Clinton presents politics as the art of the possible, with change coming incrementally through good governance, a skill that she has honed in her career as advocate, First Lady, and senator. This is the real meaning of the remark she made during one of the New Hampshire debates: "Dr. King's dream began to be realized when President Lyndon Johnson passed the Civil Rights Act of 1964, when he was able to get through Congress something that President Kennedy was hopeful to do—the president before had not even tried—but it took a president to get it done."

In the overheated atmosphere of a closely fought primary, this historically sound statement set off a chain reaction of accusations, declarations of offense, and media hysteria, and for a few days the Democratic Party seemed poised to descend into a self-destructive frenzy of identity politics. The *Times* editorial page scolded Clinton for playing racial politics and choosing a bizarre role model in Johnson; the columnist Bob Herbert accused her of taking "cheap shots" at King. But Clinton was simply expressing her belief that the presidency is more about pushing difficult legislation through a fractious Congress than it is about transforming society. In the recent debate before the Nevada caucus, Obama, who confessed to being disorganized, said that the presidency has little to do with running an efficient office: "It involves having a vision for where the country needs to go . . . and then being able to mobilize and inspire the American people to get behind that agenda for change." In reply, Clinton likened the job of president to that of a "chief executive officer" who has "to be able to manage and run the bureaucracy."

Similarly, if this campaign is, among other things, a referendum on the current occupant of the White House—as elections at the end of failed presidencies inevitably are—then its outcome will be determined partly by whether voters find George W. Bush guilty of incompetence or of demeaning American politics. Clinton is presenting herself as the candidate who is tough and knowledgeable enough to fix the broken systems of government: the intelligence agencies, the Justice Department, the legislative process, the White House itself. Last week, speaking on the phone from California, she said that a president allows advisers to oversee the running of government at his or her peril. "Otherwise, you cede too much authority, and although it may not be immediately apparent to the public, the government picks up on those signals," she said. "What we now know about how Dick Cheney basically controlled the information going to Bush means that we'll never really know how much responsibility Bush should be assumed to have taken with respect to serious decisions. The water will flow downstream, and often pool in great reservoirs of power that will then be taken advantage of by those who have been smart enough to figure out how to pull the levers. And I know from my own experience, and certainly watching how deeply involved Bill was in those areas that he thought were important, what it takes to try to get the government to respond. It's not easy. We're talking about this massive bureaucracy . . . and you have to be prepared on Day One to basically wrest the power away in order to realize the goals and vision that you have for the country."

Although Clinton didn't utter her chief rival's name, Obama seemed to be the subtext of many of her remarks, such as when she mentioned reading Michael Korda's recent biography of Eisenhower, and compared the portraits of Ike and Field Marshal Bernard Montgomery—"who was given great marks for being so brilliant and inspiring of his men, but often had a difficult time making a tough decision, often dithered about it, and claimed he needed yet more information before he could pull the trigger." If elected president, Clinton acknowledged, she would have to use unifying rhetoric and reach across partisan lines. But Clinton is less sanguine than Obama is about the possibilities of such efforts; she is readier to march ahead and let those who will follow do so. "It's also important to say, 'Look, there are certain things we have to do as a country. You may not agree, but let me explain why, and let me try to persuade you. But if I can't persuade you, we have to go forward anyway.' And I think that that kind of understanding of the combination of using the bully pulpit but also producing results—managing the government so it doesn't manage you, so it does act as an instrument of the policies you're actually implementing—will give proof to what it is I'm saying."

These rival conceptions of the presidency—Clinton as executive, Obama as visionary—reflect a deeper difference in how the two candidates analyze what ails the country. Obama's diagnosis is more fundamental: for him, the illness precedes the Bush years and the partisan deadlock in Washington, originating in a basic failure of politicians to bring Americans together. A strong hand on the wheel won't make a difference if your car is stuck in the mud; a good leader has to persuade enough people to get out and push. Whereas Clinton echoes Churchill, who proclaimed, "Give us the tools and we will finish the job," Obama invokes Lincoln, who said, "As our case is new, so we must think anew, and act anew. We must disenthrall ourselves, and then we shall save our country."

Sidney Blumenthal, a former staff writer at *The New Yorker*, who was a senior adviser to Bill Clinton and is now a senior adviser on Hillary Clinton's campaign, describes the 2008 election as a chance to secure progressive government for years to come. "It's not a question of transcending partisanship," he said. "It's a question of fulfilling it. If we can win and govern well while handling multiple crises at the same time and the Congress, then we can move the country out of this Republican era and into a progressive Democratic era, for a long period of time."

Peter Wehner served in the Bush White House until August 2007, working for Karl Rove, the administration's chief strategist. Wehner, who is now a senior fellow at the Ethics and Public Policy Center in Washington, said that as a candidate, Hillary Clinton would provide a "much more target-rich environment" than Obama. Republicans wouldn't need to uncover new scandals; they would simply remind voters of the not so distant Clinton wars. "Certain regions of your brain are latent," Wehner said. "But if there's a word or a sound or a memory that you hear, that region of your brain lights up again. And I have a feeling that with Bill and Hillary Clinton, there are latent regions of the brain that will light up, and if the Democrats don't light it up, the Republicans will. And that is going to be Clinton fatigue." As for Obama, Wehner's only complaint is that he's a liberal: "I find him to be very impressive. He would be much more difficult for Republicans to handle. He has much more breakout potential."

Advisers to Clinton told me that there is something naïve, even potentially fatal, in Obama's vision of leading the country out of its current political battles. The advisers seemed to be saying that Obama considers civility and nonpartisanship to be amulets that can stop bullets. In this view, Obama will be annihilated by what members of the Clinton campaign call "the Republican attack machine." Neera Tanden, the campaign's policy director, expressed admiration for Obama but cautioned that the general election will be brutal. "You cannot let your guard down with these guys," she said of right-wing politicians. "They take people's strengths and make them weaknesses; if you give them an inch, they'll take a mile. They're not ready to give up. They're not ready to lose the Congress and the presidency. I don't think Grover Norquist"—the conservative lobbyist—"is sitting around thinking that's going to be great for him. His salary depends on it, at the very least. Both of the Clintons have

been through it and won before. But if we don't think that the Democratic nominee, whoever it is, is going to have high negatives by the end
of this process, then we're crazy."

Late last year, as the Democratic race was tightening, there was an
argument within the Clinton camp over whether to go on the attack
against Obama—an argument won by the proponents. When I described
to Greg Craig the Clinton campaign's skepticism toward the idea of
transcending partisanship, he said, "You're getting to that five percent
of Hillary that I don't like—which is to see in every corner a conspiracy or
an opponent that must be crushed. Look at her comment 'Now the fun
part starts'"—Clinton's announcement in Iowa that she would begin
attacking Obama's record. "There is a quality of playing the embattled,
beleaguered victim that I find unappealing and depressing." He added,
"I want a president who is looking to move the country with positive inspirational ideas rather than to fight off the bad guys and proclaim victory by defeating the forces of reaction. I would like us to inspire the
forces of reaction to join us in treating people better, and lifting more
vulnerable people and people in jeopardy out of their vulnerability and
jeopardy."

Of course, as Craig learned during the impeachment effort—which
he denounced as "a gross abuse of power"—the Republicans in Congress
have shown little interest in making peace with Democrats. "Yes, but the
way in which you beat them, the way in which you make progress in this
country, is not by further polarizing and further dividing," Craig said. "It's
by building the consensus around the positions that make sense—say,
the position that we should not have forty-seven million Americans uninsured. You don't win national health insurance by turning Republicans
against you. You've got to get them to join you."

Clinton's admirers counter that as a member of the U.S. Senate, she
has learned the art of compromise. In just seven years, she has mastered
the power relationships and legislative labyrinths of this most difficult
club. "Hillary believes in governing," Neera Tanden said. When Tanden
worked as her legislative director, Clinton would call again and again from
the Senate floor to gauge the effect that a new amendment would have on
a bill. Such attention to minutiae is rare in a legislator. The question,
though, is whether her indisputable virtues—hard work, intellectual acu-
ity, a command of policy—are ideally suited for the White House. A sen-

ator must convince fifty to sixty fellow politicians; a president must rouse three hundred million fellow citizens.

In the 1990s, Republicans, taking aim at an all-too-human Democratic president, liked to say "character matters"—a phrase that has been bitterly reprised by Democrats during the Bush years. If there's a flaw in Hillary Clinton's character that could keep her from becoming a successful president, or president at all, it is what Carl Bernstein, her best biographer, described to me as a tendency toward "subterfuge and eliding." In the deep and sympathetic portrait *A Woman in Charge*, Bernstein's recent biography of Clinton, a constant theme is her fear of humiliation; as the daughter of a harsh, often cruel father, she learned early to conceal any weakness and, ultimately, to protect her very humanity from exposure. In the recent Las Vegas debate, when Clinton was asked to name a weakness, all she could come up with was her impatience to get things done.

"In her personal life, she's always seemed like she had something to hide," Dee Dee Myers, who was a top adviser on Bill Clinton's 1992 campaign, and who served as White House press secretary for the first two years of his presidency, said. "She had a difficult father, and she spent a lot of time trying to create an image of a functional family when she could have just said, 'It's my family.' The burden of perfection was upon her, and she carried it into her marriage. There's always this fear of letting people see what they already know."

In *A Woman in Charge*, Bernstein writes of Clinton, "Almost always, something holds her back from telling the whole story, as if she doesn't trust the reader, listener, friend, interviewer, constituent—or perhaps herself—to understand the true significance of events." A former Clinton administration official explained his decision to support Obama by urging me to read the two candidates' autobiographies side by side. Obama's *Dreams from My Father*, unlike Clinton's *Living History*, he said, reveals a narrator who has struggled through difficult questions of identity and re- solved them, and who, as a result, is comfortable not just with himself but with the complexity and contradiction of the world. "When I'm with her, I feel she wants to impress me," the former official said. "When I'm with him, I feel he wants to know what I have to offer him."

In numerous conversations, friends of both Clintons expressed a preference for Hillary, upending the public perception that Bill is the warmer and more likable of the two. He talks; she listens, with a talent for banter that can be disarming and even whimsical. Shortly after Lissa Muscatine, a close adviser of Hillary Clinton's, went to work as a White House speechwriter, in 1993, she tried to catch the First Lady's attention as Clinton was hurrying along a corridor. "Stop—stop!" Muscatine called out. Clinton wheeled around. "Stop! in the name of love," she sang out, breaking into a boogie in the West Wing hallway. Clinton's aides are famously loyal, staying with her far longer than most staffs at the highest level of politics. Tanden, who was in her twenties when she joined Clinton's staff in 1997 and "sort of grew up working for her," found that Clinton really wanted to know what a midlevel aide thought about policy issues. "She asks questions, and she has a very high b.s. detector on people," Tanden said. "You get in her foxhole, she gets in your foxhole." In 1999, when Muscatine underwent surgery in order to determine if she had breast cancer, the First Lady asked her to telephone as soon as she had a diagnosis. The tumor was malignant, and Muscatine was too overwhelmed by the news to call, as they had agreed. Clinton phoned her and said, "If it's okay, I want to check back every few days. But if you don't want to come to the phone, that's fine." Muscatine told me, "She gave me not only her support but the license not to talk to someone of her stature. That meant the world to me." Richard Holbrooke, who served as Clinton's envoy on Bosnia and as ambassador to the United Nations, is now a foreign policy adviser to Hillary Clinton's campaign. (He is sometimes spoken of as a potential secretary of state.) He said of Clinton, "I like her because she's human. She has a vulnerable side. She's fighting for things she really believes in."

Several friends also describe Clinton as more committed to using power for social change than her husband—for example, during the health care reform effort of 1993–94, she insisted on universal coverage even after President Clinton became willing to drop it. (Her intransigence, of course, helped doom the entire effort.) John Danner, who worked for Clinton during his first term as governor of Arkansas, said, "Bill's policy wonkishness, in my judgment at least, was an application of his insatiable curiosity. People confuse that with a deep caring about actually getting anything done with the political power that he'd got. Hillary has always had a tenacity and a toughness that Bill never had. In that sense, she has cared more about getting stuff done." Danner's wife, Nancy Pietrafesa, who attended Wellesley with Hillary, also worked for Bill Clinton in Arkansas. (The two couples had a falling-out after Danner and Pietrafesa were fired.) Pietrafesa said that Hillary's fear of public exposure was connected to those early years in Arkansas. "To be so humiliated, and ruthlessly," Pietrafesa said. "In Arkansas, she went to a place she wasn't welcomed, big time. Everything was wrong with her. She didn't paint her toenails when she wore sandals, she didn't look like a cocktail waitress when she dressed up. Everybody really felt they could insult her with impunity."

Clinton's instinct to fight back was honed in the rough world of Arkansas politics. Once, when the two couples were talking about policy matters, Danner proposed a way to offer retail discounts to Arkansas's substantial elderly population. To the astonishment of Danner and Pietrafesa, Hillary responded, "The last thing we need to do right now is something for folks who didn't vote for Bill." She had, Danner remembered, "this binary view of the world, a little like Bush's comment 'You're with us or you're against us.'" In Pietrafesa's opinion, "Hillary needs enemies."

During the tumultuous early years of her husband's presidency, Clinton's ambitious political goals were too often stymied by her penchant for secrecy and combativeness. In one controversy after another—Whitewater, the travel office scandal, the Paula Jones lawsuit—she refused to compromise or be forthcoming, and allowed what might have been temporary embarrassments to become part of an endless battle that helped derail the progressive reforms on which the Clintons had campaigned, including health care legislation.

In early 1995, not long after the Republicans' sweeping win in the midterm elections, Hillary Clinton met with a dozen advisers in the White House residence to discuss how to handle the new political reality, which would include congressional investigations on Whitewater and other matters. One argument—the one that she had always made—was to "batten down the hatches, fight to the death," in the words of an adviser who attended the meeting; another was to defuse the opposition as much as possible through openness. At one point, almost as if she were thinking aloud, Clinton suddenly said, "I need people like the people JFK had around him." The adviser described the moment as "existential" for Clinton: she was saying that she wanted "people who were strong, tough, loyal, who play to win but do it in the smart, strategic way." Clinton's way had not been smart or strategic. Afterward, she grudgingly began to change her approach, withdrawing from the front lines of political battles and, as some of her aides had urged, using her platform more symbolically rather than always trying to achieve concrete results.

That year, Clinton began writing a book about children and society called It Takes a Village. The thing that Washington insiders remember best about the book is Hillary's failure to thank Barbara Feinman, the writer hired by Simon and Schuster, the publisher, as a collaborator. The truth, though, is more complicated, and shows Hillary to be less a Machiavellian liar than a woman whose guardedness leads to self-sabotage.

Editors at Simon and Schuster reacted to early chapters with dismay, and worried about the quality of Feinman's contributions, but they kept their reactions private. Over the summer, a manuscript emerged, but neither the publisher nor Clinton's aides—nor, especially, Hillary herself—were pleased with it. When Feinman left for vacation, Clinton, a Simon and Schuster editor, and a few key aides, working on their own time, continued on the book without her. (Feinman fulfilled the terms of her contract, and was never told by the publisher that her work was unsatisfactory.) In November, the Simon and Schuster editor spent three weeks at the White House, working intensively to expand and refine the material with the aides and with Clinton, who filled yellow legal pads with incorrigibly wonky prose, in "round, schoolgirlish handwriting," the editor told me. In private, Clinton was strikingly relaxed, padding around the Book Room and Solarium in sweatpants and Coke-bottle glasses, the editor said, calling her "Buttercup." Clinton's personality, the editor found, "is refreshingly sharp and clear—but she can't show it."

It Takes a Village appeared in January 1996, with an acknowledgments page that mentioned nobody. Clinton had apparently given in to the urge to pay her ghostwriter back (as had Simon and Schuster, which considered withholding the last portion of Feinman's hundred-and-twenty-thousand-dollar fee but quickly relented). Clinton's omission aroused the enmity of powerful friends of Feinman's at The Washington Post, and journalists began covering the slight, their suspicions roused by Clinton's explanation that she had forgone names in the acknowledgments for fear of leaving someone out. Hillary's triumphant return to the public eye became another embarrassment. As with so many other Clinton scandals, the press framed the story in the worst possible light, and got its essence wrong, suggesting that Feinman had written the whole book and that Clinton had stolen the credit. Instead, Clinton had micromanaged every aspect of the book's development. The episode captures her habit of undermining herself, when the worst might have been averted by a little candor and grace—a tendency that has reappeared in the past few weeks, as her campaign has responded to the shock of Obama's challenge.

In the Senate, Clinton seems to have taken the hard lessons of the White House years to heart and become a far better politician. The majority of her legislative achievements, for the most part under Republican control of Congress, have been modest, and geared toward constituent service. Richard Holbrooke pointed out that Fort Drum, outside Watertown, New York, stayed open and was even expanded during a period of base closures, and said, "To her, it's one of her most important achievements. She's incredibly proud of it." A senior Democrat on the Senate staff, who declined to be named, pointed out that Clinton's focus on New York was necessary to win over her colleagues: "She demonstrated that she was a workhorse, not a show horse." Clinton has surprised Republicans by cooperating with erstwhile enemies of her husband's administration, such as Lindsey Graham of South Carolina, who was a House impeachment manager in 1998, and Trent Lott of Mississippi, who in 2000 expressed a hope that lightning might strike Clinton before her first day in the Senate. And she has surprised the military by becoming an expert on defense policy, as New York's first member of the Senate Armed Services Committee.

A member of Clinton's campaign told me that Obama has not held a single hearing of the Senate Foreign Relations Committee's subcommittee on European Affairs, which he chairs, implying that he is a less serious senator than she is. In fact, according to *The Boston Globe*, Obama has presided over appointment hearings, but nothing more substantive: he took over the subcommittee just as the presidential campaign began, and all the candidates have been AWOL since then. As for the challenge to Obama's seriousness, the Senate staff member disputed it, describing him as a deeply thoughtful, well-prepared member of the committee who asks good questions and never tries to score cheap points. In the staff member's words, Obama can see all sides of an issue, whereas Clinton would be formidable across the negotiating table from, say, Iranian president Mahmoud Ahmadinejad.

In the Senate, Clinton has gone a long way toward neutralizing skeptics and antagonists by working hard, deferring to seniority, and deploying her underappreciated personal charm. At the same time, she became a Democratic leader in the Senate in part because she understood the powers of the presidency and the need for an overarching strategy in any major conflict with the executive branch—for example, Neera Tanden said, during the fight to prevent Social Security from being privatized. Presumably, she would turn her knowledge of Congress to her advantage should she return to the White House.

"Her Senate years are when she learned," Holbrooke said. "How could she conceivably have been such a successful, bipartisan, reach-out senator, collaborating even with impeachment managers, if she hadn't learned something?" In Holbrooke's chronicle, her Senate career has instructed her in congressional power and filled the last conceivable holes in her résumé, leaving her perfectly poised for the presidency. "Here's my view of the arc of her story," he said. "The so-called 'soft issues,' which are not soft at all—women's empowerment, HIV/AIDS, micro-credit, global health, foreign assistance—are things she mastered as First Lady. Her national security qualifications are based on her five years as a member of the Senate Armed Services Committee."

There is another view of her years in the Senate, one suggested by a few associates who have grown wary of Clinton the politician: that she's learned the lessons of the nineties all too well and become the same careful centrist that electoral setbacks led her husband to become. "'Caution' is the operative word," Robert Reich said. "Essentially, Bill Clinton's agenda ended at the start of 1995, when Republicans took over Congress. What resumed in the White House was a management operation to stay relevant and to keep the Republican Congress at bay." Clinton associates expressed concern that Hillary's chief strategist and pollster was Mark Penn, the author of *Microtrends*, who is closely associated with triangulation—

the cynical adoption of ideas from both sides of the political divide. And some of her actions in the Senate have had an air of opportunism; in 2005, for example, she cosponsored a bill to criminalize flag burning. The burden of Clinton's long and intensely public political career is that she can be faulted for both excessive caution and excessive zeal. A Clinton associate put it this way to Carl Bernstein: "I'm not sure I want the circus back in town."

Two nights before the New Hampshire primary, Clinton was more than ninety minutes late for a rally at Winnacunnet High School in Hampton, and the energy was rapidly seeping out of the cafeteria. The recorded music track was on its third or fourth round of "Every Little Thing She Does Is Magic," and the standing crowd of six hundred people (with a slightly larger number in an adjacent auditorium) was no longer amused by a campaign worker tossing out "Hillary" T-shirts like a game show host. The fearsome Clinton machine appeared to be close to breakdown. "If you're on the fence, this isn't such a good thing," a man next to me said.

Ruth Keene, a small woman of seventy-one years who wore a big blue parka, kept telling the people around us that the candidate would appear any moment. I mentioned to her that a nurse I'd met at a John McCain town hall meeting had called Clinton "bitchy." Why did so many people dislike her so much? "Strong woman," Keene said. "I'm a bitch and proud of it. I can't talk about her with some of my friends, or it would end the friendship." As for Obama, she liked him fine, but "the Republicans would chew him up."

When Clinton finally appeared, in a black pantsuit and a bright pink blouse, there was a surge of excitement, and I noticed how many people in the room were not just female but girls. One who could not have been more than ten held a placard that said HILLARY 2008, SOPHIA 2040. "I apologize for running late," Clinton said. After the loss to Obama in the Iowa caucus, she told me, New Hampshire was a matter of "do or die," and, perhaps for that reason, she almost immediately opened the floor to questions, something that she had rarely done earlier in the campaign. Whatever question the crowd threw at her, she had an informed answer, often accompanied by a multipoint plan: immigration, health care, global warming, student loans, small business, animal rights, Cuba. For well over an hour, she projected her voice across the room in the same tone, the same semi-shout, regardless of the question—even when a girl near the stage asked how her third-grade class could become more challenging. "That is really touching," Clinton said, laughing, but within half a minute she had turned away from the girl and was declaring, "We live in a much more personalized, customized world, but education is still on an industrial model."

It occurred to me that Clinton is a familiar kind of Democrat—the earnest policy junkie, like Michael Dukakis, Al Gore, or John Kerry—except that this is a wonk with a killer instinct and a passionate temperament under wraps. In our conversation, Clinton seemed to admit that she does not inspire through rhetoric and emotion. "You can also inspire through deeds," she said. "You can demonstrate determination and willingness to make difficult choices, to show backbone and courage, to confront adversity calmly and skillfully. A president, no matter how rhetorically inspiring, still has to show strength and effectiveness in the day-to-day handling of the job, because people are counting on that. So, yes, words are critically important, but they're not enough. You have to act. In my own experience, sometimes it's putting one foot in front of the other day after day." She cited her efforts on behalf of the health of workers at Ground Zero. "It's important to realize that once the lights are off and the cheering crowds are gone, you still have to go back to the Oval Office and figure out how to solve these problems. It really does mean that the buck stops there. You can't delegate it, you can't outsource it."

In the New Hampshire cafeteria, Clinton couldn't quite make an individual connection, even when listening sympathetically to a woman in the crowd who said that she held down two jobs and still had trouble paying for her asthma medicine. When a man declared himself appalled by the Democrats' weak statements about terrorism at a televised debate, Clinton snapped, "I'm sorry you were appalled by it," and moved on. She wouldn't risk the loss of control that it might take to energize the room with humor or anger or argument, or the sort of spontaneous human touch that everyone who spends private time with her notices and likes. A number of people drifted away before she had finished.

The next morning, Obama was scheduled to appear before an overflow crowd at the opera house in Lebanon. When he walked onto the stage, which was framed by giant vertical banners proclaiming HOPE, his liquid stride and handshake-hugs suggested a man completely at ease.

"I decided to run because of you," he told the crowd. "I'm betting on you. I think the American people are honest and generous and less divided than our politics suggests." He mocked the response to his campaign from "Washington," which everyone in the room understood to be Clinton, who had warned in the debate two nights before against "false hopes": "No, no, no! You can't do that, you're not allowed. Obama may be inspiring to you, but here's the problem—Obama has not been in Washington enough. He needs to be stewed and seasoned a little more, we need to boil the hope out of him until he sounds like us—then he will be ready."

The opera house exploded in laughter. "We love you," a woman shouted.

"I love you back," he said, feeding off the adoration that he had summoned without breaking a sweat. "This change thing is catching on, because everybody's talking about change. 'I'm for change.' 'Put me down for change.' 'I'm a change person, too.'"

It was the day before the primary, and Obama began to improvise a theme, almost too much in the manner of Martin Luther King: "In one day's time." It carried him through health care, schools, executive salaries, Iraq—everything that Clinton had invoked, except that this was music. Then came the peroration: "If you know who you are, who you're fighting for, what your values are, you can afford to reach out to people across the aisle. If you start off with an agreeable manner, you might be able to pick off a few folks, recruit some independents into the fold, recruit even some Republicans into the fold. If you've got the votes, you will beat them and do it with a smile on your face." It was a summons to reasonableness, yet Obama made it sound thrilling. "False hopes? There's no such thing. This country was built on hope," he cried. "We don't need leaders to tell us what we can't do—we need leaders to inspire us. Some are thinking about our constraints, and others are thinking about limitless possibility." At times, Obama almost seems to be trying to escape history, presenting himself as the conduit through which people's yearnings for national transformation can be realized.

Obama spoke for only twenty-five minutes and took no questions; he had figured out how to leave an audience at the peak of its emotion, craving more. As he was ending, I walked outside and found five hundred people standing on the sidewalk and the front steps of the opera house, listening to his last words in silence, as if news of victory in the Pacific were coming over the loudspeakers. Within minutes, I couldn't recall a single thing that he had said, and the speech dissolved into pure feeling, which stayed with me for days.

In June 1992, when Bill Clinton was running third behind President George H. W. Bush and Ross Perot, his advisers were faced with the problem of reconciling his support of the middle class with his character and biography, which, until then, the public associated with Oxford, Yale, womanizing, draft dodging, and marijuana. Their "Manhattan Project"— an effort to introduce Clinton to the country as the hardworking product of a broken family and a rough childhood—helped put him into the lead and culminated in a hugely successful campaign film shown at the Democratic Convention in New York, *The Man from Hope*.

"Hillary Clinton needs something like that," Dee Dee Myers, who worked on the Manhattan Project, said. "Too often, all we see is ambition."

Ambition, of course, is the politician's currency. "Politics has ever been about advancing yourself," Richard Holbrooke said. "The question is: Is ambition harnessed to a purpose? She has the goals to advance the national purpose, she's articulated them, she's tried to lay them out."

Blame it on the media, or blame it on the voters, but American politics requires something more. A few hours before Clinton's rally in Hampton, I watched John McCain's masterly presentation before a packed middle school gym in Salem, which included many skeptics and independents. An accountant challenged him on his willingness to make Bush's tax cuts permanent while claiming to be a deficit hawk, telling McCain, "You're in purgatory." The candidate shot back playfully, "Thank you very much. It's a step up from where I was last summer." He was witty, combative, humble, and blunt (while embracing Republican orthodoxy on almost every position). Unlike Clinton, he engaged questioners in lengthy back-and-forths that showed he was capable of a respectful disagreement. After hearing Clinton that evening, I thought that she might have a hard time beating McCain in November.

"I'm more reserved than people realize or accept of someone who's in the public eye, especially in the times in which we live," Clinton told me. "I think that the world is only beginning to recognize that women should be permitted the same range of leadership styles that we permit men." She went on, "I followed with great interest the election of Angela Merkel as Germany's first woman chancellor. Many of the things that were said about her would certainly sound familiar." She laughed. Her determination to prove that a woman could be a plausible commander in chief had led her to restrain her displays of feeling, perhaps for too long. "I wasn't quite sensitive to that," she said. "Voters were saying, 'Okay, now I can look at more personal traits.'" She went on, "My friends, starting in November or December, said, 'You're not telling your story very well.'"

The day before the New Hampshire primary, Clinton, campaigning on three hours of sleep a night, spoke before undecided voters at a coffee shop in Portsmouth. Her eyes welling with tears, she said of the grueling campaign, "It's not easy, and I couldn't do it if I just didn't, you know, passionately believe it was the right thing to do . . . I just don't want us to fall backward." Many voters responded warmly to this candid moment. As Myers put it, "There was a flash in New Hampshire—that there's another reason that drives her, a desire to help other people." Since then, Myers said, Clinton has made the mistake of continuing to *tell* the public what she feels rather than showing it. During the debate in Las Vegas, she tried to explain her commitment to social change by talking about herself, not about the people she wants to help: "It is really my life's work. It is something that comes out of my own experience, both in my family and in my church—that, you know, I've been blessed." Her response displayed the awkwardness that comes from a lifelong habit of self-concealment in the face of exposure, and toughness in the face of hurt. It's a little sad and painful that this enormously accomplished and capable woman, in her sixty-first year, had to bring her mother and daughter on a "likability tour" in the days before the Iowa caucus, and found her voice—as she put it—only on the night of her upset win in New Hampshire.

"Hillary needs to connect two things," Myers said. "What's in her heart, and what she wants to accomplish and why. There are many reasons to think she'd be a good president. She knows what she wants to do, she understands how the process works, she's shown an ability to work with Congress, she's become more incrementalist. But the presidency isn't all that powerful, except as the bully pulpit. It comes down to your ability to get people to follow you, to inspire. You have to lead. Can she get people to come together, or does she remain such a polarizing figure? That's what the campaign will be about." In other words, winning the presidency might require Clinton to transcend her own history.

The Fall of Conservatism

The New Yorker, May 26, 2008

The era of American politics that has been dying before our eyes was born in 1966. That January, a twenty-seven-year-old editorial writer for the *St. Louis Globe-Democrat* named Patrick Buchanan went to work for Richard Nixon, who was just beginning the most improbable political comeback in American history. Having served as vice president in the Eisenhower administration, Nixon had lost the presidency by a whisker to John F. Kennedy in 1960, and had been humiliated in a 1962 bid for the California governorship. But he saw that he could propel himself back to power on the strength of a new feeling among Americans who, appalled by the chaos of the cities, the moral heedlessness of the young, and the insults to national pride in Vietnam, were ready to blame it all on the liberalism of President Lyndon B. Johnson. Right-wing populism was bubbling up from below; it needed to be guided by a leader who understood its resentments because he felt them, too.

"From day one, Nixon and I talked about creating a new majority," Buchanan told me recently, sitting in the library of his Greek-revival house in McLean, Virginia, on a secluded lane bordering the fenced grounds of the Central Intelligence Agency. "What we talked about, basically, was shearing off huge segments of FDR's New Deal coalition, which LBJ had held together: Northern Catholic ethnics and Southern Protestant conservatives—what we called the Daley-Rizzo Democrats in the North and, frankly, the Wallace Democrats in the South." Buchanan grew up in Washington, D.C., among the first group—men like his father, an accountant and a father of nine, who had supported Roosevelt but also revered Joseph McCarthy. The Southerners were the kind of men whom Nixon whipped into a frenzy one night in the fall of 1966, at the Wade Hampton Hotel in Columbia, South Carolina. Nixon, who was then a partner in a New York law firm, had traveled there with Buchanan on behalf of Republican congressional candidates. Buchanan recalls that the room was full of sweat, cigar smoke, and rage; the rhetoric, which was about patriotism and law and order, "burned the paint off the walls." As they left the hotel, Nixon said, "This is the future of this party, right here in the South."

Nixon and Buchanan visited thirty-five states that fall, and in November the Republicans won a midterm landslide. It was the end of Lyndon Johnson's Great Society, the beginning of his fall from power. In order to seize the presidency in 1968, Nixon had to live down his history of nasty politicking, and he ran that year as a uniter. But his administration adopted an undercover strategy for building a Republican majority, working to create the impression that there were two Americas: the quiet, ordinary, patriotic, religious, law-abiding Many, and the noisy, élitist, amoral, disorderly, condescending Few.

This strategy was put into action near the end of Nixon's first year in office, when antiwar demonstrators were becoming a disruptive presence in Washington. Buchanan recalls urging Nixon, "We've got to use the siege gun of the presidency and go right after these guys." On November 3, 1969, Nixon went on national television to speak about the need to avoid a shameful defeat in Vietnam. Looking benignly into the camera, he concluded, "And so tonight—to you, the great silent majority of Americans—I ask for your support." It was the most successful speech of his presidency. Newscasters criticized him for being divisive and for offering no new vision on Vietnam, but tens of thousands of telegrams and letters expressing approval poured into the White House. It was Nixon's particular political genius to rouse simultaneously the contempt of the *bienpensants* and the admiration of those who felt the sting of that contempt in their own lives.

Buchanan urged Nixon to enlist his vice president, Spiro Agnew, in a battle against the press. In November, Nixon sent Agnew—despised as dull-witted by the media—on the road, where he denounced "this small and unelected élite" of editors, anchormen, and analysts. Buchanan recalls watching a broadcast of one such speech—which he had written for

Agnew—on a television in his White House office. Joining him was his colleague Kevin Phillips, who had just published *The Emerging Republican Majority*, which marshaled electoral data to support a prophecy that Sun Belt conservatism—like Jacksonian democracy, Republican industrialism, and New Deal liberalism—would dominate American politics for the next thirty-two or thirty-six years. (As it turns out, Phillips was slightly too modest.) When Agnew finished his diatribe, Phillips said two words: "Positive polarization."

Polarization is the theme of Rick Perlstein's new narrative history *Nixonland* (Scribners), which covers the years between two electoral landslides: Barry Goldwater's defeat in 1964 and George McGovern's in 1972. During that time, Nixon figured out that he could succeed politically "by using the angers, anxieties, and resentments produced by the cultural chaos of the 1960s," which were also his own. In Perlstein's terms, America in the sixties was divided, like the Sneetches on Dr. Seuss's beaches, into two social clubs: the Franklins, who were the in-crowd at Nixon's alma mater, Whittier College; and the Orthogonians, a rival group founded by Nixon after the Franklins rejected him, made up of "the strivers, those not to the manor born, the commuter students like him. He persuaded his fellows that reveling in one's unpolish was a nobility of its own." Orthogonians deeply resented Franklins, which, as Perlstein sees it, explains just about everything that happened between 1964 and 1972: Nixon resented the Kennedys and clawed his way back to power; construction workers resented John Lindsay and voted conservative; National Guardsmen resented student protesters and opened fire on them. Perlstein sustains these categories throughout the book, without quite noticing that his scheme breaks down under the pressure of his central historical insight—"America was engulfed in a pitched battle between the forces of darkness and the forces of light. The only thing was: Americans disagreed radically over which side was which." In other words, by 1972 there were hardly any Franklins left—only former Franklins who had thrown off their dinner jackets, picked up a weapon, and joined the brawl. The sixties, which began in liberal consensus over the Cold War and civil rights, became a struggle between two apocalyptic politics that each saw the other as hell-bent on the country's annihilation. The result was violence like nothing the country had seen since the Civil War, and Perlstein emphasizes that bombings, assaults, and murders committed by segregationists, hardhats, and vigilantes on the right were at least as numerous as those by radical students and black militants on the left. Nixon claimed to speak on behalf of "the nonshouters, the nondemonstrators," but the cigar smokers in that South Carolina hotel were intoxicated with hate.

Nixon was coldly mixing and pouring volatile passions. Although he was careful to renounce the extreme fringe of Birchites and racists, his means to power eventually became the end. Buchanan gave me a copy of a seven-page confidential memorandum—"A little raw for today," he warned—that he had written for Nixon in 1971, under the heading "Dividing the Democrats." Drawn up with an acute understanding of the fragilities and fault lines in "the Old Roosevelt Coalition," it recommended that the White House "exacerbate the ideological division" between the Old and New Left by praising Democrats who supported any of Nixon's policies; highlight "the elitism and quasi-anti-Americanism of the National Democratic Party"; nominate for the Supreme Court a Southern strict constructionist who would divide Democrats regionally; use abortion and parochial school aid to deepen the split between Catholics and social liberals; elicit white working class support with tax relief and denunciations of welfare. Finally, the memo recommended exploiting racial tensions among Democrats. "Bumper stickers calling for black Presidential and especially Vice-Presidential candidates should be spread out in the ghettoes of the country," Buchanan wrote. "We should do what is within our power to have a black nominated for Number Two, at least at the Democratic National Convention." Such gambits, he added, could "cut the Democratic Party and country in half; my view is that we would have by far the larger half."

The Nixon White House didn't enact all of these recommendations, but it would be hard to find a more succinct and unapologetic blueprint for Republican success in the conservative era. "Positive polarization" helped the Republicans win one election after another—and ensured that American politics would be an ugly, unredeemed business for decades to come.

Perlstein argues that the politics of *Nixonland* will endure for at least another generation. On his final page, he writes, "Do Americans not hate each other enough to fantasize about killing one another, in cold blood, over political and cultural disagreements? It would be hard to argue they do not." Yet the polarization of America, which we now call the "culture wars," has been dissipating for a long time. Because we can't anticipate what ideas and language will dominate the next cycle of American politics, the previous era's key words—"élite," "mainstream," "real," "values," "patriotic," "snob," "liberal"—seem as potent as ever. Indeed, they have shown up in the current campaign: North Carolina and Mississippi Republicans have produced ads linking local Democrats to Jeremiah Wright, Barack Obama's controversial former pastor. The right-wing group Citizens United has said that it will run ads portraying Obama as yet another "limousine liberal." But these are the spasms of nerve endings in an organism that's brain-dead. Among Republicans, there is no energy, no fresh thinking, no ability to capture the concerns and feelings of millions of people. In the past two months, Democratic targets of polarization attacks have won three special congressional elections, in solidly Republican districts in Illinois, Louisiana, and Mississippi. Political tactics have a way of outliving their ability to respond to the felt needs and aspirations of the electorate: Democrats continued to accuse Republicans of being like Herbert Hoover well into the 1970s; Republicans will no doubt accuse Democrats of being out of touch with real Americans long after George W. Bush retires to Crawford, Texas. But the 2006 and 2008 elections are the hinge on which America is entering a new political era.

This will be true whether or not John McCain, the presumptive Republican nominee, wins in November. He and his likely Democratic opponent, Barack Obama, "both embody a postpolarized, or antipolarized, style of politics," the *Times* columnist David Brooks told me. "McCain, crucially, missed the sixties, and in some ways he's a pre-sixties figure. He and Obama don't resonate with the sixties at all." The fact that the least conservative, least divisive Republican in the 2008 race is the last one standing—despite being despised by significant voices on the right— shows how little life is left in the movement that Goldwater began, Nixon brought into power, Ronald Reagan gave mass appeal, Newt Gingrich radicalized, Tom DeLay criminalized, and Bush allowed to break into pieces. "The fact that there was no conventional, establishment, old-style conservative candidate was not an accident," Brooks said. "Mitt Romney pretended to be one for a while, but he wasn't. Rudy Giuliani sort of pretended, but he wasn't. McCain is certainly not. It's not only a lack of political talent—there's just no driving force, and it will soften up normal Republicans for change."

On May 6, Newt Gingrich posted a message, "My Plea to Republicans: It's Time for Real Change to Avoid Real Disaster," on the website of the conservative magazine *Human Events*. The former House Speaker warned, "The Republican brand has been so badly damaged that if Republicans try to run an anti-Obama, anti–Reverend Wright, or (if Senator Clinton wins) anti-Clinton campaign, they are simply going to fail." Gingrich offered nine suggestions for restoring the Republican "brand"—among them "Overhaul the census and cut its budget radically" and "Implement a space-based, GPS-style air-traffic control system"—which read like a wonkish parody of the Contract with America. By the next morning, the post had received almost three hundred comments, almost all predicting a long Republican winter.

Yuval Levin, a former Bush White House official who is now a fellow at the Ethics and Public Policy Center, agrees with Gingrich's diagnosis. "There's an intellectual fatigue, even if it hasn't yet been made clear by defeat at the polls," he said. "The conservative idea factory is not producing as it did. You hear it from everybody, but nobody agrees what to do about it."

Pat Buchanan was less polite, paraphrasing the social critic Eric Hoffer: "Every great cause begins as a movement, becomes a business, and eventually degenerates into a racket."

Only a few years ago, on the night of Bush's victory in 2004, the conservative movement seemed indomitable. In fact, it was rapidly falling apart. Conservatives knew how to win elections; however, they turned out not to be very interested in governing. Throughout the decades since Nixon, conservatism has retained the essentially negative character of an insurgent movement.

Nixon himself was more interested in global grand strategy and partisan politics than in any conservative policy agenda. By today's standards, his achievements in office look like those of a moderate liberal: he eased the tensions of the Cold War, expanded the welfare state, and supported affirmative action (albeit in ways calculated to split the Democrats). "LBJ built the foundation and the first floor of the Great Society,"

Buchanan said. "We built the skyscraper. Nixon was not a Reaganite conservative."

Even Reagan, the Moses of the conservative movement, was more ideological in his rhetoric than in his governance. Conservatives have canonized him for cutting taxes and regulation, moving the courts to the right, and helping to vanquish the Soviet empire. But he proved less dogmatic than most of his opponents and some of his followers expected, especially on ending the Cold War. Reagan emphasized the first word in "positive polarization," turning the Nixon playbook into a kind of national celebration. Like FDR, he dominated an era by reconciling opposites through force of personality: just as Roosevelt the patrician became the tribune of the people, Reagan turned conservatism into a forward-looking, optimistic ideology. "We started in 1980 and played addition," Ed Rollins, Reagan's political director, recalls. "'Let's go out and get Democrats.' We attracted a great many young people to the party. Reagan made them feel good about the country again. After the '84 election, we did polling—Why did you vote for Reagan? They said, 'He's a winner.'"

The Princeton historian Sean Wilentz, in his new book, *The Age of Reagan: A History, 1974–2008* (Harper), argues that Reagan "learned how to seize and keep control of the terms of public debate." On taxes, race, government spending, national security, crime, welfare, and "traditional values," he made mainstream what had been the positions of the right-wing fringe, and he kept Democrats on the defensive. He also brought a generation of doctrinaire conservatives into the bureaucracy and the courts, making appointments based on ideological tests that only a genuine movement leader would impose. The rightward turn of the judiciary will probably be the most lasting achievement of Reagan and his movement.

In retrospect, the Reagan presidency was the high-water mark of conservatism. "In some respects, the conservative movement was a victim of success," Wilentz concludes. "With the Soviet Union dissolved, inflation reduced to virtually negligible levels, and the top tax rate cut to nearly half of what it was in 1980, all of Ronald Reagan's major stated goals when he took office had been achieved, leaving perplexed and fractious conservatives to fight over where they might now lead the country." Wilentz omits one important failure. According to Buchanan, who was the White House communications director in Reagan's second term, the president once told his barber, Milton Pitts, "You know, Milt, I came here to do five things, and four out of five ain't bad." He had succeeded in lowering taxes, raising morale, increasing defense spending, and facing down the Soviet Union; but he had failed to limit the size of government, which, besides anti-Communism, was the abiding passion of Reagan's political career and of the conservative movement. He didn't come close to achieving it and didn't try very hard, recognizing early that the public would be happy to have its taxes cut as long as its programs weren't touched. And Reagan was a poor steward of the unglamorous but necessary operations of the state. Wilentz notes that he presided over a period of corruption and favoritism, encouraging hostility toward government agencies and "a general disregard for oversight safeguards as among the evils of 'big government.'" In this, and in a notorious attempt to expand executive power outside the Constitution—the Iran-Contra affair—Reagan's presidency presaged that of George W. Bush.

After Reagan and the end of the Cold War, conservatism lost the ties that had bound together its disparate factions—libertarians, evangelicals, neoconservatives, Wall Street, working-class traditionalists. Without the Gipper and the Evil Empire, what was the organizing principle? In 1994, the conservative journalist David Frum surveyed the landscape and published a book called *Dead Right*. Reagan, he wrote, had offered his "Morning in America" vision, and the public had rewarded him enormously, but in failing to reduce government he had allowed the welfare state to continue infantilizing the public, weakening its moral fiber. That November, Republicans swept to power in Congress and imagined that they had been deputized by the voters to distill conservatism into its purest essence. Newt Gingrich declared, "On those things which are at the core of our philosophy and on those things where we believe we represent the vast majority of Americans, there will be no compromise." Instead of just limiting government, the Gingrich revolutionaries set out to disable it. Although the legislative reins were in their hands, these Republicans could find no governmental projects to organize their energy around. David Brooks said, "The only thing that held the coalition together was hostility to government." When the *Times Magazine* asked William Kristol what ideas he was for—in early 1995, high noon of the Gingrich Revolution—Kristol could think to mention only school choice and "shaping the culture."

At the end of that year, when the radical conservatives in the Gingrich Congress shut down the federal government, they learned that the

American public was genuinely attached to the modern state. "An anti-government philosophy turned out to be politically unpopular and fundamentally un-American," Brooks said. "People want something melioristic, they want government to do things."

Instead of governing, the Republican majority in Congress—along with right-wing authors, journalists, talk radio personalities, think tanks, and foundations—surrendered to the negative strain of modern conservatism. As political strategy, this strain went back to the Nixon era, but its philosophical roots were older and deeper. It extended back to William F. Buckley, Jr.'s mission statement, in the inaugural issue of *National Review* in 1955, that the new magazine "stands athwart history, yelling Stop"; and to Goldwater's seminal 1960 book, *The Conscience of a Conservative*, in which he wrote, "I have little interest in streamlining government or in making it more efficient, for I mean to reduce its size. I do not undertake to promote welfare, for I propose to extend freedom. My aim is not to pass laws, but to repeal them. It is not to inaugurate new programs, but to cancel old ones." By the end of the century, a movement inspired by sophisticated works such as Russell Kirk's 1953 *The Conservative Mind: From Burke to Eliot* churned out degenerate descendants with titles like *How to Talk to a Liberal (If You Must)*. Shortly after engineering President Bill Clinton's impeachment on a narrow party-line basis, Gingrich was gone.

Though conservatives were not much interested in governing, they understood the art of politics. They hadn't made much of a dent in the bureaucracy, and they had done nothing to provide universal health care coverage or arrest growing economic inequality, but they had created a political culture that was inhospitable to welfare, to an indulgent view of criminals, to high rates of taxation. They had controlled the language and moved the political parameters to the right. Back in November 1967, Buckley wrote in an essay on Ronald Reagan, "They say that his accomplishments are few, that it is only the rhetoric that is conservative. But the rhetoric is the principal thing. It precedes all action. All thoughtful action."

In 2000, George W. Bush presented himself as Reagan's heir, but he didn't come into office with Reagan's ideological commitments or his public policy goals. According to Frum, who worked as a White House speechwriter during Bush's first two years, Bush couldn't have won if he'd run as a real conservative, because the country was already moving in a new direction. Bush's goals, like Nixon's, were political. Nixon had set out to expand the Republican vote; Bush wanted to keep it from contracting. At his first meeting with Frum and other speechwriters, Bush declared, "I want to change the party"—to soften its hard edge, and make the party more hospitable to Hispanics. "It was all about positioning," Frum said, "not about confronting a new generation of problems." Frum wasn't happy; although he suspected that Bush might be right, he wanted him to govern along hard-line conservative principles.

The phrase that signaled Bush's approach was "compassionate conservatism," but it never amounted to a policy program. Within hours of the Supreme Court decision that ended the disputed Florida recount, Dick Cheney met with a group of moderate Republican senators, including Lincoln Chafee of Rhode Island. According to Chafee's new book, *Against the Tide: How a Compliant Congress Empowered a Reckless President* (Thomas Dunne), the vice president–elect gave the new order of battle: "We would seek confrontation on every front . . . The new administration would divide Americans into red and blue, and divide nations into those who stand with us or against us." Cheney's combative instincts and belief in an unfettered and secretive executive proved far more influential at the White House than Bush's campaign promise to be "a uniter, not a divider." Cheney behaved as if, notwithstanding the loss of the popular vote, conservative Republican domination could continue by sheer force of will. On domestic policy, the administration made tax cuts and privatization its highest priority; and its conduct of the war on terror broke with sixty years of relatively bipartisan and multilateralist foreign policy.

The administration's political operatives were moving in the same direction. The Republican strategist Matthew Dowd studied the 2000 results and concluded that the proportion of swing voters in America had declined from 22 to 7 percent over the previous two decades, which meant that mobilizing the party's base would be more important in 2004 than attracting independents. The strategist Karl Rove's polarizing political tactics (which brought a new level of demographic sophistication to the old formula) buried any hope of a centrist presidency before Bush's first term was half finished.

Ed Rollins said, "Rove knew his voters, he stuck to the message with consistency, he drove that base hard—and there's nothing left of it. Today, if you're not rich or Southern or born-again, the chances of your being a Republican are not great." As long as Bush and his party kept winning elections, however slim the margins, Rove's declared ambition to create a "permanent majority" seemed like the vision of a tactical genius. But it was built on two illusions: that the conservative era would stretch on indefinitely, and that politics matters more than governing. The first illusion defied history; the second was blown up in Iraq and drowned in New Orleans. David Brooks argues that these disasters discredited both neo- and compassionate conservatism in the eyes of many Republicans. "You've got to learn from the failures," Brooks told me. "But Republicans have rejected the entire attempt. For example, after Katrina, House Republicans wanted nothing to do with New Orleans. They were, like, 'We don't care about those people.'"

In its final year, the Bush administration is seen by many conservatives (along with 70 percent of Americans) to be a failure. Among true believers, there are two explanations of why this happened and what it portends. One is the purist version: Bush expanded the size of government and created huge deficits, allowed Republicans in Congress to fatten lobbyists and stuff budgets full of earmarks, tried to foist democracy on a Muslim country, failed to secure the border, and thus won the justified wrath of the American people. This account—shared by Pat Buchanan, the columnist George F. Will, and many Republicans in Congress—has the appeal of asking relatively little of conservatives. They need only to repent of their sins, rid themselves of the neoconservatives who had agitated for the Iraq invasion, and return to first principles. Buchanan said, "The conservatives need to, in Maoist terms, go back to Yenan."

The second version—call it reformist—is more painful, because it's based on the recognition that though Bush's fatal incompetence and Rove's shortsighted tactics hastened the conservative movement's demise, they didn't cause it. In this view, conservatism has a more serious problem than self-betrayal: a doctrinaire failure to adapt to new circumstances, new problems. Instead of heading back to Yenan to regroup, conservatives will have to spend some years or even decades wandering across a bleak political landscape of losing campaigns and rebranding efforts and earnest policy retreats, much as liberals did after 1968, before they can hope to reestablish dominance.

• • •

Recently, I spoke with a number of conservatives about their movement. The younger ones—say, those under fifty—uniformly subscribe to the reformist version. They are in a state of glowing revulsion at the condition of their political party. Most of them predicted that Republicans will lose the presidency this year and suffer a rout in Congress. They seemed to feel that these losses would be deserved, and suggested that if the party wins, it will be—in the words of Rich Lowry, the thirty-nine-year-old editor of *National Review*—"by default."

On April 4, a rainy day in New York, I attended Buckley's memorial Mass at St. Patrick's Cathedral with some two thousand people, an unusually large number of them women in hats and men in bow ties. George W. Rutler, the presiding priest, declared that Buckley's words helped "crack the walls of an evil empire." Secular humanism, he said, "builds little hells for man on earth . . . Communism was worse than a social tyranny because it was a theological heresy." The service reminded me of the movement's philosophical origins, in the forties and fifties, in a Catholic sense of alarm at the relativism that was rampant in American life, and an insistence on human frailty. The conservative movement began as a true counterculture; how unlikely that its gloomy creed took hold in America, the optimistic capital of modernity.

Later that day, the Manhattan Institute and National Review Institute held a forum on Buckley's legacy, at the Princeton Club. The panelists—mostly members of the Old Guard—remembered Buckley, traded Latin phrases, and exuded self-satisfaction. Roger Kimball, the coeditor of the dour cultural review *The New Criterion*, declared that conservatism imposes a philosophical duty on its adherents to enjoy life—to which George Will, not ebullient by disposition, later added, "Politics is fun, because politics involves inherently the celebration of America's first principles . . . Politics is an inherently cheerful undertaking, so be of good cheer. That is what Bill left us with." Kimball continued to roll up the score in favor of conservatives. Their reputation for being "un-fun," he said, stems partly from the fact that they are "realists" who are "a wet blanket on people who talk about things like 'the audacity of hope' and 'it takes a village,' just to pick two terms arbitrarily." The country, he said, "is still suffering from that post-Romantic assault on humanity that is summarized by the term 'the sixties.' This, too, shall pass."

Once the principled levity had died down and it came time for questions, I asked whether the conservative movement was dead. "It would be a sign of maturity if conservatives would stop using the phrase 'conservative movement,'" Will said. "This is now a center-right country, and conservatism is the default position for, I think, a stable presidential majority." Jay Nordlinger, an editor at *National Review*, added, "If it's no longer a movement, and really is mainstream, we owe a lot to Bill Buckley and Reagan." But Buckley himself had been more realistic than his eulogists. Sam Tanenhaus, the editor of the *Times Book Review* and the "Week in Review" section, who is working on a biography of Buckley, said that in his final years Buckley understood that his movement was cracking up. "He told me, 'The conservative movement lost its raison d'être with the end of Communism and never got it back.'"

Between the Mass and the forum, I had lunch with David Frum. His mood was elegiac and chastened. He now realized that in 2001, Bush had been right and he had been wrong at their first meeting: the party did need to change, but not in the way Bush went on to change it. "It wasn't a successful presidency, and that's a painful thing," Frum said. "And I was a very small, unimportant part of it, but I was a part of it, and that implies responsibility." Frum has made his peace with the fact that smaller government is no longer a basis for conservative dominance. The thesis of his new book, *Comeback: Conservatism That Can Win Again* (Doubleday), whose message Frum has been taking to Republican groups around the country, is that the party has lost the middle class by ignoring its sense of economic insecurity and continuing to wage campaigns as if the year were 1980, or 1968.

"If Republican politicians quote Reagan, their political operatives study Nixon," Frum writes. "Republicans have been reprising Nixon's 1972 campaign against McGovern for a third of a century. As the excesses of the 1960s have dwindled into history, however, the 1972 campaign has worked less and less well." He adds, "How many more elections can conservatives win by campaigning against Abbie Hoffman and Bobby Seale? Voters want solutions to the problems of today." Polls reveal that Americans favor the Democratic side on nearly every domestic issue, from Social Security and health care to education and the environment.

The all-purpose Republican solution of cutting taxes has run its course.
Frum writes, "There are things only government can do, and if we conservatives wish to be entrusted with the management of government, we
must prove that we care enough about government to manage it well."

This is a candid change of heart from a writer who, in *Dead Right*,
called Republican efforts to compete with Clinton's universal health coverage plan "cowardly." In the new book, Frum asks, "Who agreed that
conservatives should defend the dysfunctional American health system
from all criticism?" Well—he did! Frum now identifies health care as the
chief anxiety of the middle class. But governing well, in conservative
terms, doesn't mean spending more money. It means doing what neither
Reagan nor Bush did: mastering details, knowing the options, using caution—that is, taking government seriously. The policy ideas in *Comeback*
rely on the market more than on the state and are relatively small-bore,
such as a government campaign to raise awareness about the dangers of
obesity. As with most such books, the diagnosis is more convincing than
the cure.

Frum believes that the Republicans need their own equivalent of the
centrist Democratic Leadership Council, to make it safe for Republican
candidates to tell their interest groups, such as evangelical Christians,
what they don't want to hear: that they need to mute their demands if the
party is to regain a majority. At lunch, he said, "The thing I worry about
most is if the Republicans lose this election—and if you're a betting man
you have to believe they will—there will be a fundamentalist reaction.
Not religious—but the beaten party believes it just has to say it louder.
Like the Democrats after 1968." He added, "A lot of the problems in the
Republican Party will not be fixed."

I asked Frum if the movement still existed. "We'll have people formed
by the conservative movement making decisions for the next thirty to
forty years," he said. "But will they belong to a self-conscious and cohe-
sive conservative movement? I don't think so. Because their movement
did its work. The core task was to stop and reverse, to some degree, the
drift of democratic countries after the Second World War toward social
democracy. And that was done."

As we started to leave, Frum smiled. "One of Buckley's great gifts was
the gift of timing," he said. "To be twenty-five at the beginning and eighty-
two at the end! But I'm forty-seven at the end."

• • •

When I met David Brooks in Washington, he was even more scathing than Frum. Brooks had moved through every important conservative publication—*National Review*, the *Wall Street Journal* editorial page, *The Washington Times*, *The Weekly Standard*—"and now I feel estranged," he said. "I just don't feel it's exciting, I don't feel it's true, fundamentally true." In the eighties, when he was a young movement journalist, the attacks on regulation and the Soviet Union seemed "true." Now most conservatives seem incapable of even acknowledging the central issues of our moment: wage stagnation, inequality, health care, global warming. They are stuck in the past, in the dogma of limited government. Perhaps for that reason, Brooks left movement journalism and, in 2003, became a moderately conservative columnist for the *Times*. "American conservatives had one defeat, in 2006, but it wasn't a big one," he said. "The big defeat is probably coming, and then the thinking will happen. I have not yet seen the major think tanks reorient themselves, and I don't know if they can." He added, "You go to Capitol Hill—Republican senators know they're fucked. They have that sense. But they don't know what to do. There's a hunger for new policy ideas."

The Heritage Foundation website currently links to video presentations by Sean Hannity and Laura Ingraham, "challenging Americans to consider, What Would Reagan Do?" Brooks called the conservative think tanks "sclerotic," but much conservative journalism has become just as calcified and ingrown. Last year, writing in *The New Republic*, Sam Tanenhaus revealed a 1997 memo in which Buckley—who had originally hired Brooks at *National Review* on the strength of a brilliant undergraduate parody that he had written of Buckley—refused to anoint him as his heir because Brooks, a Jew, is not a "believing Christian." At *Commentary*, the neoconservative counterpart to *National Review*, the editorship was bequeathed by Norman Podhoretz, its longtime editor, to his son John, whose crude op-eds for the *New York Post* didn't measure up to *Commentary*'s intellectual past. A conservative journalist familiar with both publications said that what mattered most at the Christian *National Review* was doctrinal purity, whereas at the Jewish *Commentary* it was blood relations: "It's a question of who can you trust, and it comes down to religious fundamentals."

The orthodoxy that accompanies this kind of insularity has had serious consequences: for years, neither *National Review* nor *Commentary* was able to admit that the Iraq War was being lost. Lowry, who received the editorship from Buckley before he turned thirty, told me that he particularly regretted a 2005 cover story he'd written with the headline WE'RE WINNING. He said, "Most of the right was in lockstep with Donald Rumsfeld. We didn't want to admit we were losing and said anyone who said otherwise was a defeatist. One thing I've loved about conservatism is its keen sense of reality, and that was totally lost in 2006." Last year, *National Review* ran a cover article on global warming, which Lowry, like Brooks, Frum, and other conservatives, listed among the major issues of our time, along with wage stagnation and the breakdown of the family. Although the article, by Jim Manzi, proposed market solutions, the response among some readers, Lowry said, was "'How dare you?' A bunch of people out there don't want to hear it—they believe it's a hoax. That's the head-in-the-sand response."

A similar battle looms between traditional supply-side tax cutters and younger writers like *National Review*'s Ramesh Ponnuru, who has proposed greatly expanding the child tax credit—using tax policy not to reduce the tax burden across the board, in accord with conservative orthodoxy, but to help families. These challenges to dogma, however tentative, are being led by Republican constituencies that have begun to embrace formerly "Democratic issues." Evangelical churches are concerned about the environment; businesses worry about health care; white working-class voters are angry about income inequality. But nothing focuses the mind like the prospect of electoral disaster: last November, Lowry and Ponnuru cowrote a cover story with the headline THE COMING CATACLYSM.

It's probably not an accident that the most compelling account of the crisis was written by two conservatives who are still in their twenties and have made their careers outside movement institutions. Ross Douthat and Reihan Salam, editors at *The Atlantic Monthly*, are eager to cut loose the dead weight of the Gingrich and Bush years. In their forthcoming book, *Grand New Party: How Republicans Can Win the Working Class and Save the American Dream* (Doubleday), Douthat and Salam are writing about, if not for, what they call "Sam's Club Republicans"—members of the white working class, who are the descendants of Nixon's "northern ethnics and southern Protestants" and the Reagan Democrats of the eighties. In their analysis, America is divided between the working class (defined as those without a college education) and a "mass upper class" of the college educated, who are culturally liberal and increasingly Democratic. The New Deal, the authors acknowledge, provided a sense of security to working-class families; the upheavals of the sixties and afterward broke it down. Their emphasis is on the disintegration of working-class cohesion, which they blame on "crime, contraception, and growing economic inequality." Douthat and Salam are cultural conservatives—Douthat became a Pentecostal and then a Catholic in his teens—but they readily acknowledge the economic forces that contribute to the breakdown of families lacking the "social capital" of a college degree. Their policy proposals are an unorthodox mixture of government interventions (wage subsidies for lower-income workers) and tax reforms (Ponnuru's increased-child-credit idea, along with a revision of the tax code in favor of lower-income families). Their ultimate purpose is political: to turn as much of the working class into Sam's Club Republicans as possible. They don't acknowledge the corporate interests that are at least as Republican as Sam's Club shoppers, and that will put up a fight on many counts, potentially tearing the party apart. Nor are they prepared to accept as large a role for government as required by the deep structural problems they identify. Douthat and Salam are as personally remote from working-class America as any élite liberal; Douthat described their work to me as "a data-driven attempt at political imagination." Still, any Republican politician worried about his party's eroding base and grim prospects should make a careful study of this book.

Frum's call for national-unity conservatism and Douthat and Salam's program for "Sam's Club Republicans" are efforts to shorten the lean years for conservatives, but political ideas don't materialize on command to solve the electoral problems of one party or another. They are generated over time by huge social transformations, on the scale of what took place in the sixties and seventies. "They're not real, they're ideological constructs," Buchanan said, "and you can write columns and things like that, but they don't engage the heart. The heart was engaged by law and order. You reached into people—there was feeling."

• • •

Sam Tanenhaus summed up the 2008 race with a simple formula: Goldwater was to Reagan as McGovern is to Obama. From the ruins of Goldwater's landslide defeat in 1964, conservatives began the march that brought them fully to power sixteen years later. If Obama wins in November, it will have taken liberals thirty-six years. Tanenhaus pointed out how much of Obama's rhetoric about a "new politics" is reminiscent of McGovern's campaign, which was also directed against a bloated, corrupt establishment. In *The Making of the President 1972*, Theodore White quotes McGovern saying, "I can present liberal values in a conservative, restrained way . . . I see myself as a politician of reconciliation." That was in 1970, before McGovern was defined as the candidate of "amnesty, abortion, and acid," and he defined himself as a rigid moralist more interested in hectoring middle Americans than in inspiring them.

Obama, of course, is an entirely different personality in a different time, but the interminable primary campaign has shown his coalition to look very much like McGovern's: educated upper-income liberal voters, blacks, and the young. Nixon beat McGovern among the latter even after the Twenty-sixth Amendment lowered the voting age to eighteen; but times have changed so drastically that, according to Pew Research Center surveys, almost 60 percent of voters under thirty now identify more strongly with the Democrats, doubling the party's advantage among the young over Republicans since 2004. And the demographic work of John B. Judis and Ruy Teixeira in their 2002 book, *The Emerging Democratic Majority*, showed that the McGovern share of the electorate—minorities and educated professionals working in postindustrial jobs—is expanding far faster than the white working class. This was the original vision of a McGovern adviser named Fred Dutton, whose 1971 book, *Changing Sources of Power: American Politics in the 1970s*, cited by Perlstein, foresaw a rising "coalition of conscience and decency" among baby boomers. The new politics was an electoral disaster in 1972, but it may finally triumph in 2008.

If not, it will be because Democrats still can't win the presidency without the working-class Americans who remain the swing vote and, this year, are up for grabs more than ever. Hillary Clinton has denied Obama a lock on the nomination by securing large majorities of swing voters, beginning in New Hampshire and culminating last week in West Virginia. It took the Obama campaign months to realize that a 2008 version of the McGovern coalition will barely be sufficient to win the nomination, let alone the general election. The question is how Obama can do better with the crucial slice of the electorate that he hasn't been able to capture. Recently, he has gone from bowling in Pennsylvania and drinking Bud in Indiana to talking about his single mother, his wife's working-class roots, and his ardent patriotism on the night of his victory in North Carolina. But the problem can't be solved by symbols or rhetoric: for a forty-six-year-old black man in an expensive suit, with a Harvard law degree and a strange name, to walk into VFW halls and retirement homes and say "I'm one of you" seems both improbable and disingenuous.

The other extreme—to muse aloud among wealthy contributors, like a political anthropologist, about the values and behavior of the economically squeezed small-town voter—is even more self-defeating. Perhaps Obama's best hope is to play to his strength, which is a cool and eloquent candor, and address the question of liberal élitism as frontally as he spoke about race in Philadelphia two months ago. He would need to say, in effect, "I know I'm not exactly one of you," and then explain why this shouldn't matter—why he would be just as effective a leader for the working and middle class as his predecessors Presidents Roosevelt and Kennedy, who were élites of a different kind. Above all, Obama should absorb what the most thoughtful conservatives already know: that these voters see the economic condition of the country as inextricable from its moral condition.

Last month, I saw John McCain speak in a tiny town, nestled among the Appalachian coal hills of eastern Kentucky, called Inez. He was in the middle of his Time for Action Tour of America's "forgotten places" (including Selma, Alabama; Youngstown, Ohio; and the Lower Ninth Ward of New Orleans). It was a transparent effort to stay in the media eye and also to say, as his speechwriter Mark Salter later told me, "I'm not going to run an election like the last couple have been run, trying to grind out a narrow win by increasing the turnout of the base. I don't want to run a campaign like that because I don't want to be a president like that. I want to be your president even if you don't vote for me." As every new conservative book points out, the Bush-Rove realignment strategy would fail miserably this year anyway.

Inez is the place where Lyndon Johnson came to declare war on poverty in 1964. He sat on the porch of a ramshackle tin-roof house, which still stands (just barely) on a hillside above Route 3, looking a little like a museum of rural poverty in a county that has recently prospered because of coal. McCain was to appear in the county courthouse, on the short main street of Inez, and the middle-aged men I sat with in the second-floor courtroom all remembered Johnson's visit and had nothing but good things to say about his antipoverty programs. Kennis Maynard, the county prosecutor, a cheerful, thickset man in a blue suit, had saved enough money for law school from a job in the mines that he got with the help of a federal work program. His family was so poor that they were happy to accept government handouts of pork, canned beans, and cheese. The courthouse in which we were sitting was a New Deal project, circa 1938. Maynard, like the other men, like most of nearly all-white Martin County, is Republican—mainly, he said, because of cultural issues like abortion. But Maynard and the others said that McCain had better talk about jobs and gas prices if he wanted to keep his audience.

John Preston, who is the county's circuit court judge and also its amateur historian, Harvard-educated, with a flag pin on his lapel, said, "Obama is considered an élitist." He added, "There's a racial component, obviously, to it. Thousands of people won't publicly say it, but they won't vote for a black man—on both sides, Democrat and Republican. It won't show up in the polls, because they won't admit it. The elephant's in the room, but nobody will say it. Sad to say it, but it's true." Later, I spoke with half a dozen men eating lunch at the Pigeon Roost Dairy Bar outside town, and none of them had any trouble saying it. They announced their refusal to vote for a black man, without hesitation or apology. "He's a Muslim, isn't he?" an aging mine electrician asked. "I won't vote for a colored man. He'll put too many coloreds in jobs. Coloreds are okay—they've done well, good for them, look where they came from. But radical coloreds, no—like that Farrakhan, or that senator from New York, Rangel. There'd be riots in the streets, like the sixties." No speech, on race or élitism or anything else, would move them. Here was one part of the white working class—maybe not representative, but at least significant—and in an Obama-McCain race they would never be the swing vote. It is a brutal fact, and Obama probably shouldn't even mention it.

McCain appeared to a warm reception. I had seen him in New Hampshire, where he gave off-the-cuff remarks with vigor; when he is stuck with a script, however, he is a terrible campaigner. Looking pallid, he sounded flat, and stumbled over his lines—and yet they were effective lines, ones that Obama would do well to study. "I can't claim we come from the same background," McCain began. "I'm not the son of a coal miner. I wasn't raised by a family that made its living from the land or toiled in a mill or worked in the local schools or health clinic. I was raised in the United States Navy, and after my own naval career, I became a politician. My work isn't as hard as yours—it isn't nearly as hard as yours. I had an easier start." He paused and went on, "But you are my compatriots, my fellow Americans, and that kinship means more to me than almost any other association."

McCain mentioned Johnson's visit and the war on poverty, expressing admiration for its good intentions but rebuking its reliance on government to create jobs—rebuking it gently, without the contempt that Reagan would have used. He called for job training partnerships between business and community colleges, tax deductions for companies bringing telecommunications to rural areas. It was a moderate, reform-minded Republicanism. He didn't use any of the red-meat language that made two generations of white voters switch parties.

"McCain is not a theme guy," David Brooks said. "He reacts—he has a moral instinct, which I think is quite a good one." Other conservatives complained to me that he has no ideology at all. "Let's face it," Brooks said. "What McCain's going to do is say, 'I'm not George Bush. I'm not like the Republican Party you knew.'" Most presidential candidates move to the center once they've locked up the nomination; McCain, however, still has to try to win over the suspicious Republican right, and he recently vowed to appoint only judges who "strictly interpret" the Constitution to the bench. But pledges of fealty to his party's ideological interest groups diminish what's appealing about McCain. "Feeling fraudulent is very debilitating to him," Mark Salter said.

When McCain opened the floor for questions, a woman asked about border security. He replied, to general laughter, "This meeting is adjourned." Another woman asked him to discuss his religious faith, and McCain told a story from his imprisonment, about a generous gesture by a North Vietnamese guard one Christmas Day. I'd heard him tell the same story in New Hampshire; it seemed to be his stock answer, and he hurried through it. Other questions came, about gas prices and jobs going overseas and foreclosures and education costs, and McCain's answers—a summer federal gas tax holiday, a cut in the capital gains tax, charter schools, federal home loans, job training programs—didn't seem to move either him or his audience very much.

Members of the audience began to appeal to McCain with the old polarizing language, but he refused to take the bait. A state senator asked what he thought about Obama's recent comments on rural voters, religion, and guns. McCain turned the question around. "Let me ask you: Do you think those remarks reflect the views of constituents?"

"I think they reflect the views of someone who doesn't understand this neck of the woods," the state senator replied, to the biggest ovation of the day.

"Yes, those were élitist remarks, to say the least," McCain said quickly, walking away.

Judge Preston had a question. McCain had mentioned Clinton's vote for a million-dollar earmark for a museum in Woodstock, New York. Had he attended the concert? It was an obvious setup for a standard McCain joke, and he seemed positively embarrassed by it. "I'll give my not-so-respectful answer," he said. "I was tied up at the time."

It was a remarkably subdued performance. McCain doesn't try to stir a crowd's darker passions or its higher aspirations. He doesn't present himself as a conservative leader; he is simply a leader. His favorite book, according to Salter, is *For Whom the Bell Tolls*, because it's the story of a man who struggles nobly even though he knows the effort is doomed. McCain says to audiences, Here I am, a man in full, take me or leave me. This might be the only kind of Republican who could win in 2008.

The Hardest Vote

The New Yorker, October 13, 2008

Barbie Snodgrass had agreed to meet me at a Kentucky Fried Chicken outlet, on a strip of fast food restaurants and auto shops west of downtown Columbus, Ohio, but she didn't have much time to talk. Her shift as a receptionist at a medical clinic, which got her out of the house at six in the morning, had just ended, at three; the drive home, to a housing development in a working-class suburb south of the city, took half an hour. She then had a little more than an hour to eat, change clothes, let the dog out, check up on her sister's two teenage daughters—Sierra and Ashley, who were under her care—and then drive back into Columbus, where she worked the evening shift cleaning the studios of a local television station, and where her day ended, at ten. She also worked some weekends. She was forty-two, single, overweight, and suffering from stomach pains.

Snodgrass sat down at my table and refused the offer of a soft drink. She was wearing a drab ensemble of gray cotton sweatpants and a loose-fitting pale yellow knit top, and her brown hair fell in bangs just above her eyes. I asked for her thoughts about the presidential candidates, and she said, "Someone who makes two hundred or three hundred thousand a year, who eats a regular meal, who doesn't have to struggle, who doesn't worry if the lights are going to be turned out—if he doesn't walk in your shoes, he can't understand."

In Snodgrass's shoes, it hardly made sense to draw a paycheck. "You're working for what?" she asked. She hadn't finished college, and the two jobs that kept her "constantly moving" brought in a little more than forty thousand dollars a year, but after the mortgage (a thousand a month), car payments (three hundred and fifty), levies for supplies at the girls' public high school, fuel, electricity, stomach medicine, and a hundred dollars' worth of groceries each week (down from eight bags to four at Kroger's supermarket, because of inflation) there was basically nothing left to spend. She could cut corners—go out for a McDonald's Dollar Meal instead of spending seven dollars on a bag of potatoes and cooking at home. But that meant the end of any kind of family life for her nieces.

"These days, you have to struggle," she said. "As a kid, I used to be able to go to the movies or to the zoo. Now you can't take your children to the zoo or go to the movies, because you've got to think how you're going to put food on the table." Snodgrass's parents had raised four children on two modest incomes, without the ceaseless stress that she was enduring. But the two-parent family was now available only to the "very privileged." She said that she had ten good friends; eight of them were childless or, like her, unmarried with kids. "That's who's middle-class now," she said. "Two parents, two kids? That's over. People looked out for me. These kids nowadays don't have nobody to look out for them. You're one week away from (a) losing your job, or (b) not having a paycheck."

Snodgrass, who has always voted Democratic, was paying close attention to the presidential campaign—she had taped both candidates' convention speeches, and watched them when she had time—but her faith in politicians was somewhere close to zero. She wanted a leader who would watch out for people in the "middle class," people like her who had no one on their side. "I think McCain is going to be just like Bush the next eight years," she said. "I don't see how it's going to change." To her, Sarah Palin, a working mother close to her own age, felt more like a token choice than like a kindred spirit. "I think McCain picked her so women can relate to her, not because she's the best person for the job," Snodgrass said. "She's more of a show for the American family." Hillary Clinton had been better, but even she couldn't fully apprehend Barbie Snodgrass's predicament.

She remained uninspired by Barack Obama. His convention speech had gone into detail about his policy proposals on matters like the economy and health care, which seemed tailored to attract a voter like Snodgrass, but they filled her with suspicion. His promise to rescind the Bush tax cuts for wealthier Americans struck her as incredible: "How many people do you know who make two hundred and fifty thousand dollars? What is that, five percent of the United States? That's a joke! If he starts at a hundred thousand, I might listen. Two hundred fifty—that's to me like people who hit the lottery." In fact, only 2 percent of Americans make more than a quarter of a million dollars a year, but that group earns 12 percent of the national income. Nonetheless, the circumstances of Snodgrass's life made it impossible for her to imagine that there could possibly be enough taxable money in Obama's upper-income category—which meant that he was being dishonest, and that she would eventually be the one to pay. "He'll keep going down, and when it's to people who make forty-five or fifty thousand it's going to hit me," she said. "I'd have to sell my home and live in a five-hundred-dollar-a-month apartment with gangbangers out in my yard, and I'd be scared to death to leave my house."

Snodgrass reacted with equal skepticism to Obama's proposal for expanding health care. "It scares the heck out of me," she said. "If the employers are going to cover more, we're going to get less in our raises. My raise every year is like a cost-of-living raise. How are they going to be able to give me more money?" The margin of error in her life was so slim, she felt, that any attempt to improve lives with ambitious new programs could only end up harming her. Obama's idealistic language left Snodgrass cold. "He's not saying to me how he's going to make my life better," she said. She wanted to hear exactly how the next president was going to remove some of the tremendous financial weight bearing down on her—reduce gas prices, cut the cost of medicine—not in the distant future but right away. A friend of hers who worked three jobs refused to support Obama on the theory that he was a Muslim, but Snodgrass said that it didn't matter to her what race or religion the next president was, nor did the ugly tactics of the campaign have any effect other than to disgust her. What mattered was "your daily life, your daily day, job, family, what you do that keeps you from robbing the video store down the street."

Snodgrass sat talking for much longer than she had initially offered; by the end, her words tumbled out in a plaintive rush, as if under some inner pressure. "You want somebody there who's going to take care of us," she said. "I'm very scared about who they put in there, because it's either going to get a lot worse than it is or it's going to keep going where it is, which is bad." She almost gasped. "Just give us a break. There's no reprieve. No reprieve."

• • •

Until the mid-seventies, the white working class—the heart of the New Deal coalition—voted largely Democratic. Since the Carter years, the percentages have declined from sixty to forty, and this shift has roughly coincided with the long hold of the Republican Party on the White House. The white working class—a group that often speaks of itself, and is spoken of, as forgotten, marginalized, even despised—is the golden key to political power in America, and it voted overwhelmingly for George W. Bush twice, by 17 percent in 2000 and 23 percent in 2004. Thomas Frank's 2004 book *What's the Matter with Kansas?* directed its indignation at the baffling phenomenon of millions of Americans voting year after year against their economic self-interest. He concluded that the Republican Party had tricked working people with a relentless propaganda campaign based on religion and morality, while Democrats had abandoned these voters to their economic masters by moving to the soft center of the political spectrum. Frank's book remains the leading polemic about the white reaction—the title alone has, for many liberals, become shorthand for the conventional wisdom—but it is hobbled by the condescending argument that tens of millions of Americans have become victims of a "carefully cultivated derangement," or are simply stupid.

Last year, four sociologists at the University of Arizona, led by Lane Kenworthy, released a paper that complicates Frank's thesis. Their study followed the voting behavior of the 45 percent of white Americans who identify themselves as working-class. Mining electoral data from the General Social Survey, they found that the decline in white working-class support for Democrats occurred in one period—from the mid-seventies until the early nineties, with a brief lull in the early eighties—and has remained well below 50 percent ever since. But they concluded that social issues like abortion, guns, religion, and even (outside the South) race had little to do with the shift. Instead, according to their data, it was based on a judgment that—during years in which industrial jobs went overseas, unions practically vanished, and working-class incomes stagnated—the Democratic Party was no longer much help to them. "Beginning in the mid- to late 1970s, there was increasing reason for working-class whites to question whether the Democrats were still better than the Republicans at promoting their material well-being," the study's authors write.

Working-class whites, their fortunes falling, began to embrace the anti-government, low-tax rhetoric of the conservative movement. During Clinton's presidency, the downward economic spiral of these Americans was arrested, but by then their identification with the Democrats had eroded. Having earlier moved to the right for economic reasons, the Arizona study concluded, the working class stayed there because of the rising prominence of social issues—Thomas Frank's argument. But the Democrats fundamentally lost the white working class because these voters no longer believed the party's central tenet—that government could restore a sense of economic security.

Such a change in party allegiance across a vast section of the electorate takes decades to achieve, and to undo. But this year should mark the beginning of a reverse migration. When will the class war ever finally drown out the culture war, if not in 2008? Under Republican rule in Washington, wages have stayed flat while income inequality has increased; the numbers of uninsured have soared; unemployment recently passed 6 percent, its highest level since the early 1990s; gas and heating oil prices have doubled, while basic food prices have gone up by 50 percent; and the country's financial system has come closer to collapse than at any moment since 1929. More profoundly, Republican dogma no longer offers convincing solutions, and in some cases it doesn't even acknowledge the problems. (Income inequality has long been considered a nonissue in conservative free-market circles.) The question that Ronald Reagan asked voters to such devastating effect in 1980, when the white working class began turning away from Democrats—"Are you better off than you were four years ago?"—should, in theory, produce an equal and opposite effect this year.

This is particularly true in big, aging, economically battered swing states like Michigan, where unemployment is nearly 9 percent, and Ohio, where residents told me that a whole generation of young people is leaving the state to seek higher education and work elsewhere. A man in Brown County, along the Ohio River in the southwestern part of the state, said that a year ago there was one foreclosure notice in the local paper each week; now the number is six or eight, and the listings for the week of September 12 announced fifty-three foreclosure sales in a county with only fifteen thousand households. In the town of Wilmington, outside Dayton, a DHL facility with eight thousand workers—a third of the area's population—is likely to close. On September 9, the day I flew into Cincinnati, a woman named Marla Bell, attending an Obama rally near Dayton, told National Public Radio, "It almost feels like it's a dying state."

The next day, Governor Ted Strickland, a Democrat who remains popular in Ohio, announced a budget shortfall that would require painful spending cuts across the board. The state's budget director, Pari Sabety, told me, "There are a lot more part-time jobs, jobs without benefits, jobs that require a broader social safety net than we currently have. We are not creating high-value jobs at a rate that can absorb people who are losing the high-value jobs of the old economy." The economic crisis, she went on, is so grave that it has created room for a renewed discussion about the role of government in people's lives. "Here's the opportunity before us. What's happening is a slow-motion Katrina to economies like ours. I feel like we are where FDR was."

Obama has had particular trouble with the prized demographic group that once delivered the presidency to Roosevelt and his successors. Anecdotally, and in polls, unusually large numbers of working-class voters seem to remain undecided or determined to sit the election out, as if they couldn't bring themselves to vote Republican this year but couldn't fathom taking a chance on Obama. Roger Catt, a retired farmer and warehouse worker, who lives in a small town near Eau Claire, Wisconsin, characterized the choice this way: "McCain is more of the same, and Obama is the end of life as we know it."

Gloria Fauss, the longtime political director in Ohio for the Service Employees International Union, or SEIU, which backs Obama, said, "I'm very worried. The conventional wisdom is that the economy will trump this year. I'm not so sure. The economy may override social issues this year and people still might not vote for Obama." Fauss has spent years studying the results of polls and focus groups among Ohio voters, and she has learned that judgments about character and values can be decisive even among those who rate jobs and health care as more important than abortion. "You can't make the assumption that because people are suffering economically and the last eight years have been downhill and things are very bleak for them—you can't make the assumption they'll vote Democratic. There's just no basis for that."

Obama understands that he is an imperfect vehicle for an already difficult message. In April, at the San Francisco fund-raiser where he damaged himself with working-class whites by delivering a speech connecting their "bitter" outlook to guns, religion, bigotry, and xenophobia, Obama also described the situation of voters like Barbie Snodgrass acutely. "In a lot of these communities in big industrial states like Ohio and Pennsylvania, people have been beaten down so long," he said. "They feel so betrayed by government that when they hear a pitch that is premised on not being cynical about government, then a part of them just doesn't buy it. And when it's delivered by—it's true that when it's delivered by a forty-six-year-old black man named Barack Obama, then that adds another layer of skepticism."

During the first presidential debate, Obama spoke directly to "middle-class" economic anxieties several times, and he later attacked McCain for never even using the word. But Obama's middle class has no face, no name, no story. Even as he becomes more specific on policy, partly in response to criticism, he still has trouble making a human connection. Bill Clinton could always employ the drawl and roguish charm of Bubba to let the working class know he was one of them, but Obama's life story is based on upward mobility, on transcending his complex origins. There's no readily apparent cultural identity he can fall back on—no folksy or streetwise manner he can assume—that won't threaten more white voters than it attracts.

Gabe Kramer, the SEIU's chief of staff in Columbus, told me, "You talk to people about the issues and the issues resonate. But what you hear people talking about on the street and on TV and radio is the other things. Is Obama like us? Does Obama share our experience of the world? Which is not the same thing as racism, but overlaps with it." Obama, Kramer added, is "very good at talking to professionals—people who care about policy—and comes across as judicious, careful, thoughtful. But he has a harder time talking about them in a way working-class white Ohioans can relate to."

Glouster, a coal mining town with a population of fewer than two thousand (and falling), lies hidden amid the gentle slopes and thick woods of southeastern Ohio's Appalachian hills. If the state is dying, Glouster was long ago left for dead. Over the past few decades, it has lost its Baptist church, grocery store, railroad depot, parking meters, four car dealerships, ten of its dozen bars, and—crucially—all but one of its deep mines. It's become the kind of town where several generations of white families live on welfare, and marijuana is the local cash crop. I was given a tour by Bob Cotter, who is seventy-four, and Pete Morris, seventy-one, both retired from the post office. We walked in a warm drizzle along Main Street, which was nearly deserted, with a few parked cars and no pedestrians. Half the storefronts were shuttered, although a local citizens' group had arranged hand-painted furniture and traditional quilts in the show windows of some of the vacant stores. It looked as if nothing had been built since the fifties. In the middle of town stood a prominent three-story brick building with the words SAM & ELLEN'S WONDER BAR—HOME OF THE "WONDER DOG" painted across an exposed side. Morris had once owned the bar before selling it to his cousin in 1971; now it was boarded up. Farther down the street, a hotel, a restaurant, and a two-lane bowling alley had been demolished, leaving a weed-strewn lot.

Every morning at seven, Cotter and Morris had coffee at Bonnie's Home Cooking, on Main Street across from the gas station. The menu was scrawled in Magic Marker across a whiteboard, and almost nothing cost more than five dollars. On the morning I visited, a dozen men and women came in for their coffee and eggs. One of them, a retired union coal miner, was identified to me as if he were a rare species of bird. Three people, including Morris, expressed reluctant support for Obama. The nine or ten others were roughly split between voting McCain and sitting it out.

Dave Herbert was a stocky, talkative building contractor in an Ohio State athletic jersey. At thirty-eight, he considerably lowered the average age in Bonnie's. "I'm self-employed," he said. "I can't afford to be a Democrat." Herbert was a devoted viewer of Fox News and talked in fluent sound bites about McCain's post-convention "bounce" and Sarah Palin's "executive experience." At one point, he had doubted that Obama stood a chance in Glouster. "From Bob and Pete's generation there are a lot of racists—not out-and-out, but I thought there was so much racism here that Obama'd never win." Then he heard a man who freely used the "*n* word" declare his support for Obama: "That blew my theory out of the water."

A maintenance man at the nearby high school, who declined to give his name, said that he had been undecided until McCain selected Palin to be his running mate, which swung his support to Obama.

"So you're a sexist more than a racist," Herbert joked.

"I just think the guy Obama picked would do better if he got assassinated than McCain's if he died of frickin' old age in office," the maintenance man said.

Four women of retirement age were sitting at the next table. All of them spoke warmly of Palin. "She'd fit right in with us," Greta Jennice said. "We should invite her over." None had a good word to say about Obama. "I think he's a radical," a white-haired woman who wouldn't give her name said. "The church he went to, the people he associated with. You don't see the media digging into that."

"I don't know anyone who's for Obama," said Jennice, a Democrat who supported Hillary Clinton and who won't vote in November.

"If they are, they don't say it, because it would be unpopular," an elderly former teacher named Marcella said. That had not been true of Bill Clinton, Al Gore, or John Kerry, she added.

"I think the party-line Democrats are having a hard time with Obama," Bobbie Dunham, a retired fourth grade teacher, told me. When I asked if Obama's health care plan wouldn't be a good thing for people in Glouster, she said, "I'll believe it when I see it. If it's actually happening, I'd say that's good." But she and the others had far more complaints about locals freeloading off public assistance than about the health insurance industry and corporations. Dunham declared her intention to write in a vote for either Snoopy or T. Boone Pickens. "I'm not going to vote for a Republican—they've had their chance for the last eight years and they've screwed it up," she said. "But I really just don't trust Obama. He only says half-truths. He calls himself a Christian, but he only became one to run for office. He calls himself a black, but he's two-thirds Arab."

I asked where she had learned that.

"On the Internet."

In 2002, John B. Judis and Ruy Teixeira published *The Emerging Democratic Majority*, a prophecy of Democratic political success based on the growing electoral clout of professionals, minorities, young people, and women. Although they emphasized that the Democrats couldn't ignore the white working class, they were essentially sketching a new politics that could win without it.

Yet during the long Democratic primary fight it was precisely the white working class that kept denying Obama a lock on the nomination. The problem first became manifest in New Hampshire, a state that much of the media declared in advance to be the end of the road for Clinton. Two days after her victory, Andrew Kohut, of the Pew Research Center, published an op-ed in the *Times* about the failure of polls to predict the outcome. He had a theory: undetected racism among working-class whites. Clinton, he noted, beat Obama among whites with family incomes under fifty thousand dollars and also among those who hadn't attended college. "Poorer, less well-educated white people refuse surveys more often than affluent, better-educated whites," Kohut wrote. "Polls generally adjust their samples for this tendency. But here's the problem: these whites who do not respond to surveys tend to have more unfavorable views of blacks than respondents who do the interviews." This statistical glitch is different from the Bradley Effect, named for the black mayor of Los Angeles, Tom Bradley, who lost the California governorship in 1982 despite polls that had showed him in the lead, apparently because a small percentage of respondents would rather lie to a pollster than admit to opposing a candidate on the ground of his race. Still, the Bradley Effect and the Kohut Lacuna produce the same conclusion: a black candidate is likely to fare worse than pre-election polls would suggest.

By the spring, after Ohio, Texas, and Pennsylvania, polls showed Obama getting trounced two to one or more among less educated, lower-income whites. The numbers were so stark that they inspired Clinton—whom conservative pundits had long condemned as a symbol of everything hateful to red-state America—to make herself over into a shot-and-a-beer gal. Even when Obama's eventual victory seemed certain, he was crushed by forty-one and thirty-five percentage points in West Virginia and Kentucky—unheard-of margins for the party front-runner late in the primaries. By then, his campaign had begun to change its tactics, making the candidate's oratory less lofty and putting him among smaller groups, in bowling alleys and veterans' halls.

Yet the resistance remained. In April, I traveled to Inez, a town in eastern Kentucky, where McCain was scheduled to speak at the county courthouse. Afterward, I noticed a group of Clinton supporters holding signs across the tiny town's main road, next to the Straight Talk Express.

I approached a man wearing a button that said HILLARY: SMART CHOICE. He was a retired state employee named J. K. Patrick.

"East of Lexington, she'll carry seventy percent of the primary vote," Patrick said. "She could win the general election in Kentucky. Obama couldn't win." Why not? "Race. I've talked to people—a woman who helped run county elections last year. She said she wouldn't vote for a black man." He added, "There's a lot of white people that just wouldn't vote for a colored person. Especially older people." Indeed, no one among the two dozen people I talked to in Inez would even consider voting for Obama. His name often evoked a sharp racial hostility that was expressed without hesitation or apology.

These were not views that many Americans had been willing to reveal to reporters. For obvious reasons, neither Obama nor McCain wants to address the conjunction of race and class in this election. The national press corps—which more and more confines its political coverage to politicians, campaign officials, strategists, and itself—has often discussed the role of race in the campaign, but the conversation is inevitably softened by euphemism. Americans accustomed to discussing race politely, or not at all, might follow the campaign without a real sense of the potency of skin color.

Patrick himself feared that Obama's race would threaten his own security and well-being. He said that it would be only natural for a black president to avenge the historical wrongs that his people had suffered at the hands of whites. "I really don't want an African American as president," he said. "I think he would put too many minorities in positions over the white race. That's my opinion."

Trade unionists in the Obama campaign know better than anyone that their candidate is not an easy sell with the working class, including some of their own members. This summer, the Wisconsin AFL-CIO sent out a brochure offering "Straight Answers to Real Questions . . . About Barack Obama": Is he a Christian? Was he sworn in on the Bible? Was he born in America? Does he place his hand over his heart when he says the pledge? The SEIU, whose membership includes prison workers, put out a flyer in Ohio that insisted, "Barack Obama Won't Take Away Your Gun . . . but John McCain Will Take Away Your Union."

Lisa Hetrick, a registered nurse and the secretary-treasurer at the SEIU's regional headquarters in Columbus, fumed that her son was supporting McCain because of national security, and that her husband was wobbling because of firearms. Like everyone else at the office, Hetrick had a story about a racist colleague, relative, or friend. "Oh God, it's terrible," she said. "I don't know what we're going to do! They're rednecks." She mentioned a prison worker and union member down in Chillicothe who, four years ago, had berated her for not enlisting him and his colleagues to volunteer for Kerry; when she made sure to call him this time, he told her that he wouldn't work for Obama, and she understood the reason to be race.

Hetrick put me in touch with Tom Guyer, Jr., a parole officer in Lorain, on Lake Erie. A Democrat with "Republican views" about some issues and a fondness for Bill O'Reilly, Guyer confessed to being undecided. He had no enthusiasm for McCain or Palin, but, he said, "The more I hear about Obama and some of his—I don't know if character is the right way to describe it, but maybe he's not ready to lead." This idea had been the theme of McCain's August campaign ads. Guyer brought up something that he had just heard on the radio. Three days earlier, on September 7, in an interview with George Stephanopoulos on the ABC program *This Week*, Obama had said, "You're absolutely right that John McCain has not talked about my Muslim faith." From the context, it was clear that Obama was simply compressing "the idea that my faith is Muslim" into fewer words, but for anyone already harboring doubts the phrase was suspect, and Guyer wondered why Obama would say such a thing.

One evening, in the basement of SEIU headquarters, I met a group of members—nursing home workers, janitors, hospital staff—who had just returned from canvassing unionists door to door in mixed-race Columbus neighborhoods. Their score had been encouraging: out of a hundred and six contacts that day, sixty-nine had been solidly for Obama and only seven solidly against. They told me that race hardly ever came up, but other sensitive matters that might stand in for race sometimes did. Jacynth Stewart, a Caribbean-born woman who had come from New York, where she is a food service worker at Beth Israel Medical Center, to help the Ohio campaign, encountered one woman who believed that Obama was Muslim. "Didn't you see 'Obama Revealed' on CNN Sunday night?" Stewart asked, and then she explained Obama's life story—the Kenyan father he hardly knew, the white mother from Kansas. After ten minutes, the woman at the door declared that she would vote for Obama.

Another woman had read in a mass e-mail that Obama wouldn't allow the American flag to be displayed on the tail of Air Force One. She was harder to win over.

In the static-filled bedlam of viral e-mails, cable news square-offs, mangled media clips, fake-news websites, political ads, and malicious rumors, with a new lie popping up somewhere every hour, the Obama campaign faces the nearly impossible task of putting out stories before they spread across a political landscape that is often dry tinder for them. In Eau Claire, Tom Giffey, the editorial page editor at the *Leader-Telegram*, described the profusion of cut-and-paste e-mails that his page has received during the campaign. "In the old days, there were Republican or Democratic newspapers, but there was more of a level playing field and both sides had to argue from the same facts," Giffey said. "Now we're in an age when you can simply reinforce your own viewpoints. And it's hard to have a discussion of the facts when you're dealing with two separate sets of facts—two sets of talking points that came down from on high. With the Internet, all of us were going to be content producers, but it's become an echo chamber."

As Dave Herbert, the building contractor at Bonnie's Home Cooking, put it, "Partisanship has crept into every crease in this country." In 2008, a customer at a breakfast spot in Appalachia, or a worker at a union office in Columbus, is able to repeat the latest dubious campaign sound bites within days, if not hours. Everyone hates the media, and everyone sounds like a talking head.

One night in Glouster, sixteen people gathered in the modest living room of an elderly woman named Helen Walker, whom everyone called Babe. Walker had invited her friends and neighbors over to meet the Obama organizer in the area—a young woman from Arizona named Kristin Gwinn. It was clear that not all of the guests were wholeheartedly committed to the cause. Pete Morris was there because Bob Cotter had asked him to come, and Bob Cotter was there because Babe Walker had asked him to explain to the organizer why he wouldn't vote in November.

"I think the Democratic Party has kind of walked away from me," Cotter said. The issue that had alienated him from his party was its refusal to take a strong stand against illegal immigration. "It is not just Obama," he went on. "The élite of the Democratic Party, the Kennedys, the Clintons, they're pushing this thing." Cotter had contacted everyone from Howard Dean, the Democratic Party chairman, to the Athens County Democratic Party about the cost of illegal immigration to the country, without satisfaction: "Hell, nobody cares."

Gwinn, the organizer, responded earnestly, "The fact that there are two hundred staffers like me out here having this conversation with you means somebody cares. And I'll have this conversation with you every day, if you want."

Cotter said that abstaining in November still felt like his most potent option. "How are we going to get them to pay attention to us, if we don't send a message?" he asked.

Travis Post, a gangly twenty-two-year-old, mentioned that he had worked with immigrants on a landscaping crew. "These are human beings you're talking about," he said. "They come here and work hard seeking a better life just like our ancestors did. For us just to send them back? That'll never work."

"There are a lot of other things affecting your friends and neighbors here in Glouster," the organizer told Cotter. "If people who typically vote Democratic don't vote at all, we're handing this election to John McCain."

"I sent three letters to Howard Dean," Cotter said. They had gone unanswered. "The party wants my money and my vote. After that, they don't care. I think the Democrats are walking away from us people here." Illegal immigrants were rare in southeast Ohio, a sort of phantom menace; Cotter's awareness of the issue had mainly come through the media. Cotter, a mild, self-deprecating man, said with a chuckle, "I'm going to vote for Lou Dobbs, that's who I'm going to vote for. Anyway, that's my view. Maybe I'm just a turd in the punch bowl tonight."

Later, Cotter told me that he was a lifelong Democrat. "I do have liberal views," he said. "I think one of these days health care is going to have to be covered by the government. None of us want to see somebody lying out on the curb dying. Hillary was ahead of her time." He had grown up on stories of how the New Deal had saved his family, who were miners. "I can remember the hard times, I can remember the things the Democrats have done for the working people. I can remember when rent was ten dollars a month and my parents lay awake in bed wondering how we were going to pay for it. Where do people like me go? I don't think anybody cares what we think. I just wish our party would pay more attention to people down here in the grass roots."

As the guests drank sodas and ate pigs in a blanket in Babe Walker's living room, Gwinn asked for volunteers to make phone calls and go door to door. There were not many takers. "Local validators are very important," she said, with urgency. "A lot of people are secretly for Barack, but they're afraid to go public. You know everyone in this town. So if there's anybody out there with misinformation, you have to find them and say, 'It's not true. He's not a Muslim.'" Seeing an Obama sign in a neighbor's yard could make a huge difference in a place like Glouster, she said.

As I drove around southern Ohio, I saw only half a dozen Obama yard signs. Some people told me that the campaign's state headquarters had been slow to get them out to the far-flung counties; it was as if they were afraid that the signs would be torn down or defaced.

Babe Walker agreed to make phone calls, as long as she didn't have to say "ratty things" about McCain.

"Barack's father was from where? Kenya?" a seventy-one-year-old woman named Karla Cominsky suddenly asked. "Would that be any part of the world that was part of slavery?"

Gwinn explained that Obama had grown up mainly in Hawaii.

"My great-great-grandfather and grandmother came here from Morgan County," Cominsky continued. "And guess who they brought with them? A little slave girl named Dinah. She was buried in the family plot. They felt she was one of the family."

A campaign intern from Ohio University, in the nearby town of Athens, explained, "Most slaves came from western Africa, where the ships could just take them and go. Kenya's from the eastern part."

There was an awkward silence: the point of the woman's story had not been immediately clear. Afterward, it occurred to me that this was how people in towns like Glouster were accustoming themselves to the thought of a black president.

With the media coverage a cacophonous standoff, and organizations like unions vanishing year by year, the Democratic skeptics in Ohio needed someone they knew and trusted to vouch for Obama. At SEIU headquarters, I spoke with Donna Steele, a home health aide working on the

Obama campaign, about how she would make the case to Barbie Snodgrass. She said, "I've been where she is. I know exactly what it's like." A few years ago, Steele had been working in the homes of two separate clients, sixteen hours a day, seven days a week, sometimes past midnight. "I didn't know what day it was. I was numb. I fell asleep at traffic lights on my way home—woke up when someone honked." Steele, who had soft, startled pale blue eyes and a frizzy reddish-blond perm, described the "weird spiral" into which she descended: "You're afraid of change, you just keep doing what you've been doing. You're afraid if you do anything different, things will get worse. You get so negative that you don't want anything to change—you think everything would be worse than this. You don't want anything to rock the boat. One false move and you're down." Eventually, she said, this mentality would make Snodgrass physically sick.

Steele went on, "I'd tell her she doesn't have to be alone. There's other people who've been down the same road. She just needs to look at the issues and it's real simple. 'What do you got to lose? What are you doing now? Voting for Obama and pulling that lever isn't going to make you any less tired than you was before.'" With McCain, health benefits would be taxed and oil prices would go up, whereas with Obama, "I think gas prices are going to miraculously go down because of his policies." Steele used almost mystical terms to describe the process by which Obama could transform Snodgrass's life. Her language was not so different from that of conservative Christians, except that Steele's community of believers was organized around class, not religion. "If she doesn't have some infrastructure"—like a union—"that can touch her, she doesn't have a chance," Steele said. "She's afraid of change, but if she doesn't demand change she's not going to make it. When something good happens, faith has a positive effect, the aura of it. It's called hope, faith, and it's change, and you get enough people together and it's massive change."

One day in Athens, I met Latisha Price. She was a big-boned blonde of thirty-seven, with a raw complexion, an Appalachian twang, and a forthright, vulnerable manner. "I come from a very bad background," she said within minutes of meeting me. Her mother had been an alcoholic, and Price had grown up in a series of foster homes, attending fourteen different schools. From the age of fifteen, she had been on her own, falling in with a series of abusive men, about whom she didn't want to say much. At twenty, she got a job in a nursing home; she still works there, as a cook and a nursing assistant.

"I noticed the union people would stand up for themselves," she recalled of her early days on the job. "And they seemed to be like a small family, a voice. I never had that. That's how I got active, and got so gutsy and eager to always jump in—I learned that from the union. When I first started, I was like a little mouse in the corner because I had so much drama in my life. I was too caught up in staying alive." Price, who now lives on a farm with her boyfriend, thirty guns, and every kind of domestic animal except pigs, runs the SEIU's Obama office in Athens, with two graduates of Smith College working for her.

Price and I drove down Route 33 from Athens, into Meigs County and a town called Pomeroy, which once had been a loading dock for coal barges and now lay prostrate and blighted along the Ohio River. Across the river was West Virginia. Insofar as Price had a hometown, Pomeroy was it.

"Meigs County is one of the worst," Price said as we drove. "We're going to a racist area—I won't lie to you. I have heard, pardon my French, 'Get the fuck off my porch, I'm not voting for no nigger.'" A few days earlier, she had twice been chased away by dogs. Price canvassed for Obama alone day after day, with a can of Mace in the car. She had learned not to wear an Obama T-shirt. People didn't react well—they seemed to take it as someone telling them whom to vote for.

She parked on a street that ran along the foot of the rock face looming over Pomeroy. It was early afternoon. There was no sign of life on the street except for two boxers in a yard, unleashed and barking at us. Price told me that their collars would register a shock if the dogs crossed a buried wire.

"I'm not scared of my hometown," Price said. "I'm a pretty tough girl. Gotta be."

She had a list of voters—Republicans, Democrats, and independents—and we began to go door to door. Some of the residences were boarded shut, some were trailers with appliances lying out front. One or two were large, lavishly decaying houses with overgrown gardens. A front porch was sealed off by fallen branches.

A middle-aged woman in a nightdress peered out of a screen door. Price began her pitch.

"If the election was held today, have you decided who you'll vote for?"

The woman hesitated, then turned away to speak to someone inside. A man's voice called out, "We're not voting this year."

Price noted this on her sheet and thanked the woman.

She didn't leave the sidewalk to speak to the owner of the two snarling dogs. He said that he would probably vote for McCain, because he was a veteran. A shirtless young man in his underwear, who seemed to have just woken up, said that he was an Obama supporter and knew a few others. There was an AIDS ribbon tattooed on his right shoulder. "The ignorant ones that don't vote, they say Obama's a nigger and he's going to be assassinated," the young man said. "That is classic Meigs County." Farther down the street, two women and a little girl—three generations of a family—were getting out of a car. The grandmother said that she was undecided. She thought that McCain was wrong on the war, but she wasn't sure about Obama. Price left her with some literature and her phone number.

At the door of a trailer, Price knocked, then knocked again. Finally, the screen door opened a few inches. A white-haired, white-skinned ghost of an old woman identified herself as Betty.

"If the election was held today, have you decided who you'll vote for?"

"'Bama."

Recently, people in Ohio have told me that voters there have started to shift toward Obama. Gabe Kramer, of the SEIU, said that, after the first presidential debate and amid the financial crisis, union members seemed to find Obama's ideas and manner more persuasive than before. But even if Obama wins he will still have to overcome the deep skepticism of struggling Americans. For Barbie Snodgrass, who has a modest amount of stock in a retirement plan, the meltdown has turned this election into a make-or-break one, tipping her away from McCain without convincing her that she can trust Obama. "I'm going to have to pray to the holy gods that whoever I vote for is going to be honest and try to get us out of this mess," she said.

In Pomeroy, it had been a relatively good afternoon. As we drove back to Athens, Price said, "This job is a challenge, and I like that, but it's also sad and depressing. You see all these poor people that don't have anything, but they're still supporting the wrong party that's the reason they don't have anything. I've canvassed single mothers with three kids, and they still don't see what's wrong with the Republican Party." She thought for a moment. "Obama's one of us," she said. "He comes from a blue-collar family. But people don't really see that."

The New Liberalism

The New Yorker, November 17, 2008

In September 1932, Franklin Delano Roosevelt, the Democratic nominee for president, was asked by a reporter for his view of the job that he was seeking. "The presidency is not merely an administrative office," Roosevelt said. "That's the least of it. It is more than an engineering job, efficient or inefficient. It is preeminently a place of moral leadership. All our great presidents were leaders of thought at times when certain historic ideas in the life of the nation had to be clarified." He went down the list of what we would now call transformative presidents: Washington, Jefferson, Jackson, Lincoln, Theodore Roosevelt, Wilson. (He also included Grover Cleveland, who hasn't aged as well.) Then Roosevelt asked, "Isn't that what the office is, a superb opportunity for reapplying—applying in new conditions—the simple rules of human conduct we always go back to? I stress the modern application, because we are always moving on; the technical and economic environment changes, and never so quickly as now. Without leadership alert and sensitive to change, we are bogged up or lose our way, as we have lost it in the past decade."

When the reporter pressed Roosevelt to offer a vision of his own historical opportunity, he gave two answers. First, he said, America needed "someone whose interests are not special but general, someone who can understand and treat the country as a whole. For as much as anything it needs to be reaffirmed at this juncture that the United States is one organic entity, that no interest, no class, no section, is either separate or supreme above the interests of all." But Roosevelt didn't limit himself to the benign self-portrait of a unifying president. "Moral leadership" had a philosophical component: he was, he said, "a liberal." The election of 1932 arrived at one of those recurring moments when "the general problems of civilization change in such a way that new difficulties of adjustment are presented to government." As opposed to a conservative or a radical, Roosevelt concluded, a liberal "recognizes the need of new machinery" but also "works to control the processes of change, to the end that the break with the old pattern may not be too violent."

That November, Roosevelt defeated President Herbert Hoover in a landslide. His election ended an age of conservative Republican rule, created a Democratic coalition that endured for the next four decades, and fundamentally changed the American idea of the relationship between citizen and state. On March 4, 1933, Roosevelt was inaugurated under a bleak sky, at the darkest hour of the Great Depression, with banks across the country failing, hundreds of thousands of homes and farms foreclosed, and a quarter of Americans out of work.

In defining his idea of the presidency, Roosevelt had left himself considerable room for maneuvering. His campaign slogan of a "new deal" promised change, but to different observers this meant wildly different things, from a planned economy to a balanced budget. "Roosevelt arrived in Washington with no firm commitments, apart from his promise to 'try something,'" the *Times* editorialist Adam Cohen writes in his forthcoming book, *Nothing to Fear: FDR's Inner Circle and the Hundred Days That Created Modern America*. "At a time when Americans were drawn to ideologies of all sorts, he was not wedded to any overarching theory."

Barack Obama's decisive defeat of John McCain is the most important victory of a Democratic candidate since 1932. It brings to a close another conservative era, one that rose amid the ashes of the New Deal coalition in the late sixties, consolidated its power with the election of Ronald Reagan, in 1980, and immolated itself during the presidency of George W. Bush. Obama will enter the White House at a moment of economic crisis worse than anything the nation has seen since the Great Depression; the old assumptions of free market fundamentalism have, like a charlatan's incantations, failed to work, and the need for some "new machinery" is painfully obvious. But what philosophy of government will characterize it?

The answer was given three days before the election by a soldier and memoirist of the Reagan revolution, Peggy Noonan, who wrote in *The Wall*

Street Journal, "Something new is happening in America. It is the immi-
nent arrival of a new liberal moment." The *Journal*'s editorial page anticipated with dread "one of the most profound political and ideological shifts
in U.S. history. Liberals would dominate the entire government in a way
they haven't since 1965, or 1933. In other words, the election would
mark the restoration of the activist government that fell out of public favor in the 1970s." The *Journal*'s nightmare scenario of America under
President Obama and a Democratic Congress included health care for
all, a green revolution, expanded voting rights, due process for terror suspects, more powerful unions, financial regulation, and a shift of the tax
burden upward. (If the editorial had had more space, full employment
and the conquest of disease might have made the list.)

For the first time since the Johnson administration, the idea that government should take bold action to create equal opportunity for all citizens doesn't have to explain itself in a defensive mumble. That idea is
ascendant in 2008 because it answers the times. These political circumstances, even more than the election of the first black American to the
highest office, make Obama's victory historic. Whether his presidency
will be transformative, in the manner of Roosevelt and the handful of
predecessors named by FDR in 1932, will depend, in part, on history—
it's unclear whether today's financial troubles will offer a political challenge,
and an opportunity, of the magnitude of the Great Depression. But the
power of Obama's presidency will ultimately hinge on how he chooses to
interpret the "modern application" of liberalism in the twenty-first century.

During the two years that he spent campaigning for the presidency,
amid relentless media scrutiny, Obama made a greater commitment to
specific plans than Roosevelt did. Yet he, too, represented different versions of moral leadership to different groups of voters at various stages of
the campaign. Roosevelt's answer to his interviewer reflected a belief that
the presidency has both a political role and a philosophical role. Obama,
using the language of the modern age, has reflected Roosevelt's belief:
there is the "postpartisan" Obama and the "progressive" Obama. Some
tension exists between these two approaches, but he will have to reconcile them if he is to fulfill his ambition of bringing profound change to the
country.

• • •

Ask yourself what thinkers and ideas Reagan took with him to the White House and the answer comes pretty quickly: Milton Friedman, George Gilder, supply-side economics, anticommunism. Bill Clinton's presidency was ushered in by a shelf of books and papers under the not entirely convincing rubric of the Third Way, espoused by policy wonks called New Democrats. I recently asked a number of people who know Obama, both within and outside the campaign, to name a few books and ideas that will help shape his presidency. None of them could give me an answer. It's strangely difficult to identify what the intellectual influences on this cerebral and literary politician have been.

David Axelrod, the chief strategist behind Obama's victory, described Obama's influences as "very eclectic." He went on, "He's a guy who reads very widely—he reads opinion on the right and left, and scholarly treatises of the right or left. I don't think he's in the left-wing or right-wing book club. I think he's willing to draw from everywhere." Unlike Reagan, Obama has no clear, simple ideology. People who have observed him in meetings describe a politician who solicits advice and information from a variety of sources, puts a high value on empirical evidence, and has the self-assurance to reach his own conclusions. A word that comes up again and again, from Obama himself and from people who know him, is "pragmatic."

Cass Sunstein, the Harvard law professor and author, was Obama's colleague for many years at the University of Chicago Law School. Sunstein's most recent book, *Nudge*, cowritten with the behavioral economist Richard Thaler, tries to find a new path between governmental control and the unfettered free market. *Nudge*, Sunstein said, is about "ways of helping people to make better choices without requiring anybody to do anything. It's a conception of government that is reluctant to impose mandates and bans but is kind of shrewd about enlisting what we know about human behavior in good directions." Sunstein added that the book is well known in Obama's circle; Obama's top economic adviser, Austan Goolsbee, also of the University of Chicago, has read it, and Sunstein has discussed its ideas with Obama. In *The Audacity of Hope*, Obama included a proposal from Sunstein and Thaler that would have employees automatically enrolled in retirement plans, with the option not to participate, because "evidence shows that by changing the default rule, employee participation rates go up dramatically"—a noncoercive "nudge" toward better decisions. "He knows an astonishing amount about cutting-edge economic thinking," Sunstein said.

Sunstein's Obama is the postpartisan one. He calls Obama a "visionary minimalist," meaning someone who wants to pursue large goals in a way that offends the deepest values of as few people as possible. Governing in this way would make him distinctly un-Rooseveltian. FDR entered office with broad goodwill and a platform that offered almost all things to all people, but by the time he ran for reelection in 1936 his presidency had become aggressively partisan: he attacked "economic royalists" and said of them, "They are unanimous in their hate for me—and I welcome their hatred." In 2007, Paul Krugman, the *Times* columnist who recently won the Nobel Prize in Economics, commended these remarks to Obama, advising him to sharpen his ideological edge, and warning that his search for common ground with Republicans would be his undoing. But Sunstein said of Obama, "I think he believes—and this is his big split from Krugman—that if you take on board people's deepest commitments, or bracket them, show respect for them, then you make possible larger steps than would otherwise be imagined." It would not be Obama's way to trumpet the arrival of a new era of liberalism—a word, Sunstein said, that is too laden with baggage, and too much of a fighting word, for Obama's taste.

Instead, Sunstein suggested as the governing philosophy of an Obama presidency the idea of "deliberative democracy." The phrase appears in *The Audacity of Hope*, where it denotes a conversation among adults who listen to one another, who attempt to persuade one another by means of argument and evidence, and who remain open to the possibility that they could be wrong. Sunstein pointed out that "deliberative democracy" has certain "preconditions": "It requires an educated citizenry, a virtuous and engaged citizenry that has sufficient resources—and Madison sometimes spoke in these terms—that they could actually be citizens, rather than subjects." Obama links the concept with Lincoln, who was as consequential a president as Roosevelt but in ways that were less obviously partisan and ideological. In his first inaugural address, just five weeks before Southern militiamen fired on Fort Sumter, Lincoln urged his countrymen, "Think calmly and well, upon this whole subject. Nothing valuable can be lost by taking time. If there be an object to hurry any of you, in hot haste, to a step which you would never take deliberately, that object will be frustrated by taking time; but no good object can be frustrated by it."

The Audacity of Hope, written during Obama's first year in the Senate, with the clear aim of laying the groundwork for his presidential candidacy, has been criticized for burying the more revealing voice of his memoir *Dreams from My Father* under a politician's blizzard of evenhanded, unobjectionable judgments. But as campaign books go, it's a good deal more fluent and thoughtful than the genre requires. In it, Obama, who was born in 1961, presents himself as someone young enough not to be defined by the terms and battles of the sixties. His political consciousness was shaped in the eighties, and he opposed Reagan's agenda while nonetheless understanding its appeal, given the failure of liberal government to come through for the middle class. Unlike the Clintons—iconic baby boomers—Obama claims to have no dog in the culture wars; he doesn't feel compelled to defend, or mend, or end every piece of legislation passed when he was a toddler or decades before his birth. In *Hope*, he writes, "These efforts seem exhausted, a constant game of defense, bereft of the energy and new ideas needed to address the changing circumstances of globalization or a stubbornly isolated inner city." Obama found his national voice at the 2004 Democratic Convention in Boston, when his keynote address auguring the end of red-and-blue-state America made him an immediate presidential prospect.

After he declared his candidacy, in early 2007, the Obama who dominated his first year of campaigning was the postpartisan one. He won legions of followers through the sheer power of inspiration. At Dartmouth College in early January, on the night before the New Hampshire primary, a group of students expressed to me deep disenchantment with the Bush and the Clinton dynasties—the boomer War of the Roses. "Obama is the anti-Bush who could get us beyond Bush and all the polarization in Washington," one student said. Another put it this way: "He's one of us." The postpartisan Obama brought millions of young voters into his movement, and he began to peel away moderate Republicans who were sick of their party's being defined by Dick Cheney's autocratic style of governance and Karl Rove's cynical political tactics.

The real problem with partisanship, Obama believes, is that it's no longer pragmatic. After decades of bruising fights in Washington, it has become incompatible with effective government. "I believe any attempt by Democrats to pursue a more sharply partisan and ideological strategy misapprehends the moment we're in," he writes in *Hope*. "I am convinced that whenever we exaggerate or demonize, oversimplify or overstate our case, we lose. Whenever we dumb down the political debate, we lose. For it's precisely the pursuit of ideological purity, the rigid orthodoxy and the sheer predictability of our current political debate, that keeps us from finding new ways to meet the challenges we face as a country." Partisan politics, defined merely as demagoguery or stupidity, is easy to reject— but doing so doesn't take us very far. It's like calling on everyone to be decent. At its weakest, postpartisanship amounts to an aversion to fighting, a trait that some people who know Obama see in him. In the early months of the primary, Obama seemed almost physically to shrink from confrontation, and Hillary Clinton got the better of him in debate after debate.

Just before the Iowa caucus, Sidney Blumenthal, a friend and an adviser to both Bill and Hillary Clinton, told me, "It's not a question of transcending partisanship. It's a question of fulfilling it. If we can win and govern well while handling multiple crises at the same time and the Congress, then we can move the country out of this Republican era and into a progressive Democratic era, for a long period of time." Blumenthal found Obama's approach to be "ahistorical"—a simple hope that the past could be waved away. Should Obama win the nomination, members of the Clinton campaign cautioned, he would have no idea what was in store for him. At a Clinton event in Hampton, New Hampshire, a seventy-one-year-old woman named Ruth Keene told me that "the Republicans would chew Obama up."

They tried like hell. They called him an élitist, a radical, a socialist, a Marxist, a Muslim, an Arab, an appeaser, a danger to the republic, a threat to small children, a friend of terrorists, an enemy of Israel, a vote thief, a noncitizen, an anti-American, and a celebrity. Obama didn't defeat the Republicans simply by rising above partisanship, although his dignified manner served as a continual rebuke to his enemies and went a long way toward reassuring skeptical voters who weren't members of the cult of "Yes We Can." It turned out that the culture war, in spite of Sarah Palin's manic gunplay, was largely over. Obama won because he had a vastly superior organization, a steely resilience that became more evident in October than it was in January (for which he owes a debt to Hillary Clinton), and a willingness to fight back on ground on which the majority of Americans—looking to government for solutions—now stand.

According to David Axelrod, among the books that Obama has read recently is *Unequal Democracy*, by the Princeton political scientist Larry M. Bartels. It attributes the steep economic inequality of our time not to blind technological and market forces but to specific Republican policies. Bartels writes, "On average, the real incomes of middle-class families have grown twice as fast under Democrats as they have under Republicans, while the real incomes of working poor families have grown six times as fast under Democrats as they have under Republicans." For decades, rising inequality coincided with conservative electoral success, because voters were largely ignorant of the effects of tax code changes and other economic policies, those in power were unresponsive to the concerns of working-class citizens, and broader income growth occurred in election years. In other words, the causes of inequality are essentially political—an insight that suggests that Obama might use economic policy to begin reversing a decades-long trend.

Unequal Democracy is decidedly a title from the left-wing book club, and it suits a candidate whose language became more ideological in the days after the markets crashed, in mid-September. Obama began to refer to the financial meltdown as "the final verdict" on a "failed economic philosophy"—words that one of his advisers called "the key line in the campaign narrative." Another adviser told me that in the final months of the race, economic conditions pushed Obama to the left. "Barack is a progressive person but also cautious," the adviser wrote in an e-mail. "He understands politics and understands the limits it can create on progressive policy. But as the times have moved, he's moved quickly along with them." Early on, during the more vaporous and messianic phase of his candidacy, Obama took more cautious stands than Hillary Clinton did, but this fall he began to embrace some of Clinton's positions that he had once refused to support, such as a moratorium on foreclosures and a government buyout of mortgages.

Obama was able to make a powerful case for a break with conservative economics, in part, because he doesn't carry the scars of recent history. "He's not intimidated by the issue frames that have bedeviled Democrats for the last couple of decades," one of the advisers said. "There's never been a sense of having to triangulate." By the end of the campaign, Obama wasn't just running against broken politics, or even against the Bush presidency. He had the antigovernment philosophy of the entire Age of Reagan in his sights.

So events in the homestretch crystallized Obama's economic liberalism. But anyone who has read *The Audacity of Hope* already knew that Obama is no moderate when it comes to the purpose of government. On social and legal issues—guns, abortion, the death penalty, same-sex marriage, the courts and the Constitution—Obama's instinct is usually to soften the left-right clash by reconciling opposites or by escaping them altogether, to find what he called, discussing abortion in his final debate with McCain, "common ground." The phrase is a perfect expression of what Sunstein says is Obama's determination to accommodate disagreement to the extent possible. On issues of culture and law, Obama's liberalism is more procedural than substantive: his most fervent belief is in rules and in standards of serious debate. Given the abuses of executive power and political discourse under George W. Bush, this trait will bring no insignificant cleansing. But Obama's personal caution and conservatism, his sense of rectitude, as well as his idea of politics as a mature calling, shouldn't be mistaken for split-the-difference centrism on every issue. On questions of social welfare—jobs, income, health care, energy—which don't immediately provoke a battle over irreconcilable values, he has given every indication of favoring activist government. When I asked Axelrod if the conservative era had just ended, he said, "From the standpoint of values, I wouldn't say that. But from the standpoint of economics, yes— American history runs in epochs like this." He added, "That's what the theory of our race was—that this is one of those periods of change we encounter every once in a while in our history."

A chapter in *The Audacity of Hope* titled "Opportunity" describes why "the social compact FDR helped construct is beginning to crumble" and begins to sketch a new social compact for a new century. Obama makes a point of incorporating some of the insights of the Reagan era—such as the importance of market incentives and efficiency—but his conclusion, which is unmistakably Rooseveltian, is a call for the renewal of "widespread economic security." Similarly, in a speech on the economy at New York's Cooper Union last March, Obama said, "I do not believe that government should stand in the way of innovation or turn back the clock to an older era of regulation. But I do believe that government has a role to play in advancing our common prosperity, by providing stable macroeconomic and financial conditions for sustained growth, by demanding transparency, and by ensuring fair competition in the marketplace. Our history should give us confidence that we don't have to choose between an oppressive government-run economy and a chaotic and unforgiving capitalism." Since then, Obama has made it even more clear that he wants to lay the ghost of Reagan to rest.

In September, the John F. Kennedy Presidential Library in Boston held a forum on presidential leadership. Cass Sunstein was one of the participants; another was Robert Kuttner, the cofounder of *The American Prospect* and a liberal economics journalist. The two argued over what it would take for Obama to be a great president. In Kuttner's view, nothing short of a return to New Deal–style government intervention will be enough to prevent the dire economy from dooming Obama's presidency. This summer, Kuttner published a short book titled *Obama's Challenge*, which he described to me as "an open letter" to the candidate. "Obama will need to be a more radical president than he was a presidential candidate," Kuttner writes. "Obama, in his books and speeches, has been almost obsessed with the idea that people are sick of partisan bickering. Yet he also has claimed the identity of a resolute progressive. Can he be both? History suggests that it is possible both to govern as a radical reformer and to be a unifier, and thereby move the political center to the left." According to Kuttner, the next president must be willing to spend at least six hundred billion dollars—a Keynesian outpouring—on public works, health care, energy independence, unemployment benefits, mortgage refinancing, aid to state and local governments, and other programs. Otherwise, the country will slide into a depression that will rival the one Roosevelt inherited. (When I ran the six-hundred-billion figure by Paul Krugman, he agreed.)

"Sunstein's minimalism is exactly what's not called for," Kuttner told me, and he later added, "We're on the verge of Great Depression Two. All bets are off. The people who talk about postliberal, postideological, they have been completely overtaken by events. It's the same abuses, the same scenario, that led to the crash of '29. It's the same dynamics of the financial economy dragging down the real economy—these are enduring lessons. Everybody who was talking about being in a kind of postliberal world, they're the ones who don't have much purchase on what's going on. The question is whether Obama will come to this." The answer will depend in part on the advisers he chooses. In Kuttner's mind, the deficit hawks and deregulators of the Clinton administration—Robert Rubin, Lawrence Summers—have been discredited by the financial crisis, and he thinks that it would be a big mistake for Obama to give them powerful roles in his administration. (Summers is considered a likely candidate for treasury secretary, and his top economic advisers are connected with the Hamilton Project, a center-left affiliate of the Brookings Institution.) But, beyond macroeconomics, Kuttner, who plans to hold a conference in Washington called "Thinking Big," shortly before Obama's inauguration, thinks that the Democrats have a clear political agenda: "the reclamation of an ideology."

This is not an ambition that Obama has ever publicly embraced. In *The Audacity of Hope*, he specifically rejects such talk. "That's not Obama," Robert B. Reich, who was Bill Clinton's first labor secretary and now teaches at the University of California, Berkeley, said. "Obama is not about the restoration of government as a progressive force per se." He added, "Were Obama to approach this in an ideological way, talking about this as 'We are now going to affirm the importance and centrality of government in the future of the nation,' I think the public would walk away."

Reich, who holds Obama in high regard—he supported his candidacy over that of his old friend Hillary Clinton—bears his share of scars from the Clinton years, many of them inflicted by other members of the administration. He fought and lost a number of first-term battles against Rubin and other centrists, who persuaded Clinton to balance the budget rather than spend more on public investments. Obama will take office with a number of advantages that were unavailable to the last Democratic president. The party is more united, the Democrats in Congress energized by their recent return to a majority. As stagnant wages and pressing public needs have become the focus of Democratic domestic policy, the old line between deficit hawks and economic liberals has dissolved—last week, the *Times* published an op-ed piece cowritten by a leading representative of each group: Rubin and the economist Jared Bernstein, respectively. (They met somewhere around the forty-yard line on Bernstein's half of the field.) Bill Clinton began his presidency as the country was coming out of a recession, and Alan Greenspan, the semidivine chairman of the Federal Reserve, could hold the new president hostage to Wall Street. Now Greenspan, in retirement, has confessed to Congress that his free-market worldview was flawed; Wall Street lies prostrate after suffering something like a paralyzing stroke, and with the country entering a deep recession, both deficit spending and financial regulation are givens. More profoundly, the conservative tide was still high when Clinton entered the White House, and it quickly swamped him. Obama will take power at its lowest ebb. It is for all these reasons that 2009 will be more like 1933 than like 1993.

Nonetheless, in our conversation Reich kept returning to the many ways in which President Obama's ability to act quickly will be compromised. "We are not in Hundred Days territory," Reich said. "We may be, if the economy goes into free fall—the public may demand dramatic action. But there are so many constraints on dramatic action." New presidents make mistakes—in Clinton's case, Reich said, they included the push to integrate gays into the military, the botched effort to reform health care, and a failure to establish priorities. Even with a solid majority in Congress, Obama will have to deal with the Blue Dog Democrats, who represent states and districts that are more conservative. Reich recently met with one Blue Dog, in the Southwest, who "felt that it was going to be very difficult politically to make the case" that increasing the deficit during a recession was the right thing to do. On the other hand, unions will likely pressure the administration to curtail trade agreements, in the interest of preventing the further loss of industrial jobs to other countries.

Finally, there will be a Republican opposition. Given the widespread sense of national emergency, David Axelrod said, "I don't know that Republicans can afford to take a laissez-faire kind of approach. I think there are going to be a fair number of Republicans who are going to want to cooperate because they're not going to be on the wrong side of the debate." Kuttner implied that Obama can govern without them. Reich regarded them with the wariness of a crime victim whose assailant is still at large. "They are weaker," he said. "They're not dead by any stretch of the imagination. They're in disarray and discredited, but that's partly because they've not had a clear target, and undoubtedly an Obama administration and a Democratic Congress will give them a very clear target." In Washington, the establishment is already beginning to warn that Obama shouldn't "overreach" by moving too far to the left. But the question isn't whether he tacks left or center; it's whether he demonstrates early on that government can begin to improve people's lives.

The tremendous expectations that will accompany Obama to the

White House practically guarantee that some of his supporters will be disappointed by the all-too-normal incapacities of a government founded as a system of checks and balances, and lately choked with lobbyists and corporate money. This disappointment will only feed what Reich called the "deep cynicism in the public about the capacity of government to do anything big and well."

Obama, in order to break through the inherent constraints of Washington, will need, above all, a mobilized public beyond Washington. Transformative presidents—those who changed the country's sense of itself in some fundamental way—have usually had great social movements supporting and pushing them. Lincoln had the abolitionists, Roosevelt the labor unions, Johnson the civil rights leaders, Reagan the conservative movement. Clinton didn't have one, and after his election, Reich said, "everyone went home."

Obama has his own grassroots organization, on the Internet and in hundreds of field offices. This is new territory, because those earlier movements had independent identities apart from any president, whereas Obama's movement didn't exist before his candidacy; its purpose was to get him elected. Even so, it has the breadth, the organization, and the generational energy of other movements, and it can be converted into a political coalition if its leader knows how to harness it.

Obama's advisers haven't yet worked out the mechanics of this conversion. The Internet could be used to ensure transparency; almost every activity of the federal government could be documented online, as some state governments have begun to do. The White House could use the vast Obama e-mail list to convey information about key issues and bills, and to mobilize pressure on Congress. Just as FDR used radio and Reagan television to speak to the public without going through the press, Obama could do the same with the Web. It's hard to imagine, though, how an electronic "social-network platform" would constitute a movement with the clarity and the coherence of the religious right, or the freedom marchers, or the Congress of Industrial Organizations. The agenda of Obama's candidacy is a list of issues that have different constituencies rather than a single, overarching struggle for freedom or justice. Throughout the campaign, Obama spoke of change coming from the bottom up rather than from the top down, but every time I heard him tell a crowd, "This has never been about me; it's about you," he seemed to be saying just the opposite. The Obama movement was born in the meeting between a man and a historical moment; if he had died in the middle of the campaign, that movement would have died with him—proof that, whatever passions it has stirred, it remains something less than a durable social force.

With a movement behind him, Obama would have the latitude to begin to overcome the tremendous resistance to change that prevails in Washington. Without one, he will soon find himself simply cutting deals. And here is where the two aspects of his vision of the presidency—the postpartisan Obama and the progressive Obama—converge. "Changing politics and making government work are complementary, not opposed," Reich said. "Otherwise, it's the same old Washington. It's a morass."

Does "changing politics" mean finding a bipartisan consensus before moving on to major reforms? Or inspiring a new generation of public-spirited activists? Or simply using a language and a tone that reject divisiveness and respect the intelligence of the citizenry? A more idealistic and engaged politics would be a profoundly welcome departure from an age of disenchantment and venom. Consensus seems less likely. As Paul Krugman told me, postpartisan rhetoric will be the means. Solving problems through progressive government will be the end.

Last month, Charlie Rose asked Krugman what he would like to hear from Obama's inaugural address. "'The only thing we have to fear is fear itself,'" Krugman said. "I want him to call for something like a new New Deal, saying, 'Look, we've gone off the rails. Not everything's been bad these past couple of decades, but we lost sight of having a society that works for everybody, we lost sight of a society that provides some basic security, we lost sight of a society that provides some basic insurance against chaos in the financial markets, and we need to recapture some of those values that have made us successful.'" Krugman didn't say what a "new New Deal" would be.

There is a mysterious cycle in human events, but it doesn't swing back and forth like a pendulum. Arthur Schlesinger, Jr., building on his father's work, observed that American politics alternates between thirty-year periods of conservatism and reform—between the idea that we're on our own and the idea that we're all in this together. But the movement of history incorporates everything that went before, always inching ahead even as it oscillates, and anyone who governs as if the experience of entire eras could be reversed is bound to fail. (The Gingrich Congress, driven solely by a desire to dismantle government programs, comes to mind.) "It would be a mistake to surmise that the new era is somehow a return to the New Deal," Axelrod said. "The one theme that I think travels is the notion that there is a role for government to play. It may be just as a catalyst; it may be using the bully pulpit. But I think the progressive idea that government has a role to play in making sure there are rules of the road, that people get a fair shake, and so on—I think that is very much what people are looking for today."

If you dip into the literature of the New Deal, what immediately strikes you is its desperate radicalism. Next January, no one will use the kind of apocalyptic language with which Arthur Krock, of the *Times*, described Roosevelt's inauguration: "The atmosphere which surrounded the change of government in the United States was comparable to that which might be found in a beleaguered capital in war time." In his inaugural address, with the Depression in its fourth year, FDR demanded wartime powers. He took office amid protests by military veterans clamoring for their bonuses, and not long after his inauguration he came up with the idea of sending many of them, along with a couple of hundred thousand other unemployed men, to clear firebreaks in the country's national parks. After a century and a half of American individualism, his Brain Trust—an advisory group of economists and lawyers—put the government in charge of organizing the economy. Vast programs costing millions of dollars and requiring entirely new agencies took shape overnight while Americans starved to death. Critics, including some Democrats, compared Roosevelt to Hitler, Mussolini, and Stalin. Demagogues and mobs sprang up around the country, calling for communism, for fascism, for old-age pensions. Out of this churn came the mixed economy, and Social Security.

Reagan couldn't cancel Roosevelt's legacy; Obama won't be able to obliterate Reagan's. The past few decades have generated a great surge of private energy and private pursuits, and for some Americans they have been years of dizzying abundance and creativity. Laptop computers and microbrews are just as characteristic of the Age of Reagan as financial derivatives and outsourcing. Next January, legions of earnest, overworked, slightly underfed young men and women won't flock to Washington to map out new government bureaucracies; instead, legions of healthy, casually ironic, extremely nice young men and women will flock to Washington to map out the green revolution. When it comes, it will look more like Google than like the Tennessee Valley Authority.

But November 4, 2008, is one of those infrequent dates when one historical age and one generation, with a distinct political and economic and cultural character, gave way to another age, another generation. The new era that is about to begin under President Obama will be more about public good than about private goods. The meal will be smaller, and have less interesting flavors, but it will be shared more fairly. The great American improvisation called democracy still bends along the curve of history. It has not yet finished astounding the world.

Acknowledgments

Many thanks to the men and women who assigned, edited, and published the pieces collected in this book: Alex Star at *The Boston Globe*; Mitchell Cohen, Mark Levinson, Brian Morton, and Michael Walzer at *Dissent*; Monika Bauerlein and Roger Cohn at *Mother Jones*; Katherine Bouton, Megan Liberman, Gerry Marzorati, and Adam Moss at *The New York Times Magazine*; Lawrence Kaplan at *World Affairs*; and, with special gratitude, David Remnick, Dorothy Wickenden, and Daniel Zalewski at *The New Yorker*.